Professional Photoshop 6

*The Classic Guide to
Color Correction*

DAN MARGULIS

John Wiley & Sons, Inc.

New York · Chichester · Weinheim · Brisbane · Singapore · Toronto

Publisher: Robert Ipsen
Editor: Cary Sullivan
Assistant Editor: Christina Berry
Managing Editor: Marnie Wielage

Library of Congress Cataloging-in-Publication Data:

    Margulis, Dan 1951–
       Professional Photoshop 6 : the classic guide to color correction / Dan Margulis.
         p. cm.
       "Wiley computer publishing."
       Includes index.
       ISBN 0-471-40399-7 (pbk. : alk. paper)
       1. Color computer graphics. 2. Adobe Photoshop. I. Title.
     T385 .M36362 2000
     006.6'869--dc21

                      00-050278

Printed in the United States of America
10 9 8 7 6 5 4 3 2

Contents

3

The Steeper the Curve, The More the Contrast

Give the most important areas of the image an extra dose of detail by careful control of curve shape.

4

Sharpening with a Stiletto

Unsharp masking can bring images into focus—or destroy them with halos and graininess. Those who aim well can sharpen more.

5

Plate Blending as Poetry

In bright objects, contrast depends not on the dominant inks but on the weakest—the unwanted color. If you don't have a good one, *make* one.

6

In Color Correction, The Key Is the K

GCR and other black generation decisions and their effect on printing, color correction, and retouching.

7

RGB Is CMY

Once you realize that the two are basically the same, you're in a position to exploit their differences.

8

HSB Is LAB

These two separate color from contrast. That philosophy can be the start (and heart) of effective corrections—of certain kinds of pictures.

9

All Colorspaces Are One

Each colorspace has its own strength, and each can handle easy corrections. As the assignments get tougher, the smart operator switches often.

10

Making Things Look Alike

The key to calibration today rests on a shockingly simple concept: that the best way to tell whether things look alike is to look at them.

11

Managing Separation And Color Settings

With its color interface overhauled, Photoshop 6 offers all the tools for good separations—and a challenge.

12 The Great Dot Gain Gamble

If you're surprised by overly muddy results in print, you probably haven't compensated properly for one of the most difficult concepts in all graphics.

13 Friend and Foe In Black and White

To get color images into B/W, look to the individual channels. Rely on your friends, be ruthless to your enemies.

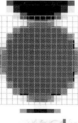

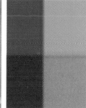

14 Resolving the Resolution Issue

The abbreviation *dpi* is used for too many things. This chapter sorts it all out and suggests better terminology.

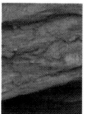

Math, Moiré, and the Artist: A New Angle on Descreening

Prescreened originals need not be a problem if you keep two words in mind during the entire process.

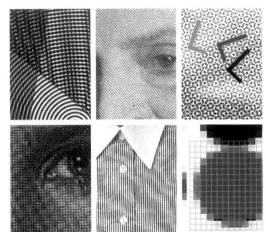

Every File Has Ten Channels

Introducing a powerful new technique: think of each color image as if it had to be converted into B/W. And look for an opportunity for a luminosity blend.

There Are No Bad Originals

We close with images that need a variety of techniques, and a two-page checklist of what to think about when confronted with a tough opponent.

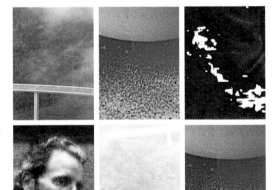

Introduction

Deceptively simple, hideously complex. Vastly easier, considerably harder.

The study of color correction is a bottomless pit, if you let it be, but an inexperienced person can become quite proficient at it without too much pain by following certain simple rules—a by-the-numbers approach, if you will.

That approach is so effective that people who master it wind up with much better-looking pictures than many of those prepared by so-called professionals.

This is a big deal. The desire to have good-looking pictures in print is not limited to graphic artists. Clients want it, too, and they are both more sophisticated and more demanding about it than they were even two years ago, when the last edition of this book came out. There was once a time when a newspaper or a large-format printer that could produce any kind of color was such a novelty that clients didn't even care that the grass turned out orange and the sky green. No more. Now, not only do they expect more, but they provide less. In comes an amateur digital capture, and if it doesn't print well, the client wants to know how come it didn't look as nice as the professionally shot, drum-scanned image in somebody else's ad on the next page.

Because of the explosion in the use of color, and a shortage of knowledgeable technicians, the inevitable has occurred. As I write this in late 2000, it's the hottest job market that color technicians have ever seen. Since the first edition of this book appeared in 1994, salaries for people who can do what this book teaches have nearly tripled in several metropolitan areas.

While this is a tribute to the skill involved to get to the highest level, the truth is that most of what these people do is readily understandable by beginners. Teaching it is what this book is about, and the objective is to do so in a simple way.

And why not? The objective, after all, can be stated as follows: *We want to make the picture look better.* How hard is that to comprehend? Do you need an expert to tell you what it means?

Accordingly, most of this book is perfectly suitable for beginners or even people who never use Photoshop at all. If you follow the by-the-numbers advice in the first six chapters, you will discover what so many have—it works. Your pictures will look better.

What's in a Mask?

If you're not an expert, you'll be stubbing your toes on many of the techniques here. For example, although we start from scratch with the most basic treatment of curves, the book makes the ludicrous assumption that you know how to make a serviceable mask. While this is partly to avoid a hundred extra pages, it's more because this a book of concepts. You don't need to know how to construct a mask to understand what the point of the mask is. And then, if you conclude that you need to make accurate masks, there are a number of good resources for learning how.

Chapter 17 is an interesting illustration.

It's based on the technical portions of a column I wrote in *Electronic Publishing* magazine about my friend and editor Tom McMillan, who died in 1999. It wrapped the story of our friendship, which had nothing to do with imaging technique, around one of the most fiendishly difficult color corrections imaginable.

Not being Photoshop experts, most readers of that column would have had better success piloting a spacecraft than they would have trying to execute those image moves. But a remarkable thing happened. Scores of them wrote in saying that although they had never heard of the particular commands I was using, they *did* follow the logic of what was going on.

That's really the way it should be. This book emphasizes ideas, philosophies, not specific methodology. In many ways it isn't even a Photoshop book at all.

The Changes in the Book...

This edition has changed to reflect the changing marketplace, new ideas about color correction that I've come up with, and helpful suggestions from readers of past editions. Close to half the material is new. Readers of past editions will find Chapters 1–6 quite familiar, although I've replaced several images where I've found more instructive ones, and I've rewritten several sections of Chapter 2.

This is not too surprising. The basics of color correction are timeless, little affected by changes in Photoshop. Every exercise you'll find in this book could have been done, perhaps a little less efficiently, in Photoshop 3, which came out in 1994. (Before that, the program didn't have layers, which are essential to some of the moves shown here.)

Chapters 2–5, for simplicity's sake, stay in CMYK, ignoring the fact that most images don't start there. Chapter 6 introduces the separation process, with great emphasis on the role of GCR. It leads into three chapters, which have been substantially changed from the last edition, on the relationship between colorspaces, and when it's advantageous to work in LAB or RGB.

Everything pertaining to calibration and the accuracy of the separation process is found in Chapters 10–12, which are all new. Chapter 10 discusses basic principles; Chapter 11 the color settings of Photoshop 6; and Chapter 12, in response to reader demand, deals exclusively with the most misunderstood and complicated topic in calibration, the impact of dot gain. As in past editions, we concentrate on basic principles rather than drown in minutiae specific to this version of Photoshop.

Historically, the *Professional Photoshop* series has synthesized for the first time in print certain secrets known only to the top echelon of retouchers, such as using curves to target specific objects or exploiting Photoshop's GCR possibilities. However, it has also introduced several techniques that were never heard of before, which have since been widely adopted by professionals. Among these are the extensive use of LAB, channel blending, and unsharp masking targeted to specific channels.

I believe that Chapter 16 will continue this trend. It introduces a method—luminosity-based blending—that I've been experimenting with over the past few years and have concluded is very powerful.

To pave the way for this new concept, I've completely redone Chapter 13, which covers how to convert color images into black and white. That chapter itself was very much an innovation when it first appeared in 1994, and I left it basically unchanged in the 1998 edition. The philosophy is still the same, but I think you'll find the explanation of it a bit easier.

Chapter 14, which discusses the various kinds of resolution we have to cope with, and Chapter 15, which covers moiré generally and prescreened originals particularly, are pretty much as in the 1998 edition. The final chapter ends with the same happy example, but otherwise is entirely new.

On pages 336 and 337, a box appears for the first time on how to develop a strategy. By the time the last chapter comes around enough tools have been introduced to confuse almost anyone. This section summarizes the thought process that one should be go through when first approaching a new image.

...and in the Package

For the first time, this edition includes a CD. This is a trend I've resisted for some years, because to get good at color correction, you have to learn to think for yourself. It's accordingly much better if you follow along with the text using your own images and applying the lessons of my examples to them, rather than simply aping what I'm doing. Obviously, my suggested methods work on those specific images, otherwise they wouldn't be in the book. The question is, will they work on yours?

To aid in finding out the answer (hint: it's yes) let me state that I include the images in Chapters 2, 3, and 5 under protest and that you shouldn't use them. The concepts of those chapters work on all images. I am less doctrinaire about the other chapters, which discuss methods that work on some types of images and not on others.

We've also taken advantage of the format to dump some of the editorial content from last time to make room for more good stuff. The chapter on how to deal with fifth and subsequent colors and how to create good duotones has migrated to the CD. This has opened up space for the expansion of several chapters of more general concern.

Also, having the CD avoids having to waste space on the thorny topic of how to migrate to Photoshop 6 not from Photoshop 5, but directly from an earlier version. Photoshop 5 changed color settings thoroughly, and there are further major changes in Photoshop 6. Chapter 11 explains how to move from 5 to 6, but that method won't work if you are starting with something more ancient. There is, however, a section on the CD that explains how to do it.

The Changes in the Market...

The secrets of making images look good have been known for a long time. If we could magically transport a retoucher from 1991 into a modern Photoshop studio, that person would have approximately zero problem adjusting. He'd have to pick up layers, and realize that computers had gotten hundred of times faster, but that would be about it. By contrast, a 1981 retoucher transported to 1991 would not have had Cluc One as to what was going on.

So much for the conventional wisdom that we are in a time of revolutionary technological change. Instead, the changes are in what the work is and in who does it.

The work is more challenging. Back when color was very expensive, those who could justify using it could also justify using a professional photographer. And, of course, color was so expensive because it required the use of very costly (and very good) drum scanners, most of which were operated by people who could sling curves around with the best of us.

Now, though, the image may come from a variety of more dubious sources. The scan is apt to be poorer, and the photo less likely to be professional. This trend will continue. The biggest technical development of the decade—although many don't realize it yet—has been the advent of cheap, high-quality digital cameras. Even at this writing, there are sub-$1,000 units capable of captures that are perfectly suitable for professional imaging.

As these units get even cheaper and even better, it's inevitable that graphic artists will become their own photographers, resulting in shorter turnarounds, the elimination of scanning, and some of the worst photography ever yet seen.

Meanwhile, the possibilities of where the work may go, and the disasters that may occur to it when it gets there, mount. The advent of the Web means that a workflow that ignores RGB altogether is a bad idea. The work may go to some kind of high-quality digital device that has many but not all of the characteristics of the offset presses that most color technicians are familiar with. Or, it may go to some desktop or other device of lesser quality, which may behave more or less like other devices of its class, or which may have some type of undocumented color management going on, written by an engineer who believes that if a product works predictably it doesn't have enough features.

As for who is going to do all this more difficult stuff, take a look in the mirror. Anybody seriously interested in quality today has to do their own work, and do it without much help. The traditional service providers—printers, prepress houses, and service bureaus—no longer have the skilled personnel they did ten years ago.

Moreover, the decentralization of the industry means that you'll have little chance to learn from your peers. Few graphics operations now have more than a dozen employees, a stark contrast to a decade ago, when larger groups were the rule.

…and in What We Know

The 1994 edition of this book was quite state of the art, and is still emphatically correct in its basics. The problem with it was, neither I nor anybody else at that time had had much experience trying to bring video captures and other such horrors up to professional standards. As a result, we had never worked out how to deal with them, and assumed doing so was impossible.

Since then, we have been forcibly reminded that necessity is the mother of invention. The result has been a blizzard of new techniques that use the traditional foundation but move off in exciting directions that were unknown seven years ago.

The question may therefore be asked, how do I know that my recommended techniques are the right ones?

I offer no guarantees that better methods won't be found in the future; in a couple of places here I have recorrected images that appeared in earlier editions and have gotten better results by using some new trick that I've since thought of. However, I can say with considerable assurance that these are the best tricks currently known.

For the past few years, I've been teaching hands-on master classes in color correction. Experience has demonstrated that the best learning method is sink or swim. That is, a group of seven people each work the same image, using whatever method they like, and then we compare the results side by side. I often participate in these exercises. Though my vision is not what it was in my twenties, I am not yet so blind that I can't recognize when somebody else has done a better job than I have.

In something like the horrible image introduced in Figure 17.3, for example, there are an infinite number of possible approaches. However, I've seen at least fifty experienced people have at it in different ways, and none of them have had any luck except with methods substantially similar to what I describe.

The same goes for choice of colorspace. Sometimes one works a bit better than the others on specific images. At other times there's just no comparison; if you don't use the right one, you're booked for Mudville. In a situation like Figure 6.11, which is a stalking horse for all manner of images with critical detail in the darkest blacks, I say that this is the type of image that can *only* be effectively corrected in CMYK, even if your final output must be RGB. This is no wild guess. It's a reaction to having seen several hundred people work the image, none of whom came even close to the desired result without doing the shadow enhancement in CMYK.

Another great thing about this experience is seeing what points trip people up. The most glaring example: most folks have no problem grasping how to decide whether to force one or more points in an image to be neutral, or close thereto. Unfortunately, a significant percentage find this concept extremely difficult. I've responded here by completely rewriting that section of the book and adding several more example images.

You may not have a problem figuring this neutrality business out, but there will be some other area that will confuse you. That's part of the price of being human and being asked to absorb a complicated topic. Fortunately, being human, you can console yourself with the thought that nobody else is exempt. If you like, you can ask yourself why, if I understand so much about color, the excruciatingly powerful methods of Chapter 16 don't happen to appear in any earlier edition.

Of Crutches and Complexity

For all these experts-only tricks, we always get back to basics. We are simple folk, just trying to make the picture look better, nothing more.

This book has been successful because it expresses complex topics in simple ways. That's why, although it was first aimed at professional retouchers, it's been hijacked by photographers, desktop generalists, and a lot of other people who don't spend eight hours a day running Photoshop but do care about quality color.

Furthermore, it's about ways that work. If your pictures look lousy you won't be told to go calibrate your monitor or buy 15 plugins. You'll be told how to figure out the likely causes, and what to do about it.

No mercy, however, is shown to those interested in crutches. All commands that come under the description of kid stuff will be avoided. There is no need for Levels because we use curves. There is no need for any of the sharpen filters other than Unsharp Mask. And, as mentioned earlier, we breeze by silhouetting and masking. If you're an advanced user, you already know how to do this; I prefer to concentrate on talking about when it's necessary, because most users who consider themselves advanced resort to masks far too frequently.

We assume the likeliest scenario, that you have to prepare an image for CMYK output, although we'll touch from time to time on the exigencies of RGB output, such as for the Web. We don't know where the files we are working on came from, or in what colorspace they arrive. The assumption is that printing conditions are roughly those of magazines, although we discuss how to cope with different ones, such as those of newspapers. And we assume we don't have forever to work on the images.

None of the original images in this book were sabotaged to make the "correction" more impressive. Also, if we are talking about curves, the corrected version will not have more unsharp masking, say, than the original. If we are talking about a single plate and its impact, the other plates will be unchanged from original to correction.

The Lifelong Learning Curve

The topic of color has fascinated the finest minds, some of whom pay us a visit during the text. This indicates that a certain amount of serious thinking is necessary, and I hope to provoke you to do it. That's why it's written this way, with no hot tip boxes or lists of shortcuts.

For sure, you can skim the top of this book and learn how to color-correct without thinking.

Once you've seen how easy it is, however, you can make it as hard as you want. This topic is more art than science, and has tripped up the likes of da Vinci, Morris, and Ansel Adams. No wonder the conventional color wisdom is so often wrong!

Also, there seems to be no limit on learning. In fact, the opposite occurs, as one understands more the pace of learning increases. When the first edition of *Professional Photoshop* came out in 1994, I thought I was nearing that limit.

What a laugh. The 1998 version left it in the dust. And, annoyingly, I think I've learned more since then than in the four years preceding. I shudder to think of what mistakes I may find in *Professional Photoshop 6* in two more years.

So very hard, so very easy. It's appropriate to end with the last words of the 1994 edition, which didn't appear in 1998. The first paragraph, for students of such matters, refers to the seed that grew into Chapters 8, 9, 16, and 17 of this edition:

I have learned, for instance, to consider the use of the L channel in LAB to aid in correcting a CMYK image. This is a more effective way of adding sparkle, I have found, than the methods I used to employ.

Then again, two years from now, I expect to be much better at color correction than I am today. If you are uncomfortable with some of the methods discussed here, don't worry. The basics can be acquired. Improvement will never stop.

Photoshop evolves, gets faster, comes up with new techniques, becomes better in every way. With any effort, with any luck, so will we.

Professional
Photoshop

6

Preflight: What Shall We Do with This Image?

Before tackling color correction, a fundamental question needs to be answered: is the idea to reproduce a photograph as accurately as possible, or to reproduce what a viewer who was in the position of the camera would have seen?

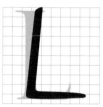et there be light, the Lord said, and since then it's been nothing but headaches for those of us interested in quality color printing.

The big problem is not so much that the Lord created such a large visible spectrum, but that He also endowed us with an acutely sensitive and highly adjustable visual apparatus. The combination of these two factors makes it quite impossible to create digital images that even remotely resemble the clarity of real life.

Can a camera capture the majesty of the Grand Canyon? Anyone who has ever been there knows that it cannot. To generalize further: photographs can never rival reality. Their tonal range is too small. More important, when the human eye is confronted with a preponderance of similar colors it adjusts unconsciously, gaining sensitivity to those colors at the expense of others. A camera lacks this flexibility. A camera faithfully records what it sees, even if the human eye would see something different.

Figure 1.1 *A scene from Grand Canyon National Park. It's a fine image, but it isn't prepared for print as well as it should be. To see what one touch of curves and another of unsharp masking can do, turn ahead to Figure 1.2 on Page 7.*

When we look closely at the Grand Canyon, with its rich redness, our eyes compensate to let us pick up a greater variety of reds. The camera sticks to its original settings. Even if it could magically make itself more sensitive to reds, though, it could not record nearly the range of colors that the eye can see.

Defining "Quality"

We can probably agree that a color photograph is "worse" than the image would appear in real life. Similarly, an amateur photographer using a $12.50 disposable camera will surely produce a "worse" image of the Grand Canyon than a professional with a first-quality instrument.

If we convert the image recorded by either photographer to digital information, we will get a "worse" image still. Just as between real life and a photograph, between a photograph on positive film and a digital scan there is a decrease in the range of colors that can be portrayed, and a loss of some detail.

Next in line of deteriorating quality comes the printed piece. Again, image quality and color space is lost, all to the detriment of realism.

There is yet another quality leap between color printing on reasonably good paper, such as is used in this book, and printing on poor stock, such as newsprint. A final indignity that can be imposed on an unfortunate photograph is to lose its color altogether, on those occasions when we must print it in black and white.

Now that I've trashed the entire printing process, I should point out that the news is not all bad. If we can't achieve real-life or even film-like quality on the printed page, well, neither can anyone else. The viewer,

consciously or not, understands this and cuts us some slack. The viewer judges the quality of a printed picture in comparison to other printed pictures, not against original transparencies, and certainly not against what the viewer might perceive in person.

The *really* good news (or, for the lazy, the really *bad* news) is that, even in our relatively low-quality world, skill means a lot. Just as there is a huge gap between the work of a professional photographer and someone who just points a camera and clicks the shutter, the difference between the work of a color technician and that of a dilettante will be obvious even to the most inattentive observer.

That analogy can be carried further. In photography, a number of crutches have emerged that enable the less skilled to improve their pictures. Things like auto-focus and automatic exposure are a big help to people who don't know how to set these things manually, but the camera's judgment will never be as good as a professional's. In our own field, there are similar crutches, such as Photoshop's Auto Levels command.

The similarity with photography breaks down in one important area, however. The objects that the photographer takes pictures of, whether outdoors or in the studio, are generally just as easy or as difficult to shoot as they were five years, or 50 years, ago. That is not true for us: technology has reduced the price of capturing the base product, the digital file, that we work with, but it has also reduced its quality from the days when drum scanners reigned.

Plus, now we have much more of a range of printing conditions to plan for. Back then, it was pretty much output to film, print on an offset press. Now, we have a bewildering variety of desktop printers, digital proofers and presses, large-format printers, color copiers, and platesetters, not to mention the Web and desktop devices that don't like CMYK input at all.

Our job, therefore, *is* harder than it was five years ago. Of course, that means that we will have to be *better.*

The Goals in Color Manipulation

Before charging into color correction with both guns blazing, we'd best have some idea of what we're aiming at. This is a ticklish topic, one that many people ignore.

Leaving aside the cases where we want the printed piece to be at odds with the original (as when the sky is overcast in the photograph but we want happier-looking weather), the standard instruction in the industry is "match the art." By this, we are supposed to understand that we are to produce something that reminds the viewer as much as possible of the original photograph, granted that we are smashing it into a grotesquely smaller range of colors.

Plainly, we can't be too literal about this. If the original photograph has a scratch or dust on it, nobody would question that "match the art" means take it out.

Next, there is general agreement that if the photograph is flat, it's our job to fix it. By "flat" we mean lacking contrast, which means lacking a good range, which means that either the whites are too dark or the blacks too light, or both.

In printing, our color range is so limited to begin with that we can't afford such flat images, even when the original photograph itself is slightly flat. So, to most professionals, "match the art" means set the lightest white in the original to the value of the lightest white that we can print and still show detail, and set the darkest black in the original to the darkest combination of inks that we can conveniently accommodate. The results of this approach cause no end of astonishment to the uninitiated. Nobody thinks that a snapshot will reproduce as well as a high-quality transparency, but that is because the transparency has so much more of a dynamic range. Once we scan and correct the two, they'll each have the same range, and as long as the snapshot was as detailed as the transparency, it will print just about as well.

Should We Match the Art?

Another major issue, particularly in dealing with photos taken outdoors, where lighting conditions are unpredictable, is that when we compress the colors of the original into our colorspace, we sometimes exaggerate an existing color cast.

Color casts are — well, Figure 1.1, that's a color cast, albeit a mild one. If you compare it to Figure 1.2, it looks like there's a yellow piece of Saran Wrap lying over it. Every color is affected.

Casts are usually caused by suboptimal lighting conditions, but they can also be introduced or aggravated by lousy scanning. Casts come in every conceivable color strength, and some affect only certain lightness ranges. Even a relatively mild one can damage an image, because casts play havoc with neutral colors. By neutral colors, we mean whites and grays. Neutral colors, as will be repeated over and over in these pages, are one of our chief torments. They must be carefully balanced, or they won't stay neutral. The lighter the gray, the easier it is to mess up.

Annoyingly, many things in life are of a neutral color, and if our image shows them otherwise people will think we don't know what we are doing. Paper, asphalt roads, elephants, shadows, packaging materials, porcelain—the list is endless. In Chapter 2 you will encounter a picture of a horse that your logic will tell you must be white, yet is distinctly pink on the page.

The question is, should we correct this, assuming that the horse is actually pink in the original?

The argument against correcting is simple. If we horse around with the color balance, we may change a lot of things besides the horse. Although a pink horse does prove that a color cast infects the original, perhaps the photographer or the final client *likes* the way it is affecting the other areas.

As against that, if we were looking at the horse ourselves, rather than at a photograph, we would see a white horse, not a pink one. Human eyes are highly efficient at rejecting color casts in ambient light. Cameras are not so good at it. Probably the lighting conditions at the time *were* slightly pink. Our eyes would have compensated. The camera didn't.

I find this to be a convincing argument. So do most other color professionals.

The problem with this philosophy, however, is that it's only the start of a slide down a rather slippery slope. In knocking out the cast to make the image look more natural, we cater to a feature of the human visual system known to scientists as *chromatic adaptation*. Unfortunately, there are many other ways, some subtle, in which we see things differently than cameras do. And it seems only logical that if we adjust for chromatic adaptation, we should adjust for the others as well.

The major areas for consideration are:

- In darker environments, the human

visual system adjusts and sees everything as lighter, but the camera does not.

- If similar colors are in close proximity, humans perceive more difference in them than if they were far apart. This explains why the lake in Figure 1.1 looks so flat. It *has* to look that way because cameras have never heard of this anomaly, which is called *simultaneous contrast*. A human observer automatically and unconsciously breaks the greens apart, seeing many more shades of green than the camera does.

- The human visual apparatus sharply reduces the perceived intensity of reflected flashes of light, but the camera puts in catchlights wherever it sees them.

- When humans concentrate on one object, that object gains contrast and everything else loses it, but the camera is egalitarian. Also, the human observer loses color perception in uninteresting areas, but the camera doesn't.

- The darkest parts of a scene are usually seen as colorless by humans, even when the areas are part of something with a pronounced color, such as the darkest folds of a green garment. A camera usually sees the folds as a very dark green.

Matching the Meaning

Success in color correction depends very much on the imagination. We need to visualize the kinds of changes that are possible and the effects they may have.

Instead of showing you a picture of what I am starting to talk about, I would like you to *imagine* a couple of pictures. As we go along, there will be quite a few more of these hypothetical situations.

Figure 1.2 *A quick correction of Figure 1.1, using techniques discussed in Chapters 2–4.*

First, please imagine a picture of your own yard, taken at 15 minutes before sunset on a day with pleasant weather.

Ready?

The first question is, did you imagine what your yard looks like at that time of day, or how it would look in a *photograph?* There's a big difference. At that time of day, it is much darker than at, say, noon. Once again, though, our eyes would have compensated by becoming more sensitive to dark colors. Once again, the camera would not. Even if the lightest and darkest areas of the photograph are correct, overall the image will be darker than you remember.

This is exactly what occurs when we are in a relatively dark room with the lights out. We adjust to the environment and after a while it seems normal to us. If the lights get turned on suddenly, we are dazzled; we rub our eyes, and it takes time for us to start to discern obvious visual details.

When our vision adjusts to changed surroundings, it's not as if we can see more colors. We just evaluate them differently. If we increase the range of dark colors we see, we have to decrease how many light colors we can perceive. When we are staring intently at the incredible reds of the Grand Canyon, we lose the ability to see the normal range of greens.

As it happens, color correction by computer can work in exactly the same way. The question is, should we do it? In other words, Photoshop lets us do exactly what our eyes do at 15 minutes before sunset: lose discrimination in lighter colors so as to be able to make finer distinctions among darker ones. Thus, we will see moderately dark tones as lighter than they are in the original photograph.

It seems to me that if we are going to correct a pink horse to agree with what our eyes would have seen, it must follow, as the night the day, that we must correct this sunset as well.

As you can see, the simple decision that color casts should be corrected leads to some unexpected logical consequences. Let us extend the concept further, with one final, more agreeable imaginary picture. Imagine, please, an attractive individual of whatever sex you prefer. This person is wearing a bathing suit, drinking a piña colada, and standing amid tropical foliage at a resort hotel somewhere in the Caribbean.

Relaxing, isn't it?

In deciding what to do with this image, we color technicians need to know more. Imagine further, then, four different possibilities. Suppose that this is:

a. A picture of a family member, for personal use and enjoyment

b. A posed picture to be used to sell bathing suits in a clothing catalog

c. Intended as a promotional piece for the hotel

d. A shot for a horticultural magazine article discussing the flora of the island

I put it to you that these four scenarios require four different corrections, even though the basic picture is the same. Part of the reason is just a matter of commercial priorities: in cases a, c, or d we do not care particularly whether the color of the bathing suit exactly matches the original, but in case b we care very much indeed. Mostly, though, it is just a matter of placing ourselves in the position of an actual observer. We would be concentrating on whatever most interested us. Whether that happened to be the person, the bathing suit, or the palm trees, that particular area would gain definition at the expense of things that were not as important to us. Furthermore, those unimportant areas would lose color: they would seem to us to be grayer.

What the camera saw was accurate. But it was not real. That, in short, is the case for aggressive color correction.

You Be the Judge

We now embark on more than three hundred pages of image evaluation and enhancement. A few words on procedure first.

Many of the images in this book come from commercial CDs of stock photography. None have been sabotaged so as to create something easier to correct. When the correction is not done in CMYK, it is converted using the Photoshop separation settings

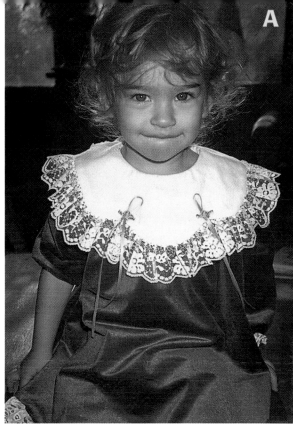

Figure 1.3 Some 500 people have evaluated these three images as if they had to choose one for an unknown client. They were asked to pick the "best" one, with no definition of what that means. How do you think they voted?

suggested in Figure 6.2 on Page 100, and printed without further changes.

Many corrections are therefore incomplete—certain steps, such as fine-tuning a highlight or sharpening, are omitted so that you can see how a certain technique affects the result.

If you wish to follow along—and it's not obvious that you do; you may be better off trying the methods on your own images—many of the ones in here are on the enclosed CD. Those that are have the CD icon inset into the original version.

A book about color manipulation is not like other instructional books. There is much more room for the reader's opinion. The basic question, after any color move, must be, *does the picture look better now?* You do not need fifty years of experience and twelve advanced degrees to answer this. If you disagree with my assessment in certain cases, you shouldn't be surprised.

Color means different things to different people. Varying interpretations of what is important in a picture are possible, as we saw in our imaginary trip to the Caribbean. Possibly more important, individuals do see color differently.

It's therefore somewhat difficult, to put it mildly, to predict what people will like. Test yourself with Figure 1.3. Which of the three versions do you like best? Do you think the world at large will agree with you? Let me rephrase. I've asked around 500 people this same question. How many of them do you think voted for each version?

From my point of view, version C stands out a mile. It's sharper, higher contrast, has better hair color, and is generally more believable. Around five years ago, I had a jury of ten professionals evaluate this and some 50 other sets of three images by secret

ballot under controlled lighting conditions. All 10 jurors agreed that C is the best.

Whereupon, I wrote an article stating that the other two were unacceptable, because it was obvious that nobody could possibly prefer either one of them.

This turned out to be a miscalculation. I then started asking my classes to evaluate the same three images, among others, and a most annoying trend evinced itself. Every now and then someone would vote for version A. Well, maybe a bit more often than now and then. A gets around 20% of the vote, and C 80%. Nobody votes for B.

If you yourself voted for A, the rest of the world disagrees with you by a 4-1 margin. The reason is briefly stated: if the choice comes down to good color vs. good contrast, contrast usually wins.

If, like me, you voted for C, you should probably give some thought to why there is a minority view. In fact, the explanation is simple. Those choosing A always state that they think the face in C is jaundiced. They cheerfully concede that in every other way it's a superior image. But they think the face is so obviously the most important area that they sweep away all other arguments and vote for A, notwithstanding that the face is no work of art there either.

So, there is a method to the apparent madness. And we have to cater to the fact that people may decide that certain objects in the image are more important than we would rate them ourselves. There's nothing irrational about this.

What would be irrational would be if a client preferred version B. Considering that it's running 0 for 500 at this point, it's fair to say that B is an inferior image.

To *correct* means to make better. Given this unanimity, it is certainly fair to say that either A or C is a *corrected* version of B: not just different, but *better.* Your clients know that thay are better just as well as we do, and if you persist in giving them images that look like B when A or C is possible, you will pay a price, sooner or later.

The CMYK Standard

People involved with color printing for a living tend not to be very tolerant of those who preach other standards than the one we all use, which is CMYK. Within about a hundred pages, I think, you will be a believer, if you are not already. For the time being I ask you merely to accept that CMYK is the system that all printers and virtually all prepress professionals employ, and the one that will be used throughout the first part of this book.

CMYK is the abbreviation for the four inks—cyan, magenta, yellow, and black—that are used in normal printing. These four are sometimes referred to as the *process colors. K* is the abbreviation for black because at one time it was customary to refer to cyan as *blue* and to magenta as *red,* so the letter *B* is ambiguous. In the pressroom, *blue* and *red* are still synonyms for cyan and magenta, which can lead to confusion. In this book, *blue* and *red* mean what they do in everyday English.

Every color that the press can reproduce with these inks is expressed in terms of percentages. $70^C 0^M 100^Y$ means 70 percent of the maximum cyan plus the absolute maximum yellow, with no magenta. If the black value is zero, we omit it.

The numbers just given describe a color known as Kelly green. If you are to become a color corrector you will have to understand this intuitively: you must know approximately what will result from any mixture of colors. Similarly, you must know the general impact of changing any of these numbers slightly. Suppose, for example, that we increase cyan. This will move us toward a color we might call forest green. If we remove cyan, on the other hand, we will tend toward chartreuse, and eventually, if enough cyan comes out, toward yellow.

Yellow cannot go higher, since it is already maxed out, but if we reduce it we will start to see a purer, yet less intense, green. Magenta cannot go lower, since it is at zero now, but if we increase it, interesting things will happen, and happen fast.

In a situation like this, where two of the three colors predominate, the odd man out (the magenta here) is called the *unwanted color.* This is a misnomer. It is not unwanted at all by the intelligent artist: we want it a whole lot, because we can do more to add punch to the image by manipulating it than we can with the dominant plates.

The unwanted color controls how "clean" or "dirty" the dominating color appears. When working with green, the addition of magenta moves it toward gray. Magenta has such a powerful impact on green that if we can engineer detail into the magenta we are certain to see it in the green, even if the cyan and yellow plates have poor contrast. The unwanted-color channel is so surpassingly important that, if need be, we will construct one out of fragments of other channels. We will spend all of Chapter 5 discussing this.

In previous editions of this book, this has been the occasion for a brain-teaser. I provided the four channels that made up a CMYK image and asked readers to guess which was which. Exploiting the strengths of the individual channels is one of the hallmarks of a good retoucher, so it was a fair question. Most people got it wrong.

We live in a cruel world, and over the years life has gotten ever crueler for the color technician. Figure 1.4 is truly a cruel thing, a puzzle too difficult even for most experts to solve. If you think you're an expert, by all means spin your wheels in it.

If not, skip on to the next section. But in either case, once you get through this book you will probably be able to nail it.

There were three originals, one in RGB, one in LAB, one in CMYK. The A and B channels of LAB are omitted, leaving eight. Your mission is to identify which channel is which. If you're not a gardener, this is a

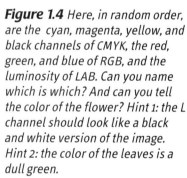

Figure 1.4 Here, in random order, are the cyan, magenta, yellow, and black channels of CMYK, the red, green, and blue of RGB, and the luminosity of LAB. Can you name which is which? And can you tell the color of the flower? Hint 1: the L channel should look like a black and white version of the image. Hint 2: the color of the leaves is a dull green.

rhododendron, whose leaves are dull green. The flower can be almost any color.

If you absolutely must have another hint, you can turn the page and look at Figure 1.5, which shows the image in color. That, of course, is the coward's way out. Come up with your answers before reading the next few paragraphs.

Sorting Out Eight Channels

The purpose of black is to strengthen dark areas. Consequently the black is invariably the lightest of the four CMYK channels, which are themselves lighter than the RGB channels. That means that version D here is like the free space in bingo. It's the black. That leaves seven toughies to untangle.

Versions A, E, and H share an anomaly. Notice how the darkest areas have been flattened out, especially in A and E? This identifies them as CMY channels. If you know why, you understand a lot more about the characteristics of CMYK than do most of the folk who work at prepress houses.

In CMYK, the printer usually imposes an arbitrary limit on the total amount of ink that can be laid down in the darkest areas of an image. With 100% being the maximum in each channel, 400% is theoretically possible. Nevertheless, the printer will impose a limit of somewhere between 225% and 350%, with 300% being what is known as the SWOP (for Specifications for Web Offset Publications) standard. 300% is also Photoshop's default.

In RGB, where there are no inks and therefore no ink limits, channels can be completely solid in the darkest neutral areas. In CMY, they can't, except in the black itself.

Now that we know which ones are the CMY channels, it's time to pair them off

with their RGB counterparts. Many retouchers don't realize how similar the two are. We'll discuss this in Chapter 7. For the time being, take my word for it that the cyan will resemble the red, the magenta the green, and the yellow the blue.

Fair enough. Excluding D as being the known black, it's obvious that E and G are a pair. It may take a second or two more to observe that A and F are also partners.

Whether H mates with B or C is a tough call. The relationship in darkness between flower and leaves seems to match up best between B and H. That means that C, the odd man out, is probably the L of LAB.

To narrow down the identity of the remaining six, we need to turn to our color knowledge. We have no clue as to what color the flower is, but we do know that leaves are green. Even in a dull green, yellow and cyan will dominate. Since A's leaves are clearly lighter than those of its CMY partners, it's the magenta, and its cousin, F, is the green.

Notice how much harder it would have been if we had to distinguish the green channel from the red and the blue—there never is as much color variation in RGB as there is in the CMY channels.

Another such anomaly helps us sort out the others. In RGB, the deepest shadows should be roughly equal in every channel. That's because equal values in RGB make a neutral color. But in CMY, they don't. More cyan is needed. H is darker in the shadows than E. That pinpoints it as the cyan, E the yellow, and E's partner, G, the blue.

The lighter, contrastier shadows also confirm that C is the luminosity of LAB, making B the red.

This may seem like a useless trivia contest. If that's what you think, you may be

Figure 1.5 *Here's the actual image on which Figure 1.5 was based. Were your guesses about which channel was which correct?*

And black kills everything.

You should also adopt professional terminology regarding color ranges. The darkest significant neutral area of the image is called the *shadow*. This can be confusing, since we often deal with literal shadows. For graphic arts purposes, the *shadow* of Figure 1.1 is in its lower right. There are several potential shadows in Figure 1.3, such as directly above the girl's left shoulder or next to her left hand.

We call the lightest significant white area of the image the *highlight*. In Figure 1.1, the highlight is where the waterfall hits the pool. In Figure 1.3, it's somewhere in the little girl's collar.

Quartertone, midtone, and *three-quartertone* are the intermediate ranges of the picture. There is no set demarcation between these areas. A value of 25% is plainly quartertone and 50% is midtone, but what about 35%?

This is not as ambiguous as it sounds. Since nobody can guess color values with single-digit precision, we need more inclusive words. If you look at what you perceive to be Kelly green somewhere in an image, you can't possibly (I don't think) tell whether it is $65^C2^M97^Y$ or $71^C4^M93^Y$. You can, and should, think to yourself, cyan three-quartertone, magenta highlight, yellow shadow. That way, if you are planning some other correction in the image that would affect the cyan three-quartertone, you will realize that it may also have an impact on the Kelly green.

Though the exact numbers were unimportant there, here is one that you *do* have

surprised by the number of times this puzzle will be referred to in the following pages. Twenty-first-century color correction can be in any colorspace, and often the problems can be so severe that we need to choose the right one. These characteristics that we've seen—that the weak channel in CMY is lighter than in RGB; that in RGB the shadows are equal but in CMY they aren't; that in RGB shadow detail is distributed everywhere, but in CMYK it lives in the black—are the keys to figuring out the right way to attack challenging images.

Colors and Their Complements

You need to have confident knowledge of the circle of colors, especially in terms of the complementary colors that they damage so effectively. Magenta falls between red and blue. It kills green. Cyan falls between blue and green. It kills red. Yellow falls between green and red. It kills blue.

to wear next to your heart. $5^C2^M2^Y$, approximately, is the magic number that defines the minimum highlight that most presses can carry and still show detail. Most images have bright white areas somewhere, although many, like Figure 1.5, don't. Our eyes are acutely sensitive to variation in light colors. Consequently, setting the highlight properly is crucial to the success of the overall image.

The darkest shadow is not nearly as important a number, because we lose a lot of color perception in dark areas. Also, this value varies a lot depending upon what kind of paper and press the job is being printed on. If preparing the image for magazine work, we must be conservative and assume that $80^C70^M70^Y70^K$ is the darkest shadow we can use if we expect to see any detail. An image with no area that can legitimately be made into a shadow is unusual, although some do exist, as Figures 2.3 and 9.11 will demonstrate.

Obviously, we can get much higher and lower than these two endpoints. There is nothing in Photoshop to stop us from making areas $0^C0^M0^Y$, or for that matter $100^C100^M100^Y100^K$, although employing that kind of a shadow is a good way to make a lifetime enemy of one's printer.

Our biggest disadvantage is that we don't have access to as wide a range of colors as a photograph, but we still can't push the envelope that far. Not all presses can reproduce a 1% dot. On the shadow side, every press reaches a point where detail can't be held, and this point is usually in the 80s or, if we are lucky, low 90s.

Not that we can't cheat in certain cases. Figure 1.6 demonstrates the perils of dogmatic adherence to numbers. It is not so much a color correction as a *range* correction. All it takes to recognize its effectiveness is a little common sense.

The center of the lava flow is the lightest area of the image. Orthodoxy suggests setting that value at $5^C2^M2^Y$. But what is the point? Do you see any detail there? The defining characteristic of white heat is its brilliance. We have nothing to lose by zeroing it out, and by doing so we open up valuable real estate.

In just the same way, the danger of an excessively dark shadow is that it will lose detail and seem to be nothing but an area of solid black. In the area on the cliffs just to the left of the lava flow, that's what we've got already. So how can we hurt things by going beyond the usual limits? By increasing the range of the image, we get more contrast everywhere. Do you see it in the cliffs?

If you agree that the second version of this image is palpably better than the first, it seems that you must also agree that before doing anything to a picture, a careful analysis of its strengths and weaknesses is key to success.

And, in the process, we will make the image look more vivid, more lifelike, by making it look more like what a human observer would see and less like camerawork. At the risk of being repetitive, we need not match the art, but match the art's meaning.

The Power of Curves

Photoshop is one of the most terrifying applications around in terms of the number of capabilities, tools, and commands thrown at the user. Luckily, the professional can ignore most of them when correcting color. However, in the arsenal we will bring to bear against inadequate color in the coming chapters, the most useful weapon is also the most frightening.

Input-output curves (found under Image: Adjust>Curves) are by far the most important correction tool in Photoshop or any other color manipulation program. They operate in close conjunction with the density readout provided in the Info palette (if it isn't visible on the monitor, go to Window: Show Info).

Curves can remap an entire image, affect only a limited range of one color, or anything in between. If we leave a particular color's curve alone, we will get a straight line at a 45° angle. If we start adding points, we may get sections of the curve that are steeper or flatter than others. In the areas that are steeper, the image will show more contrast, and in flatter areas there will be less. When the curve is higher than the original 45° line, the image will be darker than it was at first, and in areas where the curve is lower, the image will be lighter.

Photoshop lets us enter curve points directly from the keyboard, or we can move the points up and down with the mouse. We can check Preview in the Curves dialog box to get an interactive feel as we manipulate. However we decide to do these things, the density readout in the Info palette will show both the present value and what will happen if the new curve is implemented.

The power of curves is immense. We will come back to them over and over. If you understand how to apply curves you will get great color even if you never use any other feature or tool in Photoshop.

Obviously these other things have their uses. I will list the principal ones in a moment. First, however, now that we have defined the most underrated feature of the program, a word about the most overrated, the one that most often snags nonpro-fessionals into needless or even counter-productive correction cycles.

Photoshop makes it seductively easy to "select" areas of an image to be worked on in isolation, so that any changes will affect only the selected region and not the rest of the image. Human nature makes us want to fix things that are obviously broken. So, upon encountering a pink horse, the natural, understandable reaction of most Photoshoppers is to select it and make it white.

This is not the best approach. A pink horse may be the most blatant problem in our image, but it won't be the only one. Whatever caused the horse to appear pink will also have an impact on the rest of the picture. It will be subtler, probably because we are seldom as sure about what colors are impossible as we are about pink horses. An overall correction is likely to make everything look better, not just the horse.

There are certainly times when we have to select. Clearly, if we are silhouetting part of an image or extending a background, there is no way around making a selection first. When one important area of an image is horrendously defective and the rest is more or less OK, we also need to select. If we are trying to enhance some small area with one of our retouching tools, it may make sense to isolate it from any surrounding areas that are much different in color or texture. And when we encounter a shot that has two conflicting light sources, a selection is usually the only way of reconciling the color throughout the image.

To think like a professional, when the idea of selecting crosses your mind, take your hand off the mouse and sit on it. Make a selection only when you are sure there is no other sensible way to handle the problem you are trying to fix.

All the Tools You'll Ever Need

Although we will be covering a wide variety of color problems, the fraction of Photoshop's tools that we will use is rather small. All the rest are unnecessary unless we get involved in heavy special effects, and sometimes not even then.

So, without further ado, and from left to right on the monitor, here are the tools of our trade. There will be a brief explanation of some of them when they are first introduced, but if you are not familiar with them ahead of time and are a coward by nature, recourse to the manual may be an option.

Starting with the toolbox, at the top we will need (although not as much as you probably think) the selection tools: the lasso, the magnetic lasso, marquees, and the magic wand. In conjunction with these, the various simple commands located under the Select heading in the menu bar.

Next, the *practical tools:* there is nothing elegant about cropping off part of a picture or rotating it, but in the real world we frequently have to do it for efficiency's sake. So we will need the crop tool and the Image: Rotate command. We also have to be familiar with the Quick Mask feature in the toolbox, and the Foreground/Background color change box.

The retouching tools for our purposes consist of the rubber stamp tool, the airbrush, the blur/sharpen/smudge tool, and the dodge/burn/sponge tool.

On to the menu bar. Edit: Fade, formerly Filter: Fade, is a highly useful item that we will be discussing more in later chapters.

Edit: Color Settings replaces in one neat package four separate dialogs of Photoshop 5, including RGB Setup and CMYK Setup. We used to have to visit CMYK Setup a lot to make changes for individual images, but

that's no longer necessary. Now, we do this in the new Image: Mode>Convert to Profile command, which is to its predecessor, Photoshop 5's Profile to Profile, roughly as a Ferrari is to a moped with engine trouble. We now use Convert to Profile to change the method of black generation, as discussed in Chapter 6, to adjust for different dot gains and/or ink limits, as discussed in Chapter 12, and occasionally for really weird purposes, such as to create false

Figure 1.6 *Cost-free color correction. There is almost no detail in either the brightest or darkest areas of this image. This means that we can go beyond normal limits in portraying them (bottom), giving ourselves more contrast without losing anything of value.*

separations from which we can steal channels for later blends or masks.

Mode eventually has to be CMYK, our bread-and-butter correction colorspace. But it isn't always the best one to work in, particularly in the case of seriously troubled images. In Chapters 7–9, we'll get heavily into the attractions of other options: RGB, HSB, and especially LAB.

The awesome capabilities of Image: Adjust>Curves overshadow other important options under the same menu bar item. With Image: Image Size we control resolution, and with Image: Canvas Size we can arrange to have two files at the same exact size, a prerequisite for compositing.

Image: Extract is a new and reasonably powerful way to create masks. I don't find it as flexible as stealing the masks out of various channels, but other people do.

Image: Duplicate makes a second version of a document, which is very important in correction. As

shown in Figure 1.7, Image: Apply Image allows us to crossbreed channels.

Image: Adjust>Selective Color lets us get at particular colors wherever they occur, without affecting the rest of the image. It is more accurate but less flexible than Image: Adjust>Hue/Saturation. Both of these commands should be used *after* basic curve corrections, because the presumption is that a global curve change will make all colors fall into place.

Photoshop's mathematical Filter options give creative artists lots of exciting choices. Here is where one can find twirls, mosaics, and motion blurs, and here is where we will

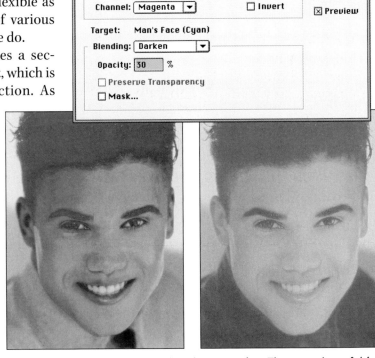

Figure 1.7 *Mathematical blends of two plates are a recurring theme in color correction. The cyan plate of this image (left) is weak and lacking in facial detail. The magenta plate (center) is more desirable. To create a cyan that is more detailed yet still lighter than the magenta, Photoshop lets us average the two: the image at right is a 70–30 blend, but only in areas where the magenta was originally darker, to protect the color of the shirt.*

THE PREFLIGHT ANALYSIS

✓ Despite the maturity of the prepress process, there is no general agreement on a very fundamental question. Should the color technician try to match the original photograph or what human observers would have seen had they been in the position of the camera?

✓ Humans and cameras do not see things the same way. If you have decided to make your images match the meaning of the art rather than the art itself, several sorts of correction will become very familiar.

✓ Our color perception changes so that colors we know to be white or gray appear that way to us, regardless of the ambient lighting. The camera, however, will see a color cast if there is one and will incorporate it into the photograph.

✓ When we focus on a certain object we will see more detail in it and less in surrounding objects. The camera will treat them all equally. This means that some pictures must be corrected differently in different contexts.

✓ When looking at an image with an obvious color defect, do not go charging in to fix it. Corrections are generally best made to the image as a whole. The horrible defect you see may be your biggest problem, but it won't be your only one.

✓ Since printing has a smaller color range to begin with than does an original photograph, it's imperative not to waste any of it. This means that special attention must be paid to the lightest and darkest points of the image to make sure that they are close to the limit of what the press can reproduce.

✓ Individuals often disagree on which of two variations of an image is better. However, there is a certain category that virtually every viewer prefers, namely, images with more detail. The things people disagree on usually concern color.

✓ Photoshop has a dazzlingly complete suite of commands and tools, but there is no need to be intimidated. High-level image enhancement and color correction require only a fraction of them. The overwhelming majority of professional color correction work is done through manipulation of input-output curves.

✓ Color casts that are nearly invisible on the monitor can be quite offensive in print. The only way to ensure that the image doesn't retain such a cast is to examine color values in the Info palette and correct if necessary.

leave them. In our world, the only filters we need are Unsharp Mask and its complement, Gaussian Blur, for which Dust & Scratches is sometimes a good substitute.

The options under Layer have great significance, although perhaps not as much for us as for those who do lots of special effects. The Layer Mask is, in my view, the most important tool in heavy-duty retouching. And layering can be an important safety net, allowing us to cancel, in whole or in part, some Photoshop butchery we've inflicted on the image.

Select: Feather lets us achieve soft edges when we are silhouetting or are forced to make a locally selected correction. Used to an extreme degree, it can also be an effective fadeout tool. Select: Color Ranges is a useful way to isolate individual colors.

Of the palettes accessible under the Window command, the ones we will be visiting constantly are the density monitor (a.k.a. the Info palette) and the toolbox. There will also be frequent side jaunts to the Layers and Channels palettes. If you never make mistakes that you discover much later, you won't need the History palette, which allows multiple undo; the rest of us probably do need it from time to time.

In the Layers palette, in certain commands, and in most painting tools we have several blending options. The one called *Normal* is self-explanatory, but many people have trouble grasping Darken and its opposite, Lighten. *Darken* really means, don't lighten; only make the change in areas where it will make the result darker, and ignore it elsewhere. In Figure 1.7, we're blending the center version into the left one, Darken mode. The center version has a darker face, but a lighter background. The background therefore is excluded from the blend, while the face gets darker.

We also frequently use Luminosity mode, but that takes several chapters to explain, so please be patient. And occasionally we even use other modes.

There you have it. With this small group of tools, the whole gamut of professional color is accessible. Provided, of course, that we bring along the most important tools of all: our eyes and good judgment.

2

Color Correction By the Numbers

When looking at an image for the first time, we often see what we perceive to be many small problems. Normally, they are all part of one bigger problem, which can be solved all at once with an application of Photoshop's most powerful tool, curves.

Monkeying around with the color balance of photographic images is not a sport for the timid, or so goes the conventional wisdom. Believing this, people go through the most simian sorts of shenanigans trying to make their color look believable. They select this area, sharpen that one, call up histograms, apply strange filters, and generally try to demonstrate that if an infinite number of art directors employ an infinite number of digital tweaks somebody somewhere may throw them a banana.

And yet, most color correction could be handled by monkeys. This chapter and the next introduce a numerical, curve-based approach calling for little artistic judgment. To be sure, one can go much farther—that's why the book has 250 more pages—but all the advanced techniques are inevitably based on these surpassingly simple ones.

The by-the-numbers rules can be stated in a single sentence.

Use the full range of available tones every time, and don't give the viewers any colors that they will know better than to believe.

To see how this deceptively simple concept works in practice, here is an imaginary problem that may at first seem ridiculous. Figure 2.1 is the black and white image of me that used to grace my magazine column. The question is, supposing the unsupposable, that it were in color, what would our by-the-numbers objectives be in correcting it?

At this point you may say, how can we possibly know what a black and white image should look like in color, any more than we know how colors would look to us if we were Martians?

That attitude assumes that we know nothing about the colors of this image. Actually, we know quite a bit. True, we have no idea what color my tie should be, but what about my hair? As you can see, I don't use Grecian Formula. What color hair do you think I have, green?

Similarly, we have no clue as to what color my jacket is, but men in business attire usually wear shirts that are either white or some distinct other color, not some muddy combination. This one happens to be white; if we saw a rendition of this image in color, regardless of how bad the monitor, we'd realize this.

And, though my skin is dark, there are limits to the range of normal skin tones.

These considerations are very typical. The giveaways of problems in color reproduction are almost always fleshtones and neutral colors—grays and whites.

A General Approach to Correction

If we are to use the full range of available tones, we must find the whitest and darkest areas of the image, and make them as light and as dark as we can, given our paper and printing process. Many pictures are complex enough that we must mosey around quite a bit to find these endpoints. Here, though, the lightest point is evidently somewhere in my collar, and the darkest is in the stripes of my tie.

At this juncture, we decide how strictly we will adhere to our general guidelines on highlight and shadow. This decision depends on how significant we believe the endpoints are to the overall picture. In the case at hand, I would say that preserving detail in the white shirt is important, so we should try to stick with a conservative highlight, but I am not particularly enamored of holding detail in the stripes of the tie, so I would not go to excruciating lengths to stay within normal shadow range.

All that remains is to enforce our numerical decisions by means of curves. Since there are both neutral colors in this picture (the hair and the shirt) and fleshtones, we must check, before applying the curves, that these colors stick to certain standards, which I am about to discuss.

Throughout the next four chapters, the

Figure 2.1 *This image is in black and white, but we can make generalizations about how we would treat it if it were in color.*

images begin in CMYK, and this is the colorspace we will work in. This is for simplicity's sake. If, for the time being, you absolutely must use RGB, you can, by clicking on the eyedropper icon in the right side of the Info palette, display RGB and CMYK equivalents simultaneously. But if you do this, you are a sissy. Sooner or later you *will* correct in CMYK—why not now?

The Magic Numbers

As a first step, we must force the image to meet four numerical requirements. Three of these cater to the most illogical feature of CMYK: the weakness of cyan ink.

In RGB, a neutral gray, regardless of how dark it is, has equal values of red, green, and blue. One might suppose that the same would be true in CMY, but it isn't. Magenta and yellow must be equal, true, but cyan has to be higher. If not, the gray will actually print somewhat reddish, because the cyan ink is supposed to absorb red light, and it does a lousy job of it.

Correction by the numbers is the foundation on which all quality rests. The fact that further improvement is possible beyond merely setting numbers is why this book has more than 300 pages. Be that as it may, those whose basic numbers aren't correct condemn themselves to third-rate color, regardless of their Photoshop skills. A numbers-conscious monkey could do better; a color-blind person could do better.

In the 1994 edition of this book, having no monkey available, I backed this provocative statement up by actually training a color-blind person to color-correct. His work was impressive, better than that of many students with perfect color vision but the wrong mentality.

Having made the point, I see no reason to repeat those images here, but Figure 2.2, which didn't appear because it was one of his failures, is a fitting way to start the discussion. Although it is a failure, it is also a success in a way, due to his adherence to the following numerical rules.

- The **shadow** is the darkest significant neutral area of an image. Around 99 percent of images have *something* we can use for a shadow. Figure 2.3 is the exception.

In principle, the shadow should be set to the heaviest value we believe that the output device can hold with detail. Thus, for sheetfed commercial printing, the shadow value should be higher than for this book, which in turn should be higher than for a newspaper. If unsure, use what I'm using here: $80^C70^M70^Y70^K$. One or more of these numbers can be higher in a deep color. Navy blue, for instance, might be $95^C65^M15^Y50^K$.

Many printing applications put a set limit on the sum of all four inks, the better to allow ink to dry. The better the printing condition, the higher the allowable number. SWOP, the industry-standard Specifications for Web Offset Publications, mandates a maximum of 300, which most magazines tweak down to 280. My suggestion, $80^C70^M70^Y70^K$, sums to 290, close enough.

290 is not close enough, however, when preparing images for a newspaper, which is apt to ask for 240, or even for some desktop printers. If a lower number is necessary, we reduce the CMY colors and increase black in roughly equal amounts.

People don't have good color perception in areas this dark, so, if need be, we can take liberties with one or two of the ink values. Don't do this without a good reason, though. An unbalanced shadow often is a symptom of a color cast that may be subtly hurting other parts of the image.

Figure 2.2 *The bottom version is a "correction" of the original, top. It was executed by a color-blind person, and it looks it. But this was a skilled person, who works by the numbers. Can you figure out how he went astray?*

• The **highlight** is the lightest significant part of the image, with two qualifications. First, it cannot be a reflection or a light source. These things are called *speculars,* or *catchlights.* We ignore them. Second, it must be something that we are willing to represent to the viewer as being *white.* Assuming that all these requirements are met, use a value of $5^C2^M2^Y$.

Other experts suggest different things. They may tell you $4^C2^M2^Y$, $3^C1^M1^Y$, $5^C3^M3^Y$, or $6^C3^M3^Y$. But everyone agrees that magenta and yellow should be equal, and cyan a couple of points higher. There is such universal agreement because this highlight value is critical. We humans are quite sensitive to light colors, so a variation of two points in any ink could result in an unacceptable color cast.

Doubt the impact of an incorrect highlight? Then return to Figure 2.2. The "correction" by Ralph Viola, the color-blind person, has a lot to be said for it, as by-the-numbers corrections always do. There seems to be more depth, more snap, than in the top version. But the color is wrong.

That problem developed when Ralph set his highlight. He knew enough not to use the top of the wine glass: that's a reflection. He was looking for something very light, yet nonreflective, and *white.* And he thought the bottle's label *was* white, because he can't see yellow. So he arranged to set a highlight in the label, *making* it white.

This torched color balance and created a blue cast throughout the lighter half of the image. Darker objects are not affected as much, since Ralph's curves introduced the cast into a light area. The wine bottle isn't that bad. But the wood is now gray.

Those with normal color vision have no

trouble detecting that the label shouldn't be white. A lot of people, though, fall into the same kind of trap when the off-color isn't quite as obvious.

Looking for the Sure Thing

Like any brute-force approach, our by-the-numbers approach requires certainty. In Figure 2.3, we can be certain that there is a white somewhere in the clouds, and almost certainly in the statue as well. So we force the lightest point to be a white.

Ralph's folly, on the other hand, doesn't have a palpably white point. The label is definitely the lightest significant nonreflective part of the image, and it's definitely yellow. How yellow it is, logic can't tell us. But logic does say that the cyan and magenta should be minimum. We have, in other words, two-thirds of a highlight. Rather than the $5^C2^M2^Y$ we'd use in Figure 2.3, we have to go with $5^C2^M?^Y$.

So, what should Ralph have done with the yellow value? The answer is as obvious as it is frustrating.

He should have guessed. That's what we do when we aren't sure. And because we hate being tossed about in a sea of guesses, we always have to be on the lookout for anchors, colors that are sure things. The most common example of that is colors that logic tells us must be neutral.

• For an area that is supposed to appear **neutral,** that is, white, black, or any shade of gray, the magenta and yellow values should be equal and the cyan higher. How *much* higher is an open question; two or three points ought to do it in the highlights, six or seven in the midtones, nine or ten in the shadows.

I used to think that if there was a problem meeting this requirement, it is better to

Figure 2.3 *This image has no shadow at all, no point that can be considered to be a dark gray or black. Such images are rare—try to locate another one!*

be too heavy in the cyan than either of the other colors, since bluish grays are less obtrusive than greenish or reddish ones. I've changed my mind; the grays themselves may be more believable, but overall the image is likely to be worse. Even slight cyan casts are disagreeable. Slight casts in the direction of a warm color are often pleasing.

The statue of Figure 2.4 is gray. Our logic tells us so, even if we've never seen it in person. So, here I've made it a nearly perfect gray. I've measured a point in the arm as $20^C15^M15^Y$; other points are comparable.

But is this the only possibility? Could this not be yellowed with age as well, or perhaps brownish? Here's a quiz. Let's raise each ink, in turn, by 5%. There are a total of six possibilities, counting combinations of two inks. For example, $20^C10^M10^Y$ would imply a slight cyan cast. $15^C15^M15^Y$ is higher in both magenta and yellow, which combine to make red. Therefore, it's a reddish, or warm, or brownish, cast.

The other four possibilities are $20^C15^M10^Y$, $20^C10^M15^Y$, $15^C15^M10^Y$, and $15^C10^M15^Y$. They yield (but not in this order; you have to figure it out) yellow, green, magenta, and blue.

That part is so easy that I won't waste space on the answers. The harder question is, which, if any, of these six possibilities do you think is a reasonable alternative to pure gray? Come up with a response before you turn the page to Figure 2.5.

• **Fleshtones** should have at least as much yellow as magenta, and up to a third again as much in extreme cases. Where the yellow is equal to or only slightly higher than the magenta, this implies a very light-skinned person, such as a small child or a blonde. For Caucasians, the cyan value should be a fifth to a third as heavy as the magenta, depending upon how bronzed a person is. For a dark-skinned person like myself, $15^C50^M65^Y$ will do; lighter-skinned people can go $7^C35^M40^Y$ or even lower.

Finding an image's typical fleshtone is easy enough with experience, but if you haven't tried it before, there are some snares to avoid. Measure only areas that are in normal lighting, not a shadow or a semi-reflection. Also, avoid any area where there's likely to be makeup, such as a woman's cheeks. You may wish to make a small selection of what seems like an appropriate area, use Filter: Blur>Gaussian Blur at a high value to make the selection take on a uniform color, and then measure that before cancelling the blur.

Except in persons of African descent, it is not customary to have black ink in a fleshtone, but it sometimes happens, particularly when using nonstandard GCR settings (see Chapter 6 for more on this). If there *is* black in the fleshtone, count it as additional cyan, because it does the same thing: it pushes the color away from red and toward gray.

Writing Curves: A First Step

To start, we open up the image and check the ink values, using the Info palette, in the highlight and shadow areas, plus fleshtones and any area you are certain is close to neutral. First, though, click on the eyedropper tool, and set its sampling to 3×3 rather than the default single pixel, which can give a false view of what is going on.

In simple pictures, we can keep these numbers straight in our heads, but as they get more complex, writing down the density values and what we propose to do with them can be helpful. To the extent the image does not meet our target numbers, we apply curves to force it closer to them.

To do so, open Image: Adjust>Curves. Ignore the default, or master curve. Go directly into the individual colors. To agree with the examples in this book, please be sure that shadows are set to the right and highlights to the left. This is done, if necessary, by clicking on the light-to-dark bar at the bottom of the curves panel.

The horizontal axis of the curve represents the original values of the image. The vertical axis is the values the curve will cause the image to take, when we click OK.

The default curve is not a curve at all, but a straight line at a 45° angle. If we decide that we are going to change it (and we may well decide to leave it alone) we can

Figure 2.4 *This garden statue surely should be gray— approximately. But should it be exactly gray? This one is, according to measurements in the arms. Turn the page to see some other possibilities.*

A Plan for Using This Book

To jump-start your effort to correct by the numbers, here's some advice, as well as some common problems readers have run into over the three previous editions of *Professional Photoshop.*

For the first time, we're including a CD containing many of the originals used here. These are indicated by the CD icon next to the uncorrected image. Although, in deference to those readers who demanded that I do so, images from most chapters are included, I recommend that you *not* use the CD for Chapters 2–5. The reason is, you should use your own. The techniques in these chapters apply to almost all images and I think you'll be more impressed if you apply them to ones you're more familiar with. Later, particularly in Chapters 16 and 17, which show techniques that are right for certain images and not for others, you should probably use the ones on the CD. Also, in those images I used a lot of blending percentages that are really personal preference, as opposed to the curves in earlier chapters, which I think are basically the one and only best way. By working on these blend images yourself, you can get a good idea of what the other options are, should you decide you don't like my choices.

This and the next three chapters assume CMYK files. For the moment, never mind how they got into CMYK. This is discussed in Chapter 6. Also, ignore the possibility of correcting in RGB or LAB. These options are discussed beginning in Chapter 7. The reason for this organization is that if you are preparing files for print, knowledge of CMYK correction is indispensable. A CMYK-only workflow isn't particularly smart, but one can get by with it. A CMYK-never philosophy is another story.

If you are converting your own files into CMYK and trying to follow the numbers, you'll have a problem if you use Photoshop defaults, which will give you strange shadow values. The quick fix is to enter Edit: Color Settings>Working CMYK and choose Custom CMYK. Skip ahead to Figure 6.2 on Page 100 and copy its values. You'll need to know why later on, but it's not important now.

To maintain your sanity, I strongly recommend that you make a decision as to which side of the curves dialog should represent lightness and which darkness. By default, Photoshop sets lightness to the left in CMYK, but to the right in RGB. This has blinded generation after generation of users to the essential similarity of the two colorspaces. If you make these settings uniform, the shape of the correction curve in the cyan channel of CMYK will be very similar to what it would be in the red if you did the work in RGB. The green correction would resemble the magenta and the blue the yellow. Because my background is CMYK, I've set lightness to the left in both colorspaces throughout the book. It doesn't hurt to reverse this if you are more comfortable with it, but then you have to reverse my curves in your mind. To reverse the sides of the curve, simply click on the gradation line beneath the horizontal axis of the curve.

As with previous editions, many sets of images have circular color swatches inset, with their CMYK values indicated. This was by reader request and is intended to help you start to visualize what colors various CMYK combinations produce. The swatch represents an important color in the image. The swatches in the corrected version(s) show what that same color has been changed to.

Finally, you should commit the basic colors to memory, ignoring black, which is neutral. If there are two strong CMY channels and one weak one, this creates red, green, or blue. If only one is strong and two are weak, the overall color is cyan, magenta, or yellow. Thus, $20^C90^M90^Y$ is a red; $20^C20^M90^Y$ is yellow; $20^C70^M90^Y$ is a yellowish red; $20^C40^M90^Y$ is a reddish yellow.

Figure 2.5 *Even when the precise color of a near-neutral object is unknown, logic and experience can exclude certain possibilities. Obviously this garden statue could be gray, but it might have a slight color. Here are six possibilities, all generated by five-point increments in the CMY values at a certain point in the neck. Clockwise from top left: red, magenta, blue, cyan, green, and yellow casts. Which ones do you think are plausible? If you encounter one of the others, correct it!*

keep it a straight line by changing one or both of the endpoints. Normally, though, we insert one or more intermediate points and adjust them up and down. If we do so, the straight line will become a curve.

If the entire new curve falls below the original 45°, the corrected image will be lighter than the original. If it falls above the default, the new image will be darker. Most of the time, we will want curves that fit neither description, but that make some parts of the image darker and others lighter.

Parts of such a curve will end up steeper than 45°. To compensate, other parts will have to become flatter. When the curve is applied, areas that fall in its steeper parts will gain contrast, and objects located in the flatter parts will, sad to say, lose out.

To locate highlight and shadow, I personally prefer to run the cursor over several likely areas and watch the Info palette. This lets me choose the second-lightest area as a highlight, if I decide that the real lightest area isn't important to the image.

If you are uncomfortable with this, you can open Image: Adjust>Threshold and move its slider until it becomes obvious where the light and dark points are.

In the imaginary color image of me, suppose that we measure the lightest area of the white shirt and discover that it is $12^C10^M18^Y$. Measurements of the stripes of the tie find $70^C65^M85^Y50^K$.

We start by adding two points to each curve. In cyan, we want what is now 12^C to become 5^C, since we are shooting for a highlight of $5^C2^M2^Y$. We will also insert a point that brings 70^C up to 80^C. Similarly, we adjust each of the other colors so that we hit the targets for highlight and shadow.

Before clicking OK, we run the cursor across the neutral areas of the picture. The Info palette will tell us both what the values are currently and what they will become after applying the curve. Ideally, the neutral areas will have equal magenta and yellow and slightly more cyan; if not, we will have to make further adjustments to the curves.

Avoiding the Impossible: How the Pros Know the Numbers

There's a popular misconception that the best retouchers know exactly what numbers to shoot for no matter how esoteric the subject matter. In real life, the key is more to avoid numbers that can't possibly be right. If we find any such in the image, we have to twist curves or whatever to avoid them. Here's a brief guide to familiar colors, starting with the easiest.

GREENS are nominally equal combinations of cyan and yellow, with much less magenta. In practice most greens favor their yellow neighbor. Cyanish greens are quite rare. Often yellow is as much as half again higher than cyan. In the natural "green" of a plant, equal cyan and yellow would be impossible. On the other hand, if the cyan is so low that it's closer to the magenta value than the yellow, then it's a greenish yellow rather than a yellowish green. That's impossible, too. If we discover either situation in our picture, we have to correct. We may not get the right color, but it has to be better than an impossible one.

REDS are nominally equal combinations of magenta and yellow, with much less cyan. If the magenta is slightly higher than yellow, it's a rosier red. If yellow is higher, it's an angrier, more orange color. Faces are close to equal, but when they aren't, it's always a yellowish red. Reddish yellows, and magentaish red, are impossible in faces. In other things that are red, anything goes.

BLUES would, in a perfect world, have equal amounts of cyan and magenta. Photoshop commands like Hue/Saturation and Selective Color that are capable of targeting "blues" in fact make this assumption. The sad fact is that equal cyan and magenta makes purple, so any real blue will have decidedly more cyan. The color of most skies is even more heavily skewed; many skies are better described as bluish cyan than cyanish blue.

Intelligent retouchers therefore look at suspect areas of an image and ask, are these color values even *possible?* If they are, we don't try to mastermind the operation by guessing at how they might be better. But if the colors are impossible, we have to change them, even if we aren't positive of what to change them to.

For example, if you were asked to define the hair color known as *blonde,* you would probably say it was yellow. Pure yellow, in the sense of equal cyan and magenta, is in fact possible. More commonly, though, the hair is a *reddish* yellow, meaning yellow first, magenta second, cyan third. A greenish yellow, with cyan higher than magenta, is impossible. If the image features greenish yellow hair, this has to be changed. I can't tell you to what, but you can't let it be green.

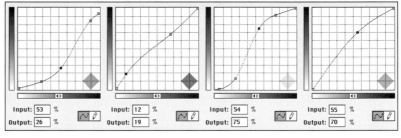

Figure 2.6 Correcting this image requires picking its lightest and darkest significant points, and forcing neutrality into at least parts of the clouds. Right, the curves that transform the original, left, into the version at right.

If a major amount of work went into these curves, we should take advantage of the Save option in the Curves dialog box before doing anything else. If we do this and then decide that a slight modification is necessary (or, heaven forfend, if we make some big mistake and are forced to File: Revert to the last saved version of the image) we can cancel the changes, then reopen the dialog box and choose the Load option to reinstate the curves. Or, we can save the curves within an Adjustment Layer, which will allow us to change the curves later even if there are other intermediate changes, such as airbrushing and/or cloning.

That's really all there is to color correction, and if you truly understand curves, you know how they can eliminate color casts, increase contrast, and make the image more lifelike, all at once, without any local correction, without using any esoteric program functions.

So much for theory. Let's roll up our sleeves and correct some color.

Give Me Your Tired Images

The Statue of Liberty of Figure 2.6 is straightforward. The first questions are always shadow, highlight, neutrals, fleshtones. Here there aren't any fleshtones, leaving us with three issues.

• There are several candidates for shadow. The doors at the base, the large half-oval windows beneath the statue, or the dark area to the right of the base. They all measure about the same in the original.

In such cases, we choose the one that seems most significant. Here, since I didn't care whether the doors closed up, I chose the farthest window to the right. It measured $85^C70^M56^Y53^K$, similar to the doors.

• Highlight is trickier, and it illustrates the danger of taking things too literally. The lightest pixels of this image can be found, if we magnify the picture enough, in the white shirts that some of the strolling people are wearing, or in the whitecaps of New York Harbor. These all measure around $13^C1^M9^Y$. The only reasonable alternatives, Lady Liberty's scroll and the brightest parts of the base, are significantly darker.

If you want to choose these white areas as the highlight, fine. That'll make for a snappier picture. It isn't the best approach, though. You need to ask yourself whether those points are really significant enough that you would care if they were lost altogether. The danger of forcing a highlight into a point other than the lightest in the image is that anything lighter will get zeroed out, leaving a blank area on the printed page. That's usually very bad. In the picture of me, for example, it wouldn't do to have blown-out areas in the shirt. Some kind of dot, however light, is needed to retain the sensation of seeing a fabric.

But here, suppose that there's no dot at all in these tiny shirts and whitecaps? Do you care? I don't. They're inconsequential. Therefore, I'd go with a point in the second base, at $15^C2^M19^Y$. I prefer something relatively neutral to the statue's scroll, which might be green.

• Speaking of neutrals, the only thing we can be sure of is that parts of the clouds are white. Not every part, to be sure: the sky is cyan or blue, and the clouds could be picking up some of that. But some part of the cloud has to be white. Right now, no part is. The typical value of the clouds on both sides of the statue is $45^C10^M25^Y$.

Summing up: the highlights are cyanish green. The clouds are greenish cyan. The shadows are cyanish blue. This indicates a cast favoring the cold colors, hardly what we'd want on a sunny day like this one.

The correction curves therefore come in different shapes. The magenta goes up; the cyan and yellow go down. This forces neutrality, grayness, into the clouds. The yellow goes up especially sharply on the right side, to neutralize the shadow.

A common problem beginners have is to look for "the" neutral point of the image. There may not be one. In Figures 3.2 and 3.4, there's nothing lighter than a shadow that we can guarantee is gray or white. So, we don't force neutrality into anything.

The reverse of this error is to ignore other areas of known neutrality once "the" neutral point has been found. That's what needs to be avoided in our next image.

Give Me Your Tired Vehicles

It can be awkward if there is no obvious highlight or shadow. Figure 2.7 has no such problem: the original has plenty of choices for each.

There are four reasonable guesses for highlight: the top of the small truck in the foreground, the street signs, the jacket worn by the woman in the lower left, and the trailer at the extreme left. The unreasonable guesses would be the reflections on the cars, which are catchlights, and the sky, which we can't guarantee is white.

Measuring all four of these likely suspects, the street signs turn out to be much darker than the other three, so they're out.

The truck is typically $3^C3^M7^Y$, the jacket $5^C4^M4^Y$, and the trailer $6^C8^M8^Y$. So much for the trailer, which is slightly darker in all three colors. Our choices are to set highlight either in the truck (in which case the jacket is slightly blue) or in the jacket (in which case the truck is slightly yellow). The second alternative seems more logical.

This shows how sensitive we are to variations in light colors. There's very little difference in the two values—but doesn't that truck look yellower than the jacket?

A $5^C4^M4^Y$ highlight is fairly good already. The shadow is another story.

The rear windows of the building under construction are literally darkest, but surely the body of the black car at the right is more significant. It currently measures $84^C67^M60^Y47^K$.

With the cyan four points high and the yellow ten points low, this isn't really a black—it's a navy blue. And if a blue car is set as a neutral shadow, the picture will turn yellow, just as the picture turned blue when Ralph thought a yellow

Figure 2.7 *Concrete buildings are normally neither pink nor blue. By forcing them to become neutral with curves, and by proper adjustment of highlight and shadow, the original, top, gets transformed into the image at bottom.*

label was white. Yet I asserted confidently that the car is *black*. How can I be so sure?

I can't be sure just by looking at it. Nowadays, slightly off-black colors are fashionable, so the car could certainly be navy blue. But I am sure, quite sure, that tires are black, not navy blue. So, whether this car is darker or lighter than the tires, if it is black there will be the same relation of the CMY colors as there is in the tires. If it's blue, its yellow value will be much lower.

Upon investigation, the nearest tire reads 84^{C}67^{M}58^{Y}32^K. Remembering that a neutral black would have equal magenta and yellow and 10 or 12 points more cyan, this tire is navy blue also. We thus deduce (color correction is like detective work, in a lot of ways) that not just the tires but the car must be made black.

Two more things remain to be found out out about this image before we can start writing curves. One of them, fleshtones, we don't have to worry about, because there aren't any. But how about neutral colors? It's true that there's nothing that has to be a pure gray in the sense that my hair, or the statue of Figure 2.3, have to be. But certain things here should be *close* to gray: the street itself, and the buildings at left and right. Are they?

Not hardly. The street is 51^{C}45^{M}11^Y— very blue. The light building at left is 11^{C}23^{M}9^Y, distinctly magenta. And the right-hand building is 64^{C}54^{M}32^{Y}5^K, blue, though not quite as blue as the street.

By clicking on the eyedropper tool in the toolbox and changing it to the sampling tool, we can expand the Info palette so that it shows the color val-

ues from each of up to four fixed spots in the image. With something as complex as this street scene, this can help. Figure 2.8 shows the points I chose here for the highlight, the shadow, and as representatives of the two buildings at the sides of the image.

Incidentally, at this point, one can turn the monitor to grayscale. It's all monkey work from here on in. Now that we have a general read of the picture, we can color-correct in black and white just as easily — and the screen display refreshes ever so much faster.

Whether you are willing to take that particular plunge or not, it's pretty clear what has to happen here.

The cyan is just right in the highlight. In the light building, it might be OK, but in the street and the dark building, it's too heavy, and in the shadow it's four points too high.

The magenta is the major headache. It's two points too high in the highlight, way too high throughout the quarter- to midtone range, but three points too *low* in the shadow.

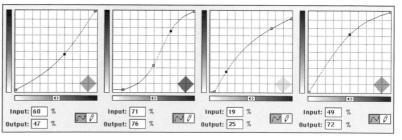

Figure 2.8 *The Info palette, left, shows before-and-after values during curvewriting. Fixed sampling points, such as the one in the building, also aid in understanding the numbers. Below, the curves used in Figure 2.7.*

The yellow needs a big boost, especially in its quartertone, so as to neutralize the street and the buildings. A bigger boost there, in fact, than in the shadow, where it's 13 points too low.

And the black is simplest of all. It's too weak. We need to bring 47^K up to 70^K.

The curves that do these things are shown in Figure 2.8. Notice how much better the color of the scaffolding, and of the reddish building itself, are. And yet, no attention was paid to these, or even to other objects of approximately that color. This is very characteristic of this method of correction. If the basic colors are right the others fall into place, as if by magic.

Also, try doing this with Levels.

The Intent of the Photographer

At this point, you may throw up your hands in disgust and ask why photographers never get it right. Actually, they do. The incredible human optical system is what causes problems.

Everybody knows that when we are in a darkened room, our eyes adjust to the environment and become more sensitive. When somebody turns the light on suddenly, it dazzles us.

Not everybody realizes that the same thing takes place in color perception. Our brains want to reference everything to a neutral environment, so when we are flooded with light of one color we compensate by making our eyes less sensitive to it—all unconsciously.

Figure 2.9 In Figure 2.2, the cast was obviously undesirable. That isn't always the case. Is the blue cast above an aesthetic choice, or should we balance the image as at bottom?

The quick summary of what just happened is that we corrected the image to be what human observers would have seen had they been where the camera was. Humans ignore color casts. Cameras don't. We found a cast, so we deep-sixed it. Obviously, that is not "matching the art."

Perhaps you can think of a reason why the photographer might have wanted, for artistic reasons, the look of the original of Figure 2.7. I surely can't. Figure 2.9 might be something else again. The blue cast sets mood. I would like to think that the photographer did it on purpose.

But suppose that the decision is made that the cast is incorrect, that we are to do exactly what we did with the first two images of this chapter.

The analysis works the same way. Highlight? There isn't one. The pants are the lightest nonreflective thing in the image, and they aren't white.

Shadow? Pretty clearly in the black door to the left. Currently $81^C66^M68^Y68^K$, which isn't bad.

Fleshtones? For sure. A typical value in the woman's arm is $29^C45^M44^Y1^K$. By the standards set out earlier, this is illegal, cyan being twice as high as it should be, and yellow being slightly low.

Neutrals? Yup, virtually everything that's made of stone. The front part of the first step reads in its lightest area $24^C9^M1^Y$, a heavy cyan cast, as if we didn't know.

What to do? That's easy. We have to blow away the cyan that contaminates the highlight. The yellow has to come up sharply in the lighter part of the image, and the magenta has to come down slightly, to get neutral stone. Note that this will also correct the balance between magenta and yellow in the fleshtone. And the black plate is OK as is.

So, we now have an interesting blue cast version, and a nice-looking normally lit one. You can take your pick, but there's no need to limit yourself to these two choices. Photoshop allows us to split the difference any way we like: 90–10, 50–50, whatever.

I am not a professional photographer myself, but I am given to understand by some of my friends who are that this business of shooting something with an intentional subtle cast is not as easy as a simian might think. If I were a photographer, and if I wanted the image to look more like the top half of Figure 2.9, I think I'd deliberately shoot the image too blue. Color-correcting a copy of it by the numbers as in Figure 2.10 and then blending the two versions together is a useful safety net to have.

And there's another plus for the curve-savvy photographer: certain difficult lighting conditions can now be ignored. For example, suppose you are shooting a hockey game. Odds are, you have to shoot through glass, which will donate a slight green cast to the image. For my money, it's a lot easier to apply curves in Photoshop later than to experiment with magenta filters. The results will look better, too, trust me.

Figure 2.10 *The curves used for the bottom version of Figure 2.9.*

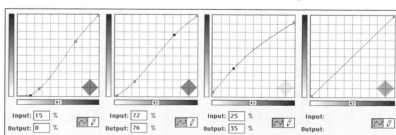

Input: 15 %	Input: 72 %	Input: 25 %	Input:
Output: 0 %	Output: 76 %	Output: 35 %	Output:

Behold a Paler Horse

If you have never seen a purple cow, nor ever hope to see one, you should probably find another field of endeavor. For a fourth variation on a familiar old theme, we'll do battle with a purple horse.

In Figure 2.11, we begin by rounding up the usual suspects. Highlight: the forehead of the near horse, $2^C2^M2^Y$. Shadow: blinder of the far horse, $71^C57^M71^Y30^K$. Known colors: the horses obviously should be white,

Figure 2.11 *The pink horses below are clearly wrong, but are merely the most obvious of many problems.*

but the readings are $7^C26^M7^Y$, $10^C31^M16^Y$, and $15^C32^M18^Y$.

Fixing the color balance here is straightforward. We need to set highlight and shadow and then twist the curves somewhat to make sure that the horses become neutral.

The cyan is slightly too low throughout. We know this because in three nicely neutral areas — the highlight, the shadow, and the horses — the cyan is roughly equal to the yellow, whereas it is supposed to be a few points higher. Since there is no specular highlight in this image, we can start our correction curve by making 0^C move to 3^C and keeping all other values correspondingly higher.

Rather than raise the cyan shadow directly, we place a point at 13^C and increase *that*. The horses need a bigger boost in cyan than the shadow does, so this should work well.

The yellow's highlight and shadow are OK as is. But we still need to reshape it in the quartertone, because in the horse, it needs to be equal to the magenta, which starts out around 15 points higher.

The magenta behaves peculiarly. It is correct in the highlight, too heavy in the quartertone, and too light thereafter. That sounds more difficult to fix than it actually is. We construct a curve that gives a minimum value of 2^M and is completely flat for a while, meaning that anything that was 9^M or lower will now stabilize at 2^M. It starts its climb slowly, so that 30^M becomes 15^M, and then skyrockets so that the midtones will in fact increase.

And the black plate gets very steep very fast. So now we have correct highlights and shadows, and neutral horses. That's what Figure 2.12's numbers say. Good numbers usually imply a good picture.

Betting the Image

I use that horses image in hands-on classes, and many students louse it up by misapplying the principles of this chapter. In their quest for known neutral colors, they assume that the building is one, and they force it to be gray.

Readers from the New York City area will be familiar with the building's architectural material, which is indigenous to the area. It is called *brownstone.* We don't call it that because it's gray.

If we've never heard of brownstone, we should ask ourselves whether this building is really gray. The answer to that is yes—probably. Most such walls would be close to gray. But the next question is the big one: are we ready to bet the image that we're right?

This is an important principle. Ralph bet the image that the wine labels were neutral. He lost. We have to do better. I'm not willing to bet that the building is neutral, but I am willing to risk the image that the horses are. I'll also gladly bet that the light parts of the flags are neutral and that the horses' blinders are too.

This thought process happens over and over. I won't bet that a very dark car is black, but I will bet that its tires are. I won't bet that any given part of the clouds behind the Statue of Liberty is neutral, but I will bet that somewhere in the clouds there is a point that's neutral.

Figure 2.12 *Since magenta starts out too high in the light areas and too light in the darks, the shape of the correction curve is eccentric. Cyan and yellow have to increase in the quartertone to eliminate the pink cast in the horses, while the magenta drops. And the black plate increases drastically throughout.*

Figure 2.13 shows how to use—and misuse—the by-the-numbers method. At first glance it looks easier than any of the others, because there aren't known neutral colors and the fleshtone areas are too small for us to get reliable measurements. It looks as though we can do nothing more than set highlight and shadow.

Fine. The highlight is obviously the back of the matador's collar, which starts out at a reasonable $6^C5^M2^Y$. The shadow, on grounds of significance, should be either the bull or the matador's hair in preference to the background signs. The matador's hair is $64^C73^M98^Y43^K$. The bull's left shoulder is substantially darker, $81^C60^M80^Y62^K$.

That needn't be an obstacle. There's so little detail in the bull that we shouldn't worry about losing it by making it too dark. So let's suppose we choose the hair.

The bottom half of Figure 2.13 moves the collar to $5^C2^M2^Y$ and the hair to $80^C70^M70^Y70^K$. I guess it's better than the top version; there's more snap for sure. But it looks like something Ralph Viola might have done. Can you analyze why?

The bottom image looks much cooler. The dirt is gray, rather than the yellowish-brown of the original. This proves nothing. We've all seen gray dirt and we've all seen brown dirt. We can't bet the image that either one is correct.

But we've already placed a similar bet. The matador's hair is black, we think. But the original CMY values of $64^C73^M98^Y$ have a strong warm cast, suggesting that the hair is really dark brown. Is that possible? I don't think we can bet the image against it.

I would be, however, prepared to bet the image that the bull isn't

Figure 2.13 *The original, above, is flat. The corrected version, below, assumes that the highlight is in the matador's collar and the shadow in his hair. What do you think of the colors?*

COLOR CORRECTION BY THE NUMBERS

✓For 90 percent of the correction work we face, the rules can be stated in one sentence: Use the full range of available tones every time, and don't give the viewers any colors that they will know better than to believe.

✓In each uncorrected image, we must find the highlight—the lightest white with detail—if there is one. Also, we must find the darkest area, or shadow. We will use curves to move these areas to the minimum and maximum values we expect to be able to hold detail with on press. Absent specific information to use different numbers, use $5^C2^M2^Y$ for highlight and $80^C70^M70^Y70^K$ for shadow.

✓In choosing a highlight, speculars, meaning areas that are reflecting light or portraying a light source, should be ignored. Values of zero are acceptable for them. Similarly, dark areas without important detail can be allowed to print heavier than the recommended shadow values.

✓Most pictures have some colors that are known to the viewer. The known colors are generally either fleshtones or areas that must logically be neutral.

✓Neutral colors, of which there are plenty in nature, should have equal amounts of magenta and yellow, and slightly more cyan. The amount of black, if any, is irrelevant. If there is a slight cast, viewers prefer it to be a warm-color imbalance; if you must depart from this formula, a reddish gray may be better.

✓The best highlight isn't necessarily the literal lightest nonspecular. Ask yourself: do I care if all detail in this area vanishes and it prints without a dot? If you don't care, choose some other point to be the highlight.

✓Except in small children and other very light-skinned persons, yellow is always higher than magenta in fleshtones. Cyan is always at least a fifth of the magenta value. As skin tone gets darker, these imbalances increase. A dark-skinned individual may have a third more yellow than magenta, and cyan a third the strength of the magenta.

✓Do not be seduced into a local selection of an area where the color is obviously wrong. Whatever is causing the undesirable color is also doing it in the rest of the picture, but it may not be apparent. Applying correction globally will cause overall improvements that you might not anticipate.

Figure 2.14 *A corrected version of Figure 2.13, using the bull as the shadow and maintaining neutrality in letters of the sign at top left.*

In short, once he got the hang of curves, there is absolutely no reason that an orangutan could not get these results. Years of retouching experience, artistic talent, and mathematical aptitude wouldn't hurt him, but they are not really needed.

Notice how these numerical adjustments have the habit of helping areas of the image that we never even thought about. Things like the red scaffolding on the brick building, the flags behind the horse, and the matador's cape.

Artists who worry their images to death tend to see such shortcomings immediately and plunge happily and vigorously into a morass of individual moves. They sponge out the flags and select the horses; they isolate the scaffolding and work on it; they apply Selective Color to the cape, and after eight hours or so of labor they have 12 layers, 18 alpha channels, an 800-megabyte file, and an image that's not as good as what the curvewriting orangutan would have achieved in seconds.

Neutralizing our artistic judgment along with the color casts gave us images that came out much better than the originals—yet not as good as they might have been.

Determining that the horses are more important than the building, or that the statue is more important than the sky, are the kinds of logical decisions that are too difficult for either apes or calibrationists. In the next chapter, we will exploit our superior intellect, and with a combination of good numbers and curves that improve contrast in the critical areas of the image, we'll get the color correction monkey off our backs forever.

greenish yellow. That's what the original numbers say. Furthermore, although the color of the dirt is anybody's guess, the large letters in the sign at upper left are probably white or gray. I'm ready to bet the image that they aren't cyan, which is what happened in the bottom version of Figure 2.13.

Therefore, we balance the bull, not the hair. This may still be wrong: for all we know he's brown, not black. But it has to be better than leaving him yellow-green.

Figure 2.14 uses the bull for the shadow and deliberately maintains neutrality in the letters. There's also a little better contrast because, reasoning that the collar had no significant detail, I set a light highlight of $2^C1^M1^Y$. ¡Olé!

Of Values and Judgments

In the corrections to these five images, we made almost no "artistic" judgments. It was all numbers, numbers, numbers. There was no need even to use a color monitor. And every single change was made to the image as a whole.

The Steeper the Curve, The More the Contrast

Color correction is a give-and-take operation. Once an image uses the entire available space, there can be no gain in one area without sacrifices in another. Every improvement thus has a price. Fortunately, there are real bargains out there.

Color correction is like life. We are forever having to make decisions involving allocation of scarce resources. I have eight hours free during which I would like to improve my skills; should I spend it making sure I understand every feature of a program I already know pretty well, or should I learn a new one? I have a couple thousand dollars available to spend on hardware: should I buy a disk drive, more RAM, a portable viewing booth, or a new CPU?

Tough calls like this are what put the fun in color correction.

As we saw in the last chapter, there *are* some free lunches available. There, we avoided being shortchanged by making sure we used the full available tonal space, every time. And we adjusted curves so that colors that were supposed to be neutral got that way.

Those moves were unconditionally positive. They improved things at no cost to any aspect of the image. Best of all, very little judgment was called for.

Once there is a full range in an image, however, we pay a price for any further moves. Sometimes the price is too high, but it is sometimes astonishingly cheap. To be an adequate color technician one need only grasp numbers. To be good at it, one must be a bargain hunter.

Figure 3.1 *Below, each row shows the result of a single curve applied to each of the three originals, above. Can you guess the shapes of the three curves that created the three rows?*

To illustrate, we will use the same rules as last time. In correcting, local selection is not permitted. Neither is the use of any retouching tool. All moves must affect the image as a whole. The colorspace will be exclusively CMYK, and all corrections will be accomplished by means of curves.

As Long As It Catches Mice

In Spanish, there is a saying that goes, in the nighttime every cat is a gray one. Entirely too many computer artists amend this to say that all cats are gray as long as the highlight and shadow are correct. If that was your impression, consider Figure 3.1.

The top row is the original version of each of three felines. I have preadjusted each to have a good highlight and shadow, which for black and white work on this kind of paper is 3^K and 90^K, respectively. (If you are wondering why this shadow sounds a bit higher than its color equivalent of $80^C70^M70^Y70^K$, it's because with four inks in play it's harder to see detail in such areas, and in CMYK there is often an arbitrary limit of 300 or less on the sum of the values of all four.)

Each of the other three rows shows what happens when a certain curve is applied to each of the three images. As you can see, the original was not the best possible reproduction of any of the three cats, because in each of the lower three rows, there is one cat that's better—and two that are worse. You'll see the three curves that made these rows in a minute. Meanwhile, can you figure out what they must look like?

The images in which we set highlight and shadow in Chapter 2 were all fairly busy, by which I mean they contained several important objects or colors. Some images are like this, but many more are not. Product shots, fashion shots, images of animals, food shots—all generally have only one or two color ranges that are important. The rest is just background.

So it is with Figure 3.1. Each image is about a *cat*, not a background. If the price for improving the cat is making the background lose some detail, so be it. Just as I have only a certain amount of money to spend on computer hardware, I have only a certain amount of contrast to spend on this image. And, in these pictures, I propose to spend it on cats, not backgrounds.

I'm starting the discussion with black and white images because they are simpler: there's no need to worry about how the plates interrelate. Now, let's talk about why setting highlight and shadow works, and how we can extend the principle to bring out more detail in the important areas.

Consider a black and white image in which the highlight value is correct, but the darkest value is only 60^K.

Correcting this invariably creates a staggering improvement. A simple curve that leaves the zero point alone and moves 60^K up to 90^K will not just darken the picture: it will profoundly hike contrast throughout. Every detail will become more pronounced because there are now around a third more tones available. Any two locations in the picture will have more variation between them than before the correction. This variation is what gives an image snap.

This by-the-numbers method is a great start, but it is somewhat wooden. As we saw, it can even be mastered by a colorblind individual. Without such a handicap, the intelligent artist can do better.

Curvewriting boils down to this: the steeper the curve, the more the contrast.

The default curve is a straight line at an angle of 45°. If we change the default in any way, certain areas will become steeper than 45°, and certain others will become flatter. Any objects that fall in the steeper areas will improve. Unfortunately, anything that falls in the flatter areas of the curve will get worse.

In our hypothetical example the curve was steeper between 0^K and 60^K—and much flatter between 60^K and 100^K. We don't think about that part, because nothing in the image falls in that range. The correction therefore has nothing to lose. The curve damages an area of the picture that does not exist.

If you accept that, it is only logical to damage areas that *do* exist, but are not important. It is thus possible to trade quality in unimportant parts of the picture for extra mustard in the parts we care about.

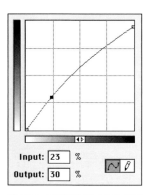

Figure 3.2 *The three curves that created the alternate rows of Figure 3.1. Left, second row; Bottom left; third row; Bottom right, bottom row.*

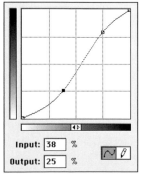

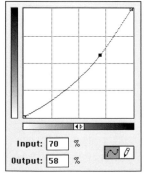

A white cat lives in the light end of a curve. A black cat, in the dark end. A gray cat, somewhere in the middle. That's enough information for present purposes, but normally one would like to narrow it down a little and find the exact range. This can be done by running the cursor over the lightest and darkest area of each cat and recording the resulting Info palette numbers. Alternatively, with the curve of a single channel open, we can move across the image while holding down the mouse button. This will generate a circle on the curve that will indicate the value of whatever is currently beneath the cursor.

Granted that the highlight and shadow start out correct, it still is possible to write curves, as Figure 3.2 shows, that are steep where a specific cat is found. Provided, that is, that we agree with what any of these cats would say, which is, anyplace a cat is not is a place unworthy of our attention.

Now, one last question before we look at the curves. Each of these three curves is intended to make a single cat purr, at the expense of the other two. The first part of the question is, which row hosts the two *worst* cats? I assume you agree that it's the second row from the bottom. The gray cat there is great, but the other two are much the worse for wear.

Why are the black and white cats so poor in the row that favors the gray one, even compared to what happened to the white and gray one in the row that favored the black one? (Hint: if you know, you are a long ways toward also knowing why the best retouchers write curves in CMYK rather than RGB—but we won't get into that for another few chapters.)

There is a big difference between a single image of three cats, and three images of one cat. If all three cats were in the same picture, we'd be stuck with the original, if its highlight and shadow were correct.

But if even one cat is missing, this opens up space to maneuver. This kind of retouching is much like shopping: it's one thing to know what you'd like to buy, and another to find the money to pay for it. Or, to use a better analogy, it's like horsetrading. To get what you want, you need to find something you're willing to part with.

The curves of Figure 3.2 each get steeper in the region occupied by one particular cat. To pay for it, they get flatter in the tonal ranges of the other two cats, squashing contrast. It would also be possible to write a curve that helped *two* cats at once, paying for it by damaging the third.

And why are the black and white cats hurt so disproportionately badly by the curve that is aimed at improving the gray cat? It's all a matter of range. The gray cat originally had the most variation in its color of any of the three (the white one, by a narrow margin, has the least). Therefore, the area it occupies on the curve is longer, more expensive to correct, requiring more of a sacrifice elsewhere.

High Key and Low Key Images

Discussing black and white at such length in a book about color is not a waste of time. To be successful in CMYK, we have to realize that we are working not with a single color image but with four black and whites. Each one can be treated individually, and yet the four together constitute a family whose relationships must be respected.

Consider an image where the highlight is correct, but the shadow is $70^C 70^M 70^Y 70^K$. This value indicates a red cast, because there isn't enough cyan ink. We need 80^C, not 70^C. So, we have to fix it.

The obvious way to do so is to grab the 70^C point of the curve and drag it up 10 points. A second way would be to grab the top right point of the curve and move it to the left, preserving the straight line, but making it steeper. And there are many other ways of making 70^C become 80^C, as illustrated in Figure 3.3. Which one should we use?

In real life, it would be unusual to have all of these choices, because we still have to meet the four basic requirements set out in Chapter 2. Namely, we need not only a good highlight and good shadow, but neutral colors where appropriate, and valid fleshtones.

Figure 3.3 *If the objective is to make values that were 70 percent increase to 80 percent, any of these curves will do the job—but they will have very different effects on the overall image.*

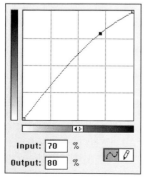
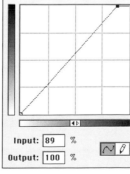
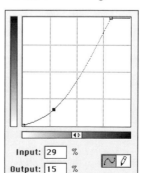
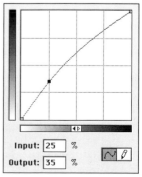

If the image has no neutral colors or flesh-tones in it, we may be able to use any one of these four curves. But most images are not like that, so the chances are we can forget about two or three of these shapes.

Which may still leave us with a choice.

When a choice exists, we resolve it in favor of the option that makes the important areas of the image fall in steeper areas of the curve. A professional might use the term *keyness* here. The picture of the white cat is a *high key* image, meaning that the important areas are light. The black cat is a *low key* image. As far as I know, there isn't a specific term for the image of the gray cat.

Figure 3.4 is a rare specimen, an image that's simultaneously high key and low key. Everything of importance here is either light or dark—there is nothing in the middle. The correction is obvious: steepen the ends of the curves, flatten the middle in all three CMY colors. In the black, there is no need to bother about steepening the light end. As the color circles indicate, the ice is so light that there's no black in it at all.

Most color images are simultaneously high and low key, but in a far different way. Consider a picture of a lawn. The lawn is green. CMYK greens are mixes of yellow and cyan. And in the greens of nature, yellow always predominates. In a lawn we would see heavy yellow, semi-heavy cyan, and light magenta.

In other words, the yellow, if it were a black and white, would be a low key image, whereas the magenta would be high key.

Or, to put it another way, the yellow is a black cat, the magenta is a white cat, and the cyan is a gray cat. The three curves we would use to correct such an image are in principle those of Figure 3.2.

Three different curves for three different cats. That is why we use the individual channels rather than the master curve, because we have already seen what happens when we try to correct all three cats with the same curve.

And while we are discussing why we do things one way and not another, let me bring up why we use curves rather than the Image: Adjust>Levels command.

Levels is nothing more than a curve with only three points: the two endpoints and a point in the exact center. Like curves, it can be applied to each channel individually. Effective moves are possible with it. High key and low key images can be handled with Levels by moving the midpoint up or down. This isn't quite as accurate as raising or lowering the exact point at which the main object of interest ends. In other words, light objects don't just end at 50 percent for our convenience; they are just as likely to pick 42, 37, or the square root of 1,500.

But this is a technical argument. I suspect that if I had corrected the white or black cat using Levels nobody would have known the difference. The gray cat is another story.

When the interest object falls in the center of the tonal range, rather than the ends, one really needs four points on the curve. One needs to make what some people refer to as an S curve, of which the second version of Figure 3.2 is a mild representative.

This can't be done in Levels, An S curve suppresses detail in highlights and shadows in the interest of developing it in the midtones. That's usually OK, but blowing the highlights and shadows out altogether, as Levels would do, is not.

Two of these three cats, then, could be corrected effectively with Levels. That's not bad. The only thing is, we work mostly with color, not black and white images, and a color image is made up of three or four channels, and almost invariably one or more of them resemble the gray cat.

On to Bigger Game

As color can be seen as a bigger, more complex, and more dangerous relative of black and white, so does Figure 3.5 relate to the kitties of Figure 3.1.

Correcting this image doesn't stop with setting a highlight and a shadow. Here, unlike the images of Chapter 3, we have one obvious object of interest, one object that defines the whole picture. We would like to bring out detail and definition in the tiger, and if that should happen to harm detail elsewhere that is just too bad.

This is done just the way we handled the cats, except that here we have to do it four different ways, one for each channel. The black channel resembles the white cat. The cyan and magenta channels resemble the gray cat, and the yellow resembles the black cat. Knowing this, if we were sloppy we could actually take the appropriate curves directly out of Figure 3.2, apply them to this image, and see a substantial improvement.

It's much better, however, to measure the exact range of the tiger and be surgical with the curve. The more accurately the curve targets the tiger, the more precise the cor-

Figure 3.4 *The term* high key *means an image where most important detail is in light areas;* low key *means important darks. This unusual image can be said to be high key and low key simultaneously. The corrected version, below, closes up some of the unused space in the middle in favor of more detail in both highlights and shadows.*

rection, and the less the undesired impact on the background.

Too many people select the tiger and correct it without touching the back-

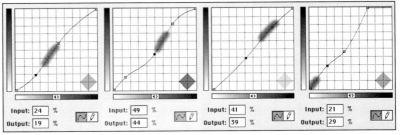

Figure 3.5 *By making the tiger (brown patches on curves) fall in steep areas of at least the CMK curves, detail is enhanced. It also emulates the phenomenon of simultaneous contrast, breaking the animal away from the background.*

| Input: | 24 | % | | Input: | 49 | % | | Input: | 41 | % | | Input: | 21 | % |
| Output: | 19 | % | | Output: | 44 | % | | Output: | 39 | % | | Output: | 29 | % |

ground. This invariably looks unnatural, regardless of how careful the selection. The curves method is the method of the eye.

This particular exercise is useful in understanding not only color correction, but also human evolution. We discussed earlier how we perceive colors differently depending on what is next to them. Figure 3.5 shows why. Tigers like to prowl in areas just like this, where their color blends into the background. It was obviously rather useful for our prehistoric ancestors to know whether a certain stream had a tiger in it before going in for a swim.

After all, we don't run as fast as most other animals. We can't smell tigers as well as other animals can. And we certainly don't match up well *mano a mano* with a tiger. Aside from our impeccably designed hands, our biggest physical advantage is, we see color better than other animals do. And, per Darwin, evolution will enhance the advantages that animals already have. Hence, our unique sense of simultaneous contrast, which enables us to detect such slight variations as a tiger in a yellow stream when there is a yellow bank in the background.

Notice how, in addition to enhancing the tiger, the correction changed the color of the water, making it greener. This effect makes the true calibrationist howl as if several tigers were after him: sacrilege! This is not in the original art!! The water didn't change color just because a tiger happened to be in it!!!

But yes. Yes. Read *Origin of Species*. The way the human visual system works, water *does* change color when a tiger wades in. This is a preface to a tirade against color scientists that will commence at the start of Chapter 10. It is also why the bottom half of Figure 3.5 looks so convincing.

Do We Suppress the Snow?

Figure 3.6, yet another feline, is a further variation on the theme of give and take in color correction. In Figure 3.5, most people would agree that the tiger is of such paramount importance that we would be willing to let all lighter and darker objects lose contrast. This time, it's not so clear.

The bobcat's range can be enhanced in the same way the tiger's was. This time, the animal being more neutral than the tiger, all three CMY channels resemble the gray cat of Figure 3.1. If we apply that shape of curve to the three channels, the bobcat will gain detail—but the snow will lose out. And the delicate detailing of the snow is one of the more interesting features of the image.

So there you have it. The more you are willing to suppress the detailing of the snow, the better the bobcat you can have in return. The more you want to concentrate on the bobcat, the lower you make the lower point of the bobcat's range on the curve in each color. The more you do this, the flatter the snow will become. Your priorities on how far to go may be different than mine. Almost everyone would think that the middle version of Figure 3.6 is better than the top one. The vote might well split on whether the bottom one is better than the middle. The curves that produced both corrected versions are shown in Figure 3.7.

The successful retoucher is always on the lookout for something to suppress, some means of financing the improvement in the important areas. This means a continual hunt for ranges that are not in use.

As images get more complex, seat-of-the-pants responses have to give way to

Figure 3.6 *The bobcat in the original, top, is obviously the focus of the image. But is the snow important as well? If it is, the middle version preserves it, while extending the range of the cat into the shadows. The bottom version sacrifices the snow in favor of an even more detailed animal.*

more careful analysis. Often, horrors, we actually have to take out a piece of paper and start writing down some readings, but the extra time is worth it, because usually we can find unused color ranges. When we do, we will mercilessly compress them.

Figure 3.8 is the most difficult correction so far. Because it's a busy picture it resembles more the images of Chapter 2 than the cats we have been working with so far.

If this were a black and white image, the strategy would be fairly clear. The lightest significant areas are the lights themselves, and they don't carry a lot of detail. The second lightest significant area seems to be either the rugs or the column in front of the desk. Whichever, it is much darker than the lights, and therefore, the range we can compress is everything between. Probably, we would treat the lights as specular highlights and blow them out to zero. We could then find the value of the lightest portion of the column, and lower that to about 5^K. That would certainly steepen the curve.

Unfortunately, this is *not* a black and white image, so this approach won't work. Do you see why?

Figure 3.9 shows the magenta and cyan channels of the color image. In the magenta, the plan works just as outlined above. The lights are still the lightest object, and the columns are the second lightest. So we compress the range between them, not caring even if we take a sledgehammer to detail in the lightest areas.

But in the cyan plate, the second lightest object is not the column but the red floor. And there, detail is critical because it establishes the grain of the wood. We definitely can't afford to crush the highlight the way we did in the magenta. And the black channel will have a similar problem.

Some quick measurements: the lightest spot in the original image is in the chandelier to the rear. It starts out at $7^C4^M4^Y$, a little high. The darkest point, $66^C77^M73^Y66^K$, is in the shadow beneath the farthest chair. A typical value for the red floor is $17^C94^M100^Y4^K$, and for the column is $30^C33^M53^Y1^K$.

We can't bet the image that the lights themselves should be white. Therefore, there is no particular need to have a balanced highlight. And, as the lights carry no detail to speak of, there should, contrary to usual practice, be no objection to having a zero value in any or all channels.

The shadow value suggests a red cast, but further investigation is necessary. It *looks* like it should be neutral, but it's in the middle of a red floor, and that could contaminate the readings. It's a good idea to check the chair itself, which should definitely be black, although it's slightly lighter than the shadow itself. And the chair measures $68^C78^M66^Y61^K$—still red. (Reminder: a neutrally balanced shadow has roughly equal magenta and yellow, and about 10 points more cyan, with the black being irrelevant.)

For all this picture's complexity, that shadow value is our only restriction, the only thing that *has* to be fixed. After all, the other areas that normally concern us don't exist here. There is no highlight, there are no neutral colors, and there is no fleshtone.

Therefore, there is considerable flexibility on how to write the curves. Naturally, we make them steeper in the areas that matter. Here's my approach:

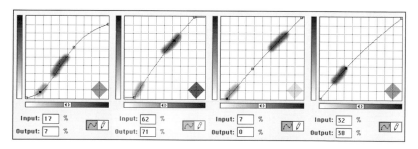

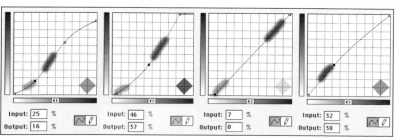

Figure 3.7 *The curves that produced the bottom two versions of Figure 3.6. The bobcat's range is highlighted in brown and the snow in gray. Note, in the bottom curve, how much flatter the snow ranges of the magenta and, to a lesser extent, the cyan are. This accounts for a better bobcat—and poorer snow. Was it worth it?*

Figure 3.8 *The original, top, has little happening in the quartertone. The second version horns into this unused space. The third adds a Selective Color move to darken the windows.*

- **Cyan** needs to be strengthened in the shadow, but that doesn't mean just a wooden raise of the curve. Instead, let's emphasize the contrast in the floor, and between the walls and the darker areas of the image. So, since I don't care whether the lights have a dot or not, I make the curve start at the lightest point of the red floor, and raise the light part of the curve to make it steeper. Next comes a relatively flat area, reaching the range of the walls. This helps keep the second half of the cyan curve steep, adding definition in the shadows and breaking the windows away from the interior.

- **Magenta** is more straightforward. With no important detail in the highlights, I wipe them out. The shadow point needs to come down, but that is accomplished by finding the lightest point of the columns, and dragging *it* down until the shadow becomes reasonable. This, of course, makes the entire second half of the curve steeper.

- **Yellow** is such a weak ink that curve-steepening doesn't add much contrast to the image as a whole. Here, there is a modest gain by lightening the center part of the curve, representing the interior of the room, while holding the shadow point constant by moving the top right endpoint of the curve to the left. This last move will cause large parts of the floor to print solid yellow. We can get away with this in the yellow plate, but it would be a bad idea with any other ink.

• **Black** is handled like the cyan, with a couple of differences. First, there is no need to reduce the highlight, since we don't start with any black in the lights. Second, we really want to have a very steep top half of the curve, because there's detail in the darkest part of the foreground chair that a good black can help bring out.

The second version definitely beats the first, but you might wish, on artistic grounds, to darken the sky to make the interior seem lighter by comparison. So, using Image: Adjust>Selective Color, I added cyan, magenta, and black to cyan. There is no pretense that this reflects what is in the original image. Omit it if you like.

Correcting a Machine Correction

In early 1997, I did a lengthy review of various scanner-control packages that try to color-correct without human intervention. They often get striking results. Novices think that this is magic, and in a way they are right. Set highlight and shadow properly, and the image magically looks a lot better. These programs try to identify the highlight and shadow point. If they are successful in doing so, bingo. Some are able to analyze color casts to some extent as well.

The big problem with such packages is that they don't think. They do just about as well as you or I would on images where the overall color balance is reasonable and where the highlight and shadow are easily identifiable. The horse image of Figure 2.11, on the other hand, was part of the test suite, and every program messed it up pretty badly. Most of them made the horses even pinker than they were in the original.

Figure 3.9 *Above, the cyan, left, and magenta, right, plates of the original of Figure 3.8. Below, the correction curves that produced the middle version.*

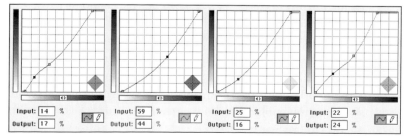

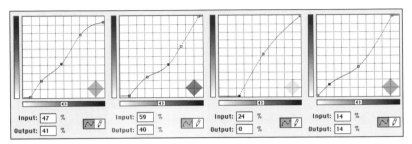

Input: 47 %	Input: 59 %	Input: 24 %	Input: 14 %
Output: 41 %	Output: 40 %	Output: 0 %	Output: 14 %

Figure 3.10 *The original, top right, has a reddish cast. Also, an automated correction chose the wrong highlight. The curves at left correct this but also add contrast to the walking area around the pool, the pool itself, and the trees.*

Similarly, images like Figure 3.9, where there's a range of choices of highlight and shadow and finding the right one is critical, are quite difficult for nonhumans. Results like those obtained by the color-blind person in Figure 2.2 are not uncommon.

The top half of Figure 3.10 has in fact already gone through such a correction, one that's become much more common than people realize. It's a capture from a digital camera with an automated range and color adjustment, very similar to, if not as sophisticated as, the programs I tested. As this is also a rather complicated image, it's a good real-world test.

About two-thirds of the way to the right of this image, some 15 feet from the far side of the pool, a guy wearing a white shirt is bending over his lounge. The camera felt that this shirt should be the highlight. For the shadow, it picked someplace in the trees.

Since we couldn't care less whether that shirt blows out, it shouldn't be the highlight. In fact, I'd forget the umbrellas as well and go for the far lounges. They start off at $12^C11^M24^Y$. There's not much to be done with the shadow. Other than the chaises there's nothing we can bet on being neutral. The people are much too small for us to measure fleshtone accurately.

There is, however, another known color that we can use for guidance. While we can't know exactly what hue a given tree is, it doesn't seem like too much of a stretch to say that it ought to be some species of green.

The trees in this original aren't. A typical value is $57^C64^M100^Y38^K$. This is a dark yellow, actually closer to orange than it is to green. We don't know how much, but the magenta surely has to go down and the cyan come up.

In writing the curves we also have to consider where we want to gain contrast. This picture is rather busy, but I think the areas to go for are the pool itself, the trees, and the mosaiced terrace around the pool.

In addition to lightening the highlight, therefore, I arranged for the curves to be steeper in these areas, to the extent this was possible while lightening the center of the magenta curve.

- **Cyan** is the unwanted color in the terrace, so it's important to have the lightest part of the curve be steep. The pool and the trees are both found in midtone to three-quartertone, so steepening that area helps both. The shadows and the quartertones pay the price.
- **Magenta** is difficult. The center has to come down if the trees are to become green. This, however, will make the shadows quite green as well. What I'd really like to do is move the top right endpoint sharply over to the left, to make the darker half of the curve extremely steep. Unfortunately, that isn't possible here. Some sunbathers

are wearing red shirts, with values of 90^M and higher. Moving the endpoint any further to the left than what's shown would posterize them. The steepening of the highlight area of the curve is, of course, for the terrace.

• **Yellow** is, as pointed out earlier, not a big contributor to contrast. Here, though, it's important to steepen it for the effect it will have in creating color variation in the pool. As both pool and terrace are relatively light in yellow, this curve is simpler than the three others. All that's needed is to raise the midtone.

• **Black** is also easy. The trees are dark, everything else is light. There's almost nothing in between. So I steepened both ends of the curve, flattening the middle.

Remember, by the standards of Chapter 2 the numbers in the original aren't so bad. But with these four dissimilar curves, a substantial improvement can be had.

Of Contrast and the Paycheck

This two-chapter series of color corrections demonstrates that there really is a place for the thinking artist. No automated system can hope to equal the work of someone who can make intelligent judgments about which areas of an image need emphasis and which can be sacrificed.

Yet the conventional wisdom still is that the changes we have just seen are impossible. Here is a quotation from a book on halftone reproduction that was published in 1993.

It cannot be emphasized too strongly that the quality of all photographs reproduced by the halftone process depends entirely on the quality of the original. No

printing process, however refined, can compensate for a sloppy original. While a good process technician might well be able to enhance part of an image, it is usually at the expense of a tone elsewhere. For example, if lighter tones are heightened, the blacks could at the same time lose some of their density.

*   *   *

Right.

Such sanctimonious piffle gets disproven every day. Anybody would prefer to start with the best image possible, but life isn't like that. As we have seen, a lot can be salvaged from second-rate originals.

No question, when we make an improvement, "it is usually at the expense of a tone elsewhere." But the author of these remarks did not grasp that this expense can be quite reasonable, in the hands of a thinking artist. It is quite true that every change suggested in this chapter had a cost. Fortunately, a lot of the time, the price was right.

When we go to the bank to cash our paychecks, the bank does not give us an extra percentage because we happen to be graphic artists. We are given a fixed amount of money, which we then have to allocate to best advantage.

Your spending decision can be entirely different from mine. It all depends on our priorities. If you wish to take a Caribbean vacation this winter, this may mean no meals in fancy restaurants for a while. If you are saving for a child's college education, you may have to skimp on the type of car you drive.

Few people seem to have trouble with this concept, and yet everybody says that color correction is difficult. Go figure.

COLOR CORRECTION AS HORSETRADING

✓If the full range of colors is in use, there will be a price for any further improvement of the overall image. We should therefore always be awake to the possibility of a favorable tradeoff, where detail in an unimportant area can be exchanged for contrast in a more vital one.

✓Any change in the default curve will make some areas steeper than they were before, and others flatter. Objects that fall in the steeper areas of the curve gain contrast; objects that fall in the flatter areas lose contrast.

✓Applying contrast-intensifying curves globally is easier and faster than selecting parts of the image and working on them locally. Most of the time, the result is also more believable.

✓Two separate images of two objects would, in this method, be treated entirely differently from a single image in which both objects appeared. Furthermore, the separate images each would look better than the composite.

✓When we look closely at a certain object, it gains detail, while everything else in our field of vision loses out. The camera, on the other hand, is egalitarian. We are fully justified, therefore, in emphasizing the details that we would like the viewer to focus on, at the expense of those we consider less important.

✓Before beginning, take an inventory. List all the ranges in each color that fall in important areas. Use it as a guide not only to the areas that deserve extra contrast but to those that can be sacrificed.

✓Writing curves to increase contrast does not excuse us from the obligation to keep neutral colors neutral and to keep appropriate highlight and shadow values. Before applying the curves, check the Info palette to make sure that none of these requirements is being violated.

✓The conventional wisdom in color correction is that everything depends on the quality of the original. That can become a self-fulfilling prophecy. With proper attention, decidedly mediocre originals can yield professional results.

✓Yellow ink adds color balance but is too weak to help detail. Therefore, curve-steepening maneuvers are much more effective in cyan, magenta, and black.

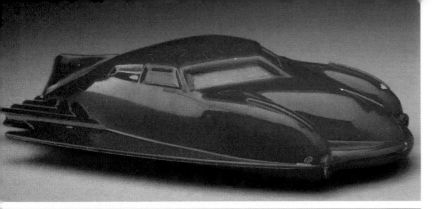

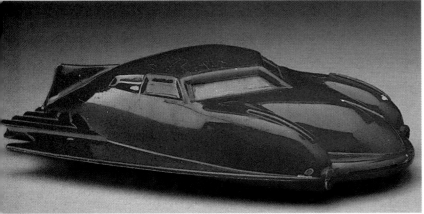

Figure 4.1 *These sets of images differ only in that Photoshop's Unsharp Mask filter has been applied to one version of each. The filter uses deception—the introduction of false light and dark areas known as halos—to fool the eye into seeing what seem to be stronger transitions. If USM is used improperly, the halos become obvious and the image looks artificial. Used carefully, however, very high amounts of USM can be introduced, resulting in much crisper-looking images. The key lies in understanding the three fields in Photoshop's USM dialog box.*

Sharpening with a Stiletto

Unsharp masking, an artificial means of making an image look better focused, is a powerful tool, especially for larger images. How much of it should you use? As much as you can get away with, of course. By choosing which channels to sharpen, and with accurate use of Photoshop's controls, you'll be able to get away with a lot more of it.

ou enter the boss's office under that most tense of circumstances: you are about to ask for a raise. It is possible that negotiations will ensue, so you have to be prepared with a number. How much more money should you ask for?

The stakes are all too clear. Ask for too little, and you may just get it; ask for too much, and you may get booted out of the office with nothing.

It is also clear that the amount you can get away with asking for is not fixed, but varies sharply depending on your technique. People who, during the meeting, tell the boss what a kind, sweet individual he is and what a joy to work with, as a rule can ask for more than those who imply that, were it not for their own contribution, the boss's boss would realize what an incompetent dolt he is.

And it is also clear that it depends on the character of the boss. Should you mention that another company may make you an offer at a higher salary? Some bosses respond well to this type of thing. Others, like myself, are of the crabby variety, and are apt to suggest that, should you decide to change jobs, you not allow the door to hit you in the backside on the way out.

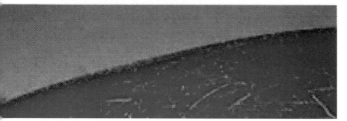

Figure 4.2 *Enlarged copies of sections of one of the images of Figure 4.1. The sharpened version, below, shows the characteristic light and dark haloing in transition areas.*

The fact is, you should ask for as much as you think you can get away with under the circumstances, but the circumstances are very much under your control. This is exactly analogous to unsharp masking.

How USM Fools the Eye

Unsharp masking makes images appear more in focus. It is useful in virtually all graphic scenarios, except when we expect someone else to rescan our work, as when we are outputting to a high-resolution film recorder. Whether preparing for a large-format output device, an inkjet or other digital proofer, a JPEGged file for Web use, or any type of print work, accurate USM is a big deal. The larger the image, the bigger a deal it is.

Before discussing how USM works, let's point out that it *does* work. The only difference between the two sets of images in Figure 4.1 is the USM, but it's a pleasing difference. And the car, at any rate, is quite an extreme example: sharpening isn't as

effective when the object is basically all one color, as the car is.

In Figure 4.2, the process is put under a microscope. Where car hits background, one would expect the same nice, crisp line of demarcation between red and green we might perceive in real life. Instead, in the raw scan, top, we get several pixels that are neither fish nor fowl: dark, colorless blurs caused by the real-life line of transition being narrower than the scanner can resolve, possibly even than the film of the original photograph can resolve.

The technical workings of unsharp masking are not as important as the result, which is an exaggeration of transitions, such as where the car hits the background. USM, as the bottom of Figure 4.2 shows, puts the suggestion, the hint, of a black border, or halo, on the car's exterior. Furthermore, a second, lighter halo appears around the first. If done subtly enough, the viewer won't notice these halos when the job is printed at the proper size.

That this particular scam is highly effective at hornswoggling people into believing they see stronger transitions, and thus better focus, is not a big secret. Artists have been doing it for centuries. El Greco didn't use Photoshop, but as you can see in Figure 4.3, he knew all about unsharp masking.

The Four Deadly USM Sins

As with asking the boss for a raise, the objective is to do as much unsharp masking as possible without being so obnoxious as to be counterproductive. USM is artificial, and if we overdo it, the image will look artificial as well. Fortunately, if we pinpoint, and avoid sharpening, the things that may look artificial, we can get away with more USM overall, much to our advantage.

The four problems that may limit how much USM we can apply appear in magnified form in Figure 4.4. From top to bottom, they are:

• **Color shift.** The idea of USM is to make the image look more focused, not to introduce new colors. But that is just what is

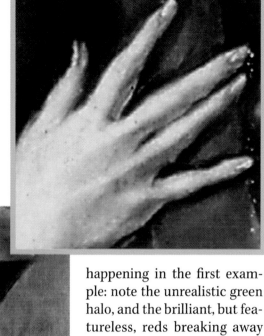

Figure 4.3 Desiring to have Christ's upper hand stand out from the cross, El Greco (1540–1614) resorted to a double-haloing maneuver indistinguishable from today's unsharp masking.

happening in the first example: note the unrealistic green halo, and the brilliant, but featureless, reds breaking away from the more orange body of the car.

• **Unreasonably wide halos.** USM only is believable when the characteristic haloing isn't obvious to the naked eye. Here, it would be.

• **Intensification of unwanted detail.** USM makes the picture look more focused, which is fine unless the things that are being focused are not things we want to see. Here, the plastic car has some scratches in its roof. Although this is real detail and not mere noise, I cannot imagine why a client would want us to emphasize it.

• **Exaggeration of grain or noise.** Random pixels in the background are being made more prominent. If we allow the image to print this way, the background will look strangely grainy.

All these problems can be finessed, provided we are willing to treat USM as a stiletto, not a shotgun. There is a lot of flexibility in how to apply it, although every program has different strengths and weaknesses. Photoshop can do everything we need, but sometimes requires kludgy two- or three-step operations. But before discussing specific Photoshop settings, let's attack the four sins in a conceptual way.

Taking Aim at the Problems

The brilliant greens of the first example in Figure 4.4 came about because hitting an entire file with USM actually applies it to each channel individually, as though each were a black and white image.

(You should already be thinking: is that really the best way of doing things? Because we can certainly apply the filter to some channels and not others, or apply it in a different colorspace altogether.)

Recall that USM places a dark halo at the edge of the darker of two objects, and a light one at the edge of the lighter. This explains the color-shift problem: in the magenta channel, the car is darker than the background, but in the cyan, the background is darker than the car. So, at the transition just outside the car, USM darkens the cyan but lightens the magenta. This is a recipe for bright greens.

A partial solution, as hinted above, is to sharpen the weaker channel only. But for an image as soft as this one, the real answer is to eliminate channel-by-channel sharpening totally, in favor of an approach that only considers the lightness and darkness of the image as a whole, not its color.

This technique, luminosity-based sharp-

ening, is better than the defaults of Photoshop and most other programs. The second example in Figure 4.4, for all its other problems, is a luminosity sharpen, and it has none of the color shift of the top version.

If you wish to sharpen by luminosity, and you should, there are two ways of doing so in Photoshop without getting into Layersville. Easiest is if the document is in the LAB colorspace rather than RGB or CMYK. Guess what the L in LAB stands for! Sharpening the L channel is one of the many attractions of this colorspace, which we will explore in Chapters 8 and 9.

When in RGB or CMYK, Photoshop allows the same thing, albeit in two steps. After applying USM, choose Edit: Fade, which has moved: it's been Filter: Fade until Photoshop 6. Its main function is to reduce the impact of the last action, in this case, USM. But it also permits us to change the application method, such as to use it only to lighten or darken—or to act on luminosity. So, if we set Fade to 100% intensity, but Mode to Luminosity, as in the bottom of Figure 4.4, we wipe out the color shift. (Note: this only works if you are sharpening the image overall, not channel by channel.)

The second sharpening sin that will deter us from our goal of using as much USM as possible is the exaggerated haloing shown in the second example. Or rather, it is *one* of the halos. This points up an irritating Photoshop weakness.

USM's double haloing scheme causes a problem when one of the objects to be sharpened is relatively dark and the other is medium. The difficulty is that the car can absorb a pronounced dark halo fairly well, but the light halo at the edge of the background becomes painfully obvious.

You can try fading the filter as above

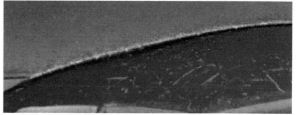

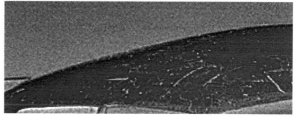

using Darken mode, which will wipe out the white halo altogether, but if you are not inclined to waste time, let me tell you in advance that the image will look ridiculous if you try. No, we need to tone down the white halo, not blow it away.

The ability to control white and dark sharpening independently is an assumed feature of any drum scanner or high-end retouching workstation. But it slipped through the cracks in Photoshop, so to achieve it involves another kludge, which I will demonstrate at the end of the chapter.

Reduction of white-line sharpening would also help deal with the scratches in the top of the car. Even though those scratches are real detail and not noise, we certainly don't want to emphasize them, as is done in the third example.

The better way, though, is simply to avoid sharpening the darkest channel, which here is green in RGB or magenta in CMYK. That is where the scratches are best defined, because the background of the car will be dark, but the scratches light. By comparison, the lightest channel—red in RGB or cyan in CMYK—will have very little difference between car color and scratch.

Are you beginning to see a pattern here? Even if the image can be sharpened overall, the weak channel can usually be sharpened more. Leaving the magenta unsharpened would have virtually eliminated the problems in the first and third images, and gone a long way toward eliminating the grain in the fourth. Meanwhile, reducing the lightening while retaining the darkening aspect of USM would have substantially improved all four of our problems.

To this point, all of our maneuvers could have been done with Photoshop's greasy kid stuff, the filters Sharpen, Sharpen More,

Figure 4.4 *The four deadly sharpening sins, top to bottom: an overall color shift; halos that are too pronounced; enhancement of an unwanted detail (the scratches in the roof of the car); and exaggeration of simple noise. Below, an undocumented feature, the very desirable ability to sharpen by luminosity even when in CMYK.*

and Sharpen Edges. Divest yourself of these popguns in favor of the vastly more flexible Unsharp Mask filter.

Are These Crops Tight Enough?

In large images, judicious USM is every bit as potent as the other big weapons in the retoucher's arsenal: appropriate highlights and shadows; good allocation of contrast;

strong detail in the unwanted color; and careful use of the black plate.

In smaller images, the various USM options aren't nearly as important. Small images do need sharpening, don't get me wrong, but the exact setting won't make or break quality, the way it will in large ones.

And yet, virtually all existing documentation, from Adobe's manuals to third-party Photoshop how-to books, illustrates the USM options with images the size of postage stamps.

The reason for the thumbnail approach is, of course, that it's expensive to print large color pictures in documentation. I have that limitation here, too—note the excruciatingly tight crops to make everything fit—but it's just too hard to see the detail

Figure 4.5 *Faces are the biggest unsharp masking problem. The original, bottom left, is too soft. But a careless sharpen, top, can create the illusion of a skin disease. By avoiding the sharpening of channels that contain facial detail, the hair and eyes can be made more realistic, as at bottom right, without damaging the skin.*

otherwise. Remember, if these images were printing larger, the sharpening defects would be even more evident than what you see here.

A Few New Wrinkles

So far, we've discussed how to avoid introducing what might be termed *artificiality*. Examples of this would be applications of sharpening that exaggerated the grain of the film or random noise.

The detail in the face of the young woman in Figure 4.5, however, is not grain, not noise, nothing artificial at all, just the natural variation of her skin. The skin of humans, even relatively young ones, is made not of alabaster, but rather of a flexible epidermoid integument, highly useful for insulation and in resisting injury, but somewhat unforgiving of acne scars, and entirely too prone to wrinkling.

What that means in English is, careless USM can make Cindy Crawford look like Louie the Lizard. While doing so would be all right with my wife and certain others, it's not likely to be what an art director wants.

And yet, the original seems too soft, especially in the hair. Note that even in the version with the reptilian skintone, the hair is not overfocused. The question is how to get such hair and at the same time a natural-looking, yet not overdetailed, skin.

You may think of somehow selecting the hair, or rather, deselecting the skin, before sharpening. That approach, in my experience, always falls short: one winds up with what looks like two images pasted together.

Better alternatives are to sharpen by luminosity only, which reduces the impact of the facial imperfections by not allowing them to get so red, and/or to employ a relatively high Threshold in Photoshop's USM dialog box. This will eliminate the sharpening of some of the subtler detail at the cost of limiting the sharpening of the hair. Some of the more pronounced wrinkles will still be accentuated.

But the best way of all is to finesse the whole problem by doing the deed where it can do no harm—in other words, to hit the image where the facial detail isn't. And I can tell you exactly where it isn't, by means of a simple rule that applies not only to faces, but to any image:

In all things red, green, or blue, there will be more subtle detailing in the two darkest channels than in the other(s).

A face is red. The two dark channels are magenta and yellow, if we are in CMYK, or green and blue, if we are in RGB. These are the channels we need to avoid sharpening.

USM is even more dangerous in the face of older people, whose skin is always more irregular. The man in Figure 4.6 has pepper-and-salt hair. You wouldn't know this from the original, where it looks like a flat gray. That will never do. We must attack, but not at the cost of making him a Methuselah.

The leatherlike magenta plate of Figure 4.7 is therefore the absolutely last thing we would want to sharpen. Compare it to the cyan plate, and to the black, where the face is virtually a blank. These two channels can therefore be sharpened with a heavy hand. If there's no detail there to begin with, USM won't make it materialize out of thin air.

With the image of the woman in Figure 4.5, I didn't even bother with the cyan. The only channel I used was the black—but I really hammered it. Were Photoshop's maximum Amount not 500%, I'd have sharpened it still more.

There is a huge advantage to doing this kind of sharpening in CMYK rather than RGB, where the weakest channel will still be heavier than either of its two CMYK counterparts.

Consider the bottle image of Figure 4.8. The noise in the first sharpening attempt is worse even than in the fourth version of Figure 4.4.

One way to sidestep this problem is to sharpen a channel that has no noise in it, such as the black. This happens frequently, especially if we have generated the black plate using UCR or Light GCR. One should always take a look at the black plate to see if it can be sharpened—even if one has already sharpened the image as a whole.

And one should always look at the unwanted color as well, if there is one. Here, the image being greenish, the unwanted color is magenta. Because the background magenta is so light (and the background black nonexistent) these two plates will have less detail, and hence much less noise, than the dominant cyan and yellow.

Figure 4.6 *The older the face, the more care needs to be taken. The original, left, doesn't do justice to the man's pepper-and-salt hair. The key to the version on the right side is to avoid sharpening the magenta plate.*

By the Numbers

In addition to our God-given ability to apply sharpening to specific channels and not others, an acceptable USM implementation needs to give us four things:

• Control over how strong the sharpening effect is, in other words, how dark and light the halos get.

• Control of how wide the halos are.

• Some means of suppressing noise.

• Independent control of lightening and darkening.

Every application has its own way of doing these things. Two things that all seem to have in common are a dialog box that is incomprehensible to the typical user and a failure to document how it works and for what types of images each option might be useful.

They nevertheless have to be deciphered, and they can be, if one keeps in mind the purposes described above. In Figure 4.9, we'll compare Photoshop to Heidelberg Color Publishing Solutions' Lino-Color Elite scanner-driving software.

Start with the obvious, the need to control the strength of the sharpen. Here, Photoshop uses the word *Amount* and Lino-Color *Intensity*. Both terms

are clear enough, except for Photoshop's insistence on using a percent sign, which seems designed specifically to bluff people into never using a number higher than 100, when 500 is the actual maximum. Anyway, with both applications, the larger the number, the stronger the sharpen.

I doubt that most people would understand *Radius* or *Size* to refer to the width of the sharpening halos, but that's what they do. Again, the larger the number, the wider the halos. Photoshop's flexibility with this is tops in the industry; note the paucity of choices in LinoColor.

Stopping USM from enhancing noise as well as detail depends on allowing it to ignore small variations and concentrate on big-ticket items. The higher the value

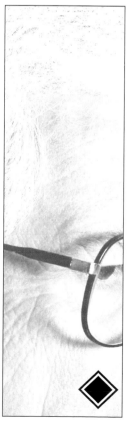

Figure 4.7 *Dominant-color channels always have more detail, meaning we should sharpen the weak ones. Left to right, the magenta, cyan, and black plates of the original version of Figure 4.6.*

in *Threshold* or *Starting Point,* the less likely the filter is to exaggerate noise—but it isn't always possible to get this right. In the image of the red car, setting a high Threshold will indeed kill the noise in the background without harming the car, but the detail in the bottle image is no more pronounced than the speckling in the background. To sharpen the bottles correctly, you need to go channel by channel.

As for independent control of lightening and darkening, LinoColor has it and Photoshop doesn't but should, for reasons that will be made clear later.

The Eyes Have It

Knowing where to sharpen is one thing, and knowing how to do it another. Time, then, to shift attention to Amount, Radius, and Threshold, the three variables in Photoshop's USM filter.

Figure 4.8 When background noise is heavy and detail light, a high USM threshold can't always separate one from the other. In such a case, sharpen the weak colors—here, black and magenta. Top right: the original cyan plate has noise in the background, but the black, bottom right, has none. At left, top to bottom: the original; a careless all-channel sharpen; and a version with USM applied only to the black and magenta.

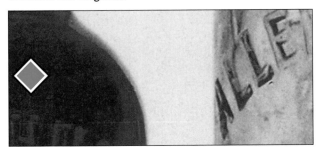

Threshold is the most straightforward. As it increases, variations between areas of similar darkness get ignored in favor of bigger-ticket items. This would work to some extent in the magenta plate in Figure 4.7: there's a huge difference between a white hair and a black one, but not as much between normal flesh and an old scar. A high Threshold setting is a good way to avoid sharpening mild noise. It is somewhat less effective in faces, where the idea is not to suppress noise but to avoid accentuating actual detail.

The Radius and Amount settings define what happens when Photoshop encounters a transition area. Both settings emphasize the transition, but in different ways, as Figure 4.10 indicates.

Granted that the transition between colors in the original is razor-sharp, why do we need to emphasize it? The answer is surprisingly simple: the digital file may look great, but we print with halftone dots, and those dots are wider—a lot wider—than the line of transition between purple and gold. Result? Blursville.

If this were a real photograph and not something generated artificially, there would be a further complication. The line of transition would also be narrower than a scanning sample. So, the scanner would add even more blurriness on top of the contribution of our lousy printing process. This, in short, is why all images need some kind of sharpening. The question is, of course, what kind.

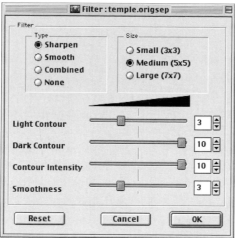

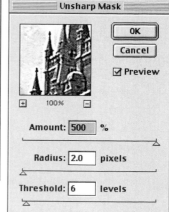

Figure 4.9 *The basic USM menus of LinoColor Elite, left, and Photoshop, bottom.*

The Radius setting, to my mind, is the most important of the three options. It regulates how wide the characteristic sharpening halo will be. The Amount setting, on the other hand, determines how ferocious the effect is, but not its width.

There is no such thing as an image that is too much in focus. We want to sharpen as much of it as possible without being detected. If we use too high an Amount or too low a Threshold, we *will* be detected, because the image will seem too noisy, even if the Radius is correct. And if we use too high a Radius, we will lose subtle detail, even if the Amount is right.

In their eternal search for mathematical verities, calibrationists have been known to suggest that the Radius should depend on the resolution of the scan. This is like saying that the larger a suitcase is, the heavier it will be. There is a kernel of truth there, but the fact is that the contents of the suitcase have a considerable impact, and that a small suitcase filled with lead weighs more than a larger one filled with clothes. And so it is with images, even if we set aside the obvious point that certain photographs have more grain than others of the same size, and thus cannot be sharpened as much.

Imagine that Figure 4.5 was a woman shown from the waist up, rather than in a tight closeup of the face. One need not be Einstein to realize that this would present an entirely different sharpening problem, because the size of the detailing would not match, even if the two images themselves were of identical resolution.

Accordingly, there is really no substitute for thinking. Given this tiresome necessity, here are some of the things you should think about.

Using a large Radius to widen objects can be very effective. Notice that in spite of the softer face, the entire area of the eyes in the correctly sharpened image of the woman is better than in the oversharpened version. That's the Radius at work. The eyelashes are wider. So are the dark parts of the iris. And there is a hint of added weight in the eyelids, digital eyeliner, if you will.

This is all very nice, but before wheeling out a big Radius, we have to be sure that there is nothing in what we are sharpening that has subtle detail, of which big Radii are the enemy.

Small and subtle are not the same thing. An eyelash is small, but not subtle. The variations in the skin of the man are subtle, but they are not small.

In larger images, the details are more crisply defined. Hence, in principle a larger Radius will do less damage. But don't be afraid to use a big Radius on a small image, provided you have the right small image. If you don't agree, check out Figure 4.11.

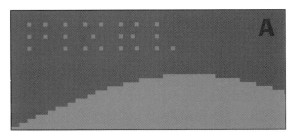

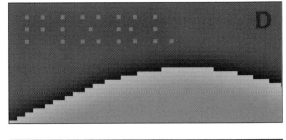

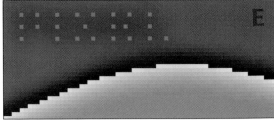

Figure 4.10 *Greatly enlarged, the differing effects of Photoshop's Radius and Amount settings are visible. A: the original. B: 200% Amount and 1.0 Radius. C: 400% Amount and 1.0 Radius. D: 200% Amount and 3.0 Radius. E: 400% Amount and 3.0 Radius. Inset in caption: the size at which the graphic would normally appear.*

Where is the subtle detail inside the bottle? Where is the big color difference between bottle and background? If you don't see these things, I don't either, and I conclude that a wide Radius will work better. Do you agree?

The character of the image, therefore, plays a much bigger role in determining the best Radius than resolution does. Ask yourself, is there fine detail or not?

A person's hair or eyelashes, a wine bottle, the bubbles in a glass of soda: these things want a wide Radius. The bark of a tree, the skin of a fruit, a field of grass, the fabric of the soldier's uniform in Figure 4.12, the grain in wooden objects, all have subtle detail that a large Radius would kill.

But where both kinds of detail appear, we are forced to go with the least common denominator, and choose a narrow Radius, even though it is a second-best way of sharpening gross objects. We need to find a channel that does not have subtle detail. In a face, that's the black, and often the cyan, too.

So, with the woman of Figure 4.5, I was able to use a Radius of 3.0 in the black channel, because as a practical matter the black contains only the eye area and the hair. And the Amount? I used Photoshop's maximum, 500%. If you hit the ball accurately enough, it doesn't matter how hard you hit it.

Figure 4.11 *When an image doesn't have subtle detail, consider a wider Radius. Above right, the original. Below left, 250% Amount and 1.0 Radius; below right, with 250% Amount, but Radius increased to 3.0.*

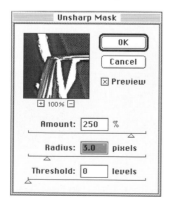

Glitter and Be Gay

The Unsharp Mask filter by itself does not yield a perfectly sharpened image. The careful artist needs to work with Photoshop's sharpen *tool* as well. The tool isn't as flexible as the filter, but it's useful in dealing with small areas, to add that last touch of believability. At the very top of the wine glass, there is a tiny sparkle of reflection on the left side where the glass touches the background. That little highlight should be sharpened. The sharpening tool will make it lighter and wider.

In fact, we'd be happy if there were no dot at all in this particular sparkle. And that is the key rule for this tool. Use it on anything that glints, because for such objects the brighter the better, meaning a zero dot.

More of these targets are hanging around than you might think. Let's take a quick look at the images in this chapter, starting with the young woman of Figure 4.5. She is wearing earrings and a necklace. They glint. They should be sharpened with the tool. There is a sparkle in the center of her eyes, very important in seeming to wake the face up. That, too, should be sharpened. And, just as we should sharpen small areas where a pure white is desirable, so should we attack those where we wouldn't mind a pure black. Namely, the eyelashes, eyelids, and possibly parts of the eyebrows as well.

The older man of Figure 4.6 is not kind enough to be looking at the camera, so we can't sharpen the center of his eyes. But wire-rimmed glasses are a tempting target, especially the lighter metal of the hinge. This guy's frames are black. If they were the more typical gold, it would be even more important to sharpen them. Such glasses vanish right into the skin without it.

There are a couple of places in the stem of the wine glass of Figure 4.11 that could stand sharpening, in addition to the area pointed out previously. And the image of the soldier in Figure 4.12 has more objects that glint than Photoshop has goofy filters.

It's more than a little doctrinaire (and certainly not recommended) to sharpen only with the tool and not the filter, as I have done here, but it isn't hard. The tool is crude enough that we can't vary its settings much, unlike the USM filter. Personally I vary the brush size, but I always use 40% pressure with mode set to Luminosity.

Location, Location, Location

As for the numbers one should use with the USM filter, I will admit to having been somewhat evasive. Unlike most other areas of color correction, fixed formulas and rules don't apply. A certain amount of playing around is necessary.

If you are working with large, important images, it is well worth the time to experiment with different sharpening settings. With experience, adjusting the three numbers becomes intuitive. But if you are (for the moment) uncomfortable with how they interrelate, here is a tip.

The Amount setting is easier than the other two, so save it for last. Start with a setting of 500%, the maximum, a Radius of 1.0 pixel, and a Threshold of zero. Although this will often seem hideously harsh, it will also show whether you are sharpening noise and/or unwanted detail. If so, start adjusting the Threshold upward.

After Threshold is set, turn to Radius. Increase it until you seem to be starting to obliterate needed detail rather than emphasizing it. And once you know the proper Threshold and Radius values, it's simple to

Figure 4.12 *Local areas that sparkle are natural targets for Photoshop's sharpen tool. Note how many such areas there are in the original, left. The image at right is sharpened only with the tool, not with the normally more powerful Unsharp Mask filter.*

adjust the Amount down. But if you start with a proper Amount, it's not as easy to figure out what the right Radius and Threshold should be.

Brute force is no match for intelligence. The biggest gain in sharpening remains avoiding the channels with unwanted detail, allowing a much heavier sharpen of the weaker ones that add contrast.

Also unlike most other areas of color correction, here we really have to rely on the monitor to figure out whether our sharpening settings are sufficient or whether we have gone overboard. That's a tall order, since the phosphors of a monitor don't correspond to the realities of either desktop printers or presses. We have to make the

best of it, though, by being resolution-savvy. First of all, we should view the image in Photoshop at 100%. Lower magnifications are unreliable on most monitors; higher ones cause needless ulcers by displaying defects that will not be visible in print.

More important, though, if our file departs from the normal rules of resolution we need to make an adjustment for it in our minds. Normal resolution, experts agree, is between 1.5 and 2 times the screen ruling, times the magnification percentage. This book, for example, uses a 133-line screen, so normal resolution for my digital file is between 200 and 266 pixels per inch. The images here are all around 225, and I am printing them all at 100% magnification. If

I were printing one at 75% magnification, that would result in a higher than normal range (225/.75 = 300).

When resolution is higher than normal, or if output is to an inkjet printer, the printed image will appear markedly softer than it will on the monitor. When resolution is lower than normal, the printed image will appear harsher. Be warned! If, as so many people do, you scan at 300 samples per inch regardless of the screen ruling, your monitor will be lying to you about how effective your USM is.

Beware the Whitening Halo

Our final sharpening exercise is an important one, because it's a non-obvious big move for the better in a class of images that's more common than people think.

Knowing when to use it requires you to ask yourself two questions:

How would I like it if, not just dark, but black halos were introduced into this image?

How about not just light, but white?

Normally, these two questions will only get one answer. We wouldn't like it if parts of the red car of Figure 4.1 became black, and we wouldn't like it if parts of the green background became white. We don't like white spots or black spots in the texture of the Sphinx. We absolutely hate any white or black appearing in the face of the woman in Figure 4.5. And we love any white or black that finds its way into the hair of the man of Figure 4.6.

Often enough, though, the two questions get two different answers.

In the soldier of Figure 4.12, there's a hint of what's to come. The dark green jacket can accept black more gracefully than the light green shirt can take white.

A more drastic example is the temple of Figure 4.13A. At first glance, the sharpening issue seems to resemble that of the Sphinx of Figure 4.1. Neither has a dominating color, so an overall sharpen seems preferable to black-plus-weak-color. The two match closely for darkness. But the darkest regions of the Sphinx aren't nearly as heavy as the corresponding parts of the temple. White artifacts would be a problem in either but black artifacts are seriously objectionable only in the Sphinx.

In the temple, we can therefore use a heavier hand on the darkening than on the lightening—but the USM filter has no such control.

To concoct one, we start with the seemingly oversharpened Figure 4.13B, in which the fabric of the stonework seems to be unraveling. The lightening halos are to blame for that.

I therefore changed layering mode from Normal to Darken, creating the weird Figure 4.14C, which has no lightening halos at all.

Next step was another Duplicate Layer, this time of the top, sharpened layer. This time I chose Lighten as the method, returning me to square one: the image again looks like Figure 4.13B.

The advantage of using this sandwich method is that one can vary the opacities of the darkening and lightening layers. I left the darkening layer alone, but reduced the opacity of the lightening layer to 50%. After converting to CMYK, I now had Figure 4.13C. The Layers palette is shown in Figure 4.14, as are enlarged versions of the steps along the way.

This seems rather convoluted, but it pays off. Figure 4.13D is the logical alternative, a conversion to CMYK followed by a heavy

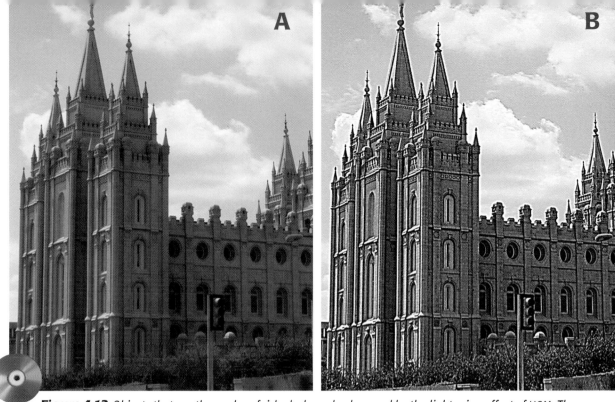

Figure 4.13 *Objects that are themselves fairly dark can be damaged by the lightening effect of USM. The solution is to control the lightening and darkening aspects separately. Above left, the original; above right, a version that seems oversharpened. Below left, the same version with lightening cut back 50%. Below right, a version sharpened only in the black channel.*

A

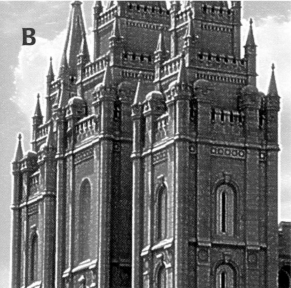

B

C

D

Figure 4.14 *In certain images, the lightening halos are more offensive than the darker ones. Greatly enlarged, version A is the original; B has lightening halos only; and C has darkening halos only. Version D is the final image, with darkening halos at full intensity and lightening halos cut back 50%, as indicated in the Layers palette above.*

sharpen of the black channel only. It's good, but it doesn't measure up to Figure 4.13C.

A truly fanatical sharpener would go further, by throwing the black channel from 4.13D into 4.13C.

Some Sharply Focused Tips

It's time to apply a little USM to this chapter, to make its points a bit crisper and its transitions more clearly focused.

• **Before doing anything, look at each channel.** Decide which ones have the detail you wish to sharpen, and which ones have the noise that you don't.

• **Sharpening by luminosity** is the best bet if you choose to sharpen the document as a whole rather than one or two channels.

• **Think twice about sharpening either the blue** (RGB) **or yellow** (CMYK) **channels**. These

KEEPING UNSHARP MASKING ON TARGET

✓Unsharp masking is an artificial method of making an image appear in clearer focus. It works by creating subtle light and dark halos in transition areas.

✓There is no fixed amount of USM beyond which one dare not venture. Try to use as much of it as possible, without making the image appear artificial.

✓The larger the image will print, the more important experimentation with USM becomes. For small images, it's OK to get by with a single all-purpose setting.

✓For overall focusing, it's best to sharpen by luminosity: either by attacking the L channel of an LAB document or by immediately fading the sharpening back to Luminosity mode.

✓For objects dominated by red, green, or blue, think about sharpening the *weaker* plates, since the stronger ones tend to have more noise. For this type of sharpening, CMYK is a much better choice than RGB, because of the presence of black.

✓The Radius setting governs the width of the sharpening halos. This makes it inappropriate for sharpening objects with subtle detail, which it may kill. It is, however, great for objects that don't have small tonal gradations.

✓To exclude relatively small variations from the sharpening process, increase Photoshop's Threshold. This works well in faces, where there is often detail that shouldn't be exaggerated.

✓The Photoshop Amount setting, being the easiest of all to understand, should normally be specified *after* Threshold and Radius have been chosen.

✓Be alert for the appearance of any or all of the four major sharpening blunders: a color shift; excessively obvious haloing; an intensification of unwanted detail; or an exaggeration of background noise.

✓In certain images, the lightening effect will be so offensive that it must be minimized. In such a case, make one heavily sharpened version, apply it to the original in Darken mode, and reapply it in Lighten mode at a lower opacity.

✓The sharpening tool is a useful adjunct to the USM filter. Use it to intensify type, logos, eyes, and anything in the image that sparkles or glints.

don't have much impact on overall contrast, yet they generally have the most noise and are thus the most dangerous.

• **Always think about sharpening the black and the weak channel** (if there is one). Or, at least sharpening them more than the others. This applies even if you've already sharpened the entire image.

• **Sharpen after tone adjustment**, if convenient. Applying a major adjustment to an image after USM can result in exaggerating the artifacts of sharpening. Furthermore, if you think there's a chance the image may be repurposed for some other printing condition later, save a copy *before* sharpening.

• **Master the Threshold setting**. If you are having trouble, set your USM Amount all the way up to 500% while previewing the image. This will make it obvious on screen whether your threshold is suppressing the noise. Once you have found the proper Threshold, you can adjust Amount to something more reasonable.

• **Be playful**, especially if the image is large. There are few set rules. In a large image, a little time set aside for experimentation with ever-higher USM settings can have a big payoff.

• **Be conservative**. If eventually you decide to sharpen a little more, it won't be the end of the world. But if after a series of corrections you discover that the image is oversharpened, you may wish to turn your stiletto on yourself—oversharpening is hard to fix.

• **Be greedy**. Remember the strategy of asking for a raise. There's no fixed limit. The best amount of sharpening is, the largest amount you can get away with.

CHAPTER *5*

Plate Blending As Poetry

In strongly colored areas, detail in the weakest ink—the unwanted color—is critical. If you don't have that detail, there's only one thing to do: get it from somewhere else. Understanding the observations of an American poet will help.

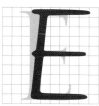

Emily Dickinson, the 19th-century American poet, was a keen observer of matters of color. She should, in fact, be required reading for Photoshop theoreticians.

Although not a Photoshop user herself, she was able to put her finger on many an issue that still plagues us. The image at the upper right of this page is a romantic icon, exactly the sort of thing most professionals have to produce over and over again.

Most of the time, that reproduction winds up being—well, I'd better leave the description to Dickinson.

It tried to be a Rose
And failed—and all the Summer laughed.

     *   *   *

Since our clients may not be so easily amused, it behooves us to do some technical analysis. I haven't seen the particular flower that Dickinson was referring to, of course. But I can tell you what its problem was. It had a lousy cyan plate, same as the one at the top of this page. Her operator should have blended channels to get a better one.

How do I know? Because that's how it is with red roses, and that's how it is with most brilliant objects. The weak ink is the key to detail.

And to understand why things work that way, one might start with the following:

Nature rarer uses Yellow
Than another Hue.
Saves she all of that for Sunsets
Prodigal of Blue.
Spending Scarlet, like a Woman
Yellow she affords
Only scantly and selectly,
Like a Lover's Words.

*   *   *

This isn't bad poetry, but as color theory it leaves a lot to be desired. The exigencies of rhyme outweighed the facts. Understandably reluctant to commence hostilities with

Nature rarely ladles Yellow
Out of a Tureen,

the poet found herself obliged to declare Nature prodigal of the wrong color. I cannot continue the rewrite: the business about spending scarlet is far too politically incorrect for the publisher to permit me to leave it in. I have thought, instead, about likening the way nature is with red to how calibrationists expend time and money on color management solutions that don't work, but I've had some little difficulty coming up with lines that scan. I would, however, end the poem thusly:

Chorus'd Nature, chanting Yellow,
Sings with more élan
Than Progeny of Press atonal
Magenta and Cyan.

*   *   *

Before you decide that poets should stick to poetry and Photoshop authors to Photoshop, let's cut Emily Dickinson a break. She didn't know her verse was incorrect,

Figure 5.1 *Two cyan plates, one with proper focus, and one that is decidedly second-rate.*

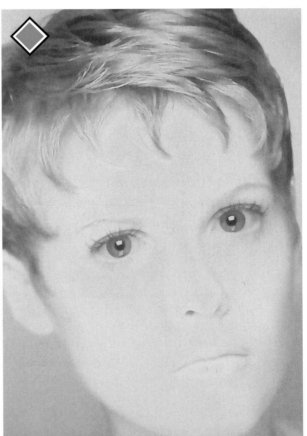

because she thought in the color terms some of us learned in school under the acronymous name Roy G. Biv: Red, Orange, Yellow, Green, Blue, Indigo, Violet. I don't know that there has been a lot of research done on this point, but my impression is that, of these seven hues, Dickinson is correct, nature uses yellow the least.

Today, we have buried Mr. Biv and are more inclined to think in terms of CGYRMB, a perfect color circle. In this model, red falls midway between yellow and magenta, magenta is midway between red and blue, and so on.

One might think that there would be no reason to think that any one of these six colors would be used more than another, but a quick check of the works of God and man demonstrates how silly that view is.

Red, green, and blue objects are far more common in nature than the other three. Bananas and other yellow objects exist, but they aren't that common. Bubble gum is magenta, and certain Caribbean waters are cyan, but outside of these I am hard put to come up with *anything* else that is magenta or cyan. And yet you could name hundreds of things that are red, green, or blue.

An interesting exercise is to walk down the street and record the color of clothes that passersby wear. I've tried this, and found ratios of from four to ten to one in favor of RGB colors as opposed to CMY.

The point of all this poetry and palaver? Simply this. In the images you work with, you are far more likely to be working with red, green, and blue objects than cyan, magenta, and yellow ones.

Figure 5.2 *When the two cyans are plugged into the same MYK image, the difference is impressive.*

To translate this into prepress language: it is extremely likely that the objects we work with will have two strong inks and one weak one, as opposed to other way around. It is that weak one, and how to exploit it, which is the focus of this chapter.

The Cavalry of Woe

CMYK, in addition to being a cockeyed colorspace, is a backwards one. Instead of choosing inks based on their positive capabilities, they have been selected for what they do *not* do. Magenta does not reflect green light; yellow does not reflect blue; cyan does not reflect red.

From this, it is not too much of a stretch to realize that much of the color correction we do is topsy-turvy: that to be effective, we have to think in color terms that are the opposite of what one might expect. When we deal with reds, we should be thinking cyan; when doing greens, magenta; and when portraying blues, yellow.

This is the religion of the *unwanted color* — the color that is the odd man out.

Because the unwanted color is so proficient at poisoning what would otherwise be a bright, clean look, it has a special importance in making an image seem lifelike. The unwanted color, even in slight quantities, is what gives an image depth.

The most obvious example of the importance of the unwanted color is in fleshtones. Regardless of a person's ethnicity, flesh is basically red. That is to say, it is a combination of magenta and yellow. Cyan is, therefore, the unwanted color.

It may be a leap of faith for you to accept that cyan is the most important color in a face. So, without further theoretical ado, let's go straight to an example. The two cyans of Figure 5.1 represent the only difference between the two versions of Figure 5.2. The other three channels are identical.

Note that there is technically nothing wrong with the poor image. The fleshtone is within proper parameters. But the picture has gone dead. The other seems to leap into three dimensions by comparison.

When there are clearly two inks dominating, the unwanted color is so potent in neutralizing them that adding it is almost like adding black. The unwanted color, however, is not quite as blunt an instrument. Also, a much bigger range, and thus a better shape, can be engineered into the unwanted color than into either the two dominants or the black. That is just a matter of numbers: in the better version, the cyan ranges from around 5^C to 20^C. There is thus four times as much cyan in the darkest area as in the lightest. Try getting *that* with either one of the dominants.

Best of all, the unwanted color is easy to adjust—or, if need be, to create. The two dominant inks must be kept carefully balanced, otherwise areas of the face will start to get too yellow or too magenta. But it will take an enormous move in the cyan before the overall color of the woman goes to something other than a shade of red. Much can be hidden in the unwanted color, and part of the normal technique of working with faces should be calling up the cyan and seeing what improvements can be made. The picture as a whole cannot be sharpened, for example, but sharpening only the cyan is possible, and that will make a small but significant improvement.

To sum up, when trying to improve sky, the professional thinks of yellow first. To correct faces, we concentrate on cyan, and for plants and other greenery we focus on magenta.

Figure 5.3 *When the interest area is the green of a forest rather than the red of a face, the key color becomes magenta rather than cyan. Above, the original image and its magenta plate; at bottom, a version with a better magenta. The two color versions are identical in the CYK channels.*

Yet I Know How the Heather Looks

Figure 5.1 wasn't a red picture, but the most important object, the face, was red. In Figure 5.3, on the other hand, green dominates. That means strong yellow and cyan, and it means that magenta is the unwanted color.

The bottom halves of Figure 5.3 make clear how critical that unwanted color is. There is no difference at all in the cyan, yellow, and black plates, but the enhanced magenta seems to bring the image to life. No other channel could make such a difference in this picture. Just as in the picture of

the woman no other channel could have had the same impact as the cyan.

Here, we simply use the technique of Chapter 4, steepening the curve in the magenta where the greenery is, roughly 10^M to 20^M. Also, I've sharpened the magenta channel. Notice how harsh the result is. That's one of the happy things about the unwanted color: it's covered up by so much ink from the two dominants that we can get away with really ugly-looking channels.

Of course, in real life we would do other things to this image besides tweaking

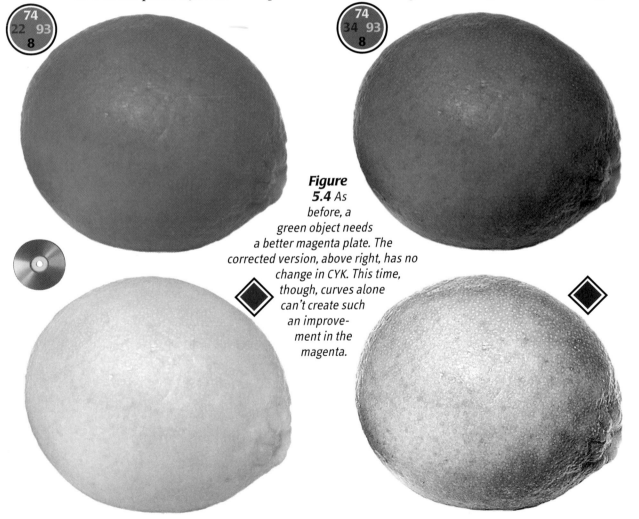

Figure 5.4 As before, a green object needs a better magenta plate. The corrected version, above right, has no change in CYK. This time, though, curves alone can't create such an improvement in the magenta.

the unwanted color, but that isn't the point. The message is, when confronted by such a predominance of one color, you'll get a lousy image if you *don't* take special care with the unwanted color.

In many cases the need for strong contrast in the unwanted color is so compelling that we have to take desperation measures. The normal desperation measure is to find a higher-contrast channel and blend it into the unwanted color, hoping not to throw overall color off too much in the process.

This is actually a watershed moment in this book, at least if you've been reading the chapters in order. Up until this point, the concepts have been universal. We *always* need appropriate highlight and shadow values. If we have a choice of the shape of curves, we *always* choose to have them emphasize the important areas of the image.

From here on, however, the strategies are specialized. Plate blending, unsharp masking tricks, unorthodox GCR decisions, the use of other colorspaces: these are all great responses to specific situations. Unfortunately, one has to learn what those situations are.

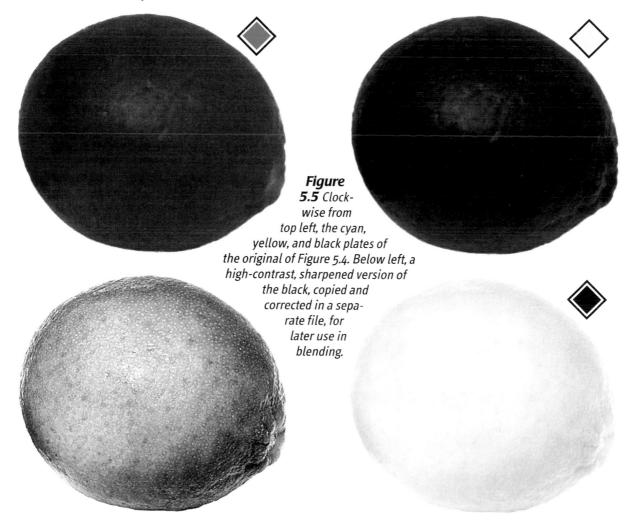

Figure 5.5 Clockwise from top left, the cyan, yellow, and black plates of the original of Figure 5.4. Below left, a high-contrast, sharpened version of the black, copied and corrected in a separate file, for later use in blending.

The Berry's Cheek Is Plumper

When everything is brilliant, nothing is brilliant. Plate blending to enhance contrast in the unwanted color is often needed when there are large areas of intense color. Fruits, vegetables, and, of course, flowers are excellent examples.

There are two main reasons this maneuver is so important. First, the human observer always tries to break apart similar colors, whereas a camera does not; therefore, humans perceive much more variation in the color of fruit than is going to be captured on film. Since our job is to remind the eventual viewer of the original subject, not what the photographer captured, we have to try to restore some of this color variation, and applying curves and sharpening alone may not do it.

Second, we want our bright objects to look three-dimensional, not like flat blobs. The right-hand lime in Figure 5.4 is a lot *rounder* than the one on the left. That's because the purer the color, the closer it seems to us. The more it tends toward gray, the further away it goes.

At the brightest spot in the center, these two limes are almost identical in color. The difference is at the edges. There, the right-hand version is grayer, less green. Those grayer edges recede, fooling us into thinking we are seeing rounder fruit.

And, not to beat a dead horse, when we have a dominant red, green, or blue object, the way to turn parts of it gray is with its enemy, with its opponent, with the ink that is specifically designed to contaminate, poison, depurify, confound, distress, and distrain it, to wit, the unwanted color.

Once having concluded that this lime needs a magenta plate like the one at bottom right of Figure 5.4, the question is how to get there from the version at bottom left. The answer is, we don't. The original is simply too flat. Curving it won't help, at least it won't help enough.

Accordingly, we need to seek assistance elsewhere. We need to find a channel with more detail and blend it into this pathetic magenta. Figure 5.5 shows the choices.

The maxed-out yellow is plainly unsuitable. The cyan is pretty flat as well, although it does have a well-pronounced hot spot in the middle. And the black? Well, at first blush it seems as flat as the magenta, but it isn't. Curving this one can bring out detail, as we will see.

The first order of business is to get a copy of the aforesaid black channel so that we can play with it. This is done by displaying the channel, Select All (Command-A); Copy (Command-C); New document (Command-N, which automatically opens a document to the same size as what we have just copied); Paste (Command-V); drop down one layer (Command-E.)

The result of all this alphabet soup is a grayscale document that is divorced from the original, meaning we can smash it all to pieces if we like.

But there is no need for such violence. Instead, what we want to do is increase contrast in the fruit, and having gone through Chapter 3, we know exactly how to do so. We create a curve that is as steep as possible in the area occupied by the lime. And for good measure, we apply heavy unsharp masking afterwards. The result is at the bottom left of Figure 5.5.

This souped-up channel is almost good enough to replace the original magenta, because the two are practically the same color. The key is understanding that contrast needs somehow to be added to the magenta. After that, how far to go is a judgment call.

With both the original file and the separate blending channel open on screen, we display the magenta channel of the original and choose Image: Apply Image. Up comes the dialog box shown in Figure 5.6. We now specify that the source is the other image and pick an opacity. Here, understanding that this is purely an arbitary decision and that you are perfectly free to think I should have gone further or not even this far, I used 75% Opacity.

Ordinarily, after a blend like this, a further correction is necessary. Blending into the unwanted color always adds detail, but it frequently changes color as well. We want a rounder lime, not a browner one. Most of our perception of color comes from the brightest area of the fruit. So we have to make sure that, after the blend, that point hasn't changed color too much. If it has, we need to apply curves to the blend plate to restore color while holding contrast.

Here, we lucked out; the color is close enough as is, another reason to favor blending with the black plate rather than the darker cyan.

If this blend seems too simple, more complicated options are readily available. We could have made two separate blending channels, one based on the cyan and one on the black, and then blended those together before blending the result in the magenta. Or we could have made a copy of the image, converted it to LAB, and used the L channel for blending. Or to RGB, and used the green. Or we could have

Figure 5.6 *The blending process, using Photoshop's Apply Image command.*

done one of these things using Multiply as the blend mode, rather than Normal.

Any of the above is a reasonable choice for dealing with this image. Giving up and leaving the magenta plate alone is not.

The Accent of a Coming Foot

The dancer's costume in Figure 5.7 looks fine in person, fine in the photograph, fine on the monitor, and lousy on the printed page. Process inks are not good at reproducing vivid colors like this red. When we bring this image into CMYK, what we get is a kind of red blob lacking most detail, since every part of the costume will be close to the limit of the press's color gamut.

This red is made up of maximum magenta plus large quantities of yellow. (If the two were equal, we would have a costume the color of a fire engine; as yellow decreases, we head toward a rosier hue.) What it will not have is very much cyan or black, because these are red-killing colors.

If we take the approach advocated in

Chapter 3, the way to create more contrast in the reds should seem as risk-free as it is obvious. After all, there is nothing in the background to be harmed. There are no neutral colors, no highlights to unbalance.

Therefore, we should steepen the magenta and yellow by dropping the minimum values of them we find in the costume by 15 points or so. Magenta is probably maxed out already, but we can increase the yellow. As for the cyan and the black, we will steepen their curves by finding the maximum values within the costume and increasing them, presuming that the minimum is near zero and cannot go lower.

The problem is that when the overall effect is so brilliant, the maximum cyan and black are likely to be near zero as well. So, the impact of our correction will not be as much as could be hoped for. In fact, the poor contrast throughout is because only one of the four plates—the yellow—has any kind of detailing in it. The magenta is essentially a solid color throughout the costume and the black and cyan are basically zeroed out. In other words, three-quarters of our color space is not being used at all.

First, then, we should apply curves to maximize whatever small contrast we can find, and along the way, make the flesh-tones more realistic. As for the costume, the way out of this mess is not to be so shockingly red throughout. Whatever the brightest part is, we should keep as saturated as possible, (i.e., no cyan or black at all) but we should subdue the rest. For that, we want the unwanted color, and as there is

Figure 5.7 *When an image contains brilliant objects, look to the unwanted color. All channels have been corrected here, but the cyan is the most important one.*

none to speak of at present, one will have to be manufactured.

In practice, we explore the image and find the brightest area. Having done so, we proceed to create the unwanted color. Since yellow is the only plate with detail, we create a new cyan that is a blend of 70% of the old cyan and 30% of the yellow.

This finagling will create a problem. There will now be a certain amount of contaminating colors everywhere in the red. The area that I have identified as lightest will have 8^C. All other areas will have more.

This conflicts with our previous goal of having the brightest area be absolutely as intense as possible, meaning no cyan or black at all. To restore these regions to brilliant red, the correction curve must move 8^C to zero. That is desirable anyway, since it steepens the cyan curve. Of course, we will steepen it further in the range of the red objects, which is the lightest part of the cyan curve. The cyan channel, before and after, is shown in Figure 5.8.

In Just the Dress His Century Wore

The interesting marbled-paper image of Figures 5.9–5.12 symbolizes a species particularly suited to unwanted-color moves. If an object has a pronounced grain, as this paper does, the unwanted color governs its intensity. When we want to make the grain more or less prominent, the unwanted color is the principal tool.

Although wood might be a more typical example of where we might want to control grain, the paper image has more possibilities. Images like these are sold to be used as backgrounds, for which they are very

Figure 5.8 *The two cyan plates of the images of Figure 5.7.*

Figure 5.9 *Left, the original. Center, removing all cyan sharply reduces grain. Right, increasing contrast in the cyan makes all patterns more pronounced.*

useful. Frequently we will want to make some custom variation of them. Here are a few examples.

Curve-based contrast boosting of the unwanted color is the best way to bring out the grain. In Figure 5.9, compare the original to a version with no cyan at all, and one with a steep contrast curve that increases cyan quartertones without adding cyan where there was none.

Unwanted colors do their work best against purer incarnations of red, green,

and blue. The overall feeling of this art is less red than magenta, although the yellow plate is much heavier than the cyan. In Figure 5.10 we make the image pure red by duplicating the magenta plate into the yellow channel. Under these circumstances, the impact of moves in the cyan is intensified. Note that one effect has gone away: a danger in working with grains is that the grain may take on the look and feel of the unwanted color. This is what is happening in the right third of Figure 5.10. Where

Figure 5.10 *When the image is shifted from magenta-red to pure red, the unwanted color becomes even more prominent. Center and right, adjustments in the cyan drastically change the strength of the grain.*

Figure 5.11 *Neutralization techniques. Left, a single overall reduction in saturation. Right, curves that aim for more neutral colors. Center, swapping the cyan and black plates gives less color variation.*

the cyan is heavy, the pattern is becoming distinctly blue. That is not necessarily a problem with this art. If we were working on a reddish wood, however, a bluish grain would be just as easily achievable, but far less desirable.

The center image of Figure 5.11 suggests a way of avoiding this. Earlier, I asserted that adding the unwanted color is roughly as powerful as adding black. To test this proposition, I actually transposed the black and cyan in the center image. If we would

like a strong grain, but don't want any of it to have a blue tinge, this is the way to go.

This version is flanked by the right and the wrong way to get a less pink, more neutral effect. On the left, Image: Adjust>Hue/Saturation reduces saturation throughout the image. This floods everything with unwanted colors, and although it does make the image more neutral, it also neutralizes a lot of its appeal.

The blunt instrument of Hue/Saturation adjustment should only be used for its

Figure 5.12 *Special effects. Left, increasing cyan sharply overall by blending 50 percent of magenta into it. Center, an inversion curve on the cyan. Right, using the entire available colorspace through drastic curves.*

ability to isolate a certain color. When acting on the image as a whole, curves will always be more effective, as in the version at the right of Figure 5.11. This was treated just as we would any other image with a cast. I found areas that I wanted to neutralize and forced a gray in them. This retained plenty of interesting color variation throughout the image, since places with relatively heavy magenta, yellow, or cyan continued to display it. The only issue was where to set the highlight and shadow. This is one of the rare images that, in the interest of softness, should probably not make use of all available color space. So, I set my highlight at $10^C10^M8^Y$, intentionally retaining a slight magenta cast, and the shadow at about 50% in all colors.

Figure 5.12 shows three fanciful variants. At left, a new cyan plate that is a 50–50 split with magenta makes for a lavender image with a much less pronounced grain. Quick! How would we add more grain?

Yes, of course, this change has given us a different unwanted color. The way to add detailing would be to alter the yellow.

The center version has a flipped cyan. That is, the start of the curve is higher than the end, meaning that places that were relatively heavy in cyan are now relatively light. This is not a straight negative version of the cyan, which would overwhelm the image, but a softer variation on the negative theme.

Finally, the right-hand version is a reminder of just how much vitality we can add to any image through curves. I simply set the lightest area of each color to zero and the heaviest to around 90%.

This series of maneuvers illustrates some of the potential offered by manipulating abstract patterns. They have interest just by themselves, but they are particularly useful as backgrounds, especially if they are not too assertive.

Give the One in Red Cravat

Our last demonstration of the contrarian school of color correction is Figure 5.13. At first glance, it isn't much like the other images in this chapter, which tend toward blazing exhibitions of a single color. Here, 90 percent of the image—the door and the woman's flesh and hair—is fairly subdued. The dress, however, is brilliant red, and when we see brilliant reds we must instinctively look to the cyan plate.

The extra bite in the door comes from moves in the L channel of LAB. We'll see how to do this sort of thing in Chapters 8 and 9. But LAB techniques won't put folds in the dress. And without those folds, the dress looks like it's painted on.

This seems like just another version of the dancer or the lime. So, after the overall correction is made, we need to think about blending into the weak channel. But this one is not as easy. The dancer image was essentially all red and the lime was all green. Figure 5.13 is neither. Unfortunately, this means that if we start blending into the cyan plate generally the door is apt to turn a very weird color.

We've avoided the practice for nearly five chapters, but here there's nothing for it but to make a selection, and blend into that. First, an examination of the channels verifies the problem. The cyan is terrible. The magenta is totally solid. The yellow is serviceable and is the obvious blending choice.

I've used this image in classes and have been astounded to see professional retouchers who are insightful enough to realize that such an unorthodox maneuver is necessary, yet so set in their ways that they take half an hour to create the necessary selection mask.

Granted, the ability to make accurate masks is one of the hallmarks of the professional. If you don't have a lot of practice at this sort of thing, imagine how difficult it would be to select, for example, the hair of the woman in Figure 5.1. In such a case, we'd be looking at individual channels to try to find the best edge and doing all sorts of other tricky things.

Here, however, there is no need to spend any time at all. Just look at the magenta plate in Figure 5.14. One can hardly ask for a more decisive distinction between dress and background. All one has to do is hit the dress with the magic wand tool, and presto, a perfect selection. I feathered it from force of habit, but this is not really necessary.

Now, with the dress still selected, flip to the cyan channel, and apply the yellow channel to it. This will leave the background unaffected. I used 50% opacity.

As happened also with the lime, this blend leaves the cyan channel temporarily too dark. Therefore, with the dress still selected, I applied a curve that brought its minimum cyan value down to what it was before the blend. I left the curve relatively steep to retain the shape of the folds.

But Graphicker for Grace

When one color dominates the image, we should not be dazzled into believing that that is the one we must attack. Instead, we

Figure 5.13 *The unwanted color at work in a selected object. An overall plate blend won't work here because it would change color too drastically in the background. By selecting the dress and blending into that, however, more detail can be built into the folds.*

should be more subtle, devoting our energies to courting the color that is prominent by its absence—unwanted, perhaps, but not unnecessary, not unloved.

Admittedly, this channel blending is tricky stuff, more so than the curving of Chapters 2 and 3. The decision-making is much less automatic. It's fairly easy, I think, to know when a channel blend might be appropriate; the hard part comes afterward.

The language of color is indeed the language of poetry. The idea that there should be fewer yellow objects in nature than red, green, or blue ones is counterintuitive, but it is nevertheless correct. Many scientifically fashionable ideas about

Figure 5.14 *Creating a replacement for the original cyan channel, left. Below, left to right: the original magenta; the original yellow; a 50–50 blend of the yellow into the dress area only of the cyan; a final cyan version in which curves have been applied to the dress to lighten it and enhance shape.*

how color should be handled have failed because their authors did not grasp facts about color that were obvious to, say, Leonardo da Vinci.

Or Emily Dickinson, for that matter. I've often been attacked, over the years, for saying what I did in Chapter 1, that photos taken in dark conditions generally need to be lightened even when the photographer has already tried to compensate. Match the art! say the scoffers. What gives you the right to think that an observer would see it differently than the camera?

A voice from 1862 answers them:
We grow accustomed to the Dark
When Light is put away.
As when the Neighbor holds the Lamp
To witness her Goodbye.
A moment—we uncertain step
For newness of the Night,
Then fit our Vision to the Dark
And meet the Road erect.

*   *   *

For all the glorious instincts of the true poet, certain things come only with experience. Appreciation of the importance of the unwanted color is one of them. For now, we should just resolve that all strongly colored

MANIPULATING THE UNWANTED COLOR

✓ Areas that are predominantly red, green, or blue are peculiarly susceptible to moves involving the opponent process plate, otherwise known, somewhat inaccurately, as the *unwanted color.* In red areas, including fleshtones, the unwanted color is cyan; in greens, the unwanted color is magenta; and in blues, it is yellow.

✓ Focus-enhancing moves in the unwanted color are very powerful, roughly as effective as moving both dominant inks at once. In adding detail, it's the most significant channel. Steepening the weak color's curve will yield dramatic results.

✓ Many bright areas appear too flat because they lack an unwanted color altogether. In such cases, applying curves will be of little help. It is often necessary to generate a shapelier unwanted color plate by means of blending detail in from another channel.

✓ After a channel blend, restore original color by lowering the minimum value of the new channel in the affected area to whatever it was before.

✓ When trying to use bright, happy colors, consider reductions in the unwanted color rather than trying to beef up the dominants.

✓ In objects with a pronounced grain, such as woods, steepening the unwanted color will greatly intensify the graininess, but at the risk of creating an unwelcome hue. In such cases, consider means of transferring some of the role of the unwanted color into the black plate. Normally this is done by blending some of the unwanted color into the black.

✓ Zeroing out the unwanted color in the absolutely brightest area is a good way to add even more contrast to a primary color, even though letting one of the CMY colors drop to zero is normally considered unacceptable.

✓ Our perception of colors is influenced by what we see near them. To emphasize a bright color even more, increase the unwanted color in nearby areas.

✓ Be alive to the possibility that an image may offer more than one opportunity for an unwanted-color maneuver. If an ink is unwanted in one area of the image and dominant elsewhere, generally it will pay to steepen the curve in the unwanted area even if it penalizes the dominant range.

red, green, and blue objects: flowers, fruits, faces, whatever—will always have high-constrast and poetically shapely unwanted-color channels in our work. In arranging this, we avoid the following Dickinsonian error of inexperience:

The good Will of a Flower
The Man who would possess
Must first present
Certificate
Of minted Holiness.

*   *   *

Phooey. The above is a crock. You want good flowers, you don't need any certificate. You need a good unwanted color. The certificate, plus the other three channels, plus a dollar and a half, gets you on the subway.

Long before the age of Photoshop, John Wiley & Sons, the publishers of this book, brought out a scholarly work on color, which offered the following wisdom:

Confusion about the elementary principles of color is very widespread, the chief reason being that words dealing with color are used very loosely in ordinary language. But the difficulty goes deeper than that. Color was an art long before it was a science, and consequently the language of color is poetic rather than factual. The words are not as a rule intended to be taken literally but rather to convey a feeling or an impression....Scientists are often infuriated by their inability to pin down an artist, or even a layman, to factual statements on subjects that might lie within the sacred realm of physics. Or, not recognizing that the artist's statements are poetic, they point out the departures from literal truth and expect the artist to retract them.

If you read about "caverns measureless to man," nobody supposes that a dedicated spelunker with modern surveying instruments would be unable to map them, if they existed. And if a lady with spike heels says "My feet are killing me" this is easily recognized as a poetic statement, on a somewhat lower plane. But if someone says "This color has some red in it," how are we to take it? This sentence sounds factual and objective, but probably it merely expresses that the speaker associates a feeling of redness with the color, and it might better be regarded as a poetic statement.

Indeed.

In Color Correction, The Key Is the K

Manipulation of the black plate is the most potent tool in color correction. Gray component replacement, contrast-boosting curves, and other black magic underline why four-channel colorspaces can be better than those with only three.

A six-year-old, a scientist, and a retoucher were each given the same test in logic. They were asked, what do the following have in common: RGB, xyY, YCC, LAB, and HSB?

The six-year-old said, they all have three letters. The scientist said, each is a paradigmatic construct enabling expression of empirical visual data in the form of unique normative values of probative color equivalence. The retoucher said, each is a colorspace, but not CMYK, so to hell with 'em all.

That the six-year-old gave the most coherent and technically useful response is the theme of this chapter, in which we will discover how to make a weapon of the anomaly that sets CMYK apart from and above other color models: the presence of black ink.

The techniques discussed in this chapter are not possible in colorspaces, however attractive, that have only three variables. Taking full advantage of a four-letter colorspace avoids a lot of four-letter words.

Black is not itself a color, but rather the total absence of color. That need not deter us from using it in color correction. In fact, it should encourage us. Since black ink blots out everything, small changes in the black content have a huge effect.

Let us begin the exploration of the glories of our four-letter colorspace by discussing two other three-letterers that are very poorly understood, GCR and UCR, and how to exploit them.

Historically, artists looking for quality separations did not need to concern themselves with this topic. Drum scanners owned by somebody else produced a CMYK file, exactly what we needed to print with, and all this GCR/UCR stuff was taken care of by the time we got the files.

As the desktop revolution has progressed, it has become more common to start with files that are *not* in CMYK. When we convert them into CMYK, we need to have some plan regarding GCR.

A Hypothetical Colorspace

If this were a perfect world, we would be able to print with CMY only. In our vale of mortal sorrows, the actual inks are not quite up to the challenge. The colors that ought to make black have a reddish-brown tinge, due to the inadequacy of cyan ink.

CMY-only printing, however, isn't all that awful. People have done it for years. Certain desktop printers use CMY only, as do a couple of large-format printers. Limiting the topic to presswork, if you skip ahead to Figures 7.1 and 7.3, you can see comparisons of printing without any black, and the CMY-only versions aren't so bad. So we are talking about adding a fourth ink to a mix that already works reasonably well. How much of an impact can it have?

This question is worthy of extended discussion not just because black is such a powerhouse, but because the same considerations apply if a fifth and/or sixth color is added to CMYK. Such added colors are now appearing in all kinds of printing devices.

Note how CMY, like the five other colorspaces referred to above, has three letters. As the six-year-old noted, there's something special about that number: uniqueness.

Take RGB. We can define any color in terms of its red, green, and blue components, but only in one way. Every color is unique, and no other combination of red, green, and blue light can produce it.

HSB is entirely different, but the result is the same. It assigns a basic hue, and then modifies it with a value for color saturation (purity) and another for luminance (brightness). Again, every conceivable color can be described this way, and again, each HSB color, except for pure grays, is unique.

And so on with the other color models, including CMY, and so it will be with any other three-letter system that may be developed in the future. Each color in the system has a unique value.

Adding a fourth variable to any of these will create alternate ways to make colors that were already possible. It also will expand the gamut of colors that can be produced. That the fourth variable happens to be black has nothing to do with it. If the fourth color were (to suggest something off the wall) tangerine, the considerations would be the same.

Let's talk about, then, an imaginary world of CMTY. This would be very useful if we happened to represent citrus growers. Imagine the bangup oranges, grapefruits and lemons we could produce if we could back up the basic yellow and magenta inks with a hit of tangerine. We might even be able to make brighter limes, because of the strong yellow component of tangerine ink.

$0^C 50^M 100^T 100^Y$ is a brilliant orange, impossible to reproduce with CMY, or with CMYK for that matter. Similarly, we expand

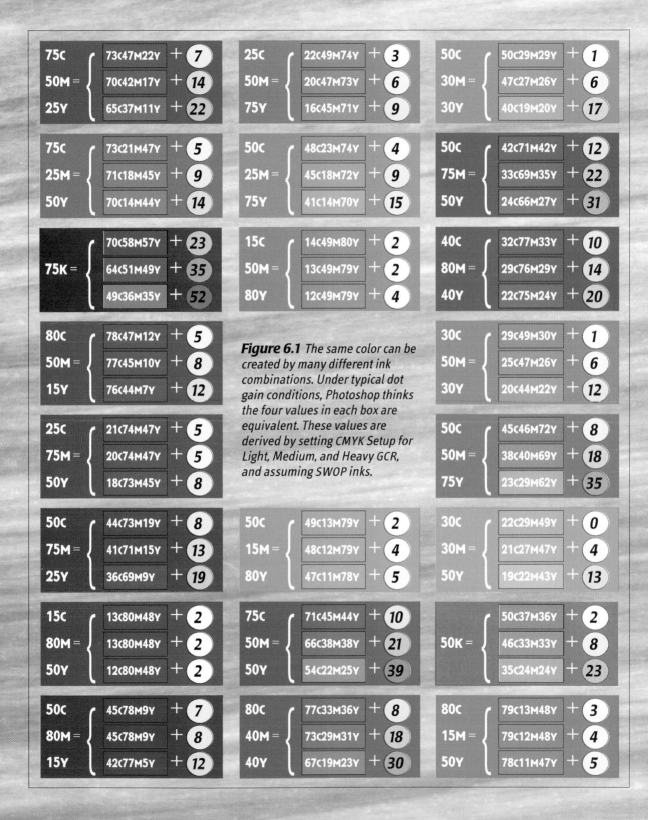

Figure 6.1 The same color can be created by many different ink combinations. Under typical dot gain conditions, Photoshop thinks the four values in each box are equivalent. These values are derived by setting CMYK Setup for Light, Medium, and Heavy GCR, and assuming SWOP inks.

the gamut in the shadows. Tangerine ink is pretty light, but adding it to CMY shadows would help a little, creating a color darker than was previously possible.

Brilliant oranges and marginally deeper shadows aren't all that tangerine has going for it. It also offers *options*—options to create colors that were already possible, but to create them with different mixes of ink.

Since tangerine could be described as a mixture of lots of yellow and a small amount of magenta ink, in principle we could put it into any color that normally contains significant amounts of yellow and even a little magenta, provided we were willing to take some yellow and magenta out to make up for it.

For example, a normal fleshtone is in the neighborhood of $10^C40^M50^Y$. $10^C39^M5^T47^Y$ should be practically the same thing. So should $10^C35^M25^T30^Y$. And so should many other possibilities. Don't hold me to these numbers, I'm guessing about dot gains and other variables, but you get the idea. If we had this problem in real life we could certainly figure out the proper numbers, with sufficient precision to obtain a colorimetric seal of calibrationist certification that the colors are actually indistinguishable.

Since there is no *theoretical* difference, we have to ask, is there a *practical* one? Would we put tangerine ink in fleshtones?

I will answer this quickly. Yes, we would. There would be less variation on press, a less pronounced screening pattern, and, most important, it would reduce the range of the magenta and yellow inks, which is significant for reasons more fully, er, fleshed out on pages 131–134.

Sorry for such a brusque answer, but we don't print with tangerine, we print with black, and it's time to face up to it.

Black as Tangerine

Like tangerine, black expands our gamut. It doesn't help at all with citrus fruit, but it does enable a far deeper shadow than was possible before. And like tangerine, it gives us options. Instead of substituting for lots of yellow and a little magenta, black substitutes for all three CMY inks simultaneously.

This discussion will be a lot easier if, for the moment, we forget about such tiresome practicalities as dot gain, different printing conditions, the anemic nature of cyan ink and other obstacles to perfection.

In this best of all possible CMY worlds, equal parts of the three, say $25^C25^M25^Y$, would result in a neutral gray. The same, in fact, as using 25^K alone. These are the extremes, but we can also split the difference: $20^C20^M20^Y5^K$ or $15^C15^M15^Y10^K$ ought to work just as well.

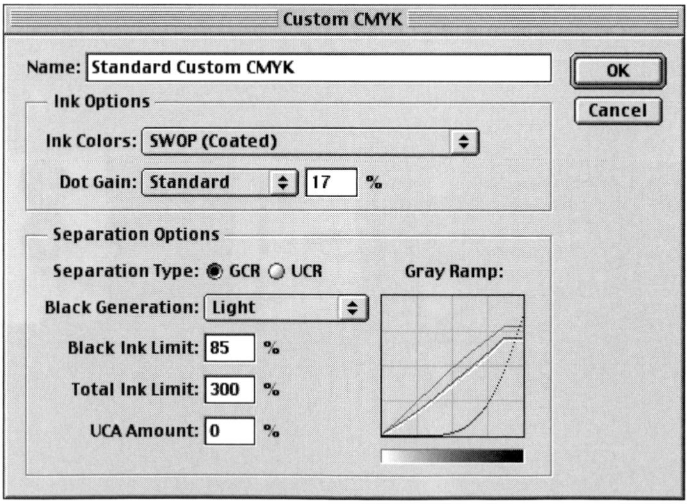

Custom CMYK

Name: Standard Custom CMYK   [OK]   [Cancel]

Ink Options
Ink Colors: SWOP (Coated)
Dot Gain: Standard [17] %

Separation Options
Separation Type: ● GCR ○ UCR   Gray Ramp:
Black Generation: Light
Black Ink Limit: 85 %
Total Ink Limit: 300 %
UCA Amount: 0 %

Figure 6.2 *These are good all-purpose defaults. For details on the dot gain curves, see Chapter 12.*

This principle could be applied not just to grays, but to any color with more than trace amounts of C, M, and Y. $75^C25^M85^Y$, which is forest green, would therefore be eligible: we could make it $60^C10^M70^Y15^K$, among many other choices.

Although forest green is not gray, it isn't pure green either. It has a gray component, which we can partially replace with black ink, the amount of said substitution, if any, being very much up to us. Hence, gray component replacement, or GCR.

Back in the real world, dot gain and impure inks dictate numbers considerably different from our ideals, as Figure 6.1 shows, but the principle is the same. We need not worry about the actual numbers because Photoshop does the math for us.

Each time we make this conversion, we have the option of generating a little black or a lot, or somewhere in the middle. The question must be, which is best? To which, happily, there is a clear and concise answer.

It depends.

GCR: When in Doubt, Do Without

Most magazines of circulation less than several hundred thousand adhere to the Specifications for Web Offset Publications, or SWOP. Among other things, SWOP dictates that total ink values in any area cannot exceed 300, which most publica-

tions adjust downward to 280. This rule exists because, at the high speeds of a web press, greater volumes of ink can cause drying problems. Worse, it can cause ink backup, which will contaminate the lighter inks and make the run inconsistent. Some titles, typically trades that print on lesser-quality paper, ask for an even lower maximum, like 260. Newspapers commonly ask for 240.

By the same token, better printing conditions imply a higher maximum. For sheetfed printing on coated paper at reputable shops, 320 is certainly acceptable, if not 340.

Enforcement of these standards is not uniform, but many magazines pay their stripping shops for a special SWOP ad inspection. Some magazine printers do the same before putting the job on press. If you are "in the neighborhood" of 280 you are no more likely to get stopped than if you go five miles an hour faster than the speed limit, but if the ink police find 300 or higher your film will bounce, and that's a lot more serious than a speeding ticket, especially if it happens late in the production cycle.

A traditional separation aimed for commercial printing might yield a shadow of

Figure 6.3 A Photoshop 6 innovation, the Convert to Profile command, allows any file—even one that's in CMYK already—to get a different black generation. The Custom CMYK being invoked here will apply to a single image only, and won't change the user's basic color settings.

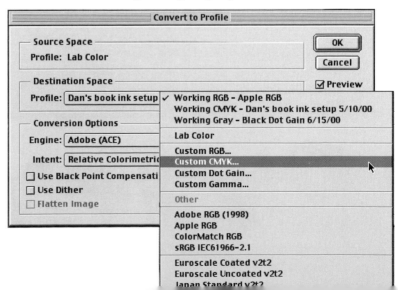

$90^C80^M80^Y65^K$, which sums to 315 and would therefore consign our magazine ad to the garbage. Yet we don't wish to lighten the shadow; the whole point of Chapter 2 was how important overall range is.

This solves the problem of whether to use GCR. We *have* to use it in the dark areas, because for every point of black we put in we can take out three points of CMY. If we adhere strictly to the 280-point rule during separation, the shadow value will be the acceptable $75^C65^M65^Y75^K$ or something close.

Allowing for nothing more than this mandatory GCR in shadows is the lightest black that Photoshop's standard settings will generate. It is for those who believe that black ink is toxic and want as little of it as is reasonable. That amount will be heavily influenced by our choice of maximum ink density in Custom CMYK.

To differentiate this species of shadow-only GCR from the picture-wide varieties, there is another term for it, a confusing one: *UCR*, for undercolor removal.

You should be aware that the above definition is generally but not universally accepted. Some people use UCR and GCR to mean the same thing. In Europe, and occasionally in the United States, another term, *achromatic reproduction*, is used to signify the use of heavy GCR.

The options in Edit: Color Settings> Working Space>Custom CMYK have a profound impact on the separation process. For the moment, I recomment you insert the values shown in Figure 6.2. The rest of the chapter will discuss why.

This looks identical to Photoshop 5's File: Color Settings>CMYK Setup, but there's an important improvement. We frequently had to change CMYK Setup to deal with exceptional images, and then remember to change it back. While that's still possible, a better way is to use the new Image: Mode>Convert to Profile command. The Custom CMYK option shown there in Figure 6.3 will bring up the Figure 6.2 dialog box, but it won't affect our master color settings; it's strictly a one-shot deal.

Convert to Profile also allows us to change the GCR of a file that's already in CMYK. In past versions, to change black generation we had to take the file out of CMYK and bring it back in.

If there is nothing to indicate otherwise, though, we should stick to our basic settings. Whether we choose Light GCR or UCR, the separation will be of the type printers have the most experience with, and which people variously describe as *no GCR, minimum GCR,* or *a skeleton black.* Black ink starts to appear when each of the three process colors is printing more than 25% and the sum of all three values is 100 or more. If the three colors get heavier the black gets heavy faster, so that the darkest area of the picture will have black values at least as high as the magenta and yellow, and perhaps even the cyan.

I think there are very mild technical

Figure 6.4 *In images with critical detail in dark areas, GCR should be avoided. An unexpected overinking of black could ruin the image otherwise.*

Figure 6.5 *Where major parts of the image are light and neutral, GCR helps guard against the possibility of color variation on press.*

advantages to using Light GCR rather than UCR as a general rule. Either one, however, is certainly a skeleton black, which is mandatory for many of the corrections described in Chapters 2 and 3. There, several examples required an increase in black throughout the image. These curves added depth, but did not make the pictures muddy. With a skeleton black, there's little if any black ink in colored areas, so such a muddying effect can't happen.

Of the other four GCR options, "None" gives, as the name suggests, no black plate at all. Use it if you are intending to print CMY only. "Maximum" wipes out CMY altogether in neutral areas and is therefore unusable for most images; who needs a shadow of $0^C0^M0^Y95^K$? It does have one specific use, which we'll discuss shortly.

The "Medium" and "Heavy" settings, though, are perfectly workable. It therefore behooves us to inquire whether there are situations where they would be preferable.

Remembering that there is no theoretical difference between using one variety of GCR and another, there are two practical ways in which one may actually be superior. One is to control problems in the pressroom. The second is to make our life as color correctors easier.

When More Black Is Better

This is not a book about printing, so why do we concern ourselves about pressroom problems? Because printers are, if possible, even less inclined to take credit for their own screwups than prepress people are. Instead, if the job looks lousy, they will blame the photographer, the art director, El Niño, and, most especially, us. Worse, the client sometimes falls for this pap, or even comes to the same erroneous conclusion without anybody's help. Preventing pressroom mistakes is therefore very much in our interest.

Black is by far the most powerful ink, and once on press, the presence of additional black has several pluses and several minuses. If the pluses seem to match what we want to accomplish with our picture it will pay to use GCR.

The most obvious way GCR can help is as a defensive measure against some of the problems caused by a variation in ink density on press. Presses and pressmen are not precision instruments, so this happens all the time. If you are working not with a press

Figure 6.6 *When creating an artificial drop shadow, don't forget GCR principles. The shadow should be partially black, to avoid color variation on press, but not all black, or there may be problems with trapping or an obvious line where the shadow ends.*

but with some kind of digital printer, it's easier to avoid such a problem, and some of these comments about black may not apply.

The nice thing about black is that it is perfectly neutral. The more black contained in any color, the less likelihood that overinking of cyan, magenta, or yellow will affect the basic hue. The bad thing is that if black itself is overinked, it is much more noticeable than any of the other three.

The shish kebab of Figure 6.4 would consequently be a very bad picture for GCR. The visual strength of this image depends on retaining detail in the three-quarter-tones. If we engineer a lot of black into these areas and the pressman overinks, the detail in the meat will close up and image quality will fall into the flames.

You may say, suppose we don't use much black, wouldn't it be just as likely that the cyan or some other color would print too heavily, achieving the same muddy mess? Yes, surely there could be too much cyan, but it wouldn't be nearly as bad. Each CMY ink darkens much less than the equivalent amount of black. And as for a cyan cast, in areas this dark our eyes are not particularly sensitive to colors. We would perceive added darkness, not blue meat.

From which, we derive:

• **Rule One**: When the most important part of the image is dark, avoid GCR.

The bridal gown of Figure 6.5 presents a neutrality problem. No matter how careful we are, there is always the possibility that for any of a number of reasons an ink may run too heavily on press and we will wind up with pink or green folds in the midst of this white fabric.

We cannot stop a determined pressman from doing this to our job. We can, however, make it a lot harder for him by using lots of GCR. The more black in the gown, the less prone it is to acquire an offensive off-color.

A less well-known extension of this rule involves items containing a grain, wood especially. The grain of yellowish wood can become green rather easily. To prevent this, use higher GCR. Distinguish these cases, though, from the marbled-paper image shown back in Figure 5.9. In that image, if the grain takes on the hue of the contaminating color, it isn't such a bad thing.

• **Rule Two**: When the most important part of the image is a neutral color and it is lighter than the equivalent of 50^K, use GCR to guard against disaster.

GCR is also useful when producing a duotone effect with process inks. If we are trying to get the look of a green duotone, we will actually use three inks: cyan, yellow, and black. No matter how good our separation is, if yellow or cyan is overinked, parts of the image may not have the uniform green tint we want. But the more black we use, the less pronounced the effect will be.

• **Rule Three**: when creating a process tritone or quadtone, use Heavy GCR.

Allowing Flexibility on Press

Sometimes color fidelity is so critical that we resort to all kinds of horsing around on press. The best-known examples are mail-order clothing catalogs. If a shirt prints in slightly the wrong shade, tens of thousands of dollars worth of merchandise will be returned by angry customers who believed the book.

In such stressful cases, pressmen and art directors do not rely on contract proofs, but on a real shirt that they hold in their hands as they try all kinds of inking shenanigans to match it.

This is not the time to use GCR, because black neutralizes everything. The more black ink, the less leeway there will be to make artistic changes on press.

• **Rule Four**: When you are expecting careful help for a critical color match during the pressrun, GCR is a hindrance.

The same principles apply if you are creating drop shadows with Layer: Layer Style>Drop Shadow, as in Figure 6.6.

This doesn't mean make the shadow *entirely* black. Anyone who does this is asking for trapping problems, and for a highly visible line of demarcation where the shadow fades into the background. A little bit of black goes a long way. I know some very good pressmen, but none who can make black ink print other than a shade of gray.

• **Rule Five**: When creating a drop shadow, specify about a third as much black as CMY inks.

Project design can also affect GCR desirability if there are areas near the image that require heavy coverage. Ink gets hard to control when a lot of it hits the paper at once. So, if our image is going to be placed on a solid black background, bet on the black coming down too heavily in the picture itself. Naturally, if one is fortunate enough to know about this before converting to CMYK, one uses less GCR.

Other hints that the black may be hard to handle are very bold headline type, or text type that contains fine lines, Bauer Bodoni being the most glaring example. Any of these factors may motivate the pressman to hike the flow of black ink.

• **Rule Six**: If there is reason to fear heavy black inking on press, avoid GCR.

Repeatability with GCR

Since black ink minimizes hue variation, if the same image appears more than once, there is a good case for using GCR.

This principle seems so obvious that we may forget that an image doesn't have to be a photograph. A flat color will behave the same way. And many designs call for repetitions of the same color, usually a pastel, in large background areas.

Light colors scarcely seem like the place one would want to introduce black. But if we are trying to insure fidelity from one page to the next—as, for example, in a company logo—it can be an excellent idea.

• **Rule Seven**: When repeatability from page to page is an issue, don't forget GCR principles, even when specifying colors in linework and flat tints.

Many people wonder why we use a K to stand for black. Mainly, it's to avoid confusion: in the pressroom, cyan is customarily referred to as *blue,* so B is ambiguous. But K is more elegant, anyway. It stands for *key,* and indeed it is the key to the final major uses of GCR.

Black is the key for registration, meaning that the other three colors are supposed to be adjusted to agree with it and not vice versa. When a job is printed out of register, then, the culprit is almost invariably one of the other colors.

This suggests an application for GCR in the growing volume of work for lower print-quality applications, especially newspapers. Because of the speed of newspaper presses, misregistration is common. A beefy black will minimize it. Warning: before trying this, make sure you understand newspaper dot gain—it is greater than in other forms of printing, and if the black is too heavy the outcome will not be attractive.

* **Rule Eight**: Where misregistration is likely, use a heavier black to control it.

The K is the key, not just in registration but in color correction generally. As the most powerful ink, it can add detail and contrast, muddy or clean up colors, and bulk up shadows in ways that three-letter colorspaces can only envy. So,

* **Rule Nine**: Before making the conversion to CMYK, ask yourself: do I want to correct this image, and can the black plate be of use?

That is a rather deep rule.

Muddiness and Custom CMYK

Beginners often go into attack mode the first time their color files hit press or printer. They are always disappointed by the lack of contrast in comparison to what they thought they saw on the monitor or chrome.

That lack of contrast is a fact of life. We compensate for it by using targeted curves that discard contrast where it isn't needed and augments it where it is. But the problem is there and can't be totally eliminated.

On the other hand, it's easy to confuse this effect with something more insidious, namely, a result that's darker and muddier than what was expected.

If this is happening to you consistently, the fault is almost certainly in your Custom CMYK. The principal suspect is your dot gain setting. That is such a complicated topic, and one that has baffled so many users, that I've broken it off into a separate chapter in this book. We'll therefore defer serious discussion until then, except for two points:

* If your images consistently print too dark, you need a higher dot gain setting.
* Dot gain in black is ordinarily higher than in any of the CMY inks.

There are no right answers for the overall dot gain number—everything depends on local conditions. But for the other Custom CMYK settings, there are definitely some *wrong* answers. To flesh out the recommendations shown in Figure 6.2, here are Photoshop's defaults—and how to do better.

* **Ink Colors**. The default is SWOP Coated. That describes most of my work, but possibly not yours. If your seps are going to a newspaper, you can still use SWOP Coated, although you'll have to raise dot gain to 30% or so. However, it's probably better to switch to SWOP Newsprint. Photoshop bases its separation on its ideas of what colors result when inks overlap. The newsprint setting assumes muddier colors, which is correct. This yields a slightly better newspaper sep in my tests.

As to the other Ink Colors defaults, I will

not pretend that I have carefully examined every one; I don't know if anybody ever has. But, if I were printing to uncoated paper or doing work in Europe, I'd use the appropriate Photoshop ink settings as a start.

- **GCR Method**. A stronger black does not necessarily imply a change in image color. Photoshop's default, "Medium" black, is heavier than the traditional standard, but not incorrect—until you pair it with its erroneous computation of black dot gain. In any event, color correction is easier with a lighter black. Also, lighter blacks are better because of the inherent unreliability of black ink in offset printing. But even if your final output is going to something other than a press, I recommend Light GCR.

- **Black Ink Limit**. Whether they use inks, toners, waxes, or dyes, all output devices fail to hold detail when the aforementioned colorants reach a certain heaviness. The worse the output device, the lighter the point at which the failure will occur. For a number of reasons, the failure point for black can be quite low. In many applications even a coverage of 80^K is likely to print as solid; even the finest presses occasionally fail at 90^K. I recommend an 85^K maximum for virtually all print conditions. Anything between 80^K and 90^K makes sense. Photoshop's default, 100^K, is a recipe for mud.

- **Total Ink Limit**. This will vary. The default is the SWOP standard, 300. If your conditions are of better quality than this, the number can go up. For sheetfed printing, it can be 320 or even 340. If worse, it'll have to go down. Most newspapers request 240, and some go even lower.

Do remember, though, that this limit doesn't protect you once the file is in CMYK. If you correct aggressively after the conversions, your relations with the ink police are in your own hands. If you show up with a 330 shadow where the limit is 300, good luck convincing them that it *used* to be 300 before you fixed it up.

- **UCA**. We haven't discussed this option before, because in Photoshop's implementation, it makes little sense to use it.

UCA (for undercolor addition) artificially adds cyan, magenta, and yellow to the shadow. This would only make sense where the normal shadow value is much less than the total ink limit, which in itself doesn't make sense. The only way this would normally occur is if GCR were set to Maximum and/or maximum black were set to 100^K. Neither of these settings should be used for a typical image.

If you are trying for a darker shadow, it makes much more sense to set a low black limit—80^K or so—and, after separation, apply a curve that brings 80^K into the nineties. This method, unlike UCA, boosts contrast in the shadows, and would therefore almost always be preferable.

The Planned GCR Correction

Several easy and efficient correction methods use GCR as an accomplice. The first is for images that need focusing or definition.

Kodak Photo CD scans are the best example. Like other scans made with a wide-open profile determined by machine readouts, they are almost invariably too soft. But since these aren't usually opened in CMYK, we get to specify whatever GCR setting we like. If we choose Light black generation, we will get a black that includes only transition areas and anything darker. We can now exaggerate the black plate with curves, normally by boosting the quarter-tone point. This adds snap to the picture in a less obtrusive way than oversharpening.

And it can't be done with any other GCR setting: had we used Medium or higher, there would have been black in the lighter colors, and they would have dirtied up when we applied the curve.

This boosting of black, at least through the quartertones, is so common a remedy for listless images that it, if there were nothing more, would justify using Light GCR as our standard method.

This kind of process can also work in reverse, to give depth to an image that is too brilliant or too dominated by a single color. In Figure 6.7, we'd like to establish more shape in the apple. At first blush, this seems like the same problem we dealt with in the lime of Figure 5.4. There, we attacked the unwanted color, magenta, making it steeper and more detailed.

That image, however, had no background to speak of. Here, messing with the magenta will be fine for the apple, but it

may turn the background purple. A better way is to hit the black—but without GCR, that won't work either. In Figure 6.8, compare the original black plates of a Light and a Heavy GCR. A curve applied to the light one would have almost no impact on the apple. In most images, that's what we want. Put black in light greens, and if black heavies up on press, we get mud.

Here, however, that *is* what we want, because it will make the apple seem rounder. And we need no help from the pressman; we can do it ourselves by separating with Heavy GCR and then bumping up the black in the manner shown, first checking that there is no black in the brightest spot of the fruit. Here, it was necessary to move the starting point of the curve slightly to the right, as shown in Figure 6.8, to do that.

Putting Snap in Neutrals

When the interest areas of an image are predominantly light and neutral, we, as per Rule Two, use GCR to prevent press error. But that's not the only reason. There are uses for it even if we are going to a digital

Figure 6.7 *Bright objects like this apple need a quick falloff in color saturation if they are to appear round. The corrected version, right, starts off with Heavy GCR, followed by a curve that increases black.*

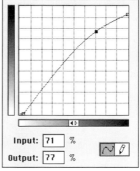

Input: 71 %
Output: 77 %

Figure 6.8 *Clockwise from upper left: versions prepared with UCR and with Light, Medium, and Heavy GCR. Note how the CMY (left sides of images) gets lighter as the black gets heavier. Above center: the curve applied to the black of the right side of Figure 6.7. It makes the fruit seem rounder. Its sides seem to recede into the background, because less saturated colors appear farther away.*

proofer, where there should be no wild swing in inking.

Figure 6.9 is a reprise of an example in the 1994 edition of this book. Except, I didn't do it as well as I should have, because I didn't keep that thought in mind.

What I did say was true enough. I pointed out that an image where the main subject is neutral, as the statues are, suggests a black correction. In most pictures we don't mind picking up a little extra color, but here we want to stay subdued. Unfortunately, when one expands range, one usually livens up color—unless, that is, we are talking about the black plate.

I added that there are two possible approaches. As the background is heavier than the statues, one could write a black curve that emphasized either the statues alone or both statues and background.

Increasing contrast in the original black was clearly better than nothing, but I had a smarter alternative available. I should have said to myself, this will work a lot better if I can engineer more detail into the black plate before I play with it. I should therefore have opened Convert to Profile, changed its Custom CMYK to a heavier GCR (this time, I chose Medium), and *then* applied my curve to the new black.

The Prince of Darkness

The role of the black plate is very important in such light neutrals, but it's absolutely critical in holding detail in shadows, because it's the only place we find any.

Figure 6.9 *Top left, the original image; top right, a conventionally corrected version. Bottom left, the same idea but with a heavier black plate to start with. Bottom center: the original black plate, generated with Light GCR. Bottom right: the black of the version at bottom left, which had been reseparated with heavier GCR.*

Remember the weird effect in the shadows of the CMY plates back in Figure 1.4? That was interesting, but academic in that picture, as it would be in most. Detail in the darkest areas isn't usually the most important thing in the image.

But every so often it is. The black cat of Figure 6.10 surely qualifies. And now, that strange effect in the CMY becomes a very big deal indeed.

What's up with that? Why is all the contrast blown away?

There's no law against very high numbers in the colored inks. In the apple of Figure 6.7, the yellow is in the high 90s, as is the cyan in the plate. And each can contribute shape, as well as color.

But these objects each have a pronounced color. The ink limit of 300 can't come into play, because there's not much magenta in the apple and not much yellow in the plate.

In something dark *and neutral,* though, like the cat, there is a serious inconvenience. The magenta and yellow can't go much above 70, or the cyan above 80, without provoking the printer to reject the job.

Photoshop must therefore suppress the natural darkness of the CMY channels during separation, creating a blown-out mess in the shadows and a correction challenge different from any we've seen so far.

Namely, *everything* depends on the black channel. As for the CMY, you can sharpen them, apply curves to them, throw them against the wall, or stomp on them, and you will not succeed in squeezing detail out of them. So, you must forget them, and work extra hard to make the black as good as it can possibly be. Let's do it.

Figure 6.10 *Important detail in very dark areas is the exclusive province of the black channel. Shadow detail in the cyan, magenta, and yellow has to be suppressed to stay within the total ink limits that most printers impose. When there's critical shadow detail, forget the CMY channels and attack the black.*

How to Hold Shadow Detail

The left-hand version of Figure 6.11 was converted into CMYK using the pure defaults, dot gain 20%. Please assume that the woman's face, pallid though you may find it, is acceptable. Instead, our job is to bring out detail in her sweater and jacket, and secondarily in her hair.

That's easier said than done. Shadow detail is notoriously difficult to enhance.

A glance at the individual channels in Figure 6.12 indicates who's to blame: it's the ink police. They insist that the sum of all inks be 300 or lower, even in the darkest areas, such as where the jacket meets the chin. Without the ink police, those areas would be in the 90s in the CMY channels. But the ink police exist. That important CMY detail has to be suppressed, held down to between 70 and 80, to let the black be as dark as usual without going over that tiresome 300 total.

The bottom line is, in terms of achieving the goal of more shadow detail, the CMY channels are worthless. We live and die by what happens in the black. If we can make it a *lot* better than the original, we win. Otherwise, the client will look for somebody who knows GCR better than we do.

The basic strategy is clear. If everything is going to depend on the black, then we'd better come up with one that has excruci-

Figure 6.11 *Images with critical detail in the darkest area, as this woman's sweater, are a major problem, particularly where dot gain is high. Often the only way to get an enhanced version (right) is to do some kind of custom separation followed by a contrast-enhancing move in the black plate. (In this correction, it's assumed that the only objective is to improve the clothing.)*

Figure 6.12 *In dark neutral areas, cyan, magenta and yellow have to be suppressed for the image to stay within the total ink limit. Therefore, the contribution of the original CMY channels to the detail in this clothing is just about nil, and everything will depend on the quality of the black plate.*

atingly high contrast. To do that, sooner or later we are going to have to apply an excruciatingly steep curve to the black plate.

With the default black, that is just not going to happen. We can't increase the shadow value because it's nearly at 100^K already. We can't decrease the lightest point of the clothing very much, because the black plate is carrying detail in both hair and face, and such a curve would blow those away.

We therefore have to forget this particular black and try some other alternatives. When the situation is as desperate as this, many rules go by the wayside. We will also forget about the normal 80^{C}70^{M}70^{Y}70^K. Increased contrast in the black takes priority; the longer the range in the black the more contrast it will have. We must plan on a black shadow in the mid-90s, with the other inks coming down to compensate. We will worry about that at the end, ignoring the ink police in the interim.

Figure 6.13 shows nine alternatives, some very unlikely. There's an infinite number of others, times an infinite number of permutations, because we could take the

black plate from a single separation and the CMY plates from a different one, or we could mix and match even further.

To start with, we try four basic variants, each with 85^K maximum. Note the similarity between UCR and Light GCR. The Medium and Heavy GCR versions we can reject out of hand. They carry too much detail elsewhere, and that will be an obstacle. We want to clear the decks, to have nothing in the way of our eventual contrast-building curves.

Figure 6.13E is something entirely different, a black generated by one of Photoshop's supplied profiles, Euroscale Matchprint (perceptual). This profile permits a maximum shadow of 95^K, which accounts for the high contrast in the clothing. But in principle, it's a lighter black generation even than Photoshop's built-in UCR setting; compare the darkness of the hair to that of Figure 6.13A.

Next, another brainstorm. The dot gain setting alters contrast in the black plate. If we separate with a false dot gain setting, we will definitely have to trash the CMY files. But it may be worth a try.

Where more dot gain is assumed, Photoshop needs to deliver a *lighter* separation to compensate for the expected gain on press. Therefore, it's no surprise that Figure 6.13F, separated at 40% dot gain, is so much lighter than Figure 6.13G, at 10%.

That extra lightness came about because Photoshop dropped the midtone of the reproduction curve more for 6.13F. Therefore, the lighter half of the curve became flatter, and the darker half steeper, and you know the rest. The lower dot gain version is absurd; it hurts contrast just where we want to gain it.

It looks to me, though, that Figure 6.13F has just lost too much detail in the lighter area to be usable, no matter what the CMY plates look like. So, as a first serious try, I'll invest in yet another separation, with the 20% dot gain we want, but UCR, 100% black allowed. The reason for these settings is, I want to be able to plug an entirely new black into the image, I want to affect non-shadow areas as much as possible, and I want to accommodate a very high black value in the shadows.

Now, yet another separation, the black of which is shown in Figure 6.13H. I raised the dot gain setting to 35%, and I cut the maximum black to 65^K. The plan was to boost contrast in it with a curve, and then paste it into the black channel of the separation I just made.

Nice idea, and probably worthwhile in slightly different circumstances, but here it didn't quite work. There is still not sufficient detail in the black to hold shape in the hair. Back to the drawing board.

Figure 6.13I uses the principle of substituting an easier problem for one that is more difficult to solve. In this version, I used 20% dot gain once more, and UCR so as to limit the amount of detail the black carries in light areas. The unorthodox thing is, I set the maximum black to 52^K.

With the maximum black that low, it's possible to apply a really drastic curve to boost contrast.

When everything rides on the black plate, one may as well go for broke by trying to sharpen it. Chapter 4 teaches that a large Radius is the enemy of subtle detail, and there's a lot of subtle detail in the fabrics. So, I went with a Radius of .8 pixel—but an Amount of 500% and a zero Threshold.

The eyepoppingly harsh result is shown next to the default black in Figure 6.14. Certainly, I could not have dreamed of sharpening the other channels to this extent, but why should I want to? They don't have detail in the areas of interest.

And the problem I substituted for the one I solved by this approach? Well, the printer of this book won't allow me to show it to you, because the shadow under the woman's chin is 87^{C}79^{M}82^{Y}94^K, 42 points higher than SWOP allows.

Compliance can be arranged by means of Image: Adjust>Selective Color, as shown in Figure 6.15. Choosing Blacks as the target, I sharply reduced the CMY inks. The reason for the slight imbalance is that I judged the shadow should remain slightly brown, rather than neutral.

Figure 6.13 *With difficult images, it sometimes makes sense to try several separation settings. At right, black plates generated by nine different Custom CMYKs. Which would you prefer to start with? Version A is at 20% dot gain, Light GCR, 85% maximum black, 300% total ink limit. The others vary from these settings as noted: B: UCR. C: Medium GCR. D: Heavy GCR. E: Using the supplied Matchprint ICC Profile. F: 40% dot gain. G: 10% dot gain. H: 35% dot gain, 65% black limit. I: UCR, 52% black limit.*

Figure 6.14 *The two black plates that produced the alternate versions of Figure 6.11. When coverage in the other three channels is so heavy, there is no need to fear a very harsh-looking black.*

the left and right sides of the image. It may seem like we are left with the tedious alternatives of local selection or blending the cyan plate, which has a decent shadow, into the black. That strategy would risk contaminating the lighter areas of the picture with black, and those areas, at the moment, are pretty good.

If We Shadows Have Offended

In the Chinese tapestry image of Figure 6.16, the fly in the ointment is also the shadow area, which is not even close to being dark enough. Normally, this would call for us to trot out some kind of curve to accentuate the heaviest blacks.

To use curves, however, we need a base image that's at least close to what we want, not on some other continent.

Lighting conditions were not right when the photograph was taken. As a result, instead of the shiny black background that usually characterizes these wall hangings, we get a translucent, flimsy-looking silk fabric, the shadow of a shadow, if you will.

As matters stand, the black is at least 30 points too light everywhere. And, in the left side of the image, certain dark areas contain only 15^K, which is maybe 45 points lower than we would like.

A standard curve might work, but it also might exaggerate the difference between

Now that we are GCR experts, there's a more effective option: a false reseparation. Using Image: Duplicate, make a copy of the image, and run Convert to Profile, using a Custom CMYK of UCR, black ink limit of 85%, and the ludicrously low total ink limit of 215. Photoshop doesn't know that no printing conditions on this planet require

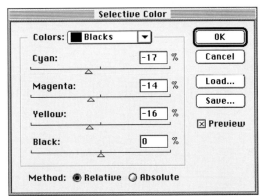

Figure 6.15 *If the total ink in a CMYK image is illegally high, this move in Image: Adjust>Selective Color can get you off the hook.*

this low of a limit; it assumes we knows what we are doing.

When this monstrosity returns to CMYK, it will have heavier shadows. Wherever the sum of the CMY values would otherwise reach 180 or so—which happens throughout the black parts—extra black will have to be generated instead, to stay within the absurd limit of 215. At the same time, the lighter areas of the black plate will be unaffected, since we specified UCR rather than GCR. This confines the damage to areas that exceed the total ink limit we specified; the bright colors in the fabric won't change.

The CMY plates of this new separation are quite worthless and should be given the burial they deserve. But when we replace the original black plate with the black from the second separation, surprise, we suddenly have a decent piece of art.

This image shows why Photoshop 6's one-shot Convert to Profile command is such an improvement over the old way, which was to take the image out of CMYK, change to the false settings, and return to CMYK. There's no quality problem with doing that, nor is the extra time involved particularly bothersome.

The bad thing about the old way is that we had to put a lethal value into the CMYK Setup—and sometimes we would forget to change it back.

Do Your Eyes Glaze Over?

A common error of beginning designers is to specify small type as a tint of three inks, just like this. It looks so nice and crisp on the screen that it's always a great disappointment to watch it break apart when ink hits paper.

Notice that the effect is worse in the text than in the subhead. This is because of the presence of fine lines in the text typeface. Trying to print these accurately with a 133-line screen is like trying to drain a lake with a slotted spoon, especially because the fine lines are horizontal and the screens of the three heaviest inks are angled.

Without such fine lines, the subhead can handle this fairly well. Switching back to images, the overwhelming majority resemble the subhead more than the text. So, in a case like Figure 6.16 we are better off with a balanced four-ink shadow than with one

Figure 6.16 *At top, the original suffers from poor shadow density. The corrected image uses a false reseparation to generate a stronger black plate.*

constructed of black alone. This is why we stick with Light, Medium, or Heavy GCR, not Maximum, for the overwhelming majority.

Those words *overwhelming majority,* naturally, imply an exception. And the exception is images that have something in common with the text type, namely, fine lines that should print in black. One such category of images appears frequently in this book. Can you name it?

Yes, indeed. I am referring to screen grabs such as Figures 6.2 and 6.3. Note the fine black lines around the dialog boxes. Printing these as a standard shadow would be about as successful as my earlier experiment with the green text type. When reproducing cartoons, which often have fine black lines, we run into the same problem. Figure 6.17 is a more difficult example.

Assume that the client insists on greater prominence and legibility for the small type elements at the bottom and the black line that borders the green type at the top. Right away, we should be thinking of Maximum GCR, to get solid black in the type.

Yet, this image is made up of dull colors, where large amounts of black are generally a poor choice. The consequences of unpredictable ink coverage argue strongly against vast amounts of black anywhere *except* in the area we're trying to emphasize.

Accordingly, we really need two separations, one with Light and one with Maximum GCR. Even if we start with a CMYK file, such as the top half of Figure 6.17, we can still fix it as follows:

• Make a copy of the original (which in this case has Light GCR) and execute Convert to Profile, specifying a Custom CMYK of Maximum GCR, 100% black ink limit.

Figure 6.17 *Images where fine type is critical are candidates for a two-step process involving Maximum GCR followed by a blend with a standard separation.*

• Still working with the reseparated copy, using the lasso tool, make a quick freehand selection of the woman and the flower, and delete this entire area. The selection doesn't have to be at all accurate, as long as it doesn't delete any of the type. This is to stop this area from being overwhelmed by black ink during the eventual blend.

• Apply a curve to what's left of the black plate by moving the top right point to the left, thus darkening the shadow. The idea is to get the type areas to be close to 100^K. The rest of the image, other than a big hole in the middle of it, will now be too dark; ignore this.

• Copy this overly dark image to the clipboard. Paste it on top of the original, making it a layer.

• From the Layers palette, choose Blending Options. As set up at the bottom left of Figure 6.18, it tells Photoshop to replace the bottom layer with the top *only* where the black plate of the top layer is heavy, meaning, only in the areas we care about.

There remains one slight problem: the image now needs to be trapped—which brings up another important use of GCR.

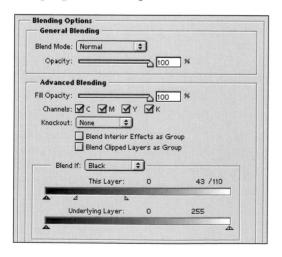

Staying Out of Traps with GCR

Trapping is desirable when two totally different colors butt one another. Without trapping, a disagreeable white line can occur if the job should happen to be printed out of register.

For example, suppose that for some stupid reason someone in authority decided that the background of this page should be magenta, the text type black as it is now, but that the subheads should be printed in cyan.

If the magenta stops at exactly the point it hits either kind of type, we are asking for trouble. If it does, and the registration of the two colors on press isn't perfect, a white

Figure 6.18 *Beefing up the type. Above, left side, the black plate. Top to bottom: the original with Light GCR; a second version with Maximum GCR; the final merged product. Left, the Blending Options dialog box set up to accept only the type from the second black version. Above right side, the cyan plate. Top to bottom: the original; after the version with Maximum GCR has been merged in; after running Photoshop's Trap filter.*

hole will appear on one side of the type and a darker overlap on the other.

To guard against such an ugly occurrence, the cognoscenti build in intentional overlaps—some of the time. In the case of the cyan headline, we would make it slightly fatter so that it would overlap the background. With the black text type, we would not interrupt the background at all—we'd just print right on top of it.

As you may know or suspect, learning how to trap isn't especially easy. Fortunately, in most of the work discussed in this book, it's unnecessary: photographs rarely need to be trapped at all.

The reason is, before trap is necessary, there has to be a knifelike edge between two colors that have very little in common, such as pure magenta and pure cyan. In a photograph, those two things almost never happen at the same time. Edges tend to be somewhat indistinct, and colors somewhat subtle, meaning that any two neighboring colors probably share certain common values and a white line or even a relatively light one cannot appear.

With Maximum GCR, however, this is no longer the case. Now, black elements, such as type, will have virtually no CMY component and thus may have nothing in common with their colored neighbors.

In Figure 6.18, note what is happening to the cyan plate after the Maximum GCR type is merged into it. The body of the type is now nearly blank. It thus is possible, if the black is sufficiently out of register, for the dreaded white line to appear.

It's not totally obvious that this is a trapping situation, because a very slight overlap already exists. But I think it makes sense to do it, particularly since Photoshop makes it so easy. Image: Trap offers us a dialog box that allows us to specify the width of the desired trap, in pixels. I chose the minimum, one pixel, and got the result on the bottom right of Figure 6.18.

A mild trap like this has virtually no impact on the rest of the picture. The only trick is knowing where it's necessary.

The Real PMS Equivalent

As previously noted, if you never use Maximum GCR, you'll probably never have to trap a photograph. But because most readers occasionally have other kinds of trapping problems, I'm reluctant to let the subject drop, because Photoshop can be a big help in solving them.

Being lazy, I think that the best way to avoid trapping problems is to avoid situations that require a trap. Figure 6.19 is an enlarged version of the drop cap that appears on the first page of this chapter. It was constructed in Adobe Illustrator, not Photoshop. In this design, no trap is necessary. There is no possible turn of events that can result in a white line. The background grid is cyan, but both letters have a significant cyan component.

Suppose, though, that the background letter were not a bluish gray, but a gray,

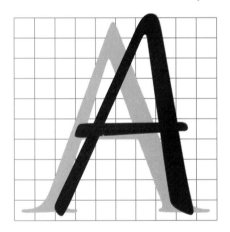

Figure 6.19 *When all graphic elements share large amounts of color (here, cyan) trapping is unnecessary.*

period. Now, it's a trap situation, if you happen to be an idiot. An idiot says that gray is a shade of black, and constructs it entirely out of that ink. And, as there is no black ink in the grid, trapping becomes necessary.

You would not, of course, do this, because you are not an idiot, and you know the theory of GCR. You realize that you can make a gray just as well with the CMY inks as with black, and a CMY gray will have enough cyan in common with the grid that trapping will no longer be an issue.

That was an easy exercise, but are you willing to carry it further, into a case where there is nothing gray? Let's assume that it's the Christmas season, and the client wants us to print with red and green. Only, we are given Pantone Matching System equivalents, which we have to match with process inks. Let us say PMS 179 for the red and PMS 342 for the green, and that we need to print green type on a red background, or vice versa.

Chances are, we aren't doing this job in Photoshop, but we could if we liked, because the PMS process equivalents are built in, as Figure 6.20 shows (to get there, double-click on either the foreground or background color at the bottom of the toolbox, and choose Custom from the next menu).

All other professional-level programs have these values built in as well, and they will all give PMS 179 a value of $0^C79^M94^Y$. PMS 342 will be, as seen in Figure 6.20, $100^C0^M69^Y43^K$. We therefore have a trapping problem. The two colors have only 69^Y in common. Yellow is a very light color. A bright yellow line appearing

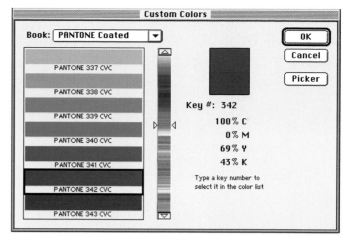

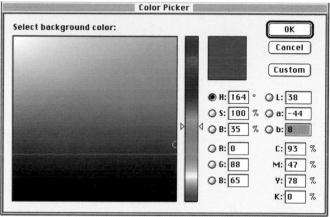

Figure 6.20 *Pantone Matching System formulations aren't necessarily the best for trap avoidance. Above, locating the nominal CMYK values in the Custom Colors submenu of the Color Picker. Below, using LAB equivalents to find a definition of the same green that uses magenta rather than black ink.*

between relatively dark green and red is no good.

Those may be the numbers Pantone recommends, but GCR theory tells us that there are many other ways of making the same green—and if we make it with magenta ink, rather than black, the green and the red will have enough in common that we can forget about trap.

Here is where Photoshop can help us in a way that other applications can't: it will tell

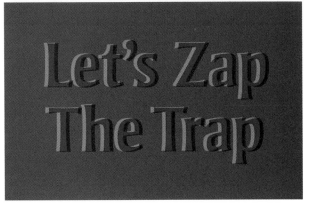

Figure 6.21 *Because one color may have several CMYK equivalents, canny users can eliminate many trapping headaches. Above left, the green type, pursuant to a Pantone definition, has a great deal of black and no magenta. Unfortunately, this means that the red and the green do not have enough in common. If the magenta prints out of register (above right) an obvious yellow line appears. But by redefining the green to a rough equivalent that uses magenta in lieu of black (lower left), such a yellow line becomes impossible. The worst that can happen is a pink line (lower right). The upper left version requires trap, the lower left does not.*

us the equivalents. To find out, call up the Color Picker by double-clicking on either the foreground or background color in the toolbox. This time, rather than clicking Custom, enter Pantone's CMYK values for the green in the bottom right.

The Color Picker doesn't work only in CMYK. It simultaneously displays the appropriate numbers in LAB, HSB, and RGB. So, when we enter $100^C 0^M 69^Y 43^K$, three equivalent values automatically appear, in my case, $0^R 87^G 65^B$, $38^L (44)^A 8^B$, and $165^H 34^S 100^B$. Whether you would know offhand that any of these colors is a green, let alone the same green, is entirely irrelevant. What you already know is that in these three colorspaces, these values are unique.

But in CMYK, they aren't, thanks to what might be called tangerine theory.

If we enter a CMYK value in the picker, Photoshop has no choice about what RGB, LAB, and HSB numbers to represent it with. But what if we start by entering the number in something *other* than CMYK? How does Photoshop then decide which of the infinite number of CMYK equivalents to use?

That's up to us. So, we close the Color Picker, and open Custom CMYK. We change the black generation preference to None. Then, back to the Color Picker, where we enter the known LAB (or whatever, it shouldn't make a difference) value and see we get for CMYK. As the bottom half of Figure 6.20 indicates, the answer is $93^C 47^M 78^Y$.

THE POWER OF THE BLACK PLATE

✓ Although black has no color of its own, it is the most powerful of the four process inks. Generally, adding black has as much impact as adding all three of the other colors simultaneously.

✓ CMYK is unique in that most colors can be expressed as more than one combination of inks, depending upon how much black is being used. This is the principle behind gray component replacement.

✓ At a minimum, there needs to be enough black to give depth to shadow areas. That "skeleton" black is the traditional method of making a color separation.

✓ Undercolor removal, or UCR, is the lightest black that Photoshop's standard settings will generate. It is only slightly lighter than Light GCR; the two will be interchangeable under most circumstances.

✓ Any time an image goes from another colorspace into CMYK, we have to make a GCR decision. Unless there is a reason to do otherwise, use Light GCR.

✓ SWOP dictates that the sum of all four ink values not exceed 300, but most publications request a 280 maximum.

✓ When the most important part of an image is neutral, using heavier GCR can avoid problems on press.

✓ Contrast-enhancing curves in a skeleton black plate are an excellent way of adding focus, commonly with a boost in quartertone values.

✓ In images with important shadow detail, the quality of the black channel will be critical. The cyan, magenta, and yellow cannot carry detail in the shadows because they must be kept artificially light to stay within total ink limits.

✓ For cartoons, critical fine type, and anything else that requires fine black lines, consider one separation with Maximum GCR merged into another with standard settings, using Layer Options to limit the merge to the black areas.

✓ Information gathered from Photoshop's Color Picker can be helpful in finessing trapping problems. Most CMYK colors can be expressed in many ways, so one chooses the numbers that avoid the necessity of trap.

Armed with this information, we go back to the application we were using, plug in the new green value, and call it quits. Since the red and green now share 47^M78^Y, a reasonably dark orange, the trap problem vanishes, as illustrated in Figure 6.21.

Incidentally, even if you don't have a trapping problem, you should use this approach to find PMS equivalents. The CMYK values that Pantone suggests assume finer printing conditions than most of us have. Assuming that we aren't printing on coated paper on a sheetfed press, using these values will give us a color that is unnecessarily dark, in comparison to its spot-color cousin.

To correct this, read the LAB values just as we did above, *and then type the same values right over themselves.* This will force Photoshop to recompute the colors using current Custom CMYK assumptions for dot gain and ink balance, and will result in a more accurate match, no matter what kind of GCR you have chosen.

It All Fits Together

If we are working in CMYK, we are well served to know what CMYK is all about. This example, where Photoshop knowledge is found useful even in a job that seems to have nothing at all to do with Photoshop, holds a lesson.

Note, also, how it is helpful to know equivalencies in other colorspaces. In the next three chapters I'll try to show how they all fit into a pattern, and how they can be exploited.

This concludes our current exercises, but not our exploitation of the awesome power of black ink as an enhancement tool. Once you master it, you will feel as much pity as I do for the scientists who, with no personal experience in color correction, preach that one should only manipulate images in a three-variable colorspace, and that GCR decisions should be made on the fly by the output device.

If ever you are forced to work under such straitened systemic circumstances, you will be able to produce pretty good color if you have become proficient at writing curves.

But if pretty good is not quite good enough for you, accept that your perpetual punishment for acceding to a three-variable colorspace will be color that can only be pretty good, forever. Through eternity, a voice in your mind, whispering ever so softly, will torment you by repeating the biggest secret in professional color reproduction. As you wail and gnash your teeth over your lack of a good image backbone, over your inability to hold neutral colors, over the missing definition, the highlights that cannot be highlighted, the voice will continue to haunt you; and whatever your color correction talents, however close you get to the sacred territory that is better than pretty good, you will continue to hear it. And you will know and understand, even without the voice, that if you wish to unlock the cell of your pretty good prison, that if you wish to be set free into a better-looking world, the lifeless, gray door *can* be opened — and the key is the K.

RGB Is CMY

Most files start in RGB and end in CMYK. When to make the conversion is up to us. Too many people make this decision because of fear of one or the other, when it should be based on the image itself. To decide which space is more effective, one has to appreciate their differences. But to appreciate their differences, one has to understand how alike they are.

 tourist, visiting New York for the first time, stops a native and asks how to get to Carnegie Hall. The New Yorker replies, "Practice, practice, practice."

Being from that neck of the woods myself, I take the same intolerant attitude toward color correction. This accounts for much missing material in this book.

For example, I see no purpose in discussing the Sharpen filter. Although it can improve certain images, the Unsharp Mask filter is much stronger and more flexible. The sooner we get comfortable with it, the better our images will be, and the more we practice with it, the more comfortable we'll be.

More provocatively, this is the only Photoshop text, as far as I know, that doesn't discuss the Levels command. Same reason: nothing wrong with Levels, but curves are more powerful. Why waste time with the second-best way? If you want to learn to swim, jump into the deep end.

The same reasoning applies—sort of—to the choice of colorspace. This book covers a lot of things, but our principal tool is curves. Anyone who is serious about print quality has to know how to write CMYK curves, because there's no such animal as a perfect separation process.

So the more practice we get, the better. That's why, up until now, we haven't even considered the uses of the two other color-spaces that Photoshop offers us for options.

Let me cut to the chase. LAB and CMYK are so different that each one can do things the other can't possibly accomplish.

RGB, however, is *not* that different. That is the problem and also the potential. If you take the doctrinaire position that you will never apply a curve to an RGB document,

Figure 7.1 *Top, a normal separation of an RGB file. Bottom, the individual RGB channels pasted into the CMY of a blank file and printed without a black plate.*

you can still get top-quality color. The same can't be said of LAB, and still less of CMYK.

It is tempting, then, to say, forget RGB, for the same reason you should forget Levels. But there are flaws in this logic, of which the biggest is the following.

If you know CMYK, you *already* know RGB. If you know RGB, you know CMYK. And if you realize why they are really the same, you will know how to exploit their slight differences.

The Ink Police Overture

In RGB, the lighter a channel is, the more light of that color is supposed to hit the viewer's eye. In a picture of a rose, for example, the red channel will be very light.

In CMYK, the lighter a channel is, the less of that ink will appear. Each ink's function is to prevent reflection of a certain color. Cyan prevents reflection of red. In a picture of a rose, for example, the cyan will be very light.

Similarly, where the red is dark, the cyan will be dark. Where the magenta is light, so will the green be. Where the blue is dark, so will be the yellow. RGB is CMY, and they even make it easy for us by putting the letters in the proper order. R=C, G=M, B=Y.

Figure 7.1 shows just how similar they are. The top is a normal separation of an RGB file. The bottom is a weirdo: it's the red pasted into the cyan, the green into the magenta, the blue into the yellow, and no black at all. No, the two images are not identical, but they aren't all that far apart, either.

Before discussing this, consider Figure 7.2, which shows the RGB channels plus CMY equivalents after a standard separation. Note the family resemblance but also the differences. The cousins, red and cyan, are both approximately the same color, but the red has more contrast. And the green similarly, in comparison to the magenta. But there is an unusual wrinkle. See how, in the magenta, the hair is washed out, lighter than the faces, whereas in the green, things are more normal.

That's the long arm of the ink police. In making the separation, Custom CMYK called for the maximum sum of all four inks in the darkest areas to be 300, in deference to the above-referenced gendarmerie.

The faces don't approach this number. Although they are dark in magenta and yellow, even if they printed at 100^M100^Y, it still wouldn't bother the flatfeet, because cyan and black are each less than, well, five-oh. So, 300 is impossible.

The hair is another story. It's a neutral color—strong in all four inks. Thus, it arouses the curiosity of the ink police. With black ink floating around 70, a sum of 300 is very achievable. Accordingly, the natural darkness of the CMY inks has to be suppressed, and the black carries all detail, just as demonstrated way back in Figure 1.4.

Figure 7.2 *The individual RGB channels are similar in color to their CMY cousins. But they have more detail in the highlights and more weight in the shadows. The unusual effect in the children's hair in CMY is the result of a total ink limit for printing. The color channels have to be restricted to make room for a heavy flow of black ink. Otherwise, the limit might be exceeded.*

The parrot of Figure 7.3 got the same treatment as Figure 7.1. The left version is a normal separation; the right version is blackless, and consists of the RGB channels pasted into their CMY cousins. But these two renditions are much closer to one another than was the case in Figure 7.1. Also, here one could actually make the case that the right version is the better of the two. When you understand why, you'll be on the road to the proper use of RGB.

Enter the Dot Gain Curve

RGB has no ink police. Nor does it have dot gain. When an image moves into CMYK, Photoshop suddenly has to cope with both factors. This explains not only the washed-out hair of Figure 7.2, but also why the bogus version of Figure 7.1 is too dark yet that of Figure 7.3 is not.

Since dot gain will cause darkening on press, the image must be lightened as it goes into CMYK. The worse the printing condition, the greater the dot gain, and the more lightening Photoshop has to do to make up for it.

The lightening will be accomplished by a curve that drops the midtone, where dot gain is theoretically heaviest. This is the "black cat" curve of Chapter 3.

Such a drop in the midtone flattens the light half of the curve and steepens the dark

Figure 7.3 *Like Figure 7.1, the right-hand version has no black, and the RGB channels have been pasted directly into their CMY counterparts. This time, though, the two versions are much closer in overall color. Do you understand why?*

half. The normal consequences of curve application have not been suspended. The steeper the curve, the more the contrast. *The separation process, by its nature, suppresses highlight detail.*

In Figure 7.1, the bottom version is darker, because there never was any such lightening, and because the image is rich in midtones. But notice how much better the definition of the chairs against the beach is. That's the extra highlight detail at work.

Not such a big deal here, perhaps, but it's more significant in Figure 7.2, and absolutely critical in Figure 7.3.

In a face, the cyan plate gives most of the contrast. We shouldn't put up with one as lame as that shown in Figure 7.2. The red channel shown is much better than the cyan, not just because the lightening curve suppressed highlight detail in the cyan but because the red does some of the shaping work done by the black in CMYK.

In a red parrot, the cyan is even more important, and that's why the right-hand version of Figure 7.3 is more detailed in the red areas. Its cyan plate—the original red channel—is better defined than that of the normal separation.

Have you figured out why overall darkness is not the issue in the parrot that it was in the beach scene?

The lightening routine is strongest in the midtones—and this bird doesn't have any. The red areas, for example, are very

Figure 7.4 *The two cyan plates of Figure 7.3. The one on the right is also the red channel of the RGB original.*

Figure 7.5 With obvious highlight, shadow, and neutral points, and a clear focus of interest, it's easy to correct this image with RGB curves.

channel from one into the cyan of the other. There is no law against mixing colorspaces during channel blends, and this is the first of many times I will recommend it.

A Simple Prologue

To summarize, RGB channels always have more contrast than their CMY cousins, especially in the lighter half. In the darker half, they may show detail that has been arrested in their CMY cousins by an overly zealous ink police.

There's a lot to be said, then, for using RGB as a blending resource. Elsewhere, the news isn't nearly so good. But before getting to that part, let's do a simple RGB correction to reinforce how much it resembles CMYK.

Figure 7.5 is a bread-and-butter kind of image that presents few difficulties. The highlight and shadow choices are clear and there is little risk of guessing wrong, as there's not much detail in either. The plane should certainly be a neutral gray or silver. And no question that the main object of the correction should be to add snap to it.

Since this is our first full-fledged RGB correction, let's review the concept. Instead of percentages, we use values of 0 to 255. The higher number indicates a larger amount of that color of *light* hitting our eyes. Thus, the higher, the brighter.

Neutrality is a simpler concept in RGB than when we have to deal with impure inks. Wherever all three channels are equal,

heavy in magenta and yellow, very light in cyan, and nonexistent in black. The other brilliant colors are similarly all highlights and shadows, with nothing in the middle.

Figure 7.4 shows the difference in the cyan channels. Not much of a competition, is it? Well, the successful retoucher is a thief. If Chapter 5 has convinced you of the critical nature of the cyan plate in red objects, your logic will convince you that this opportunity for felonious misappropriation of the version on the right cannot be passed up. With Image: Apply Image, copy the red that's neutral. This makes setting highlight and shadow values easy. We should shoot for, say, $250^R250^G250^B$ and, considering that we eventually have to print this, a conservative shadow of $10^R10^G10^B$. And we have to keep the three values roughly equal in the plane's body, so that it doesn't take on some undesirable color.

This is done exactly as it would be in CMYK. We fix all the critical values, and try to arrange to have the plane fall in the steepest parts of our three curves.

To emphasize this similarity, I reiterate an earlier suggestion: make the darkness orientation of your curve the same in both colorspaces. Photoshop's default is to have darkness to the right in CMYK curves and to the left in RGB. That's rather confusing. I prefer to know that moving the curve up always makes the image darker. So, if you'd like to follow the shapes shown here, be sure that the gradient below the curve is as you see it here. If it isn't, just click the gradient, and orientation will reverse.

In this image, the highlight is in the plane's body, just over the wing, at $235^R240^G230^B$. The shadow, in the furthest tailpipe, is at $33^R33^G43^B$. Typical values for darker gray parts of the plane come in at around $135^R150^G165^B$. Technically this shows a slight greenish-yellow tinge to the highlight, a cyanish-blue to the plane, and a small tendency toward blue in the shadow. Nothing to get unduly excited about.

This particular fighter can take off at a very steep angle, but not quite as steep as those of the center of the curves of Figure 7.6. The rate of ascent of those areas (which contain most of the plane) is so roller-coasterish that I've had to raise the zero point of each curve, so that the highlight areas don't blow out completely.

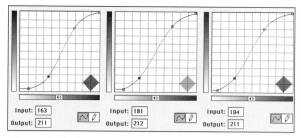

Figure 7.6 *These curves assign the aircraft of Figure 7.5 to very steep areas, in the course of correcting slight casts throughout the image.*

The result has far more snap than in the original. Also, it's about as good as one could do by converting to CMYK first and applying curves there.

Exit the Subtlety

Once we get into more complex images, the disadvantages of RGB begin to manifest themselves. Figure 7.7—another round of that old refrain, the steeper the curve, the more the contrast—shows why.

Assume that we are trying to improve a certain object in a certain channel of a certain image, and at the moment, it falls in the orange area of the top left curve. We react by steepening it, as at bottom left.

Now, suppose that the object, whatever it is, falls in the longer purple area of the top right curve. Our approach has to be the same, but we are unlikely to be as effective.

The bottom right curve is the only way to make the purple area as steep as the orange one was. That is a violent curve. We are unlikely to be able to get away with that in real life. The gentler twist in the orange one probably won't affect overall color, but in the purple one it probably will. The orange curve will diminish contrast slightly in the rest of the image. The purple one will run over it with a steamroller.

Some type of compromise is clearly

necessary. We will steepen the purple curve, but not as much. This will improve the object. It will not improve it as much as the orange curve does.

The moral of this story is, the shorter the range of the object, the more effective our curve corrections, and the less likely we are to punish some other area.

For all the reasons we've just discussed, the RGB channels are *always* longer and higher in contrast than their CMY cousins.

This doesn't mean curves don't work in RGB. If all we want to do is set highlight and shadow, there is no reason to avoid RGB. And more ambitious moves are possible.

Figure 7.7 *Contrast-enhancing curves work better when the original object of interest falls in a narrow range, as the orange object does at upper left. Given the longer range of the purple object at upper right, an overly drastic curve would be needed (lower right) to achieve the same benefit as in the lower left curve.*

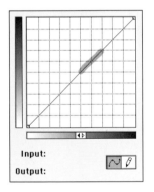

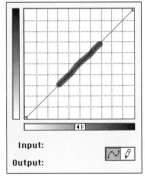

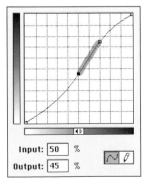

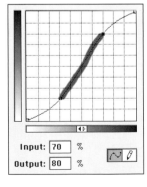

But if you're thinking of one, think CMYK. More channels, more better.

To illustrate, let's try a correction first in RGB, then in CMYK. Figure 7.8 is similar to Figure 7.5; in both one range of color is particularly significant. But here, the detail in the shadows behind the leaves is not as inconsequential as the background was in the airplane image. If these leaves were silhouetted out and placed against a pure black background, it would be as easy to apply curves to in RGB as in CMYK. Here, though, we'd also like to enhance the background to give a sensation of more depth in this rainforest.

The lightest part of this image is in the reflections off the top leaves. I found a $212^R215^G229^B$. The deepest shadow, at top right, is a Stygian $4^R4^G4^B$. There are no known neutral colors or fleshtones in the scene.

The reflections can certainly be lightened to allow more range to the rest of the image, and we would like to place both leaves and shadows in the steepest parts of our RGB curves. That's possible to a limited extent in red and blue, but not in the critical green, where the two ranges are consecutive and cover nearly the entire curve.

Making images better is pretty easy. The question always is, however, how much better could they have been? Let's do the same image from scratch, but in CMYK.

Curtain Up on Contrast

Choosing the same samples as before, the reflection is at $18^C10^M5^Y$ and the shadow at a beefy $78^C67^M70^Y83^K$. In principle the curves should be about the same as in RGB, In practice, as Figure 7.9 shows, they aren't.

The reason generally applies to all images that have more than one range of

Figure 7.8 *Should this image be corrected in RGB or CMYK?*

interest. The shorter CMYK ranges are easier to target. In CMYK the shadow region of the curve rarely is important, except in the black channel. In shadows, the CMY colors don't exceed 80%. In RGB, without a black ink to establish darkness, shadows have to be much higher. This makes it more likely that the items will share a range in CMYK, very convenient to address in curves.

Moreover, we're likely to have better results in the weak channel, and then there's that lovely, detail-rich black. Those two factors are what makes the bottom half of Figure 7.10 better than the top.

The cyan curve in Figure 7.9 is really no better than its red counterpart, and the yellow is actually a bit worse than the blue. But because the ranges of the leaves and shadows are more widely separated in magenta than in green, we can write a steeper curve in magenta. And with the interest objects at the extremes of the black curve, we can flatten out the center to gain lots of snap at the ends.

At this point, it's useful to review the five major weapons in our arsenal, the subjects of Chapters 2–6. Here's how the capabilities of RGB and CMYK stack up:

- **Setting overall range.** This is easy in either colorspace.
- **Steepening interest areas within a curve.** As we have just seen, CMYK is much better at this.
- **Working with the weak color.** CMYK's version is always weaker than its RGB cousin, making it easier to improve with virtually no risk of changing the overall color of the image. Moreover, black can often be used as a *second* unwanted color.
- **Unsharp masking.** This is more or less a subset of the last item. The unwanted color and the black can often be sharpened heavily in CMYK because they don't usually have as much noise as their darker RGB counterparts.
- **Manipulation of the black plate.** As RGB doesn't have one, CMYK wins in this category by default.

Exeunt the Flat Channels

Because of the influence of black, the CMY colors are subtler than their RGB relatives. Red makes more of a statement than cyan, green is more potent than magenta, and blue is more powerful than yellow.

This is a two-edged sword. On the one hand, complicated, finely tuned corrections such as the one we just did work better in

CMYK. On the other, when there is something seriously wrong with the image, attacking with RGB curves is a better option, but it isn't as good an option as using LAB, which we'll cover in the next chapter.

Blending, however, is an important use of RGB—and it isn't a one-way street. Whenever you see an RGB image with brilliant colors, you should keep this in mind.

Consider the red chest of the parrot in Figure 7.3, or, better yet, since we've dealt with this subject several times, consider a rose. The shape of the flower, and thus the success or failure of our work, depends on the cyan plate. The detail in the cyan is in the lightest area. When we convert to CMYK, we apply a dot gain compensation curve that suppresses such light areas.

How clever does *that* sound?

Not that the compensation degrades the image, mind you. In principle, press conditions will counterbalance the curve, and the printed piece will more or less reflect the original.

The problem is, it was a lousy photograph to begin with. The photographer

didn't capture as much detail in the rose as we now need.

How do I know this? Because there isn't any other species of photograph of roses. For reasons stated in Chapter 5, they *all* need some kind of contrast boost from us.

Since the idea is to wind up with a nice cyan plate, the direct approach is to blend something with more detail, commonly a copy of the original red channel, into it.

But this isn't the only way, and it isn't necessarily the best way. Remember, we postulate that the image didn't have enough contrast to begin with. That means that the red channel of RGB is too weak. If so, and if a blend is going to be necessary, why not get it over with in RGB?

This isn't always possible, because it can throw off the other colors of the image too drastically. But changing the red now will have more of an impact than changing the cyan later. And if a problem exists in one of the RGB plates, it will proliferate into at least two CMYK plates, if we let it.

Therefore, I recommend that, when starting with a brightly colored RGB image,

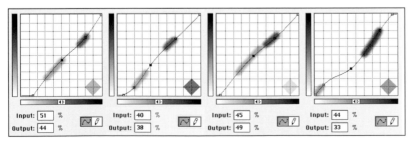

Figure 7.9 *The longer ranges of objects can hamstring those who try to target them with RGB curves. In this image, extra snap is desirable in the leaves (green range on curves) and in the shadows of the forest (brown range). In RGB, these ranges are slightly longer, in addition to being too close together in the green. In CMYK, they are easier to get at. The key channels here are magenta and, especially, black, where the two ranges are so far apart that they can be steepened dramatically without damaging color balance. No such opportunity exists in green, the RGB cousin of magenta. And RGB has no black channel.*

you check the individual channels to see if you can do now what you would otherwise have to do later.

Arranging the Lighting

As we're about to enter some really deep water, it's appropriate to have a couple of undersea shots as examples.

Figure 7.11 is brightly lit in the foreground, but the depths of the picture have the bluish-cyan cast that characterizes underwater photography. It's toning down the orange fish to the rear of the image. The background also seems too dark. And the background bubbles are ridiculously cyan, since the red channel is solid there.

Before deciding on strategy, we note immediately the possibility of Hue/Saturation or Selective Color. The normal obstacle to the use of these commands is that (1) they can throw off overall color balance; (2) they select a color that may be shared by something other than what we're trying to fix.

Neither objection applies here. The lighting conditions are unique; it's impossible to know what the real color balance should be and standard curves may exaggerate problems. As for

Figure 7.10 Top, the correction done in RGB with the top curve of Figure 7.9. Bottom, done in CMYK using the bottom curve. Note the added contrast in the leaves and shadows.

Figure 7.11 *The brilliant lighting of the foreground causes the background to appear unnaturally dark and blue. Below: the red, green, and blue channels.*

what's selected, the water is either blue or cyan, and nothing else in the image is either. The fish are either red or yellow. Yellow is shared with the coral, but red isn't shared anywhere.

Those commands alone, however, aren't enough. They can make a lighter blue background, but it would be very flat, without the darker sides seen in Figure 7.12. Also, the bubbles wouldn't be as neutral.

The solution is to blend the high-contrast blue channel at 40% into both

Figure 7.12 *After lightening the water by blending the blue, Lighten mode, into both the red and the green, followed by a Selective Color move to intensify blues and oranges.*

the red and the green. This blend must be done in Lighten mode. The idea is to lighten the water, not to darken the fish and the rocks. As almost everything in the blue channel except the water is darker than in the other two, using Lighten mode effectively selects the water for correction, but does so undetectably, unlike human-generated masks.

After these blends, the water was lighter, but more neutral. I fixed this with Selective Color, removing yellow from and adding lots of cyan and a bit of magenta to blues and cyans. I also added yellow and magenta to reds, to intensify the orange fish.

There is still sharpening and curving to be done in Figure 7.12, but the point is that we're a lot better off if we do this blend first, and that's no fish story.

A Cyan Encore

That was a somewhat complex exercise. The overwhelmingly cyan Figure 7.13 looks like it might be easier. It isn't.

For contrast, this document's red channel is worth zilch. One can't even find a diver. That explains why the image is so flat. The solution seems obvious, to repeat what we just did and blend some of the green and/or blue into it to get some semblance of detail.

I tried this, and after about ten minutes of curves, selective color, and cursing, when I converted it to CMYK it was sharkbait, worse than the uncorrected version.

Other than proving that you shouldn't get unduly upset if you find some of these concepts difficult and mess up once in a while, there's an interesting lesson here.

My plan of blending called for the water to become lighter than the divers in the red channel, just as it is in the other two. That was a stupid plan. The water is obviously supposed to be a brilliant bluish-cyan. That means that the red (or the cyan, in CMYK) *should* be maxed out. It *can't* be made lighter than the divers, without losing the intensity of the color.

One can use curves to lighten the highlights in the water in all three channels. Any attempt to steepen the green and blue to gain contrast by raising the midtone, however, runs out of air. It would make the water too neutral. So it seems that there is no blending and little curving that can be done. It's like trying to swim wearing a pair of handcuffs.

Still, if you've absorbed the last

Figure 7.13 *When brilliant objects lack detail, a maxed-out RGB channel, like the red below, is frequently the culprit. After some plate blending, the original, top, gains detail, center.*

RGB AND CMY

✓The crucial point in deciding whether to use RGB or CMYK is understanding that they are very similar. The red channel will resemble the cyan, the green the magenta, and the yellow the blue. The black is *sui generis.*

✓CMY channels seem lighter than their RGB cousins, because in the RGB-to-CMY conversion, a lightening takes place to compensate for dot gain on press. Also, in the deepest blacks, the CMY channels lack detail. This is because they have to be suppressed to make room for black ink and stay within the total ink limit that print shops demand.

✓RGB channels have more detail in highlights than their CMY counterparts. Since highlight detail in the unwanted color is vital (see Chapter 5), it frequently makes sense to use the RGB cousin channel to blend into the unwanted color channel in CMYK.

✓For curve-based corrections of typical images, CMYK has many advantages over RGB. There is a much greater chance that several important objects will fall into the same range on a single curve.

✓For corrections of very poor originals, in principle RGB is better than CMYK, but LAB is better yet.

✓Problems with lack of detail in brightly colored objects can often be traced back to one poor channel in an RGB file, which then proliferated into several CMYK plates. In such a case, since plate blending will eventually be necessary anyway, it is advisable to blend while still in RGB.

✓A number of other sophisticated blending options exist in RGB, such as blending to change colors or to enhance specific objects. Generally, this type of blending is more difficult in CMYK because of the unique role of black and because neutral colors have equal values in RGB but not in CMYK, where cyan is higher.

✓To avoid banding of gradients after the RGB-to-CMYK conversion, consider blending one or more of the original RGB channels into its CMY cousin.

✓In general, images that are headed for RGB output, such as the Web, can remain in RGB. The usual exception would be images containing critical shadow detail.

chapter, you may be able to think of a use for that wonderfully contrasty blue channel. It can't go into the red—but it can go to a fairly unlikely substitute.

After the quick highlight move in RGB, therefore, I converted the file to CMYK, still looking quite flat. But before doing so, I made a copy of the blue channel. I moved the lower left point of its curve considerably to the right, wiping out most of the water.

I then replaced the black plate of the CMYK file with the altered blue. As this made the water a little darker than previously, I then used Adjust: Selective Color to make the blue stronger.

If you insist on working only in RGB or only in CMYK, it's not clear how you could get this result, short of using a mask.

Know your colorspaces—and your colorspace conversions—and many such convenient tricks will suggest themselves. Blending an RGB channel into its CMY cousin, for example, is suggested by our knowledge of the workings of dot gain, a topic one might have thought irrelevant in this chapter.

Similarly, do you ever have problems with gradients that are created in RGB developing harsh bands when converted to CMYK, especially in deep, rich colors?

You shouldn't. We'll discuss this further in Chapter 11, but those colors are out of the CMYK gamut, and Photoshop is improvising. As for fixing it, now that you know the why, the how becomes obvious: find the CMY channels with the problem, and replace them with their RGB cousins.

Epilogue: RGB Output?

This book presupposes that eventually your files have to become CMYK. But what if the eventual destination is the Web, video, a film recorder, or a printer that requires RGB input? In that case, do you ever need to leave the womb?

If you are going to a film recorder, the answer is an emphatic no. The major advantages of CMYK are targeted corrections plus better control of unsharp masking. These things are not helpful if you are imaging a high-resolution chrome. Sharpening is, in fact, a bad idea; suppose somebody blows the image up to poster size and finds sharpening halos an inch wide?

Similarly, we don't need to force contrast into a chrome; that decision can be left to the person who takes it into print. A pansy that is too pallid on the printed page packs plenty of punch in a positive.

As for the other cases, sometimes added snap is needed and at other times it isn't. If you find that RGB curves can't deliver it, take advantage of another RGB strength: you can convert from RGB to and from LAB as often as you like, within reason, without any loss of detail. That is more than can be said for CMYK.

If we were restricted to one colorspace for corrections, it would have to be CMYK. If we were restricted to two, one would certainly have to be LAB, which brings a lot to the table because it is so different. In that case, the choice of the second wouldn't be that big a deal. CMY is RGB, remember? So, we'd choose whichever was our final output space—if we had to choose.

Fortunately, we have no such restriction. We can use whatever we like whenever we like. The choice should be made on the basis of effectiveness, not political correctness. To someone who thinks in this fashion, not only is CMY merely another form of RGB, but all colorspaces are one.

8

HSB Is LAB

For those who have tried to boost contrast in an image but come up with an unwelcome color change instead, here's a solution: a colorspace that keeps the two separate. LAB, powerful enough to be called the patron saint of lost causes, also happens to be the best space for general retouching.

 *one shall part us from each other*, goes the most breathtaking love song in all of opera, *One in life and death are we: all in all to one another, I to thee and thou to me.*

That this particular gem rears its head in the most unlikely setting possible, right after the lowest slapstick in a Gilbert and Sullivan comedy, does not diminish the impact of the lines that follow:

> *Thou the tree, and I the flower;*
> *Thou the idol, I the throng;*
> *Thou the day, and I the hour;*
> *Thou the singer, I the song.*

*   *   *

Or, to rephrase it more in keeping with our time, you are the words, I am the tune, play me. Whichever you like, the metaphor is so effective because it likens the lovers to things that nobody in their right mind would wish to consider as separate items.

Like, for example, color and contrast. So far, these items have been as inextricably bound. Every correction shown so far has involved both. Every channel in CMYK, every channel in RGB, affects both. And certainly, every one of us needs to be able to control both.

But considering color and contrast together has a downside. How many times have you tried to boost the detailing in a color picture, only to give up in disgust because you threw the colors off? There is also the matter of how clients react to our work. Many opinions are possible about color—but not about contrast. After all, when was the last time one of your clients complained because your image wasn't foggy enough, or because it seemed to carry too much detail?

This chapter introduces two colorspaces that do what RGB and CMYK do not, namely, keep contrast and color isolated from one another. That can be an extraordinary advantage—on certain kinds of images. On other kinds, the old reliables do better. With a little bit of judgment, we can have the best of both worlds.

Dicky-Bird, Why Do You Sit?

Of the two, LAB is by far the more significant, but it gets that distinction by default. Since Photoshop 2, there hasn't been full support for HSB, although a couple of important vestiges of it exist. LAB, on the other hand, is supported as completely as CMYK and RGB.

Figure 8.1 shows why it is unfortunate Photoshop no longer lets us work in HSB. For this, I wheeled out my copy of Photoshop 2.0.1 and opened up one of the images used in Chapter 7. I then converted it to HSB (don't try this with Photoshop 6!) and what you see here is the S channel.

You may ask what this exercise proves. I would answer, not much, unless we have to mask this bird, and in that case this particular channel is going to be a much better start at making the selection than any alternate method.

But enough crying over spilt birdseed. HSB stands for Hue, Saturation, Brightness. Users of Heidelberg Color Publishing Solutions' LinoColor product, a leading scanner-control package, encounter a different acronym: LCH, for Luminance, Chroma, Hue. The two mean the same thing, and you can use the commentary in this chapter to help run LinoColor, except you can go even further because in LinoColor you can write curves in HSB.

The L of LAB stands for Luminance. The letters A and B don't stand for anything in particular. The colorspace is more formally known as CIELAB, for Commission Internationale de l'Eclairage, an international color standards body, or as L*a*b*, which differentiates it from previous LAB incarnations. Adobe has chosen to refer to it as *Lab color,* although it has nothing to do with a laboratory, and as if the A and B were not the separate channels they are.

In both of these colorspaces, one channel—the L in LAB and the B in HSB—carries all the contrast, and none of the color. These channels, therefore, can be seen as black and white renditions of the color image. The other two channels define the color, but in radically different ways.

The underlying color in HSB is set by the H channel. It can be red, green, blue, yellow, or anything else. By this strange definition, the skin of a young child has the same H as does a fire engine: both are almost pure red, not tending toward yellow or magenta. The child's skin is *lighter,* meaning that it would be different in the B channel, but it also differs in *saturation,* the S, which is the most important channel for our purposes because it allows us to play certain games that aren't easy in CMYK or RGB.

Saturation defines the purity of the color, or how vivid it is. One could describe it as how much the color tends toward neutrality. Another way would be in terms of the presence or absence of the unwanted color. If we were reproducing a fire engine, we would use virtually no cyan ink, so we would say the color was a completely saturated red. The child's face is lighter, but it is also less saturated. Although cyan is light, it's there.

A less saturated red than a child's face is the color known as brick red. Less saturated than that is brown—which is a species of red—and less saturated than that is gray.

In Figure 8.1, where lightness equates to saturation, the parrot consists of highly saturated colors, hence the strong definition of the bird's outline.

Avoiding Overly Bright Colors

LAB's handling of the two color channels is even more difficult to understand than the HS of HSB, if possible. Here goes.

The L is simple—it's just a black and white version of the image. The A is an *opponent-color* channel. At one extreme it is magenta, at the other, green, and in the middle it favors neither one.

The B is just like the A, except its opponent colors are yellow and blue. If it falls in the middle, it is neither yellow nor blue, and if both A and B are in the middle then the overall color is neutral. Otherwise, the overall color is determined by a highly nonintuitive interplay between the A and B. If you can get past this obstacle, LAB is more powerful than HSB. But at least one of them should be part of your arsenal. If you use Photoshop 6, it has to be LAB. Let's set the table with a couple of correc-

Figure 8.1 *In the early 1990s, Photoshop allowed files to exist in HSB. Above, the S channel of a Photoshop 2.0.1 document. It would be nice if Photoshop 6 offered a comparably easy way to mask this parrot.*

tions that would be troublesome in RGB or CMYK.

When an image starts out flat, a correction in CMYK or RGB tends not only to add contrast but to create brighter, cleaner colors. If you go back and have a look at the corrections of Chapters 2 and 3, you'll see what I mean. In all of those images, the happier colors make sense.

Indeed, most images *do* look better with brighter colors. The problem is, quite a few don't. The glass of seltzer in Figure 8.2 is one of these. It needs a twist of something (I favor a curve rather than a lime) but

certainly not any accentuation of color. Yet it needs a violent correction: the rear lip of the glass is almost invisible in the original.

This subject is a nasty one to shoot and a nasty one to scan. Even in the pallid original, there are flashes of yellow at the bottom of the glass and other traces of color in the seltzer itself. Plus, assuming that the original, slightly reddish, background, is what is wanted, that's a delicate color, easy to screw up.

In short, any correction, let alone the big one we need here, risks letting the color get out of hand. Unless, of course, we have a channel that doesn't affect color at all.

Saturation and Apparent Distance

Ecclesiastes remarked, "Is there any thing whereof it may be said, See, this is new?"

If you are looking at the concept of LAB curves with trepidation, take what the preacher said to heart. We've already used HSB and LAB principles, even if they weren't called that at the time.

The role of the unwanted color, to which we devoted Chapter 5, is largely an issue of saturation, particularly as illustrated in Figure 5.4. There, the idea was to get a rounder-looking lime by forcing more magenta into the sides of the fruit. This pushed them away from green and toward gray—in other words, it desaturated them.

Similarly, we noted that unsharp masking sometimes introduces weird, objectionable color variations. These can be wiped out by using Edit: Fade>Luminosity after sharpening. Which is, of course, an LAB move all the way. It's not quite as accurate

Figure 8.2 *The hopelessly flat original, top, needs more contrast but not more color. This makes it ideal for an L channel move, bottom.*

as sharpening the L channel only, but the idea is the same.

Before entering 15 pages of hard-core LAB, let's dispose of the two principal relics of HSB: the Image: Adjust>Hue/Saturation command, and the sponge tool. In principle, the main use of Hue/Saturation is to isolate a single color and make some kind of alteration, without having to go through the annoyance of selecting it.

Hue/Saturation is analogous to Image: Adjust/Selective Color, which also selects a target color, but uses a CMYK model to correct it. I find Hue/Saturation a little more intuitive and Selective Color a bit more precise, so I use Hue/Saturation when I am guessing at what may be right and Selective Color when I think I know for sure.

Selective Color also has the advantage that we can choose Blacks, or Neutrals, as our target. Hue/Saturation's edge is the ability to point to a color of our choosing as the target, rather than just "Reds" or whatever. This is a big help in avoiding the typical problem of these commands, which is having them affect unintended areas that happen to be somewhat close to the color of what we were trying to change.

A good way to check for this, incidentally, is to try something silly at first, such as moving the Lightness slider all the way to the left or the Black ink slider all the way to the right. The preview of this atrocity will indicate whether the move is going to affect anything other than what you've intended.

The fault of both Hue/Saturation and Selective Color is that a lot of people use them too soon. One should assume that most lousy color will be corrected by setting the basic numbers with curves. If those numbers are correct and you *still* perceive a problem, then by all means trot out one of

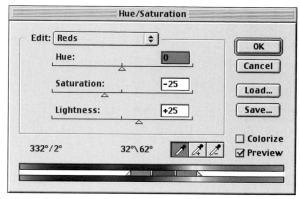

Figure 8.3 *The Hue/Saturation command allows precise definitions of the target color. The command line says Reds, but the settings actually affect oranges more. in the reds more rapidly than it does in the yellows.*

these commands. But don't do so before a general correction.

A more powerful use of HSB is in creating the illusion of distance, which is critical in product shots, as well as any other image containing a foreground object with a pronounced color.

It's that old human vision thing again: the more saturated an object is, the closer it appears. Or, more importantly, the more desaturated it is, the more it recedes.

In a case like Figure 8.4, that makes certain moves obvious. If we want to emphasize the cowboy, we should tone down the background. The best way to do that is to desaturate it, but there are actually two ways to do it. Both require a selection of the background, which can be done in many different ways.

Personally, I just grabbed a copy of the red channel before I converted to CMYK, upped the contrast, and dabbed a little with the airbrush at the edges of the cowboy and the horse. No great precision is required to make this mask; the background is going to be affected so slightly that nobody is going to notice the selection line.

When the client calls for the foreground object to get brighter and contrastier, it's amazing how many retouchers take them at their word and try to do it. It's quite a bit easier to take the indirect route: make the foreground more prominent by making the background less so.

Here, the red clay competes for our attention with the horse, which is more or less the same color, though darker. The greenery competes to some extent with the cowboy's shirt.

The obvious way to take care of this is to select and desaturate the background, using the Master setting in Hue/Saturation. Putting a number of –45 there gets us to the top half of Figure 8.5.

While this does make the background recede, I prefer the bottom half, which uses the settings shown in Figure 8.3. With Reds selected, I clicked the Hue/Saturation eyedropper on the clay to establish orange as

the target color. Then, I both lightened and desaturated it. This move did not affect the greenery, which, because it is the counter-color to the red of the horse, sets it off. Your choice of the top or bottom version probably depends on how much you want the viewer to concentrate on the cowboy as opposed to the horse.

Desaturating a relatively large area like this one is best done with Hue/Saturation; for isolated areas we use the sponge tool. The sponge works like most painting tools, with variable widths and opacities. We set it to either saturate or desaturate the area we are brushing. It's great in creating a sense of depth.

Riding the L Channel

LAB curvewriting should have a warning label saying, *Closed track! Professional driver! Don't try this with your own vehicle!*

As a further disincentive, the numbering system in LAB is designed to discourage the tourist. The actual values are diagrammed in Figure 8.6, but let's go over each channel.

The L is easiest to understand. Normal rules apply: the steeper the curve, the more the contrast. Increasing steepness in critical areas of the L curve is extraordinarily effective at bringing out detail. About the only hangup is that the numbering system appears backward: 100 represents an absolute

Figure 8.4 *When asked to accentuate a foreground object, such as the cowboy here, the most effective way is often to tone down the background. The reddish soil in this image competes with the color of the horse.*

white; 0 an absolute black. An L channel range of between 95 and 8 or 10 is sensible for most work.

The L correction of Figure 8.2 is analogous to similar moves in other colorspaces. We start by measuring the highlight, which has an L value of 93, just underneath the lip of the glass, and also in the ice cube. This is one of three images in this book (the others are Figures 2.3 and 9.11) that do not have a shadow. That is, there is no point that we really want to portray as particularly dark. The current darkest area is in the center bottom of the glass, 43^L.

The liquid itself has only 12 points of range, from 92^L to 80^L. That, obviously, is the area we seek to steepen. So we slide the lower left endpoint to the right, creating a lighter than normal highlight of 98^L. This decision seems justifiable on the grounds that there is almost no detail in the very lightest areas.

The process continues by adding a point in the quartertone and raising it sharply. This, in conjunction with the endpoint move, makes the first quarter of the curve, where the liquid resides, quite steep.

The third point is more debatable. Its positioning depends on how dark we want the pseudo-shadow to be.

Figure 8.5 *Having masked out the cowboy and horse so that they can't change, the top version desaturates the entire background. In the bottom version, the greens are left alone, but the oranges are both desaturated and lightened, using the Hue/Saturation settings of Figure 8.3.*

Finally, remembering that LAB is the sharpening space of choice, we sharpen the L channel. And, remembering the principles of Chapter 4, we use a wide Radius (3.0 pixels here) in doing so. The bubbles are what we're trying to enhance, and they have no detail for USM to blow away. Furthermore, there is no objection to a wide halo around the bubbles. Quite the opposite: it will make them seem more pronounced.

Both the Simple and Quadratical

The reverse of the seltzer correction is one that affects color only. To do this, we need to discuss the baffling numbers of the A and B channels, which are laid out in Figure 8.6.

The A starts with magenta at the light end of its curve, and ends with green at the dark end. Just to be difficult, the numbers go from +128 at the magenta endpoint to −128 at the green. In the middle is zero. The B is exactly the same, except magenta is replaced by yellow and green by blue.

Somewhat shockingly, about half of the real estate of these curves is worthless for printing. LAB is an academic colorspace, designed to encompass not just the colors of print, not just the colors of a monitor or of film, but of everything—even fluorescent colors. A value of plus or minus 90, let alone 128, is out of gamut even for the best print conditions. Plus 70 is about as intense as can be used, and that's only in the magenta and yellow parts of the curve, where the CMYK gamut is fairly good. For blue and green, −60 is flirting with out of gamut.

This extravagant way of describing colors has two very good ramifications for those brave enough to correct in LAB, and

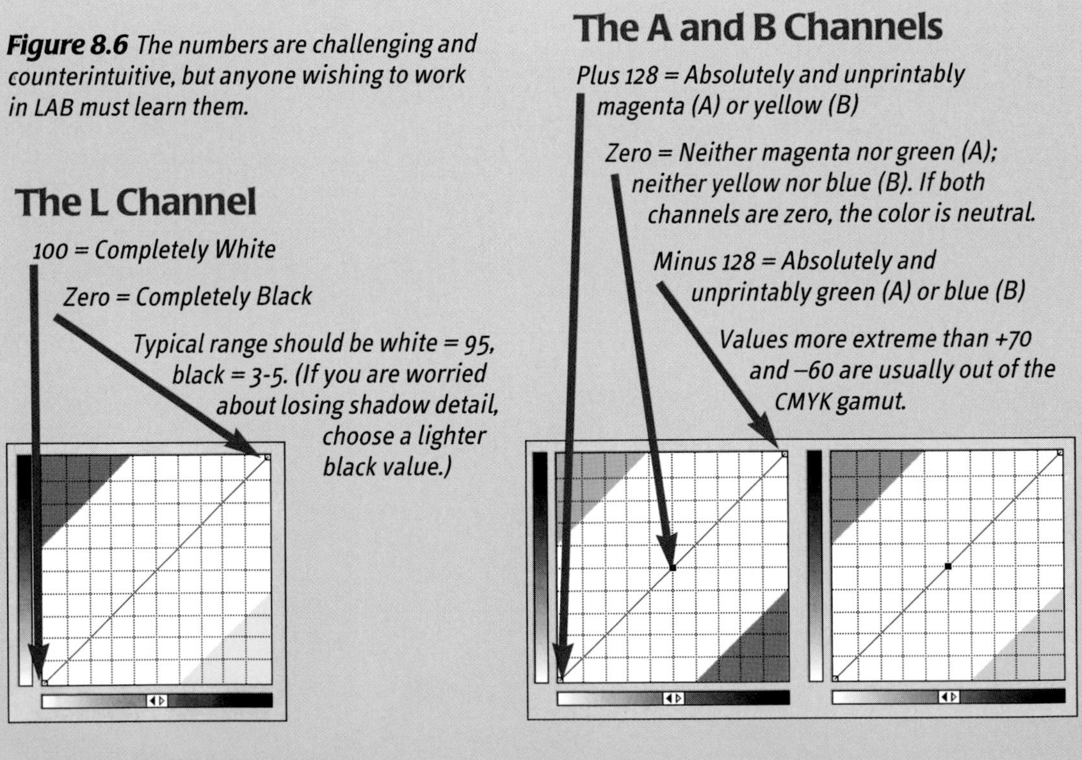

Figure 8.6 *The numbers are challenging and counterintuitive, but anyone wishing to work in LAB must learn them.*

The L Channel

100 = Completely White

Zero = Completely Black

Typical range should be white = 95, black = 3-5. (If you are worried about losing shadow detail, choose a lighter black value.)

The A and B Channels

Plus 128 = Absolutely and unprintably magenta (A) or yellow (B)

Zero = Neither magenta nor green (A); neither yellow nor blue (B). If both channels are zero, the color is neutral.

Minus 128 = Absolutely and unprintably green (A) or blue (B)

Values more extreme than +70 and −60 are usually out of the CMYK gamut.

two very bad ones. The first good thing is, there is no such animal as a color cast so bad that LAB can't zap it. Slight moves in the curves have huge consequences. When the original is somewhere near where you want it to be, think CMYK. When it's on some other continent, think LAB.

The second good thing is that it's easier to control neutral colors in LAB, because we need only balance two channels, not three. As long as we have 0^A0^B or thereabouts, it won't matter what the colorless L value is.

Furthermore, this way of describing neutrality often shows us where a problem is where CMYK or RGB would be ambiguous. Returning for a moment to the horses of Figure 2.11, they were pink because their typical value was $15^C31^M14^Y$. It's clear that something has to be done to kill that imbalance, but it isn't obvious what. Should the magenta come down, or the others up, or some combination?

LAB has no such ambiguity. The horses measure $80^L12^A1^B$; the problem is therefore in the A channel.

The very power of the A and B means that curving them is approximately the biggest and darkest dynamite factory an unwary artist can blunder into with a lighted match. One wrong move, it's curtains for the image.

The second bad thing is, you can forget about using LAB as your *only* colorspace. It's powerful, but inaccurate. There is no way to fine-tune the numbers precisely enough for the best quality. Although for the purposes of this chapter I'm taking the LAB documents into CMYK and blithely printing whatever Fortune furnishes, in real life one should make minor adjustments in RGB or CMYK after the LAB maneuvering.

It's a reasonable position, therefore, to leave the A and B alone and concentrate on the vastly more intuitive L. And yet, there is one simple AB correction technique that works on a whole lot of images, Figure 8.7 being one.

The normal questions don't become irrelevant just because we are in LAB. Highlight? Easily found. $95^L1^A(1)^B$, in the left eye of whatever this creature is supposed to be.

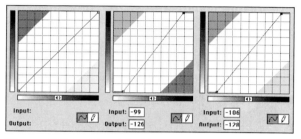

Figure 8.7 *In this original image, top, tonal range is correct, but the colors are too subdued. The curves above intensify them.*

Shadow? $7^L1^A(1)^B$, in the black paint at top left. Neutrals? The shoes, which also are close to 0^A0^B throughout, although there is considerable variation in the L. And flesh-tones? None.

For once, then, all the numbers seem to be good at the outset. The highlight is light enough, the shadow is dark enough, and both are neutral. The shoes are correct. And, in my view, no one part of the image is so much more important than the rest that it's worth fooling around with the shape of the L curve so as to gain contrast in one area and lose it elsewhere.

So, we are stuck with the L channel just as it is. Does that mean we just close the file? I suppose we could; there's nothing technically wrong with the image. But it seems to me that the colors suffer from tired blood. Let's wake them up.

By now the refrain, the steeper the curve, the more the contrast, needs no more repetition. But what about the case of a contrast-free channel, a channel that contains color information only? In such a case, the steeper the curve, the more the *contrast between colors,* the more variation between one color and its neighbor.

In this image, both the A and B are correct for neutrality, which means that the midpoints of their two curves are absolutely correct, unchangeable. And yet, we'd like the curves to be steeper, to pep up the color.

The solution is to pivot the entire curve counterclockwise around the midpoint. To do so, move the top right point to the left, and then the bottom left point to the right

Figure 8.8 *This forty-year-old print, top, has faded quite a bit with age, but is easily resurrected by moves in the A and B channels of LAB.*

until the curve—er, the straight line—goes right through the center point, leaving it unchanged from its original value, as in Figure 8.7.

Applying curves to the A and B is for the brave of heart. Dire consequences await those who misuse them. Straight-line corrections like this one, however, are easy, and have many uses. One of the most common is dealing with older, faded originals.

There Is Beauty in Extreme Old Age

Many older photos have faded badly, as in Figure 8.8, a color print from 1960. But as long as the detail has not deteriorated, the correction is easy, using LAB.

It's clear that we want not just to enhance contrast in the peacock but also to brighten colors generally. There is also a bluish-pink cast, measurable in the foreground sand, which has a typical value of $70^L5^A(8)^B$. It seems more likely that the sand should be yellow than blue.

The LAB curves, shown in Figure 8.9, are simple ones. The A and B are straight lines that cross the center vertical line above and below the center horizontal line, respectively. This brings the sand back to neutrality, while making the colors more vivid.

There are major advantages to using LAB rather than Hue/Saturation to bring up color in an image as lame as this one. Consider the tailfeathers. If we were to try to saturate greens with Hue/Saturation, they would definitely become more brilliant, but they'd also become more uniform it color. A move in the B channel, on the other hand, emphasizes yellow and blue *even where they are not the dominant colors*. Here, the correction moves parts of the tailfeathers toward yellow and other parts toward cyan. Hue/Saturation, could move the feathers

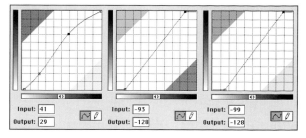

Figure 8.9 *The LAB curves used to correct Figure 8.8.*

toward either neighboring color, but not both simultaneously.

Also, colors don't always deteriorate uniformly, as they seem to have in this image. Treating the A and B as four half-curves rather than two complete ones gives us the option to address red, green, yellow, and blue individually.

And LAB gives us the option of sharpening the L channel. While it's true that options exist for sharpening by luminosity in RGB and CMYK as well, only in LAB can we *see* the channel we're sharpening. In older images, that's usually critical. Such images are commonly full of noise. We lucked out this time: the tonality of this image isn't bad, so we can just sharpen the L, convert to CMYK, correct for highlight and shadow, and print.

Experimenting With the A and B

Correcting only the L or only the A and B is reasonable. But there are plenty of occasions for some kind of combined approach. Overly flat images can get quite colorful if corrected in CMYK or RGB. Usually, that's what we want. Granted that there are a few cases like the seltzer of Figure 8.2, where we don't want any color increase at all, there are a lot more of the class of Figure 8.10, where the colors are subtle. We would like slightly more saturated reds, not canyon walls the color of fire engines.

In this image, we start with a light point of $77^L5^A(5)^B$ in the foreground river. That's a bias toward magenta and blue, which, taken together, adds up to a tilt toward purple. Do you believe this is logical? The shadow, such as it is, is in the foreground rocks, $31^L4^A(8)^B$, another purple. There are no known neutral colors or fleshtones in the image. The objects of interest are, in my opinion, the red rock formations. In the L channel, they fall in a narrow range between 55 and 40.

The overall L range of the original is thus only 46 points, which explains why it is so dreadfully flat; Figure 8.7, for example, started with a range of 88.

While LAB is made to order for the suboptimal image, we shouldn't try to hit a five-run homer with it. This image has a lot of subtle detailing in the darker areas. If we force the shadow to a value of 10 or darker, it's likely that the blunt instrument of L correction would inflict some collateral damage. Instead, my plan would be to leave LAB with a relatively light shadow, intending to darken it after the conversion to CMYK.

Hence, the L curve shown in Figure 8.11. Note the steep area right where the canyon walls occur, near the center of the curve.

As for the A and B curves, I think they need to be steepened to bring out more color, in much the same way as was done with the graffiti image. But there, the neutral colors were really neutral to start with. Here, they aren't.

A neutral color, to reiterate, is anything with values of 0^A0^B. One or two points of

Figure 8.10 *This original starts out too flat, but the normal technique of opening range in CMYK or RGB might make its colors too bright.*

difference will not be significant. But both the measured highlight and shadow of the Grand Canyon image are at least four points off in both channels. The problem is, we're not sure, from the context of the image, that our measuring points *should* be neutral.

In both the light point in the river and the dark point in the rocks, the A value is positive. This means, tending toward magenta rather than green. Shadows are normally neutral, but I can certainly believe that a shadow in the middle of red rock could itself have a magenta tinge.

But what about the water? Does it make sense that it could be more magenta than green? Not to me, it doesn't.

The B analysis is more straightforward. Here, both original numbers are negative, so both highlight and shadow are tending toward blue, rather than yellow. In the

water, brackish though it may be, I can certainly buy more blue than yellow. But not in those rocks. Yellow, maybe. Neutral, maybe. Blue, impossible.

Therefore, I conclude that the original values are wrong, and that we need to move toward green in the A channel and toward yellow in the B.

In writing the AB curves for the graffiti image, we had to make sure the new curves

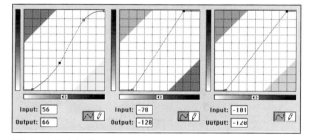

Figure 8.11 *The curves above add range in the L channel, plus a slight boost in all colors. The corrected image is below.*

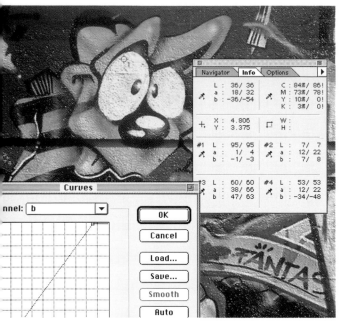

Figure 8.12 *A danger of correcting the AB channels is that they may create colors outside of the CMYK gamut. The exclamation points in the Info palette indicate that the new colors can't be matched in CMYK.*

crossed the center point exactly where they did originally, because we knew that the original neutral colors were correct. This time, we know the original center points are *wrong*. So, we make our new A curve cross the center line a little higher than the midpoint—high being the green direction—and the new B cross lower, lower being yellow.

The question may well be raised, how do I know what angle to use for the new AB curves? Truth to tell, I *don't* know. It's a purely subjective decision. This differentiates it from the techniques shown in Chapters 2 and 3. I *am* sure that the handling of the L channel is correct. I'm also sure that neutralizing the highlight and shadow is right. But how colorful to make the image, that's something on which reasonable people can disagree.

I've Got a Little List

Such straight-line corrections in the AB channels belie by their simplicity the concept that LAB is only for the brave. There are, in fact, a couple of everyday uses in which this technique is simpler, faster, and better than the CMYK alternative.

• **For newspaper use**. Normal scans don't quite cut it when prepared for newspapers. There are a number of reasons, but one of the biggest is that colors don't seem bright enough. That's because newsprint is not white. Every bright color is contaminated by the underlying dreariness of the paper. To compensate, brighter originals are needed. The formulas in this book for a fleshtone, for example, would be too gray for newsprint use: we would have to cut back on the cyan values.

The most flexible way to accomplish this, while still correcting for neutrality, is with straight-line curves in the AB.

• **For a series of smaller images**. This book is biased in favor of wringing the maximum possible quality out of an image. Some images are simply not worth that attention. And the smaller an image is to be printed, the less noticeable all these tricks are, anyway.

Furthermore, in small images we are apt to want bright, happy colors. The typical example might be a realty catalog, showing many different houses or interior shots. The client is sure to be looking for blue skies and green lawns, whether they existed in the original photograph or not. For this kind of work a quick correction and sharpen in LAB is effective and efficient, allowing us to process hundreds of images in a single shift. It's true, we have to forego finetuning the images in CMYK, but for this kind of work, who cares? If this were a magazine cover, we'd be sure to have the highlight in perfect balance. For a thousand-image weekly, close is good enough.

Photoshop's Actions allow us to be even faster. For this kind of work, write an Actions script that opens the RGB image, converts to LAB, applies Auto Levels in the L channel, sharpens the L, steepens the A and B, converts to CMYK, and saves as a TIFF. If you want to go further, have three different such scripts, each with a more drastic boost of the colors, and decide which one to apply after a quick examination of each image.

• **For conversions into RGB**. Nowadays, it is more likely than ever that a CMYK file may have to go into RGB for some reason. Maybe an image that was prepared for a print advertisement now has to go to the Web, maybe it needs to go to a desktop printer that can only take RGB, maybe it's going into video or some other kind of multimedia presentation. Whatever. The problem is, RGB has a wider gamut of colors available, but Photoshop has no clue whether to use them.

In other words, suppose we have a blue in the CMYK file that is about as bright as we can get in that blue-deficient colorspace. Should we match that blue exactly in RGB? Or should we punch it up to be the brightest blue possible in RGB?

This is a case-by-case decision, but once you have made it, the easiest way to implement it is to convert the CMYK image into LAB, apply straight-line corrections to the AB, and then move into RGB.

There's one more thing to be careful of. It's easy to go overboard and create LAB colors that are out of the CMYK gamut. If you do, you will be relying on the tender mercies of Photoshop's separation algorithm when you finally convert to CMYK.

Said method isn't too kind to out of gamut colors. So, when correcting in LAB, keep an eye on the Info palette. When exclamation points appear in the CMYK equivalents, as they do in Figure 8.12, you've gone too far.

Yet B Is Worthy, I Dare Say

There are variations on this straight-line approach. We can decide we want to hit the yellow-blue B channel without touching the magenta-green A, and vice versa. We can use different angles on each one. Or, in special cases, we can depart from the straight-line shape altogether.

Two factors in Figure 8.13 militate in favor of an LAB move. The distant New York City skyline in the original is so vague as to be nearly invisible. That suggests a drastic L move along the lines of the one done in Figure 8.2.

Also, whenever we see this much green, we should be thinking of steepening the A channel, as we've already done twice in this chapter. Confronted with this much green, human observers break it apart much more than cameras do. We need more variation.

The highlight, off in the distance, is $90^L(1)^A(10)^B$. The shadow, deep in the trees at lower right, is $13^L(5)^A8^B$. There are no neutral colors or fleshtones to worry about.

That shadow is biased toward green in the A and yellow in the B. This isn't a big surprise in the middle of a forest, and I'd be disinclined to force it to be neutral. The highlight is neutral in the A, which sounds right, and blue in the B, which doesn't.

The general approach, therefore, should be the top curves of Figure 8.14. The L curve lightens the highlight and then gets steep, to make that distant skyline stand out. The A and B remain straight lines, but steepened in the manner we're accustomed to.

Figure 8.13 *An LAB correction accentuates the vague background skyline and adds variation to the greens. But the central buildings in the middle version are also much redder than in the original, top. In the bottom version, the magenta half of the A curve was suppressed to prevent this reddening from occurring.*

The A crosses the center point, preserving the original neutrality of the channel, but the B line is slightly to the right of the center point, moving the image toward yellow and away from blue.

We now have the center version of Figure 8.13. A big improvement, but I have an issue with the reddish buildings in the foreground, which seem to have gotten distractingly bright.

That's the fault of the A channel. Our straight line exaggerated contrast in greens, but also in magentas. That's why the foreground trees are too red, too.

If those brighter reds bother you, it's time to move away from the straight-line model and go to something like the bottom of Figure 8.14, which actually suppresses the magenta component. Remember, in the A curve, green is to the top, magenta to the bottom.

And occasionally one finds an image that seems so hopeless that only a radical AB move can come to the rescue. That kind of thing is for the truly ambitious, and beyond the scope of the present discussion, but you'll see an example at the end of the next chapter.

The Best Channels to Blur

The problem of colored noise in originals has always been around. Photographs taken under poor lighting conditions or with very fast film, sports photography being the most prominent example, often display such noise.

It's gotten worse recently. Many digital camera backs occasionally throw in a disturbing colored flare at the edges of objects, and certain desktop scanners do the same thing. These artifacts are difficult to get rid of—unless you use LAB.

For the same reason that the L channel absorbs sharpening well, and is thus often our first choice, the A and B can accept blurring. This is a much better method than using a blur filter (or the Median, Despeckle, or Dust & Scratches filter) on an RGB or CMYK channel.

The reason is obvious. The last thing we want to do is defocus a channel that contributes to the contrast of an image, even if it's the weak yellow plate. Blurring the yellow may be better than nothing but it certainly isn't as good as blurring a channel that doesn't carry detail.

In Figure 8.15, the corrected blue channel seems to have lost the noise but not any contrast: it remains sharply focused. However, as the color image indicates, one shouldn't overestimate the effect of noise in the yellow plate (which is, recalling Chapter 7, what the blue becomes in adult life). The picture as a whole isn't improved nearly as much as you might expect from looking at the channel in isolation.

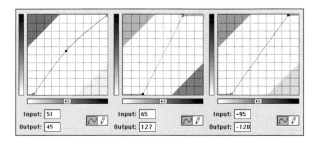

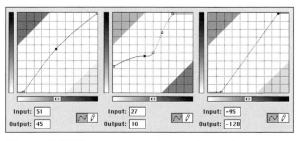

Figure 8.14 *The LAB curves that produced the center and bottom versions of Figure 8.13.*

Blurring the A and B is especially useful for the class of images that has the most noise of all—the prescreened original. We'll go into that in Chapter 15, but suffice it to say here that even a quick AB blur of a prescreened original goes a long way toward eliminating moiré.

A Declaration of Independence

LAB is, without qualification, the best colorspace in which to retouch.

By retouching, I am not referring to the common variety of removing scratches and dirt. You can attend to such simple stuff however you like. I am talking about serious moves away from the art, or the restoration of large damaged areas. The reason is not that LAB is device-independent, but that it is channel-independent.

Figure 8.16 represents the sort of thing I'm talking about. Can you guess what's wrong with this image?

This photo was taken one fall day in the Canadian Rockies. We had stopped for a break when we were visited by this lovely lady, who desired to know whether there was anything in the car that bighorn sheep like to eat. My father, sitting in the passenger seat, quickly produced a camera, and you see the result.

Unfortunately, the car window was not completely rolled down, which accounts for the wide blue line running diagonally across the picture. My father thinks that the picture is therefore a total loss, for which he blames me. A lot he knows.

The blue band is a big problem, but it certainly isn't the only one. Even if we could eliminate the color cast in it, the underlying image would still be out of focus. In fact, the defocused area extends well below the obvious blue line.

Worse than that, the entire bottom half of the image is the wrong color. It's slightly too blue, to judge by the appearance of the animal's bottom half.

As you may have gathered, in circumstances like these, one calls on the patron saint of lost causes, namely, LAB. With it, one can, with some effort, get from Figure 8.16 to Figure 8.17. Without it, good luck.

Inventorying highlight and shadow values has to be confined to the top half of the image, since the color in the bottom half is suspect. For highlights, I find $97^L1^A(5)^B$ in the bare mountain, $94^L2^A(8)^B$ in the clouds. It makes sense that the clouds might have a blue cast, but not the mountain.

For shadow, in deep areas of the trees I find $7^L0^A(7)^B$. Conceivably, the color of the trees is throwing off the B reading here, although you'd think it would affect the magenta-green A first. Just to be sure, therefore, we measure the inside of the sheep's ear at $9^L4^A(9)^B$. There's no excuse for this to be blue, so, since every reading we've taken has been to the north of zero in the B channel, it must be concluded that the image has a blue cast.

The L and A values seem good in highlight and shadow, so there's no point in changing them. But before going any further, I think we should shove down the B curve, pushing it away from blue and toward yellow, by moving the top right endpoint down.

That accomplished, we need to find out just how bad the damage in the bottom half of the image is. For that, we'll need a close look at each channel. The findings are somewhat surprising.

The L channel, first of all, was badly defocused in the diagonal blue stripe, and also to some extent for about a quarter of

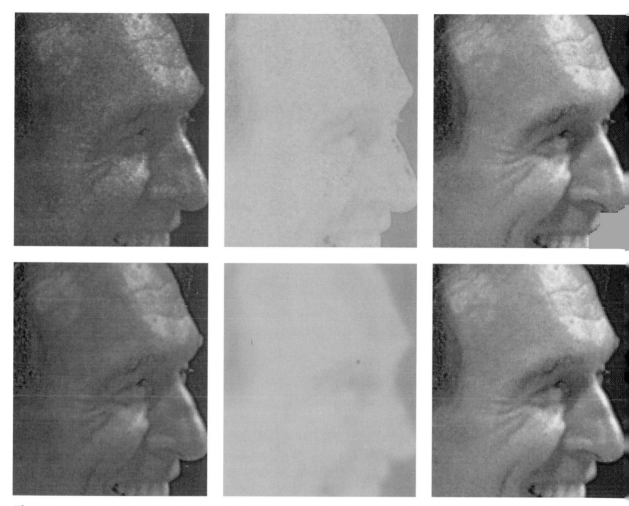

Figure 8.15 *Blurring the A and B channels is a nearly cost-free way of reducing colored noise. Above left, the man shows heavy noise in the blue channel of an RGB original. Above center, after conversion to LAB, the B channel is also noisy. After blurring the B, bottom center, and reconverting to RGB, the new blue, bottom left, is almost noise-free. At right, the color image, before and after this correction.*

an inch below it. The defocused area was not, however, significantly lighter or darker than what surrounded it.

I couldn't find any damage to the A channel at all, even when I hit it with a very steep curve. This diagonal line, it seems, is pure blue, not tending at all toward magenta or green, or toward darker or lighter.

Of course, this means that the B channel has more problems than a Mac SE running

Photoshop 6. Figure 8.18 shows the diagonal stripe clearly. To create it, I made a copy of the B channel, and applied an extremely steep curve to it, trying to have mostly whites and blacks.

As you can see, I also inverted it. Normally in the B yellow is light and blue dark. Not here. I flipped the values. I needed the blue to be *light*, because it was my intention to use Figure 8.18 as a mask.

But before applying it, we have to attend to the color problems in the bottom half of the image. It's clearly too blue, but it's hard to say *how much* too blue it is. The sheep's body, which is in the blue area, isn't going to match her face for color anyway. The gravel is blue, but who knows what color it's supposed to be. Nor is the greenery much help, because the foreground plants seem to be of a different species than the lighter ones above the diagonal line.

At the extreme right of the image, just above the line of damage, is a clump of plants that look like those in the lower half. They are the same in the L and A, and about four points less negative (meaning more yellow, less blue) in the B.

The next step, therefore, is to activate the lasso tool, and draw a line, freehand, just under the top of the diagonal line throughout the width of the image, then extending the selection to encompass the entire half of the picture that is below the damaged area.

The reason for the freehand selection is that irregular selections are tougher to detect than those based on straight lines. I doubt that this is a big factor here, since much of the damaged area is going to be replaced altogether, but what the heck.

Figure 8.16 *There seems to be a diagonal blue line across the center of the image. Can you guess the cause? How would you fix it?*

Having made the selection, the next step is to apply to it the same curve that previously was applied to the entire image, moving the B value 4 points toward the positive, moving the lower half of the image away from blue and toward yellow.

The first application of this curve could have been done in CMYK. It might have changed the overall lightness and darkness of the image, or the balance of red vs. green, but at least the image would be internally consistent.

The second move, no. If the magenta-green balance had changed, the bottom half would not have matched the top half.

Without LAB, in my opinion, this would have been a very difficult correction. Not as difficult, however, as the next adventure, restoring the damaged area itself, which is well nigh impossible without LAB.

From Here and There

You may never have had to repair damage caused by the failure of someone to lower a car window before, but you've probably had to do similar things, hopefully in not such a large area. Everybody has their own favorite method of doing this, but all techniques boil down to the same thing. We somehow have to replace the damaged

Figure 8.17 *In correcting images with physical damage, LAB is usually the best, because its three channels operate independently of one another.*

Figure 8.18 *The A and B channels can often be the foundations for effective masks. Here, an inverted, contrast-enhanced copy of the B channel isolates the area of damage.*

part with detail cloned from the remainder of the image.

The downside of doing this in CMYK (and RGB similarly) is that we can't just pick up the cyan from the left corner of the image, the magenta from the right, and the yellow and black from somewhere else. No, we have to clone all the channels simultaneously. That means that everything we paste in has to match its surroundings not just for detail, but for color.

In LAB or HSB, this ghastly difficulty goes away. We *can* clone the channels from three different areas if we like. Here, we only have to replace two channels, because the A is correct as is. We do this in two passes, vastly easier than trying to do it all in a single operation.

First, the B. Since the channel viewed alone is hard to fathom, open the Channels palette, click on the B, but then click the eye icon to the left of the LAB row. This will display the entire image, while making it impossible to alter anything except the B.

It would probably be acceptable to just slather this area with B values from elsewhere in the greenery, using large hits of the rubber stamp tool. But why take chances? It's so easy to make a mask for this (that is, if we know our LAB). So, we return to Figure 8.18, which was made prior to all these shenanigans, and load it as a selection into the main image. Now, we can slather away, confident that we are only painting into damaged areas and not elsewhere.

Having done this, we remove the mask. A detail-free channel like the B can be pasted in undetectably through a soft-edged mask; the L cannot. Furthermore, the mask did not allow us to work on the animal, which

Figure 8.19 *The advantage of repairing damage in LAB is that serious cloning only has to be done in one channel, rather than three or four. Above, a section of the original L, showing the defocused area. Below, the L channel just prior to conversion to CMYK.*

LAB AND HSB

✓ LAB and HSB are similar in that they separate color from contrast. Each has one channel that contains all the detail and two that contain all color information.

✓ The Adjust Hue/Saturation and Adjust Selective Color commands are useful, but they should be applied *after* all other color corrections.

✓ Desaturated objects seem to recede into the background. Therefore, desaturating with either the sponge tool or Adjust Hue/Saturation on a selected area can be a good way to deemphasize one object and promote another.

✓ For noisy images, digital captures, and prescreened originals, consider blurring the A and B channels, which deadens the defects without harming contrast.

✓ Older, damaged, or faded originals respond well to LAB corrections. Boosting colors in LAB is also the best way to convert CMYK files into RGB.

✓ Setting overall range with the L channel is easy. This is the method of choice when an image is flat but should not contain vibrant colors. Opening range in CMYK or RGB tends to intensify colors, which is desirable—most of the time.

✓ Because LAB has an enormous gamut, color corrections are imprecise but very powerful. Any color cast, however severe, can be eliminated in LAB.

✓ Steepening the A and B curves by pivoting them counterclockwise around the curve midpoint is an easy and effective way to liven up colors generally.

✓ Edges are often better defined in the A and B channels than they are in any channel in RGB or CMYK. Although they always have to have contrast added, they are often a good starting point for creating masks.

✓ It's easier to control neutrality in LAB or HSB than in CMYK or RGB, where neutrality depends on the interaction of several channels. In LAB, if the A and B channels have a value of zero, that's a neutral no matter what the L is.

✓ For complicated retouching, LAB is much superior to either RGB or CMYK, because the channels are completely independent. A new area can be defined based on different samples from each LAB channel, whereas in RGB and CMYK all channels must be copied simultaneously.

was too yellow in the original to be included. So we have to clone more B channel there, sans mask.

The beauty of correcting the L is that we don't have to worry about color at all. That has already been taken care of by our moves in the B. All we need do is pick up detailing from anywhere in the greenery and start cloning, in any of a variety of ways, ending with the bottom version of Figure 8.19.

The last issue is the sheep itself. The body can be rebuilt in the same way as the greenery, but there is next to no definition of the animal's edge. That's not something that can be picked up elsewhere. Unsharp masking won't help, either: USM needs to find an edge before it can enhance it.

Recalling the example of Figure 4.3, and mindful that what's good enough for El Greco is probably good enough for us, if there aren't any USM halos available, let's make 'em. My way is to use the paintbrush tool, single-pixel brush, method Darken, L channel only, L value of 25, pressure 15%. With that, I draw in subtle edges where animal hits background. Afterward, I reverse this process, with a light edge where both animal and background are relatively dark.

This hint of an edge can finally be sharpened—but with the *tool,* not the filter.

After darkening the animal's muzzle with the burn tool, set to midtones, L channel only, I switch over to the A and B. To get the muzzle to the proper color, I clone the A and B from some other likely area in the animal's coat.

Also, the blue cast of the gravel in the foreground is the sort of thing one usually needs the sponge tool for. We would like it more neutral, more gray, less blue.

LAB has a different, but equally effective, way. Set the foreground color to anything neutral—that is, to any color with 0^A0^B. Now, activating the A and B channels only, with the airbrush tool set to 50% pressure, paint over the gravel. Every time the airbrush passes over it, the gravel gets more gray, but detail is unaffected.

After this, we can at last leave LAB for the more comfortable ground of CMYK and a final tweak of the highlight and shadow values. This step is necessary in view of the inherent inaccuracy of LAB corrections.

This chapter barely scratches the surface of what's possible with LAB, other than to make the point that it's well worth the effort to master. Don't be frustrated by its intricacies: that frustration will dissipate the very first time you execute a retouch or a color correction that wouldn't have been possible in another colorspace.

Master LAB, and for you, there *will* be no bad originals. It probably can't be your primary workspace, but once you appreciate the virtue of divorcing color from contrast, it's one you will never part from. The serious retoucher, joyful yet respectful, sings to the imperious colorspace:

> *I the stream, and thou the willow—*
> *I the sculptor, thou the clay—*
> *I the ocean, thou the billow—*
> *I the sunrise, thou the day!*

All Colorspaces Are One

Though they approach problems in unique ways, each colorspace can make the basic corrections. Go beyond the basics, and certain changes are more effective in certain colorspaces. The professional has to be ready to change color models quickly but unwilling to do so when it isn't really necessary.

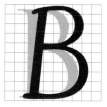

y the numbers! Monkey work! Remember those happy, mindless phrases? When we started this adventure, a few logical rules seemed to be effective for all images.

Annoyingly, just when it was starting to look easy, Chapter 6 muddied things up with, appropriately, black ink—and the sad news that some fairly serious strategic thinking is required on how to use it. As if that wasn't bad enough, it was followed by two chapters of radical colorspace alternatives to the way we had been doing things.

The foundation of Chapters 2–5 is indeed essential. To go farther, though, we now have to evaluate our options before starting work, considering many possibilities, discarding some, always remembering to just go back to the basics if there's no indication to do anything else.

The four spaces we've studied each have weaknesses—but enough tempting strengths to set anyone's mouth watering. Now, we need discipline, to know when one is enough and when to take a nibble out of several. For certain images, certain colorspaces leave a better taste in the mouth. I will illustrate with a series of images of good things to eat.

Often enough, we can enjoy all the advantages of a given colorspace without ever actually entering it. Suppose, for example, that we have

just presented a client with a first proof of some chocolates that look like the upper left rendition of Figure 9.1. Not too surprisingly, she screams at us that the image is flat, lifeless, and unappetizing. Now what?

The client objects to the lack of detail, not to the color. No matter what space we're in, we plan to make the chocolates land in steep areas of the curve in every channel. Having proofed the job, we're in CMYK, of course. The lower left version shows the danger. After the curves of Figure 9.2, more detail is certainly there—and so is a new color.

If we were instead to convert to LAB, we could use the same kind of curve in the L channel to get the same extra detail without the offensive color shift. But who needs extra work? We can, in effect, work in LAB even if the file is CMYK. All we need do, after applying the curves that generated the off-color image, is apply the Edit: Fade command, choosing 100% as the opacity, and Luminosity as

Figure 9.1 *The original chocolates, above, are correct for color, but lack snap. A normal CMYK contrast enhancement begets the version at lower left, correct for detail, but now the wrong color. Fading the curves back to luminosity creates the final version, lower right.*

the method. You do re-member, naturally, what the L in LAB stands for.

This kind of move isn't limited to CMYK, and it isn't limited to this one command. Images where the color is right and the contrast is wrong are very common. Such is the case with the raspberries of Figure 9.3.

This time, we start (and finish) in RGB. The versions have been converted to CMYK for printing purposes, but I've done no tweaking beyond the default settings.

Don't like RGB? Then you won't do much work headed for the Web, and you won't be able to do the fancy CMYK-destination corrections of Chapter 16. Don't like CMYK? Then by now you will have gathered that you won't be able to match the print quality gotten by those with no such prejudice.

A single-colorspace philosophy may have been acceptable ten or even five years ago. But today the world is different. As a singer popular a while back said, you don't need a weatherman to know which way the wind blows.

Better Use Your Sense

One's first impression is that Figure 9.3 is just a variation on the chocolates theme. The berries are properly red at the moment; all we need do is increase contrast by means of curves. This, of course, is done exactly as it would be in CMYK, by making sure that the berries fall in appropriately steep areas of the three individual curves. And, of course, the problem is exactly the same as it would be in CMYK. Chances are, the berries won't stay the same color.

The chocolates were easier because we

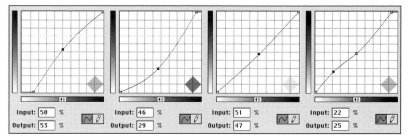

Figure 9.2 *The curves that generated the off-color lower left version of Figure 9.1.*

assumed that a client had already approved the overall color. Here, let's assume that we have no such approval, and that although the color looks good now, we are open to small changes to go along with the big change in contrast.

Under these circumstances, I'd suggest doing the correction on a separate layer. Begin with Layer: Duplicate Layer, putting a copy of the RGB image on top of itself. With this second layer active, apply curves that steepen the range in each channel that affects the berries, leaving sharp, but off-color, fruit. If you like, apply USM as well.

In the Layers palette, shown in Figure 9.4, I changed the mode from Normal to Luminosity, which accomplishes the same thing we did with the chocolates. As it happens, I quit right there, which means I could have done exactly the same thing with an Adjustment Layer.

Using a true layer, however, opens up room for experimentation. It's possible that we might think that the berries should move just slightly in the direction of the corrected color but move strongly toward its contrast. We'd accomplish this by keeping the contrast layer in Normal mode, but turning down Opacity to 10% or so. Then, we'd add a third layer, duplicating the second, but 100% Opacity, mode Luminosity. Or an infinite number of permutations.

Figure 9.3 *As with the chocolates, the original raspberries, top, are correct for color, but very flat. The corrected version, below, uses LAB techniques even though the file never leaves RGB.*

blue object depends almost exclusively on the unwanted color: magenta, in the case of a lime; cyan, for raspberries.

In the lime image, we used a brute-force approach of blending more detail directly into the magenta plate. With the raspberries, a different strategy got the same result, as Figure 9.5 shows. The new cyan plate is superior to the original.

Interesting, is it not, the way that all colorspaces treat the image differently and yet achieve the same thing?

The objective with these fruits is to create more of a range of saturation. They must be kept bright in the foreground areas, but have to fade rapidly toward gray at the edges—in the case of the raspberries, at the edges of the individual cells that make up the fruit.

The values at the left of the leftmost berry, which are highlighted in the color circles, demonstrate. They're a touch grayer in the corrected version.

These numbers show why the cyan and

Take What You Have Gathered

If you think you have seen this raspberry picture before, you have. It just wasn't a picture of raspberries, but of a lime, in Figure 5.4. The subject in both cases is brightly colored fruit. The choice is something that looks natural, or like a large blob of ink.

If you feel like exercising the first choice, there is an easy recipe. As Chapter 5 was at pains to point out, the shape of a bright red, green, or

Figure 9.4 *The Layers palette offers Luminosity as an option, even when the base document is not in the LAB colorspace.*

black plates are so critical in bright red images. Both the magenta and yellow are in the high 90s. Confronted with that heavy a flow of ink, dot structure in these two plates will not hold up when the job gets to press.

Figure 9.5 is a useful contrivance known to professionals as a *prog,* or in this case, a partial prog, short for progressive proof. Here it shows that we may be able to see detail in the magenta plate on the monitor, but it won't last when ink hits paper. Everything will depend, therefore, on how good our cyan and black are.

The prog also serves as a prelude to the discussion of the limitations of calibrationism that will start in the next chapter. If these were real berries and not just an image, the relatively dark area we've been talking about would still be extremely red. If we were able to somehow pick up this small area of berry and transport it into a picture of something else, that piece of berry would likely be, and by far, the reddest thing in the image.

In such an imaginary second image, it would be nuts to portray

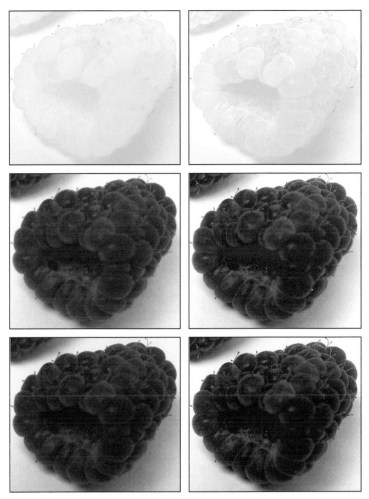

Figure 9.5 *A progressive proof shows how much more impact the RGB correction had on the eventual cyan plate than it did on the magenta. In any event, the magenta prints so heavily that it can contribute little detail. Left side: the original cyan, magenta, and cyan plus magenta plates. Right side: the same from the final image.*

that red with as much cyan and black ink as in the corrected version of Figure 9.3. If we did, all reds in the new picture would have to be even more desaturated to show they weren't as red as the berry. Faces would have to be made very gray, because we certainly can't have a face the color of a raspberry.

And so, to reiterate the point that fouls up so many beginners and calibrationists, context is everything. The color of the darkest part of a raspberry is *different* in a picture that does not contain the brightest part of a raspberry. Don't listen to anybody who says that if it's the same piece of fruit it ought to be the same color. That logic works well for colorimeters but not for human beings.

Having decided what needs to be done, all colorspaces become one. If we are using software that supports HSB curves, we write a longer saturation curve. If we are working in LAB, we steepen the L curve in the raspberry range, darkening (and thus desaturating) the edges that way. If we are in CMYK, we can blend into the cyan plate to get the extra contrast. And in either CMYK or RGB, we can use HSB principles by working with the sponge tool to desaturate the edges, or LAB principles in either of the ways shown in Figures 9.1 and 9.3.

...From Coincidence

It happens so often that we can enjoy the benefits of one colorspace while in another, that it's worth a look at some examples where we *can't* get by with such a method.

Our final riff on the bright-fruits-and-vegetables theme adds a complication: no unwanted color. Remember Emily Dickinson's philosophy of color allocation in Chapter 5? Almost all natural objects are red, green, or blue. That means, in CMY terms, two strong inks, and one exquisitely important weak one.

The pepper of Figure 9.6, however, is not red, not green, not blue. It's yellow: one strong ink, *two* weak ones.

That makes it harder to handle. Ordinarily, moves in the weak plate can't override the basic color established by the two dominants. But if only one ink is dominant, moves in the weaker two *can* change color. So, blending into the cyan and magenta channels is unlikely to work.

Let's start in RGB. Examining the individual channels in Figure 9.7, we discover two worthless voids and a decent green.

One thought might be to treat this image as we did the raspberries. Apply a contrast-

Figure 9.6 *Yellow objects are tougher to correct by plate blending than red, green, or blue ones because they have two weak inks rather than one.*

enhancing curve to the green, and then try some blending into the red and blue, ending with a layer arrangement that affects luminosity only, retaining the original yellow color.

Since all colorspaces are one, let's use LAB terms to describe what just happened. We have replaced the L channel—even though the file itself never entered LAB.

Once we realize that replacing the L is the point of the exercise, we may well ask ourselves why we are driving from New York to Boston by way of Dubuque. Let's make a copy of the image and convert it to LAB. Look at the original L channel in Figure 9.7. Pretty rancid, right? Got any ideas of where we could find a better one?

That's right. We replace the L channel with the green from RGB. Unorthodox, perhaps, but no less sensible than blending an RGB channel into a CMY one, which we've seen many times.

As with all such blends, we have to be careful with overall weight. The green is slightly heavier than the original L, so it has to be lightened. The way to do this is to find the lightest part of the pepper in the original (91^L) and, with a curve, lighten the point in the new L until it matches. Naturally, we make sure this curve is steepest in the range of the pepper.

Figure 9.7 *The original red, green, and blue channels from Figure 9.6, plus the L channel from a copy of the image that was converted into LAB.*

The difference between the two versions of Figure 9.6, therefore, is less than a minute of work: one plate blend, one easy curve, convert to CMYK, and print.

The Times Are a-Changin'

There's a significant difference between this pepper image and the two earlier examples. The chocolates and the raspberries illustrated the point that all colorspaces are similar. Although the style of the correction is different depending on colorspace, the result is the same.

Recent developments in our industry have made it highly desirable for us to be able to work in whatever colorspace we may happen to find ourselves. A CMYK-phobic

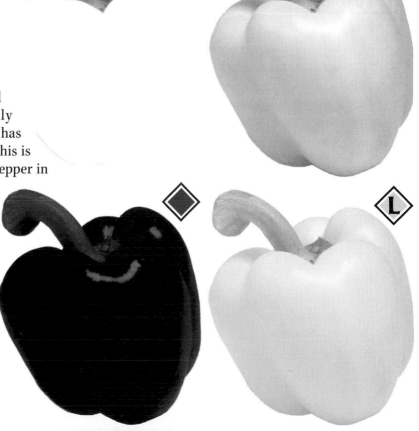

photographer may be reluctant to execute a correction as big as that of Figure 9.1 without returning to RGB. An RGB-phobic prepress type may convert Figure 9.3 to CMYK even if it has to go back to RGB because it's headed for the Web.

All this converting and reconverting is inefficient, but if that's the only way you can do it, it will work.

With the pepper, it won't. If you don't know this luminosity trick (or an equivalent method such as those discussed in Chapter 16) you are in for a long afternoon of trying to duplicate the 15-second LAB correction.

The power of the luminosity correction is such that Adobe's only recent addition to Photoshop's color correction tools is a

Figure 9.8 *When wishing a total change in the color of a product—as in transposing the colors of the garments of the two women at left—LAB is the colorspace of choice. Top left, the original. Top right, a version designed to create a red kimono. Bottom left, a second extra version for the blue vest.*

dumbed-down version of it, accessible to users of any skill level. There's always been an Image: Adjust>Auto Levels command, which sets the lightest and darkest points of each channel to predetermined levels. This usually increases contrast, but frequently changes colors, as often as not for the worse.

In Photoshop 5.5, an additional command, Image: Adjust>Auto Contrast, made its debut. It's nothing more than Auto Levels reverted to Luminosity. Sometimes it works better than Auto Levels, sometimes not.

Back to more sophisticated stuff. The objective of the chapter is not just to show the similarities between colorspaces, but also to suggest cases, like this pepper, where one is clearly better than the alternatives.

The familiar musicians image of Figure 9.8, for example, suggests CMYK. The more complexity, the greater the number of subjects of interest, the more it pays to have four channels rather than three in which to write curves.

Overall correction is not today's problem, however. The assignment is to transpose the colors of the clothing that the two women on the left are wearing.

This kind of request seems to be becoming more and more common. In RGB or CMYK, it's a real chore. Some advocate using Image: Adjust>Replace Color, which is not all that easy to control. It's tough, for example, to convince the command that the near (shadow) side of the blonde woman's vest is actually part of what we want to change.

Such gross changes in color are both easier and more convincing when done in LAB. Even if this image starts in CMYK, it's well worth it to take it to LAB in a case like this.

Tangled Up in Blue

We form our impression of overall color from the lightest portions of the object. The lightest portion of the red vest measures $49^L59^A31^B$. The lightest part of the blue kimono is at $58^L(11)^A(38)^B$.

Here's how to interpret these numbers: the higher number in the L means that the kimono is lighter. The positive numbers in A and B show that the vest favors magenta and yellow, magenta a bit more. The negative numbers in the kimono favor green and blue, blue much more than green.

The basic idea is to swap these two sets of values, but here there's a slight hitch. The kimono appears to be silk, whereas the vest is of some fabric that doesn't reflect light nearly as well. So it makes sense that the red color would lighten when we transfer it to the kimono, and the blue would darken when we take it to the vest. We therefore have to guess at the proper L value, but we should be able to match the A and B.

We start by creating two duplicate layers. The easy way to do this is by opening the Layers palette and dragging the background layer down to the paper icon at bottom. After doing this twice, we have three identical layers. The bottom remains unchanged. On the middle layer we apply curves to make the kimono red, and on the top we curve the vest into blue.

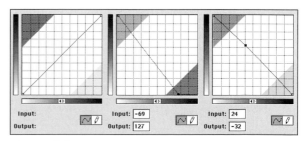

Figure 9.9 *These LAB curves turn the blue kimono red, producing the upper right version of Figure 9.8.*

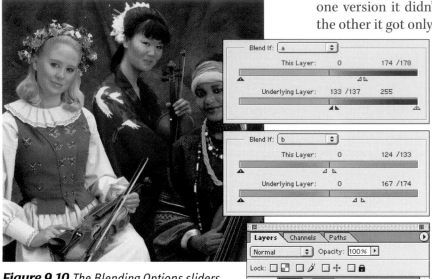

one version it didn't change at all, and in the other it got only slightly lighter.

This avoids a major problem of CMYK or RGB correction: detail gets whacked out when we make colossal color changes like this one. That inconvenience is gone, but we still face the question of how to incorporate these changed garments into the original. Fortunately, LAB helps us out there as well.

To put the red kimono (middle layer) into the bottom layer, but avoid having the purple background, blue faces, and green fiddles accompany it, we need Layer: Layer Style>Blending Options.

Figure 9.10 *The Blending Options sliders (above right) isolate the blue vest. However, they leave patches of blue in the faces and the instruments. These are eliminated with a very rough layer mask. Right, the final Layers palette; note the masks on the top layers.*

The curves that create the red kimono are in Figure 9.9. The correct procedure is not to trot out some massive curve in the A and B channels, but to turn the curve upside-down. This is mandatory. Originally, the darkest portions of the kimono are more neutral, less blue, than the brightest parts. That places them lower on the B curve. If we just shove the B curve to the left, those parts will stay less blue, or rather they will stay more yellow, and the dark parts of the kimono will go orange. By flipping the curve, those points stay more neutral, but not more blue.

Now we repeat the procedure on the top layer, creating a blue vest. The two alternate layers are included in Figure 9.8.

Ignoring for the moment the ice-maiden blue fleshtones and other peccadillos, notice how realistic the image seems to be. This is because the L channel is intact—in

That command allows us to exclude certain areas when the layers come together. For example, we don't want to blend in any place where the top layer isn't red. That excludes the faces and everything the woman at left is wearing, but it includes the background and part of the dress of the woman at right. We therefore say, where the top layer is red *and* the bottom layer is blue. That definition takes care of everything except the center woman's eyeshadow and part of the right woman's dress. But we can knock those out easily with a layer mask. The important thing is to establish the edge of the kimono without having to do any painstaking mask cutting.

The procedure is then repeated with the

third (vest) layer, and because this is the more difficult of the two, we'll discuss it in more detail.

Figure 9.10 shows two pieces of the Blending Options dialog (remember that the red kimono has already been incorporated into the base image.) The A option says to exclude things that are extremely magenta on the top layer. That kills the kimono. It also excludes things that aren't at least a little bit magenta on the bottom layer. So much for the gray background.

The B sliders exclude things that are yellow on this layer (few and far between) and things that are very yellow on the bottom layer (the yellow shirt and headband, and a lot of the fleshtones.)

Note the split sliders in the center areas where the excluded range begins.This creates a gradation, rather than a sudden stop, when excluded colors show up. In other words, it softens the edges of the blend. To split the sliders, hold Option (Alt) while clicking on them.

These settings didn't manage to exclude some of the faces and the instruments. This, however, is a non-issue. With the vest so well defined, there are several quick ways of getting rid of the other blue schmutz. My quick way: Layer: Add Layer Mask>Reveal All. Set background color to black. With the lasso tool, make a quick selection of the vest, going as far outside it as I need without actually picking up any of the other blue areas. Then Select: Invert Selection so that the vest and its immediate surroundings are the only things not selected. Now, Delete. That makes that part of the layer mask black, meaning that nothing in that area can be applied to the bottom layer.

The final Layers palette, showing the two layer masks, is in Figure 9.10.

Figure 9.11 *Very subtle colors and textures are currently in fashion, and are often impossible to reproduce accurately in print. This tile should be basically white in its raised areas, which need to be accentuated. It should have a faint green cast in the recessed areas.*

Every Grain of Sand

Another interesting use of LAB is in dealing with situations that are too subtle to reproduce. The prime example of this is fine art.

The brush-stroke texture of a painting is simply not going to be visible if a file is handled normally. Also, there are such fine variations between colors that they will probably become indistinguishable.

In such a case the least evil approach is to exaggerate the color variation by steepening the A and B curves. We also steepen the L to try to emphasize the brushstrokes, possibly with the aid of some creative sharpening. The final image is a lie, intended to suggest to the viewer what the original looked like, rather than portray its subtleties with any degree of accuracy.

The same is true in a more mundane, yet more profitable line of work: reproducing a certain modern trend: product colors that are very slightly off-neutral.

I just bought a car that the manufacturer describes as "spruce green." It looks more like silver to me and to every other person I've asked about it, but when the light hits it just right, there's the slightest of green tints. There is no more chance of reproducing that sensation in print than the car has of winning the Indianapolis 500. It's just a matter of deciding what lie we will tell.

Figure 9.11 is a similar, but even tougher problem, the boring nature of which you will perhaps forgive on the ground that it is a very typical kind of issue in product shots.

The job is to produce a catalog shot of this ceramic tile. We want the reader to get a good idea of the characteristics of the tile as well as its color. Tile is heavy and shipping it expensive, particularly if the return is at our expense because the buyer complains that the product looked nothing like what it did in the catalog.

Sadly, this is another one of these impossible-to-reproduce products. Since I can't show you an actual tile, I have no choice but to try to describe it.

Its name is "Sea Foam." It has a pronounced texture that you don't appreciate in Figure 9.11. More important, pick one up and you'll probably think it's white until you view it from several angles. The raised areas *are* white. The recessed parts have a slight green tinge, just enough so that if there's a whole floor or wall of these tiles, you'll have no doubt that they are a greenish white.

This looks like an LAB correction all the way, as we need to greatly enhance both contrast and the variation between colors. The original is extremely flat because of the following dismal readings: the brightest part of the tile, $74^L0^A0^B$. Well, at least it's a pure neutral. A suitable dark part in a recessed area, $71^L0^A4^B$. The grout above the tile: $74^L3^A6^B$.

One need not be da Vinci to scope out the L curve. The lightest point has to move to somewhere between 90^L and 95^L. There's no point in being too careful, because we have all the range we need. This is that rare commodity, an image without anything that can be used as a shadow

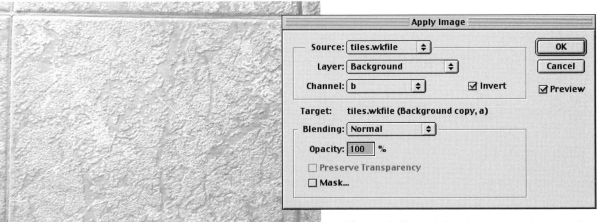

Figure 9.12 *Applying the B channel to the A for color variation. In this case, the B has to be inverted to avoid turning the tiles orange. Even this move, however, leaves the grout pink.*

point. The light range of this curve is going to get very steep, but the limit is personal preference—there's no shadow to annihilate, like would ordinarily happen if we raised the quartertone to a ridiculously high level.

The color is the problem. The dark areas of the tile measure yellow, not green. We can, and probably should, steepen the B curve, but that will just make it more yellow. As for the A curve, that can become pure vertical for all the good it will do. With both the light and dark points of the tile reading 0^A, there's no variation to emphasize, and no green at all.

It's silly to force green into the entire image; we'd have to go back and somehow eliminate it from the white "foam." One possibility is to go into CMYK and raise the quartertone in cyan. The dark parts will be affected more than the white areas, but it will be hard to control the color.

An RGB curve would be even less successful, but there's another RGB option: blend the blue into the red, Darken mode. This will remove red from the image and, thus, make the tiles greener. It will do the same to the grout, more's the pity.

There's an LAB alternative, but it's not an obvious one. We can blend the B, which has color variation, into the A.

The tiles will now turn slightly orange, which is hardly what we had in mind. Yellow values are positive in the B; positive values are magenta in the A. To make this work, we have to set up the Apply Image command to Invert, as in Figure 9.12. That command won't affect the white areas, but it will change the darker parts to green, not magenta.

From there, we can apply a further curve to the newly created A, making the color

Figure 9.13 *The final image, after using the Blending Options shown below to exclude anything more magenta than green.*

greener than it it yellow. Which leaves the problem of the green grout.

Now do you see why this is done in LAB? The blend is on a duplicate layer, naturally. Now we can use Blending Options (Figure 9.13) to exclude anything that originally was positive in the A. The grout was slightly magenta before the blend. The tiles were not. For all the complexity of these maneuvers, we never had to make a selection.

Figure 9.14 *This image, in addition to a whiter statue, is supposed to have a rich black background, with vivid coloring in the clouds.*

Knockin' on Heaven's Door

From an unmatchably dull image we move to an unmatchable one of almost unimaginable richness and majesty. The backdrop of Figure 9.14, from the Visitor Center at Temple Square in Salt Lake City, is in real life a lush black, with dark but intense purple and blue clouds and subdued planets.

We can forget about matching the impact of the actual scene, but Figure 9.15 shows that we can do a lot better than this tepid original, which comes to us in RGB.

Choosing the proper strategy calls for preflight analysis. Do any of our objectives suggest a specific colorspace?

Here, we're going to want white marble and good detail in the statue. But that's not hard in any colorspace, at least not for those who have absorbed Chapters 2 and 3. There's a slight complication in this example, however, owing to the lighting. The top of the statue starts out yellow and the bottom is blue. That argues against LAB, which can't correct both simultaneously without suppressing other yellows and blues, such as the railing and some of the clouds. In RGB or CMYK, we could use a curve in the blue or yellow channels that affects the statue but not the much darker rail.

Figure 9.15 *For a black this rich, the black plate has to be much darker than in the shadows of normal images. To retain detail in the sky it also needs to have excellent contrast.*

Second, we need to intensify the background colors. I'd prefer to do that in LAB, which will give more realism, but the option exists of correcting the image elsewhere, then goosing the colors with Image: Adjust>Selective Color or Adjust> Hue/Saturation.

Third, we have to bring the dark background to life. The translation is, we need much more detail in the deepest shadows. And *that* suggests a colorspace—the one that has a black channel.

Think all the way back to Figure 1.4 and remember where the shadow detail fell: all over the place in RGB, but only in the black in CMYK. So, when attacking such a problem, the black is ideal. It's all the detail we've got, in one handy location. Furthermore, it doesn't carry certain baggage that would otherwise hinder us.

If we want to open up contrast in the dark sky, we have to, roughly speaking, lighten the midtone. That would necessarily give less range to the lighter half of the image. And that would have the unacceptable result of suppressing contrast in the statue, *unless* the move was made in the black, which is likely to be blank where the statue is anyway. So, nothing will be hurt if we blow away whatever highlight

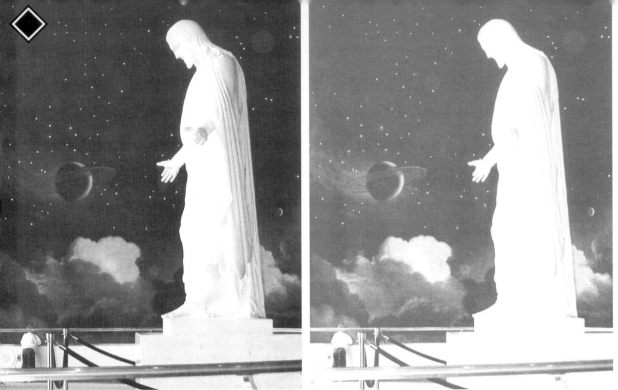

Figure 9.16 *Rather than work with the black channel of a normal separation (top left) a false separation with a low black ink limit (top right) should be the starting point. After contrast-enhancing curves and some sharpening, the final black is below right. In black areas, the CMY channels never have much detail, but they have to be suppressed even more to accommodate such a heavy black. Below left, the magenta channels that go with the normal separation (top) and the heavier black channel (bottom).*

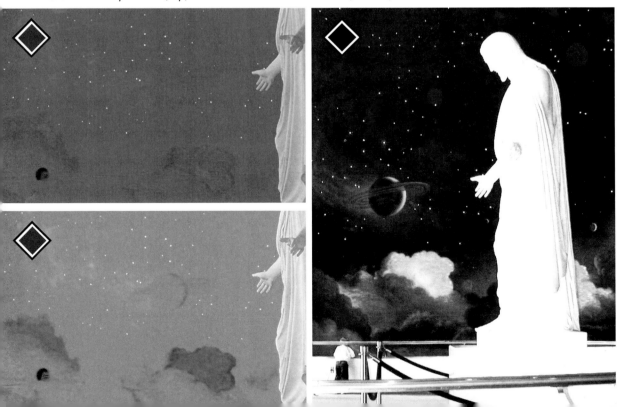

detail there may be in the black in the interest of a better sky.

Starting out in RGB, I dropped the quartertone of the blue curve very slightly, while holding its shadow. The idea was to kill some of the yellowness in the statue without harming the brass railing. This also made the base of the statue more blue, but I foresaw a way to get rid of that later.

On to LAB, for a steepening of the A and B, and an important realization. The idea is to create a spectacularly contrasty black plate, which will carry all the shadow detail. In creating this, we will snap our fingers at the detail in the statue. But the goals of the CMY channels are exactly the opposite. We know that the CMY won't contribute to a believable sky; if too dark, in fact, they'll actually harm detail. Yet we have to be quite solicitous of the statue's health in CMY, since the black will not be contributing.

There is no point trying to fry an egg and steam rice in the same pan. With two mutually exclusive goals, it's best to work with two files. So I made a copy of the LAB file.

With the one that is destined to make our black, I lightened the L quartertone so much that it blasted the statue out of the picture. Now the separation, but not a normal one. I paid a visit to Image: Mode>Convert to Profile, and specified Custom CMYK. There, I set maximum black to 60^K, and bought myself the top right of Figure 9.16.

The idea of that is to apply a very steep curve later. Even at such a low maximum, the black will have nice detail, and jacking it up to normal levels will exaggerate it. But first things first. 70^K is ordinarily satisfactory for a shadow, but not when everything depends on contrast in the darks. Let's live a little. 95^K, or even 98^K, will let the good times roll.

Mixed-Up Confusion

Returning to the second LAB file, the one that would generate the CMY, I established a highlight of 95^L in the hand. But instead of opening the sky by lowering the quartertone, my curve emphasized the statue by raising it.

At this point, I sharpened the L. That step had to be omitted in the first version because opening the black so much naturally creates a lot of noise.

Now, in Custom CMYK, I set total ink to only 240%. The point of this was to make the CMY channels quite light in the shadows, so they would not gum up all the detail I'd engineered into the other file's black. I also set maximum black to 100%, knowing that the destination of this separation's black was the same as the CMY of the first one, to wit, the trash.

Curve corrections of selected or masked areas always leave traces. Some people would automatically have selected the statue to try to bring out its contrast. Uniting the black from one sep with the CMY from the other does the same thing, but undetectably. And, as the black doesn't carry any of the detail in the statue, nobody will ever know that I blew it completely out of the version that I was separating only for the black.

Only housekeeping matters remained. The problem of the blue cast at the base of the statue and in the carpeting was solved by blending the cyan channel into the yellow with an opacity of 25%; I used Darken mode to avoid obliterating the railing or the parts of the statue that are naturally yellow. The highlight wasn't quite right and was fixed easily with curves. And I used Selective Color to exaggerate the blue fringes of the purple clouds, a personal preference that you may or may not agree with.

This correction is now over, except for a hypothetical question: what if this image is destined for RGB and thus never should be in CMYK at all?

Sshh! Don't tell anyone! If you reconvert it to RGB after doing the correction in CMYK, who's gonna know? A combination

Figure 9.17 *The pervasive yellow cast is but one of the technical problems with this original.*

of RGB and LAB techniques can solve nearly the problems that CMYK plus LAB can, with this one exception. If the image can only be resurrected by adding shadow detail, the black channel is the savior.

The Pigeons Will Run to Her

To say that Figure 9.17 has some problems is to say that it is occasionally cold in Antarctica. Let me first reiterate that the policy of this book precludes sabotaging images in order to make the correction more impressive. I *paid* for this image, and this is what I got.

The preflight analysis: some situations are almost too grim for words. Ordinarily, we don't decide whether an image has a color cast without verifying it in the Info palette. We can make an exception here. We can also make an exception to the usual rules about checking highlight and shadow until we get deeper into this mess.

Now that you are a multi-colorspace maven, however, you should be able to recognize the following color: $255^R245^G26^B$, which can also be expressed as $95^L(16)^A83^B$ or $4^C0^M90^Y$. Whichever way you like it, it's a brilliant yellow, entirely suitable for the brightest portion of the pepper of Figure 9.6—but, as a fleshtone, about as close to what we need as San José, California is to the planet Saturn.

Nevertheless, that is the current value in the woman's left arm. The blown-out area is but one of many obvious problems, including the lack of detail in the face; the desirability of holding detail in the dark brown garments; the necessity to keep good shape in the hair; the overall cast; and the lack of differentiation between flesh-tone and background.

Making something acceptable out of such a disgrace to the scanning profession will be challenging, but it can be done—see Figure 9.18—if you know your colorspaces.

A number of these issues have shown up in other corrections in this book, although not, thankfully, all at once. The immediate thought is that this is so similar to the pepper that some RGB plate blending would be in order. But it is still going to have such a ghastly color cast that an LAB correction will probably be needed. Some special separation technique may be needed to hold the detail in the clothing. Whatever correction method we use will probably destroy the color of the eyes and lips; and we still haven't even discussed what to do about the holes in the arms.

In deciding that question, a good way is to examine luminosity values. That's done by measuring the L channel, which can be done even though the image starts in RGB. With the eyedroppers in both sides of the Info palette, set the palette so that its first half reads Actual Color (RGB, at the moment) and the second half LAB.

In this way, we learn that the arm is around 97^L, and the next lightest area, the steps under her left hand, are 85^L. I believe that this makes no sense at all and that this becomes one of the rare images that requires a local selection, which means we need a mask.

The Line It Is Drawn

This is not a book about how to make a selection mask, any more than it's about monitor calibration. Never-

theless, certain techniques come up quite often—especially for those who know their colorspaces.

In situations like these, eventually we hope to cobble together a reasonably accurate selection. Then, using any of Photoshop's painting tools, we touch up whatever parts of the mask aren't correct. Finally, we Select: Save Selection, to store the mask as a

Figure 9.18 *After forays into four different colorspaces, the image is much improved.*

separate, nonprinting channel of the base file or as a separate Photoshop file, which I prefer because it saves disk space.

The question is, do we want to spend 30 seconds on this mask touchup, or 30 minutes? The key to avoiding the latter is having a decent start point, the key to that is knowing where to find edges, and the key to that is colorspace knowledge.

Here the cast is so bad that the background is practically the same color as the woman's flesh.

Which One to Use?

The three colorspaces that Photoshop fully supports have different strengths. Keeping them in mind can guide you to the right one to use for each job.

CMYK:
- Best space for enhancing shadow detail, which is localized in the black channel.
- Good for sharpening images with one dominating color (sharpening of black plus the unwanted color).
- Most precise control of curves of any colorspace.
- Can target small areas of complex images for contrast boosts.
- Directly addresses the colors that are actually in use on press.

LAB:
- Excellent for quick corrections where there's no time to fine-tune every number.
- Best way to make CMYK to RGB conversions.
- Best sharpening space for images not dominated by one color.
- Allows cost-free blurring of colored noise.
- Convenient space for experimentation when unsure of what the final colors should be.
- Easily eliminates gross color casts.
- Steepening the A and B is the most natural-looking way of creating color variation or more intense colors.

RGB:
- Great source for channel blends into CMYK.
- Works well in conjunction with a reversion to luminosity.
- Can use for gross color changes when there are countercasts that would prevent making them in LAB.
- Accepts blends aimed at correcting casts better than the others.

For getting the outlines of the woman's clothing, almost anything will work. I'd use the magnetic lasso tool myself. It might also get the shoes and parts of the legs, but it will definitely have trouble with the hair and the arms.

For those, we either need to draw the mask ourselves or find some channel that has already done the work for us. For example, suppose the background steps in this image were blue. In that case, the cyan plate would have enough definition between arm and steps that it could be used as the start of a mask. But they aren't, and it doesn't.

In images like this, with a bias toward certain colors, the best mask source is often the A or B channel. We can't use them directly, because they are too flat, too gray. But we can copy them to new documents, increase their contrast, and find the edges that way. The B channel has a good start at isolating the hair and arms.

There's also the option of Photoshop 6's new Image: Extract command. My bottom line on that is, it's quicker to do it the old way.

Better Grab It Fast

Fast forward. We have a mask. We start by examining the RGB channels. Because this picture is so dreadfully yellow to start, they resemble somewhat those of the yellow pepper. That is, the red is washed out, the blue is too dark, and the green looks nice. You can follow the progress of this correction along in Figure 9.19.

To aid in planning, it pays to make a copy of the image and convert it to LAB, to see whether we can pull the old replace-the-L-with-the-G trick. Not here: the two channels are similar. But either one can be used to engineer more contrast into the red and blue channels. Right now, these two are pretty sad.

Whichever we choose (I stuck with the green) we should make a copy of it and increase contrast. Then, we blend it in—I used 50% in each channel—to the weak red and blue.

Now, a conversion to LAB, where the curves shown in Figure 9.20 attack the cast. We've tried to stay away from oddly shaped A and B curves in the past, but there isn't much choice here: we need to slam the brightest yellows, but if we do this by moving the straight line of the B curve to the left, the brightest areas of the steps will become bright blue. Frankly, we have more than enough problems to solve already.

Note that we don't want to go overboard in darkening the L channel. There's delicate detail in the hair. That calls for something with rather more finesse than the clumsy L. Nor do we sharpen at this point:

there's too much noise in the fleshtone, noise that's present in the L but won't be in certain channels in CMYK.

With this in mind, after applying the curves and saving a copy of the LAB file, we cross into CMYK, using a relatively low black ink limit of 70% to give us room to steepen it to gain contrast in the clothing and hair.

Now, the differentiation between woman and background. Loading the mask, which makes it impossible to alter the woman, we open Adjust Hue/Saturation and kill most of the cast in the background by reducing saturation overall. Then, an LAB-like move: we apply CMYK curves that bring the lightest areas of the steps to a near-highlight value and establish a shadow in the cracks, then Edit: Fade back to Luminosity so that there will be no color shift.

Then, we Select: Invert Selection, flipping the mask so that we can work on the woman, but not the background. Two items require attention: we need a better cyan plate and we need to fill in the holes in the arm.

The cyan problem is solved by applying the L channel from the LAB file we saved two paragraphs ago. That's close to what we did in the rose image, but we won't be able to blend the yellow into the magenta, as we did there. This time, the yellow is too flat, thanks to the original cast, and mixing it into the magenta would kill facial detail.

Instead, with the woman still selected, we apply a curve to the magenta that does nothing but bring the zero point up to 15%, ensuring at least that amount of magenta in the arm. At the same time, we lighten the cyan slightly, compensating for the darkening that took place in the blend, while retaining the additional contrast.

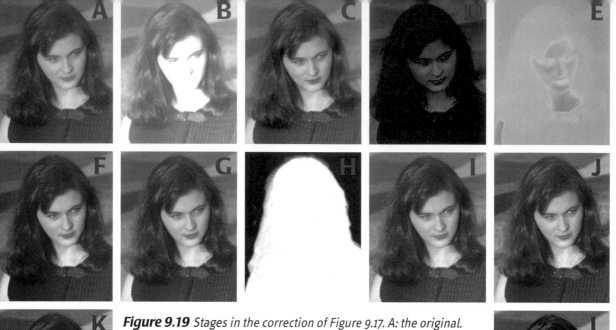

Figure 9.19 *Stages in the correction of Figure 9.17. A: the original. B–D: the original red, green, and blue channels. E: the original B channel of LAB, used to make a mask. F: after RGB plate blending to reduce the cast. G: after the LAB color correction using the curves of Figure 9.20. H: the final mask. I: the background is selected and desaturated with Adjust: Hue/Saturation. J: the background is given extra contrast. K: with the woman selected, a blend of the L channel from version G into the cyan. L: a curve adds magenta and subtracts cyan from the fleshtone. The eyes and lips have also been retouched.*

At this point, we're ready to apply unsharp masking, but only to the black and the cyan, for the reasons discussed in Chapter 4.

Finally, the local retouching. We try to restore natural coloring to the eyes and lips. With all these corrections, it would be a miracle if these features were anything like the colors they're supposed to be.

It's All Over Now

Four colorspaces in a single correction! Only the HSB move has a reasonable alternative. I could have desaturated the background with curves in any colorspace (I'd choose LAB, where just flattening the AB would do this). But the Hue/Saturation command seems easier to control, particularly in a case like this where the decision is subjective and therefore doesn't rely on numbers.

Eliminating use of the other colorspaces is another story. For many images, the plate blending in RGB can be omitted in favor of later moves in the L channel. Here, that wouldn't work. If we did an immediate conversion into LAB, we'd need to boost the quartertone in the L channel so as to add detail to the woman's face. But if we did

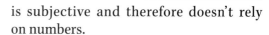

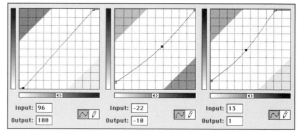

| Input: 96 | Input: -22 | Input: 13 |
| Output: 100 | Output: -10 | Output: 1 |

Figure 9.20 *These LAB curves reduce the yellow cast without turning neutral areas blue-green.*

ALL COLORSPACES ARE ONE

✓Although the style of correcting varies in different colorspaces, the result is usually the same. When dealing with a brightly colored object, for example, the desired result is a strong plate in the unwanted color. It seems as if this is a strong argument in favor of CMYK correction. In fact, moves in the other three colorspaces will eventually create a strong unwanted color, even if they don't do so directly.

✓Increasing contrast without altering color is usually associated with the L channel of LAB. However, the technique can be duplicated in CMYK or RGB by either fading curves to luminosity or by using a correction layer in Luminosity mode.

✓When making moves in several colorspaces, it's helpful to save one copy in each. You never know when they can be used for a blend.

✓As a practical matter, there is no loss of image quality in converting between RGB and LAB. The conversion into CMYK is lossless; the conversion from CMYK into LAB loses a small amount of shadow detail, which is easily compensated for.

✓When confronted with a difficult image, a sensible approach is to list all of its problems and think about which colorspace is most advantageous for treating each one.

✓If you need masks for silhouetting or any other purpose, you can save a lot of time by finding the correct colorspace. With three Photoshop colorspaces, there are ten possible channels, and one of them is likely to have the edge definition needed to get started on a mask.

✓Working in Color mode in RGB or CMYK is close to the same, but it is not as accurate as, working in the A and B channels of LAB. However, in many images it pays to work in LAB. For example, in noisy images the noise is typically more yellow-blue than it is magenta-green. This means that the B channel of LAB should be blurred more than the A.

✓Don't go overboard with the use of multiple colorspaces. Most corrections don't need them. The mark of the professional is not just understanding the colorspace concepts but knowing when a desired correction can only be done in a certain manner in a certain colorspace.

that, we'd clobber detail in the clothes and hair. There is some chance we could get the job done in CMYK instead, but it would certainly be much more difficult. By far the easiest method is what we did, correcting the original red channel with a blend.

Similarly, although the added snap that the L move added to the hair could have been arranged elsewhere, there's no good substitute for the AB curves. When the color cast is this severe, it's nearly impossible to remove outside of LAB.

Finally, the tricky separation, followed by the boost in the black and the blend into the cyan channel, is only for those who can handle CMYK.

The End of the Beginning

That result brings us to the end of the first half of our color correction adventures. Time now for an intermission to discuss several related topics, before we delve into even deeper correction techniques in Chapters 16 and 17. But first, a little retrospective on what's gone on so far.

The by-the-numbers curve techniques of Chapters 2 and 3 are the foundation on which all the advanced trickery rests. This is why beginners can learn to get professional color so easily. The recipe is simple and the image analysis required not too demanding.

The sharpening and plate blending of Chapter 4 and 5 are a little tougher, and offer many more options. Still, they are every-image tools. We always consider sharpening; we always think about ways to augment the weak color.

For the typical image, the above techniques combine nicely. They may be enough for many users or for those who, like professional photographers, have good control over the quality of the images they start with.

The professional retoucher, however, is assumed to be capable of producing professional quality not just out of ordinary images but out of those that are seriously flawed, or that have unusual characteristics. That implies a battery of specialized tricks that work on some images and not others. It also explains why frustration sometimes sets in from Chapter 6 onward.

It's one thing to have a lot of weapons, and you will doubtless agree that the last four chapters have provided quite an arsenal. The hard part is determining when to use them. The hard part is strategy, not merely tactics.

This last exercise proves the point. Every move was logical and had been discussed earlier at some point in the book. The possibility of combining things into a grand design that swept through four colorspaces is, shall we say, not very intuitive.

And so, it was an experts-only kind of correction. But the real mark of the expert is knowing that this kind of maneuvering should be saved for the really exceptional kind of image, of which this is one.

10
Making Things Look Alike

Everyone needs to calibrate, everyone needs to manage color. Getting the great results that elude those who use calibration as a substitute for thinking depends on understanding how simple the science is—and on whether you trust your eyes.

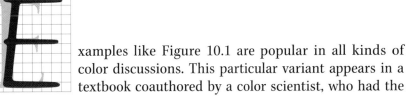

xamples like Figure 10.1 are popular in all kinds of color discussions. This particular variant appears in a textbook coauthored by a color scientist, who had the temerity to write, "To most people the green segments at the top appear to be darker than the ones at the bottom, but both are the same."

Whaddaya, blind? Give us a break. *Anybody* can see that they're different. Saying that they're the same is the sort of bogus trickery that's given color science and color management such a bad name.

We all know where the scientist is coming from. He thinks that if he wheels out a colorimeter, a spectrophotometer, or similar product, he will be able to convince us, by measuring the two greens, that they really are the same.

Despair thy charm! say I. There is an inherent defect in all artificial color-measurement devices that causes them, in situations like this, to imagine that the two greens are the same.

How tiresome language can be! If a gun were held to our heads, the two of us would probably agree on this statement: *the two greens don't look alike.*

The scientist is therefore correct, in a manner of speaking. If we were

Figure 10.1 *Are the two rows of green patches the same color? How would you go about proving whether your answer is correct?*

to modify the second part of his statement to read, "the two greens are the same, *in the unanimous judgment of artificial color measurement devices,*" we'd have to call that accurate.

There is a most unscientific error in the statement nonetheless. Can you spot it?

Sure. He said, "To *most people* the green segments at the top appear to be darker..." and of course this is not so. They appear darker to me, to you, and to everyone else, including even my color-blind friends. It's the superior simultaneous-contrast technology of the human visual system that causes us to see colors in context, just as the faulty technology of the artificial instruments causes them to have the illusion that the greens are the same.

So, are they the same, or not? It seems to me that the answer depends on who our audience is. If it consists of spectrophotometers, densitometers, and colorimeters, then the greens are the same. If the audience consists of human beings, the greens are different.

The topic of this chapter is, how do we know whether our images will look like we want them to when they go into print or otherwise take their final form?

This question is both relevant and irrelevant to what we've been discussing so far. Irrelevant, in that every correction recommended here has universal application. That is, if you take the digital file for a random original and corrected version in this book, send it to a newspaper, a flexo printer, a color copier, and also convert the file into a random RGB variant and post it on the Web, the corrected version will look better everywhere.

Relevant, in that we can plainly do better if we know a even a little bit about the output conditions. If these files go to a newspaper the corrections will still look better, but everything is going to be too dark. If we had known ahead of time, we could have compensated for it.

In addition to wanting to know about the final conditions, we usually want to have some kind of proof, or preview, to predict what the final job is going to look like, because there's nothing as depressing as discovering that the color stinks after the press has run.

Dandruff, Cancer, and Halitosis

This topic, which goes by the general name of *calibration,* isn't notably easy, but it isn't rocket science either. If you understand curves and a little bit about color, you already know how to calibrate, although it may take a bit of work at first.

Unfortunately, an ungodly amount of hype and wind surrounds the subject, coupled with enough jargon and pseudo-science to make even the most experienced color mariner turn $70^C 100^Y$ at the gills.

Calibration, a laudable goal, can sometimes metastasize into *calibrationism,* the shutdown of all mental processes in the service of the notion that this is all mathematics and that machines always do it better. One of the distinguishing marks of this syndrome is the ability to spout seemingly plausible concepts that collapse under serious scrutiny, and to do so in convincingly technical language that terrorizes others by making them feel like dopes.

Fortunately, the heyday of pure calibrationism was several years ago. Relics of it still exist, however, especially in the area described by the extremely vague term *color management.*

You, the user, have to slog through this mire and figure out a lot of things for yourself. Partly this is because Photoshop throws a lot of dangerous options at us; partly it's because you probably will need to calibrate something that can't be discussed here because it hasn't been invented yet; and partly because there are so many charlatans out there peddling color management solutions that supposedly not only turn garbage into beautiful art, but also cure dandruff, cancer, and halitosis.

Figure 10.2 wasn't prepared by charlatans, but it does illustrate this type of preposterous claim. The purpose of calibration is to get more predictable, more repeatable output. It is not, repeat *not,* to transform garbage into a work of art.

Nor is calibration a perfect an-swer even to the problems that it purports to address. The two versions of Figure 10.3 look identical on my contract proof, which ordinarily does a great job of predicting what the printed product will look like. Not this time, though, I bet. There's a well-known press phenomenon that causes areas surrounded by solid or near-solid inks to pick up increased quantities of that ink. The two images here were made with different GCRs. The one at bottom uses more black and less CMY and will, I predict, look darker in print.

Or think back to the yellow pepper of Figure 9.6. Some years ago, I had to do an unscheduled and unwelcome emergency retouch when a contract proof revealed a large blemish that was practically invisible on my well-calibrated monitor. CMYK output generally doesn't have as a wide a gamut as a monitor does, but yellow is an exception. The brilliant yellows of the proof showed variation that the monitor simply couldn't display.

So, while calibration is a good idea, it has

Figure 10.2 *A 1999 conference on color management used this misleading graphic in its advertising.*

its limitations, many of which aren't particularly obvious.

Here, therefore, is a chapter on basic principles. It's largely new; it has to be, because there's been so much change in the arguments of the children of calibrationism. But it also has to be timeless, and so, continuing past policy, I will try to defer as much as possible discussing things specific to Photoshop until Chapter 11. Also, we won't talk about particular output devices, for the obvious reason that they're changing too rapidly.

If such theoretical discussions scare you, relax. All we're trying to do is make things look alike. Does that sound so very hard?

The Essence of Spirituality

Oliver Goldsmith, an anticalibrationist, offered the following description of certain color management advocates:

> "Good again," cried the 'Squire, "and firstly, of the first. I hope you'll not deny that whatever is, is. If you don't grant me that, I can go no further."—"Why," returned Moses, "I think I may grant that, and make the best of it."—"I hope, too," returned the other, "you'll grant that a part is less than the whole."—"I grant that too," cried Moses, "it is but just and reasonable."—"I hope," cried the 'Squire, "you will not deny that the three angles of a triangle are equal to two right ones."—"Nothing can be plainer," returned t'other, and looked round with his usual importance.—"Very well," cried the 'Squire, speaking very quick, "the premises being thus settled, I proceed to observe that the concatenation of self-existences, proceeding in a reciprocal duplicate ratio, naturally produces a problematical dialogism, which in some measure proves that

the essence of spirituality may be referred to the second predicable."

* * *

Before proceeding to a concatenation of characterization that naturally produces problematical profiling, I think it helps to reemphasize that whatever is, is.

One of those things is, you can't get a whiter white than the color of the paper. If you're trying to make a newspaper reproduction match that of this book, it isn't going to happen. The newspaper can't get as bright a highlight because newsprint isn't white enough.

For that matter, its shadow isn't dark enough. More ink gets absorbed by newsprint than the coated stock of this book, which therefore supports a richer black.

If you're thinking that this doesn't really matter, that we just let the whitest white and blackest black be whatever they wind up being, and accept that the newspaper is going to be lower-contrast, well, that doesn't quite work. One reason would be a loss of shadow detail. All presses stop holding such detail at some point. The web press printing this book can fairly consistently hold detail up to about 90% ink coverage. A newspaper press is lucky to hold it after 75%. So, if the picture has a black cat in it or something else with important shadow detail, there won't be any kind of match.

Also, if we're trying to match a newspaper to a book, we probably need to play fast and loose with the highlight. We're not supposed to let the lightest areas of the image blow out and have no dot at all, but in newspapers we're so hard up for contrast that this is often the best option.

But by far the biggest difference is one of the sensation of overall darkness. This is the critical area in all calibrations. In our example, the newspaper image will seem markedly darker than the book unless we make some kind of compensation. We will now discuss the traditional, modern, and hybrid ways of doing so.

The Flawed Traditional Method

Notice that we've been talking only about presses so far. That's no coincidence. We used to be a lot more press-centric than we are today. Traditional methods cater to a workflow aimed at presses.

Said methods are, basically, to pretend that everything *is* a press, and to the extent it doesn't behave like one, make it do so.

Film-based contract proofs, such as Matchprints, did not just appear out of the 100^C70^M one day magically looking a lot like press results. Instead, their manufacturers spent a lot of research time trying to make their colorants behave like press inks.

Digital contract proofers, such as Scitex's Iris or Kodak's Signature, work slightly differently. Internal curves get set, the incoming digital file gets altered, and if it's all done correctly, the result will approximate press output.

All this is CMYK, and expensive. But it needn't be. Figure 10.4 shows two such traditional ways, both for relatively cheap devices, both of which like to get their data in RGB. The idea is the same. We play with the output characteristics of the inkjet printer until we think it behaves something like a press. We (having first made sure of our Custom CMYK settings, about which you'll hear more in Chapter 12) can horse around with the monitor settings until we get what we think is a match to press sheets.

This way works, and has for a long time, but there are some obvious flaws:

Figure 10.3 *These two images appear identical on the contract proof, but probably not here. They have different balances of black ink to CMY. The heavy inking in the background presumably throws the normal numbers off enough to make the two look different.*

- Sometimes traditionalists use this method, and sometimes not. Most gravure printers do: they mess with the incoming digital data to make it seem to the user that the characteristics of the gravure press are similar to web offset presses. Newspaper printers, on the other hand, don't. We need to give them a lighter file. Does this make any sense?
- These same lighter files that are prepared for a newspaper represent a hole waiting for us to fall into. What if somebody picks up the file and makes the traditional

(and in this case disastrous) assumption, that it was prepared for "like a press," i.e., magazine conditions.

• The flexibility of the tools that make these on-the-fly changes often leaves a lot to be desired. The high-end digital proofers named above have extensive curve capabilities. The tools of Figure 10.4 are pretty lame. We may be able to get by with them but we'd like something more powerful.

• "Like a press" is not exactly a model of clear expression. Every press is different; the same units of the same press change performance from hour to hour, let alone day to day. Contract proofs are more stable, but little more precise. Matchprints from one shop won't match Matchprints from another, let alone analog proofs from some other manufacturer.

There's a lot to find fault with, and no shortage of people who want to do it, and who suggest better ways, often at great length, often in print, often to large audiences, and often in less than dulcet tone.

The Flawed Alternative

The above-described imprecision causes calibrationists to see 100^M100^Y. Since around 1988, as nearly as I can tell, the idea has been bruited about that all these evils

would go away if everyone made one simple change in workflow.

Instead of having a vague specification like "for press," to be assumed for all files, the modern idea is to tag each file with precise information as to what colors its author intended. Then, presumably within the output device but conceivably elsewhere, that tag encounters a description of what the output conditions actually are. At this point, a translation takes place, theoretically guaranteeing that the final result is as much like what the creator of the file intended as is consistent with color science.

This concept has several attractive features. No longer will I have to worry that my newspaper file will be inadvertently picked up and used in a magazine. Plus, I don't have to worry that the output from Fred's FujiProof Emporium won't match up with that of Mark's Matchprint Store. And, as time goes on, more and more files have to be prepared for multiple output conditions. The proposed method allows a single file to be repurposed many times.

There are, however, some significant drawbacks. First and foremost, for this to work pretty much the whole world would have to be on the same page. Second, that conversion step is likely to be the occasion for a lot of errors. Third, the idea that the conversions would be perfect smacks of calibrationism: making a

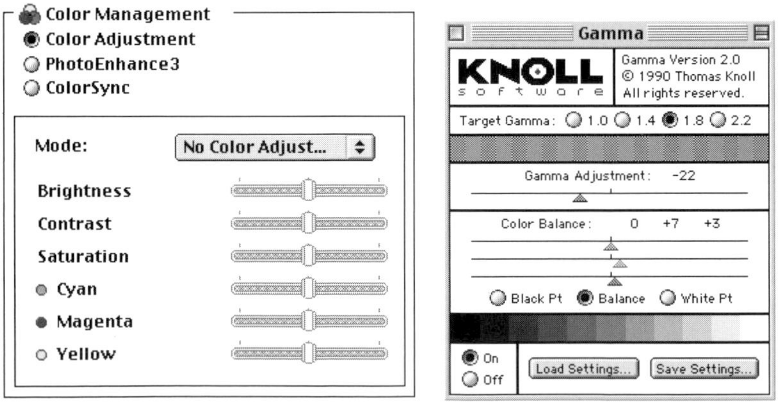

Figure 10.4 *Modern equipment but traditional calibration. These tools play with the internal settings of an Epson printer (left) or a monitor (right) to try to make them match something else, often a press.*

Making Things Look Alike   195

Matchprint look like a FujiProof is easy enough with or without human intervention; getting newspaper reproduction to resemble that of higher-quality printing is another story. And fourth, there was precious little evidence that the market was dissatisfied with things the way they were.

Whatever the merits of the new method, it didn't fly. This is not for lack of flight testing, either: for a full decade, nearly every trade publication has been trumpeting how its adoption is imminent. There were two watershed efforts to impose it on the community at large: QuarkXPress 3 in 1990, and Photoshop 5 in 1998. Both collapsed. In both cases the overwhelming majority of users who understood what was going on turned the new features off (although some users grafted the new stuff onto traditional methods), and in both cases the new methodology was withdrawn in subsequent releases of the program.

The question of whether one's files should or should not contain tags is not one of the top five or six moral issues of our decade. Nevertheless, it's been the focus of the bitterest attacks in all the graphic arts. This was so even when Quark's EfiColor XTension was released, when the advocates of the workflow scorched the service providers and those few mavericks who dared defy the unanimous judgment of the pundits by suggesting that EfiColor would not solve all color worries forever and, in fact, would not be adopted by anybody.

As soon as it became apparent that 1998 service providers weren't happy with Photoshop 5, the same silly attacks began. Things were somewhat different, however, in that this time Web discussion groups existed. This allowed angry users to give as good as they got. In response, a kind of thought

police developed, consisting of a few Adobe employees and color management vendors. This small group bullied and belittled anyone claiming to have had trouble understanding or implementing the new world order. Often, this would take the form of deluges of jargon similar to those employed by Goldsmith's squire.

A number of users responded by citing my views, which were and are, these are good features to implement for a small minority of users but not to ram down the throat of everyone, and that those seeing no benefit to the new features should turn them off.

When the program first came out, Adobe's representatives and sycophants were content to call me "highly alarmist," "reactionary," "dinosaur," and the like. But as the magnitude of the calamity became more apparent, the rhetoric got more frenzied. Eight months after the upgrade, an Adobe programmer (whose real-world production experience consists of a few months as a color copier operator in college) wrote publicly as follows: "Dan's views on color management are going to sink him and his followers just about the way computer typesetting sunk all the die-hard hot lead typesetting houses."

As I relax in my deck chair, savoring a rum punch while contemplating the bubbles coming up from the scuttled color model of Photoshop 5, I ask myself how it is that in this field so many people can be so positive about the way things will play out and yet be proven so wrong so often.

This is not a comment about Photoshop 5's color management, which is history. If you'd care to read more about that, there's a PDF of a 1999 magazine article I wrote on the subject on the attached CD. But because this sort of thing has happened so often, much to the hurt of users who have believed what they read or heard, it's worth taking a few pages, before returning to calibration, to discuss why the conventional wisdom screws up so frequently.

The Flawed Conventional Wisdom

Over the last ten years, the consensus of views found in the industry press and its major conferences has occasionally been correct. It predicted the demise of dedicated systems such as Scitex in favor of a Photoshop solution. It realized that computer-to-plate would become a big factor, as would workflows based on the Adobe Acrobat PDF specification.

On the other hand, the conventional wisdom was very late in realizing how big a deal the Web is. It missed the impact of digital cameras. It has been completely uncritical of products introduced by potential advertisers. Above all, it's fallen victim to the lure of one fantasy after another.

Part of this is the lingering influence of the cataclysm referred to by the Adobe programmer—the sudden demise of the typesetting industry. Not so much the changeover from lead to cold type, but the destruction, within around four years, of a thriving industry and its replacement by Macintosh-based publishing.

Every time a new hot product comes on the scene, therefore, the temptation for its supporters is to say that its opponents are facing the fate of the typesetters, to wit, quick annihilation.

In actuality, *nobody* ever faces this fate. The typesetters confronted a unique, unwinnable situation. None of their very expensive equipment was compatible with the new way of doing things. Almost none

of their very expensive personnel even knew how to turn a Macintosh on. This left the typesetters with less chance to survive than an ice cream cone in a blast furnace, and so they vanished.

Nobody has faced any such challenge during the decade since. Think that PDF workflow, or EfiColor, or stochastic screening, or "the RGB workflow," or ICC color management, is the Next Big Thing? Not a problem. All of these are compatible with the current way of doing things. You can adopt them gradually, over a period of years if you like.

Beware, therefore, anyone predicting a fast victory for these things. And for ideas like the above that have been around for a long time, ask which ones have made progress in the marketplace, like the PDF workflow, and which are still at approximately zero, like the others, and then ask, if they're so good, *why?*

Be skeptical, also, of anything written about potentially large advertisers. Many magazines seem to recycle the fawning reviews of their products, which are always seen through 60^M30^Y-colored glasses and always seem to merit the highest rating.

In 1997, for example, one magazine took the rare step of featuring a review's findings in a large yellow box on the cover. It read, "Quark 4.0's Knockout Punch!"

Three years later, that metaphor was recycled for a different product: "With the release of Illustrator 9, Adobe delivers a knockout punch, including transparency and Web-focused features that just may change the way we think about vector illustration programs."

The knockout punch that these featherweights delivered was to the chin of any user who tried to employ them in real jobs.

These programs were the two most incompetent and buggiest releases of the decade.

Even when a program isn't buggy, the same adulation is apt to be found. Photoshop 5 was extremely difficult to learn, and was surely the most controversial and frequently criticized upgrade of the decade.

Here's how one major magazine foresaw this, in the course of awarding Photoshop 5 five stars:

> I'm struck by the program's continued simplicity and ease of use. While the learning curve of other pixel-pushers seems to get sharply steeper with each upgrade, Photoshop still lets the casual user get out with a minimum of fuss...if you're inclined to find fault with software, you'll find slim pickings in Photoshop 5.

Slim pickings? But what of the banquet of color issues? Listen:

> Color handling gets lots of attention in this release. Photoshop's proprietary Gamma Control panel (for matching the monitor to the output) has been supplemented with support for Kodak ICC profiles, a more ecumenical solution. (The first time you open an image from earlier Photoshop versions, you'll see a color-conversion message.) Favoring Web design over Photoshop's traditional print production uses, Adobe has chosen to make the new standard RGB color space the default profile. This is intended to make image colors consistent across varied systems with disparate monitors.

*　*　*

Not to put too fine a point on it, the above is pure smoke, designed to cover the fact that the reviewer had no clue what the new color features did, and rather than reveal ignorance by finding someone to explain them to him, he declared them good.

This kind of emperor's-new-clothes syndrome has become more common as products have become more complex. People who are professional writers as opposed to graphic artists have a much harder time than they used to.

Unfortunately, most of what we read *is* written by professional writers. There are over 100 Photoshop books, for example, and at best two dozen are by people who seem to be reasonably fluent with the program. Of these, my quick count finds half a dozen whose skills are such that they could walk into a production facility today and get a job as a Photoshop operator. And of these, as far as I know I am the only one who has spent a lot of time working for service providers, which, because of its broad exposure to the way a lot of people work, is exceedingly helpful in understanding how the overall market functions.

As for general-purpose graphic arts writing, the odds of finding a knowledgeable writer get even slimmer. This accounts for a whole slew of ideas that were widely accepted as inevitable, but fizzled out in the real world. Some of these were calibrationist ideas, some were merely foolish, but the failure of all could have been—and were, by myself and others—predicted.

The Dustbin of History

In 1999, a commercial printer won an industry prize for producing, on a waterless press, a job using a halftone screen of—get ready—1,210.8 lines per inch. I was thinking of flying in and challenging the finding by saying that the screen was only 1,210.7, but I had other worries at the time, so the result stands.

What useful purpose is served by so fine a screen escapes me. Even in this book, which employs a paltry 133 lines, it's hard to detect that the pictures aren't in fact continuous-tone. And 175 lines is common; 200, even 300, is achievable without excessive perspiration on the part of those who want to do it.

And yet, for nearly two years in the mid-1990s, every industry forum trumpeted the forthcoming universal adoption of a technology called stochastic screening—the use of incredibly small (almost, say, 1,200 lines per inch) spots placed randomly rather than in a fixed pattern, to create the illusion of continuous tone. Not only that, but it would also eliminate moiré, the disagreeable image waver thought to be caused when the screening pattern—which doesn't exist in a stochastic screen—interferes with a pattern in the art.

Anybody with experience in these matters will know that moiré is as often than not found in the digital file, and in such cases the screen pattern has little to do with it. The art in Figure 15.1 would look far better with a stochastic screen, but Figures 15.6 and 15.7 will moiré just as happily as they do here. Plus, most observers can't tell the difference between a finely screened conventional reproduction and one that uses a stochastic screen. And, anyone with stripping experience would know that very small dots are hard to handle.

The technology was expensive. It did not offer enough benefits to compensate for some clear disadvantages. It now hangs on in only a few places where it has merit—in flexo and other poor printing conditions where the alternative is a very coarse screen, or for fifth and subsequent colors where there may be a screen angling issue.

Accordingly, predicting that stochastic screening would fail in the general market was a no-brainer for anyone with significant print experience. But, as usual in such cases, anybody who opposed the received wisdom was immediately called dinosaur, Luddite, etc. And this pattern has repeated itself several times in the last decade, offering some interesting lessons in the process.

Before beginning this survey, allow me to point out that, for all the flak I have taken from vendors for pointing out when their breakthroughs are hokum, on the whole I have been considerably ahead of the conventional wisdom with my predictions. I advocated Photoshop for high-end color, PDF for prepress, Kodak Photo CDs, studio digital photography, desktop scanning, the use of LAB in color correction, the Web as a business model, desktop contract proofing, and the need of photographers to expand their horizons into CMYK, years before these concepts had any wide support. Even today, I'm probably the only authority saying that the advent of consumer-priced digital cameras changes everything, and that in the near future every graphic artist will also be a photographer.

Granted, I didn't think that there was going to be any wide adoption of large-format printing, and was proved resoundingly wrong. But when I've erred it's usually been in predicting that changes will happen too soon. I thought color desktop printing for the masses would catch on earlier than it did; I thought medium-sized color separation shops would be history three years before they actually died. But I have been successful in pointing out certain products that were predestined to fail despite being supported by the conventional wisdom. Stochastic screening was one of these. Here are some others, in more or less diminishing order of ridiculousness.

• **The dumbed-down scanner**. The idea of scanning all images to exactly the same settings was forcefully advocated by Kodak in the early 1990s, the idea being to capture all conceivable detail and to match the film exactly. This naïve incarnation of pure calibrationism flopped because in real life, nobody wants to match the art, and in real life, nobody cares whether the scanner is theoretically capable of capturing data that the photographer did not happen to supply.

• **The worship of the monitor**. One of the most cherished tenets of early calibrationism was that hard proofs and by-the-numbers color would fall by the wayside, as it became possible to rely totally on monitor appearance.

While a calibrated monitor is much to be recommended, relying on it *totally,* without reference to any numbers, doesn't work, because of the human visual system's inconvenient insistence on recalibrating itself to whatever light source may be hitting it. We react to brilliant highlights by desensitizing ourselves to them, allowing us to overlook objectionable detail. And the more we look at an image with a cast, thanks to the human phenomenon of chromatic adaptation, the more the cast vanishes.

A well-maintained screen can be accurate for relations between colors and, especially, to give a sense of overall darkness. By all means, calibrate it—just don't rely on it for highlights, shadows, or neutral colors. That is why we have an Info palette.

• **The ideal separation machine**. The conventional wisdom at one time was virtually unanimous that we would all adopt an "RGB workflow." This implied that all files would be worked on and stored only in RGB. The necessary conversion to CMYK for printing would be done at the time of imagesetting, without human intervention. A 1993 magazine titled one of its lead stories "CMYK: On the Way Out" and continued: "The winds of digital change, blowing harder every day, will soon reach gale force. ...Signs, portents, and products abound: RGB will be the communications format of the just-over-the-horizon future. Graphic arts professionals, diversify."

In 1995, at the prestigious Seybold conference, Agfa, a leading graphic arts vendor, was so certain that CMYK was going away that it sponsored a session entitled "Dealing with the CMYK Heritage," which focused on how we would cope with those few quaint, antique CMYK files that might still be floating about once we had all switched over to RGB.

The market, however, didn't agree. Far from moving toward RGB for print files, typical users strode briskly in the direction of more use of CMYK.

As ordinarily happens in such cases, the rhetoric of the evangelists became more strident as it became more clear that the idea was going the way of EfiColor. By early 1997, one got up at a major conference and said, "Six months into the future, we will all discover that it's smarter to scan and save all our images in RGB and only convert them to CMYK at the RIP. Everyone will see the light one morning. We'll all wake up..."

Six months, six years, sixty years, it really matters not. The success of the RGB workflow rests on an extremely shaky, not to say nonexistent, foundation: the ability to create a perfect separation algorithm.

As we will see in Chapter 11, this is a mythical beast. RGB and CMYK are too different. Any algorithm will do well on certain images and not so well on others. In those cases, a subsequent correction will be necessary for those interested in top qual-ity. A workflow that emphasizes the use of RGB in correction is viable. One that forbids the use of CMYK under any circumstances is not.

Because I realized that the conventional wisdom had fallen victim to a calibrationist assumption that was incorrect, I was quite comfortable being the only voice in the industry saying that the RGB workflow was not going to happen.

One can't blame people for failing to appreciate this fairly sophisticated colorspace theory trap, or for that matter a corollary: that if you were to choose a workflow like this, to generate new files automatically into whatever colorspace was desired, both LAB and CMYK would be better storage spaces than RGB.

What people should have figured out, though, was that if this were going to happen it would have happened a long time ago. RGB files are only three-quarters as large as their CMYK counterparts, and all mathematical operations take three-quarters as long. This would have been a huge attraction for an RGB workflow in the days when computing power and disk space were extremely expensive.

If only it had worked. Today, far more people prepare their files for print in CMYK than they did when RGB was so unanimously declared to be inevitable.

• **The hyperactive user base**. One of the main attributes of the graphic arts is inertia. The market does change—slowly—when confronted with new proposals that are clearly much better than the existing way, but they really have to be a *lot* better. Also, it carries grudges for a long time.

There was about a two-year period in the middle of the 1990s when Macintoshes were both more expensive and less powerful than the competition. This caused a flurry of press speculation that the graphics industry would migrate to the PC. Of course, this was preposterous, and I wasn't the only one to say so at the time. The expense of retraining oneself is far greater than the pennies one might save on a different brand of computer. Plus, PCs had a bad name that they had earned several years back. Today, the Macintosh dominance among top professionals is approximately what it was back then.

This same error, overestimating the willingness of the market to make changes, accounted for a great deal of bombast in magazines in 1998 and 1999, announcing how a forthcoming product, Adobe's InDesign, was not merely a serious threat to the leading page design program, but a veritable "Quark killer."

What InDesign wound up killing was Adobe's bottom line; the company had to take a charge in 2000 when sales fell far short of expectations. Quark has never had great relations with its customers, but that's not enough to make them walk away from its product. The company's recent upgrades have been less than reliable; if that continues and if InDesign continues to improve, then in a couple of years we may see a significant move. InDesign is in many ways an impressive product, and it avoided the fatal error of an overly buggy first release. But the early coverage lavished on it was a waste of ink and paper.

The same error—supporting a method that is arguably better, but not sufficiently so to motivate many people to spend money or otherwise inconvenience themselves—has pervaded coverage of color management throughout the decade.

• **The repurposing phantom**. It's been apparent for a very long time that more images are being prepared for placement in more than one destination. Today the most common example is both print and Web, but it's not unheard of for a single image to go to half a dozen, or even more, different output conditions.

This undeniable trend has been used as an excuse to predict all manner of industry revolutions, chiefly pertaining to color management, secondarily to RGB workflows. The idea being that anyone who needs to have files prepared for more than one purpose, for, say, a newspaper ad, an annual report, and the Web, should use a single master file, which would be magically massaged by computer in such a way that the three properly configured files would emerge from it, phoenix-like.

Sounds good, but who would actually do that? A rough equality of the three images is possible, but it would be the equality of mediocrity. Somebody interested in top quality would have to forget the above scheme in favor of handling all three files individually, for sharpening reasons if nothing else. Somebody not interested in quality at all would surely not invest time or money in this solution. The potential market, therefore, is those users who are looking for good but not great quality, and are willing to spend money to achieve it.

• **The great service provider conspiracy**. In early 1996, a prominent color management advocate expressed the conventional wisdom as follows: "New types of media and new types of process color printing are also driving color management into the prepress industry...prepress shops are turning to color management solutions to deal with the new world of RGB images....Thanks to all these developments, the prepress industry is slowly beginning to see color management as a necessity rather than a threat."

The opposite happened. Prepress shops overwhelmingly rejected most of the color management innovations of Photoshop 5 and strongly advised their customers to do the same. This prompted violent condemnations from color management supporters, none of whom, to my knowledge, had ever worked in a prepress shop.

If they had, they would have realized that the way Photoshop 5 presented color management was so unwieldy as to be unworkable in that environment. Since they did not understand this, they might have been clued in by the magnitude of the rejection. Many service providers don't like a PDF workflow. Many photographers don't like to work in CMYK. But quite a few of each group have adopted these practices. This doesn't prove that the concepts are great or that they will replace past practice, but it does demonstrate that there is a certain merit to them.

By contrast, the reaction of the service providers to Photoshop 5 was virtually unanimous. In such a case, a sensible observer would have to conclude that there was something seriously wrong—even if the observer didn't understand what that thing was.

The Best of Both Worlds

The fraction of color management that some service providers adopted was a meritorious one. A standard method of conversion is an idea whose time should have come many years ago.

Guns don't kill people, the saying goes. Nor do ICC profiles kill color. One doesn't have to adopt a tagged workflow to enjoy their advantages. Instead, we can graft a profile onto the traditional system. That is, we make an assumption about the incoming file, rather than rely on a tag, and alter the colors in accord with that assumption.

To be truly a traditional workflow, this conversion has to take place in the output device. However, Photoshop lets us convert the file before it gets there, which to my way of thinking is very much the same thing.

This hybrid method has few drawbacks and a lot of advantages. Suppose that you would as soon jump out of an airplane without a parachute as use a "color management system" but that you own an color printer, which you want to calibrate.

Annoyingly, the current alternative to using an ICC profile somewhere is to embrace something like the sorry, moth-eaten excuse for a color-adjustment interface that is the left half of Figure 10.4.

That is a losing proposition. Fortunately, a hybrid method exists. Your files merely have to be consistent. And they can be transformed in the printer in the time-honored way, with an assumption about what the file is, rather than an embedded tag.

Furthermore, there is no need to hire a consultant to do this for you, although

Figure 10.5 *A typical group of swatches used to create profiles with the aid of artificial measurements.*

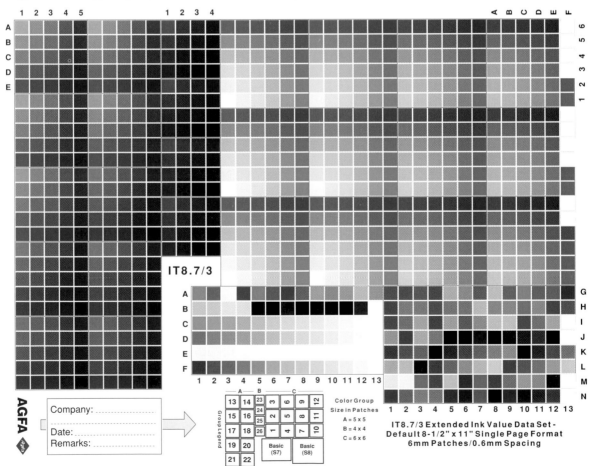

many consultants would have you believe otherwise. And there is no need to purchase measurement hardware or special profiling software, although even more vendors would have you believe that this is essential. The fact is, you can do better *without* the expensive bells and whistles.

Of Scientists and Artists

There is nothing calibrationist in the idea that a profile, or whatever you want to call the method that transforms an incoming file into whatever colors an output device needs, should be as accurate as possible. The calibrationism enters in the form of the currently politically fashionable way of generating one, which is to print something like the swatches of Figure 10.5, painstakingly measure their values with some artificial device, and let software do the rest.

This method has proven helpful to some, usually those who haven't used any method of calibration for ten years and to whom anything seems an improvement. To those, however, who can do the trick themselves, using the instruments that nature has provided, these machine-generated profiles seem as pitifully inadequate as a machine-generated poem or a digital symphony.

Calibration is, after all, the art—and to a much lesser extent, the science—of making images look alike. The human eyes are vastly better at making this determination than any artificial measurement device. Our perception of color has proven too complicated to be reduced to rules understandable even by humanity's best minds —let alone a machine.

A lot of people have thought hard about the matter. Occasionally, flashes of brilliant insight have resulted. Usually, these have come from scientists.

For example, normal correction methods call for finding a dark point, and forcing it to $80^C70^M70^Y70^K$ or something similar. Such a color is neutral, which baffles some beginners. After all, if the shadow is in the middle of a forest, wouldn't it more likely be a very dark green than a very dark gray?

Possibly to a camera, but not to a human observer. This interesting aspect of perception was first pointed out more than 500 years ago, by a scientist, no less.

This hypothesis, however, can't be reached by measurements or any other form of conventional science. Its development requires the services of a rather special scientist, one with a considerable artistic sensitivity. The particular scientist who thought this rule up, a gentleman named da Vinci, qualified in this regard.

If confronted with this imaginary photograph of a forest, da Vinci's writings indicate that he would have known why we retouchers always intensify the variation between greens. A fuller explanation of the theory of simultaneous contrast took some later work from another artistically inclined scientist, a physicist named Newton, but da Vinci basically got it.

That the photograph would also have to be gray-balanced was demonstrated by the work of a 19th-century French chemist and connoisseur of fine art, M.E. Chevreul. And here, from 1878, is another scientist's advice on our current topic, calibration:

> We forgive, then, a partial denial of the truths of colour more easily than those of light and shade, which probably is a result of the nature of the optical education of the race. For the human race, thus far, light and shade has been the all-important element in the recognition of external objects; colour has played only a

subordinate part, and has been rather a source of pleasure than of positive utility.

* * *

If there were only one thing to learn about calibration, this would be it.

This wisdom came from an American named Ogden Rood, who was a professor of physics, but one with an extraordinary aesthetic sense. If he had had to make his monitor match his proof, he would have known enough to think in LAB. And he'd have said, the L is the key; the A is far less important, and the B's impact is almost negligible.

All Greek to Them

Rood would turn over in his grave at the method used by most of the automated profile generators of today. Talk to somebody who is in the calibration biz (as opposed to the rest of us, who calibrate, but not for a living) and you will hear a lot about a very frightening-sounding concept called Δe, pronounced "delta-E." This is a mathematical model of how well colors match one another, using LAB variation as its base. Often one hears the success of a calibration or measurement discussed in terms of how little Δe (read, how little inaccuracy) there is.

Thus who are buffaloed by gamma—er, γ settings—know the power of Greek letters to intimidate. You hear them, you daren't ask questions. For example, one question my calibrationist friends ought to ask is, is Δe even remotely similar to the process by which a human evaluates color match?

The answer, regrettably, is no. If somebody tells you that your color is accurate to within 6Δe, that it's 68 degrees outside, and that the average weight of the defensive line of the 100^C100^Y Bay Packers is 280 pounds, all three of these statistics have about equal relevance to whether the color actually matches. Δe wildly understates the importance of the L, and also makes the preposterous blunder of assigning equal weight to the A and B. The intelligent color manager therefore says, Φ on Δe.

Figure 10.6 demonstrates a fundamental flaw in machine-generated profiles. To an artificial color-measurement device, these two swatches are just two colors that must be matched as closely as possible, just like any others. To Photoshop's Info palette, one is $10^C40^M10^Y$ and the other $10^C40^M50^Y$.

$10^C40^M10^Y$, as it happens, is the color of bubble gum, but of not much else. $10^C40^M50^Y$, as it happens, is a common fleshtone value for Hispanics, Asians, and dark-haired Caucasians.

These two colors are not of equal importance, folks. In deciding whether two devices match one another, one is vastly more significant. A human color manager grasps this without too much difficulty, and can make the necessary adjustment.

For example, suppose that I have software that generates profiles based on machine readings of these two colors, among others. Presumably a reasonable profile will emerge if I do nothing, but a better one is possible if I cheat by printing the bubble-gum target with darker ink values than the software is expecting.

In such a case, my cheating profile will not produce very good bubble gum. It will turn out lighter than it should, because the profile thinks the values that would actually work would instead produce something too dark. Similarly, my profile would have trouble reproducing the swatches of Figure 10.5 accurately.

Little sleep need be lost over this. We get paid to reproduce pictures, not swatches.

Those pictures are a lot more likely to contain fleshtones than they are bubble gum. The lightest parts of my fleshtones would be subject to the same effect as the bubble gum: they would print too light—in the opinion of the color-measurement device. But the opinion of the human observer would be very different. A human would evaluate the bubble gum as being too light, true. But the fleshtones would be seen as having more luminosity variation. Just as everyone sees the two greens in Figure 10.1 as being different, everyone would see the fleshtones created by my ersatz profile as being more accurate than those done the way the software is designed to operate.

Look for the Pattern

The fact that artificial devices don't do well at generating profiles doesn't mean you shouldn't buy them, any more than the fact that a person is a bad golfer means that he can't correct color. We all have our skills. Machines are very bad at telling whether images look alike, but they are rather good at telling whether a certain color is the same color that it was yesterday. In fact, they are much better at this than we are.

Accordingly, once we are satisfied that we have calibrated things, these devices are extraordinarily useful in making sure they stay that way. They are terrible at determining what the right measurements are but great at verifying that once the right ones are known, they don't change from day to day.

Similarly, although machine-generated profiles are generally going to be inadequate for the needs of color professionals, they are considerably better than nothing for persons of limited color experience. Some printers now come with automated

routines whereby they print their own swatches, scan them, and try to calibrate themselves.

Also, the price of third-party packages that generate a profile from measurements continues to plummet. A measuring device is still needed, but one can put together a package now for less than $1,000. Plus, they're getting easier to operate.

But the basic argument for using one of these has to be that the machine can analyze the characteristics of images better than you can. For typical users, that may be true. It's hard for most people to tell whether images are consistently too green or whether they aren't magenta enough.

That sort of decision requires experienced eyes, and also some discretion. The big trap that not just calibrationists but some logical people fall into is assuming that all unsatisfactory matches are the result of poor calibration techniques.

Maybe they are—but there are often other explanations. For calibration to be at fault, there has to be some kind of pattern. It may be gross, as in almost all images are too green, or something very subtle.

Either way, there's a simple test. Ask yourself, is there a pattern? And if so, would you be able to correct for it in Photoshop?

Suppose, for example, that you are trying to make your monitor agree with the results you're getting back from a certain print shop. If that is not currently happening, it's probably a bad Custom CMYK setting on your part, but it could be a lot of other things—it doesn't really matter.

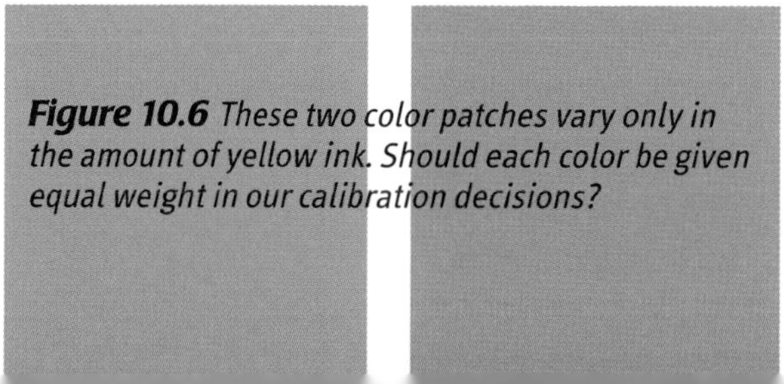

Figure 10.6 These two color patches vary only in the amount of yellow ink. Should each color be given equal weight in our calibration decisions?

It also doesn't matter whether you think the printed product looks bad. The question is, can you call up the file in Photoshop and apply some kind of curves or whatnot to make it look on screen the way it looks in print, or at least to be a closer match. If you can't, it's probably not a calibration issue, but one of capabilities. If you can, then the question is whether that same series of commands would also make most other images match the print more closely.

If it wouldn't, the issue is probably one of process control. If half of the images show up too light and the other half too dark, and half of them are too colorful and the other half too 40^K, you can try to calibrate until you turn 100^{C}70^M in the face and only succeed in making matters worse.

But if you've gotten this far in the book, you should be able to detect whether there's a pattern; you should be able to calibrate your monitor with any one of several options; and, assuming that your final output is CMYK, you should be able to generate a plausible Custom CMYK for every printer

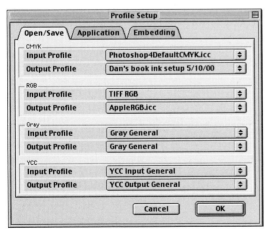

Figure 10.7 *Photoshop profiles can be used by many other applications. This dialog box from Heidelberg Prepress's LinoColor Elite uses profiles generated by Photoshop's Custom CMYK.*

you deal with, especially after you read the next two chapters. And that Custom CMYK is an ICC profile, which can be exchanged with others or used in a variety of methods.

Figure 10.7, for example, comes from the scanner-control package LinoColor Elite, but it uses profiles that I generated in Photoshop's Custom CMYK. This opens several interesting possibilities of cooperation between programs.

If you are dubious about making this kind of profile because the trade press tells you you should hire somebody with a spectrophotometer and fancy software to do it, here's an important question for you:

Whaddaya, crazy?

This is a comparison of two technologies. The cheaper one—the artificial color-measurement devices—offers repeatability from day to day, but little more. The expensive alternative—your eyes—is vastly more sophisticated, works under a far broader range of conditions, has a longer Mean Time Between Failures, detects more minute differences, evaluates colors in context, and is in every other way, except repeatability, a superior instrument.

The idea is to make things look alike. The idea that something other than the human eye can make this determination is highly dubious. Use the eye, not the machine, and your profiles will be not just cheaper and faster to produce, but *better.*

There are some scientists who argue for artificiality, but the scientists with artistic sensibility have long known better. Here's a vote for anticalibrationism from one of the very best writers the English language has ever produced. The writer, a Mr. Darwin, was also a biologist of some repute.

It is scarcely possible to avoid comparing the eye to a telescope. We know that this instrument has been perfected by the long-continued efforts of the highest human intellects; and we naturally infer that the eye has been formed by a somewhat analogous process. But may not this inference be presumptuous? Have we any right to assume that the Creator works by intellectual powers like those of man? If we must compare the eye to an optical instrument, we ought in imagination to take a thick layer of transparent tissue, with a nerve sensitive to light beneath, and then suppose every part of this layer to be continually changing slowly in density so as to separate into layers of different densities and thickness, placed at different distances from each other, and with the surfaces of each layer slowly changing in form. Further we must suppose that there is a power always intently watching each slight accidental alteration in the transparent layers; and carefully selecting each alteration which, under varied circumstances, may in any way, or in any degree, tend to produce a distincter image. We must suppose each new state of the instrument to be multiplied by the million; and each to be preserved till a better be produced, and then the old ones to be destroyed. In living bodies, variation will cause the slight alterations, generation will multiply them almost infinitely, and natural selection will pick out with unerring skill each improvement. Let this process go on for millions on millions of years; and during each year on millions of individuals of many kinds; and may we not believe that a living optical instrument might thus be formed as superior to one of glass, as the works of the Creator are to those of man?

A System that Works

The artificial instruments are at least predictable and reliable in what they do. That's a lot more than can be said for many of the output devices we have to cope with.

Certain parts of the process, such as imagesetting or photo lab work, can be very well controlled, and introduce little inconsistency into our results. Certain others, such as the monitors viewers use, and, most especially, printing presses, are so fractious and unpredictable that they threaten the viability of whatever calibration method we choose.

Quality-oriented printing firms invest a lot of time and money trying to control this variability. Even under the best of circumstances, however, the printing will be somewhat unpredictable. Temperature, humidity, the speed the press is being run at, how recently the units were washed, the order the inks are printed in, blanket pressure, the location of the images on the form, whether the printing is on the calendared side of the paper, and, most importantly, whether the pressman is in a good mood that day or not, are but some of the things that often cause surprises in print.

This quandary scares people, but there's nothing at all new about it. Printing was unpredictable long before color got to the desktop. So it is not surprising that a system evolved to take care of most of the problems. The system still works.

It relies on the skills of the pressmen, who have considerable control over the product during the run. The traditional method, therefore, is to supply them with some kind of proof, which they then attempt to match through various permutations of dial-twiddling when the job gets to press. Thus, we don't have to concern ourselves with specifics of the press—only of the proof. We rely on the printer to do the rest, which is an advantage if the printer is competent, and a disadvantage otherwise.

This sounds somewhat backwards, and strikes some who don't know much about printing as the wrong way to do things. It certainly has its undesirable aspects, but is equally certainly the lesser of the evils.

Those experienced in the field therefore calibrate to the proof, not to the press. They do this for two reasons: first, even under the best printing conditions, the proof is far more stable. Perhaps more important, the contrary approach would never work in real life with larger printers. When we send a job to them, we don't know which of their many presses it will print on; they may not actually know themselves until it's time to hang the plates.

Whether calibrating to the press and not the proof will always be the way is somewhat of a $60^C50^M50^Y$ area. A trend in press design is to make them to some extent self-calibrating. This is particularly so with the newer generation of high-speed copiers and other unconventional presses. Often these devices aren't operated by skilled people, and the vendors are trying hard to help them out.

For the next several years, however, the traditional model will dominate.

The Superior Measuring Device

Even those who sell machine-made profiles admit that they "tune" them by eyeball, often several times, before giving them to clients. This brings up the question of why bother to do the initial measurements at all, but rather just load some assumed settings, and "tune" those, as I do.

Whether profiles are better the eyeball way or the machine-measurement way is largely irrelevant. If you want to be successful, you have to learn the eyeball method. In calibrationist heaven, all owners of print shops and the like furnish us with their own custom-made profiles, which we use with great confidence.

Back on this planet, print shops give us deedledy-bop, or occasionally a canned profile of highly dubious quality. To that, some suggest asking them very politely to run color swatches for us on the press and paper that will be used for the live job. This is, in the real world, a good way to find oneself face down in an empty 55-gallon drum of isopropyl alcohol.

A lot of the time, if not

Figure 10.8 *Perception is affected by neighboring colors. A monitor with a colored background warps the view of anyone trying to evaluate the picture.*

MAKING THINGS LOOK ALIKE

✓The traditional method of calibration assumes that all output devices behave approximately like average web presses, so that one file will serve for any CMYK output condition. This may imply changing incoming files on the fly to account for the way the output device actually behaves.

✓In many cases, however, the traditional method is too inaccurate for serious work. In such circumstances, it becomes up to the user to characterize the behavior of the output device, and then create a *profile* of it, which is a snooty way of saying, figure out what it takes to make the damn thing print correctly.

✓When speaking of CMYK output, *profile* means whatever is found in CMYK Working Space under Edit: Color Settings. This can be a profile that's one of Photoshop's defaults, one supplied by a third party, or one you build yourself with Photoshop's Custom CMYK dialog.

✓When a monitor consistently doesn't match printed output, there can be many explanations, but by far the most common is that Custom CMYK is incorrect.

✓All profiles generated in Photoshop, including those originating in Custom CMYK, comply with ICC specifications, which are intended to create a uniform format. Accordingly, Photoshop profiles can often be used in other applications, and not just those originated by Adobe.

✓The human visual system has its own powerful system of color management. A color changes appearance if there is a change in neighboring colors. This ability to see colors in context is not shared by artificial devices. Humans are, consequently, much better than machines at deciding whether two images look alike.

✓Human vision is self-calibrating in that it neutralizes any color imbalance in the ambient lighting. Unfortunately, this neutralization effect also occurs when staring at a monitor. Because of this, some color casts that would be obvious in print can't be detected on the screen—or at least, people can't detect them.

✓The most important factor in calibration is luminosity, or relative darkness. If this is correct, it will far outweigh minor variations in color.

✓If you are panicked by color management, relax. Many expert opinions have been proven wrong in the past. If you understand the basic principles, it won't matter what version of Photoshop you use or how you choose to manage color.

most of the time, you'll be calibrating to new printing conditions using the by-guess-and-by-gosh method. That is, you get no swatches, no profile, what you get is a bunch of images that look too green and too dark, so you tweak a few settings and hope they work better on the next job.

Not only that, the clear trend now is in the direction of individual users making their own color proofs, using desktop printing technology. Many of these printers can achieve colors that a press can't. It is accordingly easy to produce a "proof" that has zero chance of being matched even remotely in print. When pressmen discover this during a run, they lose their sense of humor completely. These guys push around half-ton rolls of paper as though they were tennis balls. They have muscles Arnold Schwarzenegger would envy. Some of them are particularly muscular from the neck up. You do *not* want to give these people unmatchable proofs.

You therefore will learn to calibrate by eye, or you'll never be able to adjust to certain print conditions, and you'll never be able to persuade your print vendor that your proofs are reliable enough.

Beyond that, if you wish to calibrate by machine, go ahead; like almost all other color management methods, they're compatible with the general approach of this book. But even if you refuse to rely on what your eyes tell you, rely on your common sense, a commodity that is often lost in these arguments.

Figure 10.8 is an example. How many people spend lots of time and money cali-brating, and then do their work on a screen like this? The background will change color perception just as surely as it did in Figure 10.1. Unless it's gray, serious calibration of the monitor is useless.

Or, how about people who calibrate once and ignore the topic thereafter? Print conditions change over time. Monitor conditions change rapidly. Keeping calibrated requires constant discipline. Checking a monitor once a day against a proof or other known result isn't excessive.

Above all, how about people who accept the conventional wisdom blindly? How much money, how much time have they wasted studying or even buying into concepts that never had a chance?

As I hope this chapter has indicated, I *do* believe fairly strongly in calibration. But I do not make a religion of it; I insist that science and mathematics be my servants and not my master; when I see an image that looks lousy I say so even if a machine says it looks good. And so, I am not a cali-brationist, but I am a color manager.

If someone offers you what seems like a plausible scientific argument, like, say, offering to trot out an artificial instrument to measure whether the two greens of Figure 10.1 are the same, take a deep breath and think it over. If you allow yourself to be buffaloed by technology into believing things that your own eyes and intelligence can tell you are false, if you believe those two greens to be the same even though you and every other human perceive them as different—well, then, beware. Tomorrow's calibrationist could be *you*.

Managing Separation And Color Settings

Photoshop 6 picks up the pieces of Photoshop 5 and combines them into a single dialog. Getting good conversions with it depends on understanding a sad, paradoxical law: the more you try for perfection, the farther away from it you'll get.

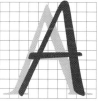

American football is played on a rectangular field roughly 50 by 100 yards, exclusive of the end zones. The field in the Canadian version of the game is about 10 yards wider in each direction.

The larger field mandates certain rule changes. For one thing, Canadian teams have a twelfth player. There are only three downs, rather than four. Although the passing game is emphasized, the same plays work in both games, and the same skills differentiate the star player from the mediocre one.

A football fan therefore adjusts easily to watching either version of the sport. But suppose that the differences were much greater. Imagine a kind of football played on the side of a hill, rather than on a flat surface, and on a trapezoidal, rather than rectangular, field, with a brook and a few trees in the middle of it.

Once you realize that in such a game the set plays and strategies familiar to fans of either version would no longer necessarily work, you are well on the way to understanding why so many people have trouble making decent color separations. To be more precise, they are having trouble making the transition into CMYK.

For that matter, we are starting to need new types of separations that involve different flavors of CMYK (as for both a newspaper and an annual report) or devices that use more than four inks or toners in an effort to get snappier color.

Prepress professionals don't have a whole lot of experience in solving this problem. Until recently, most separations were done on drum scanners that converted to CMYK on the fly. An RGB file never existed, so the question of whether the CMYK file looked like the RGB never came up.

Jumping to the conclusion that making the conversion must be easy, if only one spends enough on color-measurement devices and software, various parties have hyped "solutions" which, quite predictably, the market has emphatically rejected.

These products haven't flown, but not because of a lack of sophistication or inadequate computing power. The whole concept is wrong. Those whose quest is the perfect separation algorithm are chasing rainbows, setting traps for unicorns.

Indeed, the perfect separation method is a mythical creature, but one with a substantial sting: the closer one tries to get to it, the farther away it seems to be. This chapter will try to explain why, review the changes in Photoshop 6's color settings, and suggest how to adjust them to deliver better results.

Decisions and Damage Control

Translating between colorspaces is only hard when the rules they play by are radically different. A monitor and a transparency have slightly different gamuts, but the differences in what colors can be had are small in the overall scheme of things. So it isn't difficult to create RGB files that more or less match the chrome. It is also easy to adjust one professional digital proofing system, such as Iris, to match another, such as Approval, or to match a digital proof to a traditional film-based contract proof such as a Matchprint.

Going from RGB to CMYK is not nearly as simple. Some people say that this is because the playing field is smaller, naïvely ignoring that it is tilted as well. Let's take a quick survey of what RGB can portray that CMYK can't—and vice versa. For this, you will need your imagination. While I can tell you what colors aren't possible in CMYK, for obvious reasons, I can't *show* you.

The differences can (and should) be divided into two categories: color and contrast. Contrast is mostly a matter of how bright and how dark the white and black points are. In this area, CMYK is pretty lame. The blacks are washed out, and we can't make a white any brighter than the paper we are printing on.

Because there is less of a darkness range available, the CMYK practitioner needs to emphasize contrast. In football or hockey, a larger playing surface rewards speed and finesse, and a smaller one favors physical strength. CMYK is much the same thing, but for physical strength, read luminosity. Ogden Rood was right. It's more important to control contrast than color. The worse our printing conditions get, the more we can let the color go unmarked in the interest of getting more bite.

But the playing field, in addition to being smaller, is also weirdly shaped. The popular knock against CMYK is that is lacks the the color range of RGB. In most respects, that's correct. But in others, it has more. Let's contrast the capabilities of a monitor to those of commercial printing.

The building blocks of each are different. A monitor's phosphors are red, green, and blue, highly convenient if pure red, green, or blue appears in the image. On press, red, green, and blue are each mixtures of two inks, which is a disadvantage. On the other hand, CMYK is well equipped to produce pure cyan, magenta, and yellow.

Especially yellow. It's technically the purest ink. Under good printing conditions, a stronger yellow is available than can be seen even in positive film, let alone displayed on a monitor. Solid magenta and cyan also can be as intense on paper as they are on a screen.

As these colors get lighter, however, CMYK has more trouble with them. Bubble-gum pink is a shade of magenta, so you might think that you could portray it as well in print as on a monitor. No way. As colors get lighter, they get represented by smaller and smaller dots, and accordingly, larger and larger quantities of blank, featureless paper. The monitor has no such dot structure, and can create much more appetizing-looking bubble gum.

And the notorious weakness of print work is that cyan ink does not mix well with magenta. Therefore, although reds and greens in CMYK are somewhat worse than those available in RGB, the blues of CMYK are far worse.

Figure 11.1 shows one manufacturer's conception of the gamut differences, contrasting the capabilities of a monitor, normal CMYK, and a six-color process.

To summarize the differences: in CMYK we have better yellows, about the same magentas and cyans, but lousy reds, worse greens, and disastrous blues, in comparison to RGB. As the colors get lighter, everything changes in favor of RGB, except the CMYK

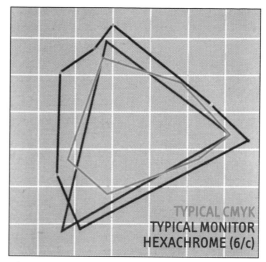

Figure 11.1 *The tilted playing field. A comparison of the gamuts of a generalized CMYK versus that of a typical monitor and of six-color printing. Note that in spite of CMYK's terrible weakness in the blue corner (lower left) it is still capable of certain colors that a monitor can't reproduce.*

disadvantage in blues is minimized. Also, CMYK lacks contrast generally.

That is a clear case of playing by different rules. When the differences are this complex, beware of anybody saying they have a foolproof conversion. They simply haven't met sufficiently talented fools.

A Question of Aesthetics

The aspen forest of Figure 11.2 speaks starkly about the injustices of CMYK. It's an outstanding image—in RGB. It loses a lot in translation to the printed page.

In the original, the sky is lighter than what you see here, but also much bluer—a nearly luminous, icy, gorgeous light blue. I have more chance of playing tackle for the Edmonton Eskimos than of reproducing that color accurately in this book.

On the other hand, part of the reason the blue is so striking in the original is that it plays off against the bright yellows of the leaves, a CMYK strength. We are not at the limit of yellow ink yet. I can make those leaves yellower still, brighter than they were in the original. But *should* I?

Granted that we can't match the original or even come close, there are many ways to try to make the best of this bad situation.

Figure 11.2 *Brilliant blues are the major weakness of the CMYK colorspace. The sky in the RGB original of this image is an almost luminous blue, a blue that can't be reproduced in print.*

Should we:
- Tone down the yellow, to keep the relative balance with the blue?
- Ratchet the yellow up, to accentuate the contrast between yellow and blue?
- Wipe out any yellow or black ink in the sky, which will wipe out detail as well, yet make the sky seem bluer?
- Increase cyan ink in the sky, to make it bluer, albeit darker?
- Or, is the answer none of the above, but rather the image just as it appears here? Not too likely: this separation was done in Photoshop 5 using the default setting, which is not good for this type of image.

I've used this as a class problem, and the consensus is that the least evil approach here is to add cyan to the sky with Image: Adjust>Selective Color. That makes the sky more colorful, but darker, than the original.

Generically, though, this is a problem without a solution. Some images will look better if we make the blues darker. Others, such as the two underwater scenes shown at the end of Chapter 7, won't. Human beings make such aesthetic decisions routinely—and accurately. Profiles and other algorithms are rather bad at it.

The EIAM and the PCCM

Now, let's consider a general approach to converting a document from RGB into CMYK. I will kick off by proposing a method so preposterous that you may have trouble recognizing its intrinsic logic.

Here it is: for every RGB color that can be faithfully reproduced in CMYK, do it. For every color that can't, do something completely random, such as translate it into lime green. Because of this uncertainty, I dub this approach EIAM, which stands for Every Image an Adventure Method.

EIAM has, to put it mildly, distinct disadvantages. For example, if it is used to convert the aspen forest image, the sky will become lime green.

If this sounds very radical and unreasonable, it is, but no more so than the team it's up against. That opponent, the PCCM, tries to force the two colorspaces into the same shape, so that the brightest red, say, in RGB becomes the brightest red possible in CMYK, with all other reds being toned down to accommodate it. Often, PCCM profiles are created by software that relies on some artificial color-measurement device measuring swatches such as the one shown earlier in Figure 10.5.

Hence, the name I have chosen for it: the Politically Correct Calibrationist Method. PCCM is the wishy-washy approach of finesse and compromise, just as EIAM is the blunderbuss method of brute force and hope for the best.

Calibrationists often showcase their methods by wheeling out something like Figure 11.3 and showing what a great separation they can make out of it. Photoshop's "Olé No Moiré" and the Kodak's "Musicians" of Figure 9.8 are similar.

Not to rain on the parade, but let's have a quick analysis of the image. Critical detail exists in both highlights and shadows, there are out-of-gamut colors everywhere, there are neutral colors that must be retained, every hue is in use, there are fabric patterns prone to moiré, there are silvers and golds, and subtle shadings even in the most brilliant colors.

As of this writing, I have worked in graphic arts production for 27 years, processing perhaps a quarter of a million images coming from every imaginable source. Except in a calibration setting, I have yet to

Figure 11.3 *The conventional wisdom suggests testing a separation method with an image such as this one above, which is grossly atypical of real-world work.*

encounter one containing all these characteristics at once. If you wanted to create an image that is as far removed from reality as possible, as grossly atypical as human ingenuity can design, you could not do better than this one.

If you ever encounter such a monstrosity—don't hold your breath—PCCM is definitely the best way to separate it. Why a practical person should care, I have no clue.

PCCM succeeds in this once-in-a-lifetime case at a considerable price. Think about the critical color, blue. In the original RGB, there are certain blues that are simply too brilliant for CMYK. Lesser blues in this image *could* be reproduced accurately, if

we made them as blue as CMYK can. That is what EIAM, the steamroller, would do.

PCCM, the great compromiser, trying to retain a distinction between the two kinds of blues, tones both of them down—along with every other blue down the food chain.

That's fine in this particular image, but what if there were no brilliant blue in the original? Then the compromise would be pointless. We would be toning down our in-gamut blues for no reason. EIAM, which does no toning down of anything, would have a decided advantage here.

Despite its match-the-art aura, PCCM guarantees that we will *never* match the art—all colors will be toned down, and all images will look flatter than the original.

EIAM, on the other hand, is for the high roller. If the art can't be matched, catastrophe! But if it can, EIAM will do it, and in those images it will outscore PCCM.

A General Law, Sad but True

Which of these two proposed methods of separation is better depends on your definition of *better*. If the definition is, which produces more *acceptable* images, PCCM wins: it is stolid, stodgy, free from ridiculous errors, and boring.

It is also a recipe for mediocrity.

Suppose, though, that the question is, which works better *most of the time?*

Guess what! Most images don't contain

Figure 11.4 Real-world differences in separation method. Both sets of images were separated from the same LAB file and not corrected further. Both methods produce nearly the same darkness, but the one on the right creates slightly brighter colors. This can be an advantage if the subject's colors are fairly dull, as in the bottom images. However, it loses detail in bright colors: note the better strawberry in the top left version.

out-of-gamut colors. And for all those that don't, that silly EIAM will kick butt. How good can political correctness be, when an *absurd* method gets palpably better results on the majority of images?

EIAM *is* absurd. In real life we don't deliberately sabotage images, the way EIAM would to anything that contains an out-of-gamut color. So, if forced to choose one or the other, we have to pick PCCM, because even if we are dissatisfied with its results, we can perhaps fix them, which is more than can be said if EIAM starts dispensing lime-green pixels all over the place.

But intermediate approaches are possible—and quite practical. When confronted by an out-of-gamut color, EIAM drops back 15 yards and punts. One can, however, visualize a smarter scheme with all the advantages of EIAM. Such a method would execute a play-fake by substituting not lime green, but something closer to the actual hue. Granted, a lot of detail might vanish in these areas as a result.

With PCCM, we have acceptable color 100 percent of the time, but if its color isn't bad, neither is it good. With pure EIAM, we have a better image than PCCM maybe 60 percent of the time. The other 40 percent of cases are unacceptable, full of lime green.

The less ridiculous version of EIAM described above does better. It may beat PCCM 70 percent of the time. An additional 10 percent of the time the image will be acceptable, yet not as good as PCCM's. The remaining 20 percent will remain, well, unacceptable.

The time has now come to state the law that governs all transformations from one colorspace to another. It is a sad law, a rock-and-a-hard-place law, but an uncompromising, invariable one. Here it is:

The better the algorithm does on the typical image, the more prone it is to do something really objectionable to ones that are not typical.

Permit me to offer a translation. Our choice really depends on whether we want as many separations as possible to be good, or whether we don't want many of them to be bad. The difference explains a lot about why people have such strong feelings about the process.

For one thing, it explains why so many people accuse Photoshop of making "bad" separations. They mean that, like its relative EIAM, Photoshop sometimes uncorks a real howler, changing blues to purples with great elan and losing detail in out-of-gamut colors. If you see enough of these stinkers, you may think that Photoshop itself is what stinks. But all it is doing is following my law: since it generally makes good separations, it frequently makes bad ones.

In preparing this book, I put together a suite of 10 LAB images, which I separated using 15 different methods from many different sources. I expected that it would show that every method did well on certain images and not on others. What it showed more convincingly was how correct Ogden Rood was. Getting the dot gain correct is far more important than getting accurate colors. Those profiles that didn't have accurate dot gain compensation lost every time, even when they had more attractive colors. This is one reason I've added a full chapter on dot gain compensation in this edition.

Figure 11.4 compares real-world versions of EIAM and PCCM. The versions on the left use the conversion settings of a friend; the ones on the right are the ones I used for this book. The dot gains aren't the same, but they're quite similar. Because of differences we'll discuss later, his approach is more PCCM, mine is more EIAM.

Matching a Photoshop 5 Workflow

Note: there were major color changes between Photoshop 4 and 5. If you're attempting to upgrade to Photoshop 6 directly from Photoshop 4, the following methods won't work. You need to study the appropriate chapter from the previous edition of this book. It's in a PDF on the CD.

• Open Photoshop 5, and choose File: Color Settings > RGB Setup. When the dialog box appears, click "Save" and store the contents somewhere.

• Ditto with Photoshop 5's File: Color Settings > CMYK Setup. After saving the file, go to the "Dot Gain" setting. If it reads "Standard," change it to "Curves" and click the mouse there. When the dot gain curves show up, click "Black." Write down the curve values you find there.

• Close Photoshop 5 and open Photoshop 6. Go to Edit: Color Settings. Click the "Advanced Mode" on; if you wish, after completing these steps, you can turn it back off.

• Under Working Spaces: RGB, click on whatever's there and choose, from a list of options, Load RGB. And load the RGB Setup you saved from Photoshop 5.

• Similarly, click on Working Spaces: CMYK and load the CMYK Setup from Photoshop 5.

• Under Working Spaces: Gray, choose "Custom Dot Gain" and change the curve to whatever you found in the black curve in Photoshop 5's CMYK Setup.

• For the Color Management settings and everything below them, unless you think you know why you should do otherwise, stick with what's shown in Figure 11.5.

• Save out your settings so that you can restore everything in one fell swoop if necessary.

These images are, obviously, quite close. But if I have to pick, I'd say his settings did better on the fruits, and mine on the volcano. As predicted, his greenery is duller, but he has better shape in the strawberry and the apples.

If forced to choose only one method for both images, I'll take his. His volcano can easily be brightened up with curves. But we probably need a blend into the cyan channel to get better reds in my fruits.

I'm not switching over, though. That fruit image isn't typical. While I don't do many volcanoes, I do handle a lot of similar images. So I'll stick with my EIAM.

But it depends on the workflow. You may handle more brilliant colors than I do. Or you may feel inclined to load different settings for different kinds of image.

Photoshop 6's New Settings Box

Having finally reached the point where we discuss the future—the specifics of the color settings shown in Figure 11.5—it becomes necessary to discuss the past. Photoshop 6 comes on the heels of the most badly thought-out upgrade in the history of the graphic arts. Photoshop 5 created chaos, not by altering its color methodology, but by booby-trapping itself and by severing reliable links between Photoshop users.

In choosing what to use in Photoshop 6, we need to consider not just what is best for us, but what the rest of the world is doing. This is a complicated and difficult-to-follow subject. If you understand the color settings of Photoshop 5, you'll yawn your way through the changes. If not (and you may be in the majority), permit me to say, for the first of several times in this chapter, I told you so. To quote *Professional Photoshop 5:*

As Santayana remarked, those who cannot remember the past are condemned to repeat it. If you find Photoshop 5's color changes incomprehensible, and look only for a quick fix, you are condemned to relive this experience at some point in your career. More likely, at several points. Photoshop 5 is not the last challenge. The principles are much more important than the implementation. Many calibrationists don't understand them, which is why their nostrums don't work. If you *do* understand them you will have little difficulty adjusting to the changes of Photoshop 5, Photoshop 6, a new type of large-format printer, or any other obstacle fortune places in your way.

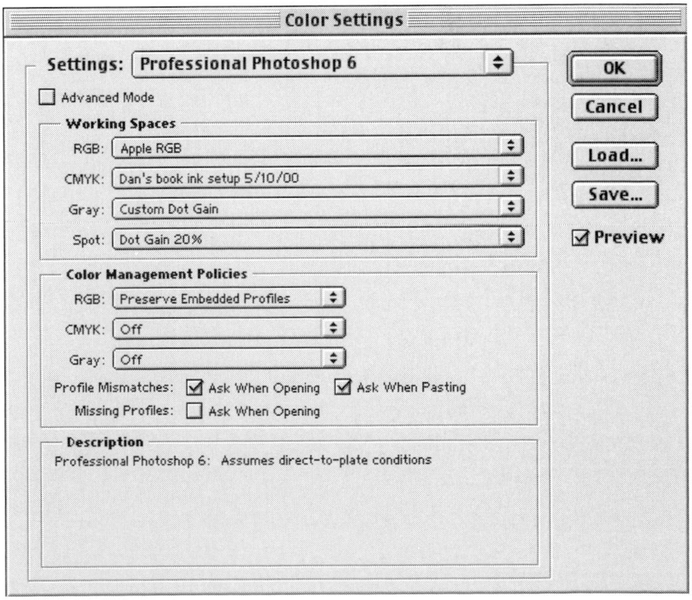

Figure 11.5 *Photoshop 6's Edit: Color Settings dialog replaces no less than four dialog boxes in Photoshop 5.*

*   *   *

Now that what I predicted has in fact come to pass—a new version with completely revised color handling—perhaps people may be more inclined to try to figure out what's going on this time. If not, on Page 218 there is a recipe for making Photoshop 6 act like Photoshop 5, if that's what you're after.

You can therefore ignore the following discussion if you like, but if you're serious about color, at some point in your life you will probably be sorry if you do.

Agreeing on a Vocabulary

Before starting this extended discussion, let's amplify some of the concepts introduced in the last chapter.

Before we can make any conversion into CMYK, or for that matter from any colorspace into any colorspace, there has to be some kind of internal definition of what colors mean. In other words, $100^R150^G200^B$, on my system, converts to $64^C24^M9^Y$. Or at least it does at the moment. Later today, it may convert to something else, because I sometimes have to change the definition of what CMYK is. It's also possible to change the definition of what RGB is, although users rarely do this once having settled on a standard setting.

We can't, however, change what LAB is, and this happy fact brings some order to the situation. My RGB definition somehow gives Photoshop the information that $100^R150^G200^B$ equals $66^L(9)^A(27)^B$. Then Photoshop looks to the CMYK definition to find out how to obtain that color, and we all live happily ever after.

A bright blue like $0^R0^G200^B$, however, would represent the doomsday defense. It converts to $26^L52^A(91)^B$, and Photoshop couldn't get that over the CMYK goal line even in a Sherman tank. The color simply doesn't exist. So the CMYK definition invents something. The invention may deliberately force other CMYK colors *not* to match their LAB equivalents. This is the method I've previously called PCCM.

These definitions of RGB and CMYK, which are changeable although many people never change them, are known to the cognoscenti as *profiles*. Sometimes the term *ICC profiles* is used to describe profiles generated by specialized software or purchased from vendors. The term is misleading, though, because all Photoshop profiles comply with the ICC specification. Every time we convert from RGB to CMYK, we're using two ICC profiles, like it or not.

Interestingly, these profiles permit conversions not just between colorspaces but between variants of them: we can convert one kind of RGB to another kind, thus changing the RGB numbers but not the LAB equivalent. An example of this is the "convert on open" option that created havoc when Photoshop 5 shipped. More constructive, in Chapter 6 we were able to change black generation for the better in certain images by means of a profile-based CMYK to CMYK conversion.

A further variation: traditionally, when we send someone a file, if the file calls for a value of, say, $64^C24^M9^Y$, that's the value we want to get on output, understanding that those values will *look* different under different output circumstances.

A long-time suggestion of what I call the *Conventional Color Management Wisdom* is that a better way to do things would be for the file to somehow carry the LAB equivalents as well, opening the possibility that down the line somebody might do a CMYK-to-CMYK conversion, giving us the colors we really wanted but were too stupid to ask for. The term commonly used for this is a file with an *embedded profile,* which is rather confusing. I prefer to say a *tagged file,* and will do so throughout this chapter.

The aforementioned CCMW is a composite of the views of half a dozen or so of the most prominent advocates of this technology, gleaned from their public writings and speeches. These people think a lot more about color than the world at large, which is a benefit; they tend to lack practical production experience, which is a minus; and most of them have a financial stake in the success of color management, which may affect certain of their views but would have no bearing on others.

I offer these views as what you would be likely to encounter elsewhere if you look for people who seem to know what they're talking about. More often than not, the CCMW agrees with me; in some notorious cases, we disagree; in several cases there isn't a CCMW as such because its constituents don't agree with one another. There are also certain areas in which the CCMW has changed its mind; I refer to these as CCMW 2000 views.

And with that introduction, let's consider the Color Settings options, what they have been, what they now are, and what you should set them at.

RGB: Out of One, Many

With the advent of cheap, high-quality digital cameras and desktop scanners, it has become impossible for CMYK-centrists to maintain a hands-off attitude toward RGB. The decision for what to put in RGB Working Space, nee RGB Setup, is more important than it used to be.

First, though, examine Figure 11.6 and decide, which two versions are the closest to one another?

• **The choices.** The concept of RGB is not a static one. $150^R150^G150^B$ will always be a gray, but exactly how dark that gray is is up for discussion. $250^R150^G150^B$ is definitely a red, but how vivid the red is needs further clarification.

Click on RGB Working Space, and the four RGBs of Figure 11.6 will pop up. If Advanced Mode is checked, you'll see umpty-nine more, but these four are now officially preferred. I started with an LAB file, which I then converted into Apple RGB. Figure 11.6A is therefore the most accurate rendition of the LAB file. The others were created by changing the RGB setting while this Apple RGB file was open on the screen.

In real life, this would never happen. We'd change the setting *before* converting to RGB. Photoshop would compensate for the variations in the RGB definition each time, and we'd wind up with four files that looked alike on the screen and that would separate to CMYK almost identically.

The RGB *numbers,* however, would be different. This means, if we sent these four identical-looking RGB files to an RGB output device, we'd likely get four different results. Furthermore, if we open RGB files from other sources into different RGB definitions, we'll get different-looking results *unless* we convert the colors—change the color data—into our RGB as we open them.

You have doubtless answered the initial question by saying that Figures 11.6A and 11.6D are the closest. 11.6D is ColorMatch RGB. Its colors are slightly more intense than in Apple RGB, but it's about the same darkness.

The other two are darker. Figure 11.6C is sRGB, which is close to Apple RGB for color.

Figure 11.6B is Adobe RGB, which was erroneously called SMPTE–240M in Photoshop 5.0. It has the most vivid colors of the four.

- **The history**. Before Photoshop 5, the standard was—loosely—Apple RGB. The others could only have been accessed by typing in numbers, hardly the sort of thing a non-expert would do.

Technically, however, everyone's Apple RGB was slightly different. Conversions to CMYK took account of settings pertaining to one's monitor; therefore, identical files would not separate identically from different machines. However, the variation would usually be less even than the difference between Figures 11.5A and 11.5D.

Believing for some reason that this slight ambiguity was a major problem, Adobe made sRGB the default in Photoshop 5, and gave users eight other unambiguous RGBs to choose from if they didn't like it.

- **What happened**. RGB users went nuts. Anybody using RGB as output to, say, an Epson printer found that their workflow had been trashed, as did those who were handing off RGB files to service bureaus and printers.

Everyone who could figure out what was happening ran away from sRGB as if it were a poisonous snake, but they ran in all directions. Panicked users could be found with almost any definition *except* sRGB.

As time went on, serious users began to converge on three options: Apple RGB (or some variant loaded directly from Photoshop 4), ColorMatch RGB, or Adobe RGB.

Figure 11.6 *The colors Photoshop perceives in an RGB file depend on the definition of RGB. The RGB values in each of these files were identical before separation, but Photoshop was told that version A was in Apple RGB, B in Adobe RGB, C in sRGB, and D in ColorMatch RGB.*

This is why Adobe changed the menu in Photoshop 6 to favor these three (plus sRGB) and this is why I don't take the space to discuss other RGB options in this book.

- **The postmortem**. The CCMW believes in wider-gamut RGBs. Its adherents were accordingly outraged by the sRGB default, which they declared was unusable. I declared this also, but have since changed my mind. Having played more with it, I don't think its smaller gamut is nearly the problem others do. The reason it was such a bad choice for default was that it wiped out a system where everyone's RGB was approximately the same and replaced it with chaos. This is the only aspect of Photoshop 5 that I would say was foolish enough to qualify as calibrationism.

For its part, the CCMW has also modified its position. At first, several vendors and some writers took the view that nine competing RGB definitions weren't enough and propounded their own, each of which was claimed to give even better results. As it became clear that the market welcomed additional RGB definitions about as much as an epidemic of venereal disease, the CCMW adjusted. Several adherents have now suggested that only Adobe RGB and ColorMatch RGB should have been added as options. CCMW 2000 prefers Adobe RGB, but accepts ColorMatch RGB as a reasonable alternative in view of the high likelihood of color management snafus. If your file is in ColorMatch RGB and somebody opens and saves it in Photoshop 4, it's not great but it's no tragedy. With Adobe RGB, a ruined job is the likely result.

I suspect that eventually the CCMW will evolve to the point that it will understand that in this area, agreement is better than disagreement. I don't endorse sRGB, but if everyone in the world used sRGB, that would be a far superior state of affairs to today's sorry one. I reiterate a statement from *Professional Photoshop 5:* "To trash a nearly universal standard in favor of such an every-man-for-himself situation is a blunder, no matter the rationale. But to replace it in the name of device independence, that takes a calibrationist."

- **The "right" way**. For those who know the secrets of color correction, the practical difference between using Apple RGB and ColorMatch RGB is nil. The impact of using one of the others is slight.

That said, the technically best choice of RGB depends a lot on the destination of the work.

If your eventual output is CMYK, ignore the whinings of the CCMW about limited-gamut RGBs. The alleged problem is that both Apple RGB and sRGB can't produce a fully saturated cyan, such as that shown in Figure 11.7. In other words, these two

RGBs can't specify a color that would convert to more than 90^C and less than 10^M10^Y.

This sounds quite horrible, but it's only another example of the CCMW falling victim to its lack of practical experience. You've never seen a pepper this color, nor almost anything else. Such a pure cyan doesn't exist in real life, except very occasionally in fashion work.

This goes back to Emily Dickinson's theories of non-random distributions of colors. Magentas as pure as the cyan pepper are also rare, but certain flowers qualify. Pure yellows occur in bananas, fashion work, and this pepper, had I not swapped the cyan and yellow plates. And pure reds, greens, and blues crop up like weeds. But pure cyans, no, unless you're trying to process a picture of the front cover of this book, which contains a color bar. Handle such images case-by-case.

If going to CMYK, the wide-gamut RGBs actually get in the way of someone who knows curves. The more colors that aren't in the CMYK gamut to begin with, the more the separation process has to guess. It will often guess wrong, as it did in Figure 11.2.

The higher-gamma (darker) RGBs emphasize distinctions in the shadows at the expense of the highlights. It's conceivable that this could help certain later corrections. Correcting for shadow detail, however, is a strength of CMYK. The problem in CMYK is retention of highlight detail, which is why one so often has to resort to channel blending.

There are two technical reasons. First, the black channel is always temptingly rich

Figure 11.7 *Mathematical purists condemn Apple RGB and sRGB because they have no way of representing the brilliant cyan of this pepper. In nature, however, this color is practically nonexistent.*

in shadow detail that can be exploited. Second, the compensation for dot gain that occurs during separation has a similar effect to the gamma correction in RGB: it emphasizes shadows and hurts highlights.

Neither of these factors exists in RGB. This is perhaps the only area in which there's a big difference between generic RGB and generic CMYK: in RGB, it's hard to work the shadows; in CMYK, it's the highlights. Consequently, Adobe RGB and sRGB are better choices if most of your work is done in RGB. If you work or output primarily in CMYK, Adobe RGB, despite having been anointed the prepress default in Photoshop 6, is actually a bit worse than sRGB. But ColorMatch or Apple RGB is better than either.

• **The practical way**. Every few weeks, some color discussion group features wailing and gnashing of teeth on the part of a user of Adobe RGB who was foolish enough to pass an RGB file on to a service provider who had never heard of Adobe RGB and had all color management turned off, thus guaranteeing a nearly colorless result.

The CCMW waxes wroth when this occurs. The service provider is called all kinds of names, great sympathy is expressed for the victim, other service providers are warned that resistance is futile, and everyone waits for the next victim to fall into the trap so that the fun can begin again.

The practical person, however, accepts the world the way it is. For better or worse, most service providers have declined to learn much about this methodology. Many would make the same error.

While it's fun to blame people, it's even more fun when the job is done correctly the first time. If you feel there's an advantage to using Adobe RGB, fine, but defend yourself

by converting your files to LAB before handing them off to others, and request that others do the same before giving you *their* RGB files.

The recommendations for the practical person, therefore, are:

For work primarily aimed at CMYK: Use ColorMatch or Apple RGB.

Work primarily aimed at non-Web RGB: If you are certain that your workflow won't let anyone convert (or fail to convert) it improperly later, use Adobe RGB. If not, use ColorMatch RGB.

Work aimed at the Web: If you believe your audience is primarily Macintosh-based, use Apple RGB, otherwise sRGB.

• **The future**. This is the one area where changes in Photoshop 6 will make things worse. Instead of a single default—sRGB—the new version has four: sRGB for the default labeled "Web" and Adobe RGB for three others labeled "Prepress."

The knee-jerk reaction of many hardcore CMYK types is going to be to choose one of the prepress options, look down the dialog box, observe those provocative words *Color Management Policies* and immediately turn everything off, not realizing that the presence of Adobe RGB changes everything.

Given the plethora of RGB practices, when a stranger's file arrives bearing a tag, it's anybody's guess as to whether the tag means anything. If the tag says sRGB, that is particularly true. Up until now, however, an Adobe RGB tag could be given a little more credence; the fact that a user intentionally chose Adobe RGB has been a slight indication of awareness of what this process is about. Furthermore, if we pass on a conservative-RGB file to someone else, the chances of that somebody else destroying it by the proven method of opening it into Adobe RGB without converting it have been pretty poor—up until now.

Whether you like a profiled workflow or not, the enemy is the nonuser who may misapply the technology to ruin your files. A legacy of the Photoshop 5 adventure is a large volume of such nonusers. This is likely to continue for years to come. It will remain dangerous for some time to pass *any* RGB files to strangers. The intelligent solution, which we'll see more and more of, is for users to convert their own files to LAB before passing them on, and letting the next person reconvert to RGB if necessary.

CMYK: Back to Basics

The CMYK setting hasn't had quite the tortured past of its RGB counterpart, but it's had its share of controversy.

• **The choices**. All CMYK definitions are now found on the same menu, recognizing that all are actually ICC profiles, even those created with what most of us know as Photoshop's built-in color engine.

• **The history**. There hasn't been much cosmetic change in the interface. Photoshop 5 combined two menus from previous versions into one, CMYK Setup, which became Custom CMYK in Photoshop 6.

Photoshop 5, however, changed the crucial dot gain definition. It left the default dot gain numbers alone, but changed their meaning. The change was not documented.

It also permitted use of third-party ICC profiles for the conversion into CMYK, but did not provide a means of editing them.

• **What happened**. CMYK users went nuts. For no apparent reason, separations began to come out much lighter than before. Many, unable to figure out what had happened, temporarily returned to Photo-

shop 4. Others blamed the dot gain problem on ICC color management, which had nothing to do with it.

• **The postmortem**. The CCMW was as appalled by the dot gain booby trap as any other rational observer. It expected, however, that many more people would adopt custom profiles than actually did, and eventually reached the correct conclusion that few would do so unless the ability to tweak them was included in Photoshop.

• **The "right" way**. Once the dot gain contretemps played itself out, people reverted to past practices. As a result, there's currently little to discuss here, particularly in comparison to the RGB situation.

None of the default offerings in Photoshop 6's Color Settings gives an adequate separation. One has to become comfortable with changing the Custom CMYK dialog. This complicated topic was largely hashed out in Chapter 6 on pages 106 and 107. But as a footnote to the EIAM *v.* PCCM discussion, I'll briefly discuss editing the Ink Colors table of Figure 11.8.

We access that table in Custom CMYK by changing "Ink Colors" to "Custom." If you've never changed these previously, they'll be Photoshop's SWOP Coated set.

The numbers come up in the xyY colorspace, which presumably is Greek to you. Fortunately, a checkbox allows us to convert them to the more familiar LAB.

The Photoshop separation method was cobbled together many years ago and has many eccentricities. Actual measurements of what your inks read have little value. But certain tweaks may help certain people.

Photoshop default separations are close to EIAM. They do well with mundane images, but crash and burn when given bright colors that are out of the CMYK gamut.

If brilliant, saturated colors are an important part of your work, you may wish to change the ink values to be more pure. This would be done by moving all the A and B numbers (except the bottom three) further from zero: positive numbers more positive, negatives more negative.

This persuades Photoshop that fewer colors are out of gamut, and that everything is more colorful than previously. This will produce a slightly duller overall look, but more detail in the saturated colors.

In short, it will move you in the direction of PCCM. This is the method used by my friend in Figure 11.4. Neither of us use standard ink definitions, but his assume purer inks than mine.

In *Professional Photoshop 5,* I discussed at length some of the potential advantages of using separation methods prepared by third-party profiling software. Among these were the ability to create eccentric seps that would, say, emphasize green and blue but not red (a realtor might want this). Also, there was a case to be made for loading such profiles for previewing purposes, mainly because they allow us to fake a non-white background where necessary.

•   **The practical way**. With most CMYK users sticking to traditional methods, there aren't as many traps to fall into as in RGB. So the practical user is limited to looking for more efficient options among the various new tools. One is shown in Figure 11.9.

I recently had occasion to prepare a small color brochure for a lecture. I wanted to use certain images I had previously used in magazines, but this brochure was to be printed on a color copier. Output from this copier looks no more like a magazine than Doug Flutie looks like Abraham Lincoln, so I was in a spot. I could have just guessed

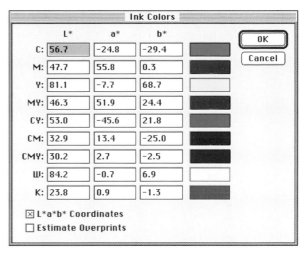

Figure 11.8 *Photoshop's separation method relies on its profiles of the four inks and what happens when they overlap one another. Edit these values at your own risk.*

that the copier would print much darker, and lightened the files to compensate, but the copier's owner provided a more effective solution.

He gave me a copy of his CMYK settings. As it happens, he was using a profile that he created using third-party software, but this makes no difference; he could have been using Custom CMYK.

Having loaded this profile into my computer, the old-fashioned way would have been to convert all of my images into LAB, using my own CMYK settings. Then, I would have changed the color settings to his CMYK, and reconverted everything and saved it under a new name.

Photoshop 6 saves a step. I opened the files, and changed each in Image: Mode> Convert to Profile.

•   **The future**. Adobe's failure to include a full-fledged ICC profile editor in Photoshop 6 guarantees that the traditional Photoshop separation engine will remain dominant. The serious user needs to be able to make quick changes in black generation, at least. A method that requires exiting Photoshop to tweak the profile is not going to fly.

There will be a peripheral role for well-prepared third-party profiles, mostly to cater to output devices such as inkjet printers and high-speed color copiers.

Printers and service bureaus will likely continue to be hostile to the CCMW for many years to come. They have an inordinate impact on the practices of the general public. If all the service providers say that color management doesn't work, it really doesn't matter whether they're right.

A More Adult Way to Play Tag

The ability to embed a tag indicating what our intentions were at the time we created the file sounds like a fine idea. In the real world, the possibility that someone or something may make unauthorized

changes to the color based on that information makes the topic a bit spicier.

• **The choices**. Photoshop 6 is what Photoshop 5 should have been. We now have the ability to tag or untag files individually each time we save them, without having to change our color settings each time. When a tagged file comes to us, we can ignore the tag, use it to convert the file into our own CMYK or RGB, or, in a major development, retain the tag.

Also new in Photoshop 6: we can, with Image: Mode>Assign Profile, put any arbitrary tag into a file. The Image: Mode>Convert to Profile command, unlike its Photoshop 5 predecessor, Image: Mode>Profile to Profile, allows us to embed the *correct* tag should we decide to convert a file.

• **The history**. The ability to embed and read ICC tags didn't exist in Photoshop before the 1998 release of Photoshop 5.

Figure 11.9 *Practical profile use. The version at right is the desired color, but it was necessary to print the picture on a color copier for other purposes. The owner of the copier provided a CMYK profile, and the Convert to Profile command transformed the image into the version at the left, too light for this book. On the copier, however, it produced a result acceptably close to that shown on the right here.*

Its defaults were not just to embed the tags, but upon opening incoming files (including files prepared in previous versions of Photoshop) to convert the data into whatever CMYK or RGB Setup called for.

* **What happened**. The entire Photoshop user base went nuts.

Service providers universally condemned the new settings and urged clients to turn them off. A few actually refused for a time to accept files prepared in Photoshop 5. Some inhouse operations forbade their freelancers to use the program. In a magazine article, I called Photoshop 5 "a major disservice to the industry." Adobe customer support was flooded with calls; online newsgroups saw an unprecedented level of namecalling and Adobe-bashing.

One year later, Photoshop 5 had still not completely supplanted previous versions, a rarity. However, the market finally realized that, properly configured, Photoshop 5 would not bite, and adoption was rapid in the latter half of 1999.

Some users, mainly photographers, began to use third-party profiles, mainly as a way to calibrate their proofers. But that's about it for the experiment. Some people embed tags for philosophical reasons, but workflows that depend on embedded tags are at this point nonexistent. Service providers continue to recommend against any workflow involving conversions. Few if any honor tags unless their client specifically instructs them to do so.

* **The postmortem**. The CCMW has been fragmented throughout this experience. Most adherents were delirious with joy when Photoshop 5 came out, but author Bruce Fraser, a prominent historical supporter of color management, correctly stated at the time that the release had made

rocket science out of fairly simple concepts, and that many users would be baffled. Other hardliners, however, blasted users for being too lazy to read the manuals, Adobe's documentation for being inadequate, and service providers for being too set in their ways to adopt anything new.

That view has changed. CCMW 2000 has come to agree that the convert-on-open default was a big mistake. Also, it has backed off somewhat on the question of embedding tags. RGB tags are generally thought desirable. Grayscale tags are not, owing to various reported problems and a lack of any real benefit. CCMW 2000 is of two minds on the question of CMYK tags. It likes the idea in principle, but understands that most of the CMYK world doesn't, and that attempting to ram it down people's throats may be counterproductive.

The CCMW also has finally concluded, or is at least on the verge of doing so, that its ideas are going nowhere unless implementing them gets a lot simpler. While this new attitude is welcome, I cannot resist a final quote from the last edition of this book:

> ...considering that you, as a reader of this book, identify yourself as being well above average in sophistication, let me ask you: how easy do *you* find the material in this chapter? This entire area has proven itself much too difficult for the typical user. For people who do not understand the theory behind it, mistakes are inevitable.

* **The "right" way**. In a perfect world, all files are tagged, since in a perfect world a tag is never misused by an ignoramus of the human or machine variety.

As for whether to honor tags in files presented to us by strangers, Photoshop 5 offered us the choice of death by hanging or

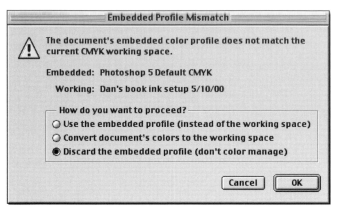

Figure 11.10 *When "Ask When Opening" is checked in Color Settings, this dialog appears when opening a stranger's tagged file. Photoshop 6, for the first time, allows retaining the tag, which is almost always the right thing to do in RGB. If the incoming file is CMYK, sometimes it will make sense to retain the tag, but in many if not most cases it should be discarded.*

by poison. If we ignored the tag, a dissatisfied client could have some color management yahoo condemn us on every online newsgroup. If we trusted the tag and converted the colors, a dissatisfied client could produce affidavits from the best service providers in the country stating that tags are known to cause warts, Hodgkins Disease, and hemorrhoids, and that reputable concerns always ignore them.

If we had opened and saved the client's file without converting it, it would then have incorrectly gotten *our* tag, or no tag at all, depending upon our settings. The only way to resave it with the *client's* tag intact would have been to change settings in two different Photoshop 5 dialogs. Most operations rightfully declined to do this—too much chance of destroying a series of future jobs by forgetting to change the settings back afterward.

Photoshop 6 corrects this horror. We can still convert if we like or ignore if we like. But most of the time we should do the obvious, *maintain* the tag, especially if the

file is RGB. In Photoshop 6, one file can be open in Apple RGB and another in Adobe RGB. If we open and save somebody else's image, the tag won't change.

• **The practical way.** Even if you are anti-color management, you should check "Ask When Opening" rather than "Ignore." If somebody hands you a tagged file, its a good idea to know it. What you choose to do at that point is another story.

Retaining the tags in an RGB file supplied by a stranger seems to me to be a no-brainer. CMYK files don't have such an easy answer.

Retaining the profile has the advantage—or disadvantage, depending on your workflow—that it overrides our current monitor settings, and theoretically displays the image as it would have appeared on the stranger's monitor. The chances that it actually does this are slim to none, but the point is that it won't look the same on our monitor as if we had opened it without retaining the tag.

In RGB, that's unlikely to hurt. In CMYK, it might. If we've got a nice Custom CMYK loaded that's accurate for our printing conditions, retaining the tag will override that and we won't see the file as it will print. For some people that's a problem and for others it isn't. For me, it makes sense to discard the tag most of the time. The good thing, though, is that I don't have to do it *all* of the time. If "Ask When Opening" is checked and a tagged file comes in, the dialog of Figure 11.10 pops up, with my usual preference—trash the tag—preselected. But if for some reason I decide to keep the tag on this particular file, it's a one-click operation.

Embedding tags ourselves continues to be a two-edged sword. Unless you are one of the few people in the world with a workflow that absolutely depends on the presence of the tag, you need to ask whether the potential gain of tagging the file outweighs the risk of doing so. Having had two major jobs ruined myself by faulty tag management elsewhere, I can assure you that it's not risk-free. A file saved without a tag is less likely to be converted by mistake.

Of my two disasters, one was human error, abetted by the design of Photoshop 5. I was reprinting an older job, and forgot that the files had been prepared in Photoshop 4. Since Photoshop 4 files *can't* contain tags, as opposed to later versions, where tags are optional, the later versions treat them differently. They can be set up to convert the colors of all such "legacy" files immediately upon opening, the assumptions to be used in this conversion being specified by the user. The boneheads who worked my job had specified that Photoshop 5 was to assume that "legacy" files had been prepared for newspaper printing, which was unfortunate for me, as mine had been prepared for magazines.

The other disaster, I can't explain. Somebody opened and recropped my files, in doing so carelessly embedding an incorrect tag. This should not have made a difference, as the tag was not that far off from what I intended, and the workflow didn't call for any conversions.

And yet one happened, a big one, apparently automatically, possibly in the page layout application, possibly in the RIP, I don't know, nor does the supplier, nor will anyone else ever know.

Color-handling programs are complex and subject to all kinds of bugs. Photoshop itself goes through an exhaustive beta-testing period, with thousands of reasonably expert users reporting any irregularity, and still the shipping versions usually have minor flaws.

Few use the sorts of workflows we are talking about, especially in the CMYK world. So, testing is inadequate. One recent version of ColorSync, Apple's enabling mechanism for color management, turned tagged files into negatives when they were placed in PageMaker. ColorSync 3.0, which shipped in early 2000, had several serious glitches. One sometimes turned screen displays bright yellow when the monitor tag was changed. Another, when a file was saved as a TIFF with a tag originating from certain vendors, prevented Photoshop from ever opening the file again.

These are not exactly minor issues. And if bugs as blatant as these can slip through, one can only imagine what other land mines may be lurking, waiting for us to step on them.

For these reasons, I would recommend against embedding tags in CMYK files, unless you have a particular reason to do it. One such reason is inherent in the left side of Figure 11.9.

If a CMYK file has no tag, one assumes it is set up for "SWOP." This is a vague term, but decades of experience have shown that the market feels little need for more precision. The deer at the right of Figure 11.9 will print slightly darker in most SWOP contexts than it does here—but acceptably so.

The left side is another story. That file is an accident waiting to happen if somebody picks it up and thinks it's a normal CMYK file. The chances of this are slim, but why take a chance? I've therefore warned the next user by naming it !HP_Only!_deer.tif.

I've also tagged the file. This hypothetical person who picks up the file in three years may know from the name that something's up. But she'll have to take a guess at what that something is if there's no tag.

For the right-hand version, if I embed a tag and it gets ignored, it's no big deal, but if the tag gets misused, it's a major problem. The left-hand version, though, is the opposite. If the tag gets ignored, *that's* what's deadly. If the tag gets misused, I'm no worse off. So, I tag one, but not the other.

For similar reasons, if I used Adobe RGB, I'd tag every RGB file. It's all part of the pattern of driving defensively. For files that never leave our premises, it makes no difference whether they're tagged or not. We have to consider the possibility that they'll fall into the hands of strangers. If it would be almost as bad for the stranger to ignore the tag as it would be to misuse it, then the tag belongs there.

• **The future**. The sensible changes of Photoshop 6 will help, but still, for the next few years, nobody is going to be able to rely on tags in files that come from strangers. Plus, certain hardware and software combinations will occasionally create havoc for those few who embed tags. For these reasons, few large operations, especially those who interact with outsiders, will want to have much to do with a tagged workflow.

One possibility is that service providers will start making their separation method available to their clients, as mine did with Figure 11.9. This step is strongly advocated by the CCMW, and I endorse it myself.

I question, however, whether this is going to occur. Many CMYK-oriented operations consider the separation method of little importance, as they intend to correct everything afterwards anyway. Others are disinclined to let the competition know what they think their dot gain is. Most of all, however, printers and service bureaus could have done this ever since Photoshop 2, which is almost 10 years ago. The fact that the practice has never yet taken off doesn't speak well for the chances it will.

Filling In the Blanks

There are two other straightforward options in the Color Settings dialog. If you want to use a custom setting here, Advanced Mode has to be checked.

• **Gray** (Grayscale). The default is 20% dot gain for grayscale images, which is fair enough, but if you have a good Custom CMYK, you should just take the gray dot gain setting from that and plug it in here, using the Custom Dot Gain option.

• **Spot Colors**. The default is again 20%, and I would leave this alone: spot inks often have higher dot gains than process inks. In *Professional Photoshop 5*, there was a whole chapter on the problems of fifth colors. For space reasons, we've omitted it this time, but a PDF of the chapter is on your CD.

An Overrated Topic

For all the aggravation this topic has caused users, and for all the hype expended on it, its importance is much overrated. One method is better on certain images and another on others, but most of the time, the exact method is almost irrelevant.

The volcano of Figure 11.4 is a perfect example. The two competing versions are quite different—but neither is good enough. Both need to be corrected both for color and to add contrast to the hills surrounding the crater.

In doing so, it does not make the slightest difference which of the versions we start with. The correction techniques would be identical on the two. Only the numbers on

MANAGING THE COLOR SETTINGS

✓CMYK and RGB have very different color gamuts. CMYK has better yellows and sometimes better magentas. As against that, it has very poor blues. Because of these differences, a perfect separation algorithm is a contradiction in terms.

✓The better a separation method is at handling exceptional situations, the worse it will be on the average image. Conversely, the better the method does on average images, the more likely it is to do something really bad on occasion.

✓Photoshop 6 corrects many of the serious color handling errors of Photoshop 5. Four dialogs are combined into one, Color Settings. Also, a new command, Convert to Profile, is very flexible and eliminates a lot of possibilities for error.

✓U.S. service providers are generally hostile to workflows involving tags and conversions. When supplying files to them, or to any stranger, you should not assume that your tags will be honored unless you have made your wishes clear.

✓Unlike Photoshop 5, which offered a grab bag of RGB definitions, Photoshop 6 suggests only four. Those skilled in color correction will get close to the same results with any, assuming no color management mistakes along the way.

✓Because the RGB definitions are so different and adoption of proper workflows so spotty, it's currently very dangerous to hand off RGB files to strangers. Convert them to LAB first, and let the stranger reconvert to RGB.

✓Certain users can benefit from the use of embedded profiles. If you aren't sure you're one of them, you probably aren't. In that case, you are probably better off disabling Photoshop's color management.

✓A disadvantage of separating with third-party profiles is that changes in black generation or small tweaks to the algorithm are time-consuming and require special software, which at the moment is rather expensive.

✓Retaining an incoming file's tags, a new option in Photoshop 6, is generally the right thing to do in RGB. As it impacts monitor display, it can be wrong in CMYK.

✓For knowledgeable users, the exact method of separation—except for black generation—is nearly irrelevant. Almost all images will still need later correction, and small variations in the initial file won't make a difference in quality.

the curves would vary. Neither would be in any way more difficult than the other. Neither would take more time. Neither would have the smallest advantage in quality once we were done.

Even in the four versions of Figure 11.6, which differ from one another far more than any sensible separation methods would, the impact of the difference, to a skilled retoucher, is nil.

There is no point in avoiding the easy changes that make the separation more accurate, such as increasing Photoshop's dot gain adjustment when separating an image for use in a newspaper. But an accurate separation only goes so far.

If there really were one best way to convert into CMYK, it would have been discovered a long time ago. Meanwhile, there are many reasonable variations within Photoshop and elsewhere. If you don't much care about image quality, it won't much matter which one you use. If you do care, and if you know the right way to get there—well, then it won't matter much, either.

The way it will matter, unfortunately, is if somebody screws up a color setting along the way and destroys the job. This is the major reason for all the controversy when the new capabilities were introduced in Photoshop 5: limited opportunities for gain, unbridled ones for disaster.

The sensible changes in Photoshop 6's color handling are a test for the responsible user. When Photoshop 5 came out, I was quite sure of what would happen. This time, it's a bit dicier. Will the users take advantage of the relatively painless new features, like Convert to Profile, and the new options in Color Settings? Or will they, disgusted by Photoshop 5, immediately turn all color management off and move on?

You've got the ball now. Let's see if you can run with it.

The Great Dot Gain Gamble

If you're having trouble making your monitor or your desktop color printer match the results you're getting in print, there can be any number of explanations. But the principal suspect is always that most ephemeral, unpredictable, incorrigible, and tiresome of concepts: dot gain. Here's how to compensate.

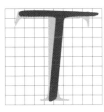

The green bar at the bottom of Figure 12.1 was meant to be an optical trick to illustrate simultaneous contrast, just like the one we saw earlier in Figure 10.1.

In a magazine article, I asserted that the circle at the bottom right of the bar would seem a very different color from that at the extreme left of the green bar, although the ink values were the same.

Refusing to take my word for it, a couple of calibrationist readers unlocked their trusty spectrodensitometers from their belts, took some measurements, and fired off correspondence accusing me of being, in rough translation, a highly untruthful individual.

For quality reasons, I'd normally show a screen grab, but this is a scan of the actual page. What do you think? Is that circle really darker than the green at the left?

If not, it sure fooled the scanner, which found around 3 points more cyan, 10 points more magenta, and 15 more yellow in the circle than in the green at left. Yet in the original TIFF, the two are the same. They were the same on the contract proof, too. What in blazes is going on?

I'll explain shortly, but first we need to discuss some of the facts of life of offset printing.

If we output a file to film and print from it in a newspaper, you can bet that the result is going to be noticeably darker than if we had given it to a local commercial printer who printed it on a sheetfed press. If we had printed it in this book, the result would have been somewhere in the middle. If we had sent our digital file directly to a color copier, it's likely that it would have been closer to the newspaper than anything else. If we had used a desktop inkjet printer, the result might have been almost anything. And on and on.

This predictable variation in darkness is known loosely as dot gain. Somewhere during the process, somebody has to take it

into account. Guess who that somebody is? If you don't understand it, you're likely to get a surprise when the job goes to press. The nature of such surprises is that they are rarely pleasant.

Dot gain is next to impossible to measure. Mathematical models of it don't work. The numbers used to define it are incomprehensible, and the industry can't even agree on what they mean. In typical conditions it changes constantly, and it also isn't the same in every color.

No wonder that virtually all Photoshop books and documentation wimp out on dot gain, saying, ask the print shop what to do.

That is absolutely ghastly advice. I would sooner go to a local psychic than ask the printer. The advice would likely be of equal validity, but at least with a psychic there is less chance of us being bluffed by a reassuring manner. Exact dot gain numbers are irrelevant to most print shops' workflow. If they did know them, they probably wouldn't tell you. Higher dot gains often indicate poorer print conditions.

In short, the documentation won't help, your service bureau and your printer won't help, and a color-measurement device won't help. No, you're in the deep water all by yourself, and if you refuse to try to swim, your jobs will drown in excess ink.

The Few Things We Know

There aren't many generalities one can make about dot gain other than, the more you spend, the less of it you're likely to see. The same image printed on different paper usually seems to be darker on the cheaper stock. Similarly, the more a press is built for speed, the less it is built for quality. Very fast presses usually seem to print darker than more conservative ones.

Figure 12.1 *The circle at lower right is set up to have the same ink values as the left side of the green stripe. Your eyes aren't fooling you—even a colorimeter would find that the circle is darker. How and why did this occur?*

Even these sketchy rules have exceptions, however. About the best we can say for sure is, if the image is going to print on newsprint, it will seem darker than it would on better papers. Consequently, we have to, by hook or by crook, produce a *lighter* final image than usual if we are intending it to appear in a newspaper.

Everything else is a matter of probabilities. Sheetfed presses are slower, and therefore usually seem to print lighter than web (rollfed) presses. Bet on this by assuming a lower dot gain for sheetfed printing—just don't bet your life.

It's especially a matter of probabilities because in the pressroom, dot gain changes not just minute by minute, but one can commonly have different dot gains at the same moment on the same unit of the same press. Where the press form is large, the outside pages of a signature frequently suffer higher or lower dot gains than those printed on the inside. Similarly, on web presses, pages printed on the inside of the paper roll often show more dot gain than those printed on the relatively smoother side of the paper on the outside of the roll.

Whether you followed that last paragraph or not, it should be clear that this is very much a by-guess-and-by-gosh adjustment. It's possible to do it all in one's head, not changing any Photoshop settings but simply producing lighter separations and hoping for the best.

Most people, however, find it more sensible to adjust the dot gain percentage, either permanently in File: Color Settings>Working CMYK>Custom CMYK, or temporarily by making the separation through Image: Mode>Convert to Profile.

The two halves of the woman's face in Figure 12.2 illustrate our predicament. Both

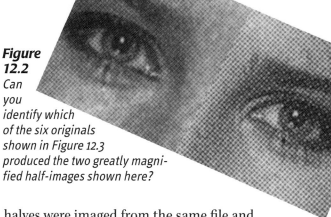

Figure 12.2 *Can you identify which of the six originals shown in Figure 12.3 produced the two greatly magnified half-images shown here?*

halves were imaged from the same file and printed under what purported to be similar conditions. I have scanned and greatly magnified the results. The dot pattern is much better defined in the right half.

In real life, the dots in either half will be too small for viewers to perceive, but because of their different structures, they'll see two different images. What do you think those differences will be?

How Predictable Is It?

The age of electronics has spoiled us. Computers, platesetters, and film recorders are reliable instruments. Their performance doesn't vary much from day to day.

Unfortunately, at the very end, a mechanical dinosaur stomps all over this parade of precision. A press slathers ink which varies in color from hour to hour over a series of rollers of questionable reliability to a plate that wears down during the run. At enormous speeds, that plate smashes into, and transfers ink to, a big slab of rubber. The rubber's performance depends very much on how old it is and how tightly it is locked into position.

The rubber, in turn, applies ink onto paper. The paper's ability to accept this is affected by press speed, humidity, temperature, and several other factors. Also, the performance of one side of the sheet is typically not the same as the other.

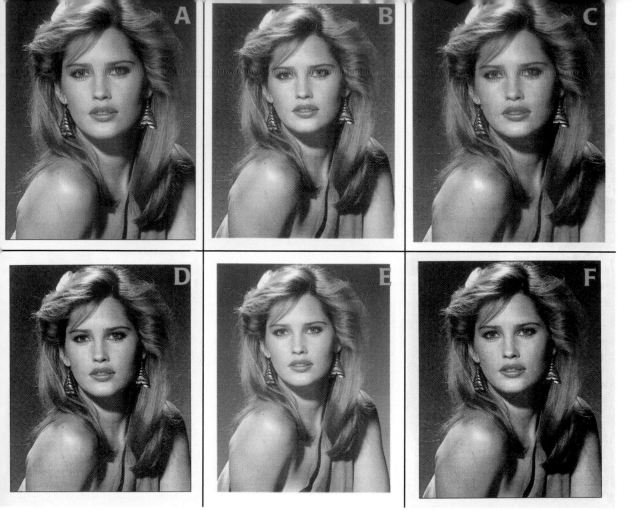

Figure 12.3 *Real-life dot gain variation. This digital file has been printed in six different publications that nominally have similar printing conditions. As you can see, they don't. Which of these do you consider to be close enough that you would say they "match"?*

The picture shown in Figure 12.3 has appeared in six different publications at very close to the sizes you see here. All came from the same digital file. All were scanned with the same settings. Although I have corrected them to eliminate problems associated with rescreening, the same moves applied to all six, so there was no change in relative colors. In the area around each image, you can see the color of the paper. Figures 12.3A, 12.3C, and 12.3E printed with a 150-line screen. The others used 133.

These are all supposed to look alike. As you can see, they don't. Let me try to explain why, and also why in certain cases it could have been predicted and in other cases not.

Figures 12.3D and 12.3F appeared several months apart in two U.S. magazines which both used the same film source and printer, who apparently had their processes well under control. The highlight areas in 12.3D are slightly lighter but I think that's because the paper is lighter—check out the added darkness behind 12.3F.

Figure 12.3A, the largest of the bunch, ran in a third U.S. magazine. It resembles 12.3D and 12.3F, but is flatter and darker, suggesting a higher dot gain. Part of this may be due to the slightly finer screen. Anyway, the reproduction is within reason.

Figure 12.3E is from a Russian magazine. Alone of the six, it was printed on a sheetfed press. These ordinarily have lower dot gains than the webs, or roll-fed presses, that print most magazines. Moreover, in Europe it is customary to image and strip with positive film, rather than the negative film used in the United States. The use of positive film actually counters dot gain, although it causes other problems.

It's therefore no surprise that this image is the lightest of the six. Could we have predicted this result? Well, no. The lightness is about right, but something went wrong: the picture is drastically weak in yellow.

Picture C also was not printed in the United States. It appeared in a South American publication. Like E, it isn't particularly close to the others, being both darker and redder.

Figure 12.3B is from *Professional Photoshop 5*. It's lighter than the rest, because it was imaged direct to plate. This eliminates an intermediate step—the contacting of film to a plate—which reduces dot gain.

And now, look again at Figure 12.2. Can you identify the two images from which it was made?

Dot Integrity and Color Integrity

The whole dot structure of the right half is much crisper, better defined, than on the left, where you see dot gain in its most classic form. The dots are bleeding into the paper, losing their shape and seeming to be wider. This creates the illusion than the left half is darker.

Not only that, the left half is redder. Partially that's because the magenta and yellow dots, which dominate in fleshtones, are getting bigger. But the cyan dots, which moderate red, are practically missing. You can, especially if you take out a magnifying glass, see flecks of cyan in the right half, but not in the left.

The left half therefore comes from the reddest of the six images, Figure 12.3C. The right half comes from 12.3B. It owes its sharpness to dots that were written directly on the printing plate, as opposed to an intermediate piece of film followed by a photographic exposure to the plate.

Somebody needs to have a word with the printer of Figure 12.3C. In addition to the heavy dot gain, they are having trouble holding the lightest dots, which is why the cyan is missing in action. These things suggest they should be using a coarser screen. They also suggest that many of the things that seem related to dot gain in fact are not.

Similarly, the extra darkness in Figure 12.3A could be dot gain—or it could be that the printer's magenta ink is slightly contaminated, too red. Or, perhaps there's something odd about the printing units that are laying down the magenta and yellow inks. It's better to think of the job as being printed on four separate presses rather than one. It's completely normal for the dot gains for each ink to be different.

If a job doesn't print as expected, the cause could be any of the above. Or, it could be completely random. Maybe the humidity was too high that day. Maybe somebody forgot to wash a press unit on schedule. Maybe the press wasn't running at its normal speed. Maybe the copy of the magazine I got isn't typical of the rest of the pressrun. Or, likeliest of all, maybe the pressmen were asleep during this particular reproduction.

Your eyes may glaze over at this point,

and with good reason. Only a handful of people, mostly pressmen, are capable of whipping out the loupe that resides permanently in their pocket, and correctly analyzing all the factors that contributed to second-rate quality.

On the other hand, most everybody is capable of determining that one set of images looks darker than another. It doesn't really matter what the cause is. If you assume that it's dot gain you can act to take better control of your final product. Doing so is appallingly simple: if images consistently seem to print too dark, move your dot gain setting up. If too light, move it down.

Pick a Number, Any Number

In Photoshop, the default dot gain is 20%. If you don't know what that figure is supposed to mean, the chances of your being able to deduce it by logic are nil. I therefore am privileged to inform you that, for reasons best known to others, the dot gain figure is the number of points—not the percentage—by which a 50% dot appears to increase. In other words, a 35% dot gain means that a 50% dot would seem to the viewer to be 85%.

Try figuring out a way to measure this, and you'll understand why the specific number has little meaning. Where dot gain is high the printing is more than a little irregular, so artificial devices have a tough time getting a handle on it. Furthermore, there's the best-behavior-syndrome problem. Like many people with a prepress background, my customary manner of speaking contains, as a grammarian would put it, certain substandard usages. You will not find any of these in this book, because I have cleaned up my act, knowing that the editor will delete such peccadillos anyway.

It should not come as a great shock to learn that pressmen behave in the same way when printing swatches that they know are about to be measured for the purposes of checking press quality. The very fact that they are printing sample sheets calls into question whether the samples are representative of real printing conditions. You can bet that they won't be *worse* than in real life.

Not to mention, many of the people who design the swatch patterns that they ask to be printed in order to measure with some artificial device don't appreciate the realities of the pressroom. Printing something like Figure 10.5 isn't like the tree in the forest that nobody hears when it falls. As we saw in Figure 10.3, in Figure 12.1, and are about to see again, what one prints alters press behavior. Big chunks of nearly solid color alter it quite substantially.

There is also the lack of any history. In the days before desktop publishing, there most certainly was no consensus on what "35% dot gain" meant. So, although we didn't admit it, we guessed. We made arbitrarily lighter separations and told the world that we were being scientific about it.

The bottom line is, 35%, 20%, or whatever, are almost random numbers. We try them out, and if the resulting separations look too dark, we raise them. If they look too light, we lower them.

As for what Photoshop's default dot gain number should be, one might as well ask what the default waist size should be for the pants of each Photoshop user. *Any* setting is going to be too dark for certain uses and too light for others. The box on Page 244 will get you started.

Don't fall for the old line about asking your printer, either. Most printers have no clue what their dot gain is, I regret to say. And, even if they think they know it, they are likely to understate it, for two very understandable reasons. First, if they tried to measure it, the press sheet that they measured is itself suspect, and real-life conditions are probably worse. And perhaps more important, higher dot gains suggest poorer printing, so the printer has a strong motivation to embellish the truth.

If you are trying to figure out the dot gain of a press, be sure to have at least half a dozen image samples, preferably printed at different times. Remember, a press is extremely variable. If you calibrate to a single printed image, that's certain to be the one that ran while the head pressman was out for a beer or on the day some lamebrain spilled black ink in the magenta fountain.

Plus, there's the impact of the monitor. We adjust the dot gain setting until the monitor matches the actual printed samples. While all properly calibrated monitors should show approximately the same colors, there is certainly no guarantee that the dot gain I set for 22% using my monitor shouldn't be 20% or 24% on yours.

The Setting's Effects

The dot gain setting lives in Custom CMYK (Photoshop 6); CMYK Setup (Photoshop 5) or Printing Inks Setup (previous

versions). If you are using third-party profiles for separation, you have just run into one of their major limitations: you can't adjust dot gain.

For a file that is now and forever in RGB or LAB, altering the dot gain setting changes nothing. For a file that is now and forever in CMYK, changing it does nothing to the file—but it does change the way the image appears on screen. Raise the dot gain setting, and it will look darker, even though it's the same file.

A more accurate monitor display is not to be sneezed at, but the big return is more accurate separations. Consider two copies of the same RGB file. Let's separate one with 10% dot gain. Ordinarily, we'd make such a

Figure 12.4 *The same original LAB file separated at 10% dot gain (left) and 30% (right).*

weird one-time conversion by means of Image: Mode>Convert to Profile, to avoid having to make a change in Edit: Color Settings, but for present purposes we have to assume that it was done by creating a new Custom CMYK for Color Settings.

We now have one RGB and one CMYK file. They match on screen, more or less.

Now, change dot gain to 30%. This darkens the CMYK image, but not the RGB. So the images no longer match.

Finally, make another copy of the RGB image and convert it to CMYK, dot gain still at 30%. This new CMYK matches the RGB, but it's much lighter than the first CMYK we produced.

If we now change the dot gain setting to 20%, none of the three images will match.

Which is better? That depends on what use it will be put to. The actual dot gain for this book (in current Photoshop terminology) is around 15%. Assuming too little dot gain, as in Figure 12.4A, makes the image too dark. Assuming too much, as in 12.4B, makes it resemble Casper the Friendly Ghost, highly suitable for a newspaper but not a book.

Note the funky things an incorrect setting can do not just for darkness, but for color. Dot gain affects midtones more than light or dark areas. In this picture, the magenta plate is in the midtone range both in the pink house and the grass. Assuming too little dot gain makes Photoshop separate the file with too much magenta in these areas. That makes the house look pinker, since no other ink is competing with the dominating magenta. But in the grass, magenta poisons the dominating green color.

Thus, some colors are suppressed and others enhanced. The greens are livelier in

the right-hand version but the pinks are more vivid in the other.

The bottom line is, if you know in advance what the destination is, and set up dot gain appropriately, your original separation will be a lot more like what you want.

This will be so even if we have to guess—and often enough, we do. Maybe Figure 12.3C was an aberration. But if I had to prepare another file specifically for that magazine, I'd add two points to my dot gain setting before separating into CMYK.

Again: accurate assessment of dot gain is the key to a successful calibration. As Ogden Rood pointed out in Chapter 10, luminosity is far more important than color accuracy.

This is why profiles done by knowledgeable, experienced people are usually better than those done by machines measuring swatches. Dot gain is notoriously a matter of perception, not of measurement.

And besides, to go anywhere in the color world, you pretty much have to be able to do this anyway. In calibrationist heaven, every output device has a reliable profile, reliably generated by reliable instrumentation reading reliable swatches.

Back in the real world, we get no supplied profile. We get a picture or two that look worse than we expected, and from there we have to wing it.

The Parrot Uncertainty Principle

And speaking of guesses, were you able to come up with an explanation for what fouled up my demonstration in the column shown in Figure 12.1?

Allow me to cut to the chase. The parrot did it.

When we ask an offset press to print a large area with very heavy coverage in one or more inks, it becomes almost impossible to maintain a normal density of those inks in that zone of the page.

Ordinarily, this effect manifests itself when an art director calls for a design element that has a huge component of one ink in it. It takes close to 100% coverage of one or more inks in an area at least a couple of square inches to trigger the problem, and that rarely happens in a photograph.

But in the parrot image, it does happen. The bird's red chest is close to 100% in both magenta and yellow. That virtually guarantees that anything falling below it will get much more of those inks than it should. The extra magenta seriously contaminated the green circle.

This accounts for the drastic change in the magenta and yellow components of the circle. The cyan increased, too, but that's just the way it is with offset presses. Three-point variation across the sheet is always possible. We can't blame the bird for that.

I'll bet that this parrot can do it again, in a different context. He appears at full size in Figure 7.3. The same file appears at a much smaller size in Figure 8.1. In *Professional Photoshop 5,* the massive area of red in Figure 7.3 fed on itself and produced a far more vivid (and less orange) color than in the smaller version. Did it happen again?

This is one of the many reasons that basing dot gain decisions on a single image is silly. What we need is a suite of 10 or 20 of them, and have the printer run off some tests of each, preferably at at least three different times of day.

Let's get real.

Having to guess at what the printing conditions may be is unpleasant, but it happens all the time. You shouldn't be afraid of tampering with Photoshop's dot gain controls, and saving a setup for each printing condition you have to work with.

The whole phenomenon, after all, is hugely subjective. Especially under poorer conditions, printing isn't consistent across the sheet. Even if it were, what would you measure? As noted earlier, a bunch of swatches, like the industry-standard IT-8 of Figure 10.5, may be appropriate for a digital printer. On press, however, there is what might be called the Parrot Uncertainty Principle. The very presence of such a large, heavily inked area changes ink flow—and invalidates the measurement.

It doesn't matter which version of Photoshop you use, or whether you understand that they compute dot gain in different ways, or why. What does matter is that if your prints consistently look too dark you should increase the dot gain setting a little, and if they look too light you need to decrease it.

As hamhanded as this approach seems, the results are actually quite consistent. Limiting the discussion to the four images that were printed in the United States, reproduction was quite predictable. Because I'd worked with the magazine for a long time, I'd developed accurate dot gain settings, so Figure 12.3F agreed closely with what I saw on my monitor. Figure 12.3D, with the same service bureau and the same printer, is highly similar.

The slight extra darkness of Figure 12.3A is the normal result of a finer screen. The lightness of Figure 12.3B is the usual consequence of going direct to plate. These two came out almost exactly the way I thought they would. In this particular case great color fidelity wasn't an issue, but if it were, I would have made a dot gain adjustment before working on them. I would therefore

Taking Your Best Guess at Dot Gain

Some pressmen can tell what kind of a dot gain a certain paper will have by running it along the underside of their tongues. If learning that method sounds too difficult, try using the following in Photoshop's setups. If you go to more than one type of output, you'll need more than one set of dot gains. This is for presswork only. As for ink-jet or toner-based color printers, the technology is changing quickly and each device is different, so you'll have to fend for yourself. After setting the base figure, remember to lessen cyan and increase black dot gain (see Chapter 6).

These recommendations are conservative, because we are far better off overestimating the dot gain than we are underestimating it. If the pressman has to adjust ink to match our proofs, we want him adding ink, not subtracting and making everything look mangy. These values assume coated paper, and are starting points only. Obviously, as you see more results from a given process or press, you'll be able to tweak these numbers (down, usually) to get more accuracy.

Waterless sheetfed printing If handled properly, this is the highest quality offset printing available. Set your dot gain for 6%.

Sheetfed offset The standard for short-run jobs. Use 11%.

Default If you haven't got a clue where the job is going, assume web offset conditions. It's a lot easier to darken a file if you must than it is to lighten it; similarly, pictures that print too light are less objectionable to most people than overly dark ones. 17%.

Web offset These high-speed presses are quite variable. Start with 17%. If the press has on-line ovens (heat-set offset), subtract two points.

Gravure Unless you are printing hundreds of thousands of copies, you won't run across this technology. If you do, assume that the dot gain is somewhat lower than normal web, tempered by the fact that the paper is probably cheaper. 17%.

Eccentric substrates If you print on plastic, metal, fabric, fertilizer bags, cardboard, canvas, or the like, your dot gain will be high, but there are few rules beyond that. Try 40%.

There are a number of factors that would modify these recommendations. If any of them apply to you, make the following additions or subtractions:

The stock For supercalendared (ultrasmooth) uncoated paper, +3. For standard grades of uncoated paper, +5. For high groundwood uncoateds (you should be able to perceive tonal variation in this paper), +8. For newsprint, +12.

The film If your job is imaged on positive film (common practice in Europe, but not the U.S.) −3.

Direct to plate If your job is going to a commercial press—not a hybrid such as Xeikon or Indigo—and the plate is imaged directly from your digital file, with no use of film, −3.

The halftone screen Unless you are printing waterless, if your job is using a 175 LPI screen, +1; if higher +4; if a stochastic screen +8.

While it pays to try to get it right, remember that all this is guesswork. Normal pressroom variation is at least four points in either direction. At least two more points could be blamed on the inaccuracy of your monitor. So, a 10 or 12 point total variation, which is huge, is possible, though uncommon.

have been adequately calibrated to both printing conditions even though I had never seen a proof or worked with these printers before.

Preparing a file for press is always a guess, always a gamble. Understanding the dot gain setting, and being willing to change it, is a fine way to improve the odds.

Of Liquids and Papers

Dot gain describes a complex interaction between ink, dye, or toner, and paper. It afflicts any print device, not just presses. The continuous-tone look of most printed pictures comes from very small dots; how well their shape is held determines final quality.

When liquid hits paper, some gets absorbed. This rule of physics is not suspended just because the liquid happens to be ink. We attempt to print a dot, and the dot spreads into the paper. The more it spreads, the larger the dot will seem from viewing distance, creating the illusion of greater darkness.

But a sense of added darkness isn't the only impact: dot gain can shift colors, as well. It discriminates most cruelly, ignoring light and dark areas and saving its full fury for midtones.

In other words, if a certain ink is supposed to print between around 30% and 60%, it ordinarily will seem to darken more than the others. If you are trying to evaluate dot gain in an image of a woman wearing a bright red dress, therefore, look to the face. Forget the dress. It's heavy in magenta and yellow, light in cyan, and dot gain isn't much of a factor. Stick with the faces, which are a lighter, subtler species of red.

Across all races, faces have mid-range amounts of magenta and yellow. This invites dot gain, and there isn't much cyan

to hide it. When you see an unduly red face in print, it probably doesn't mean that the subject is embarrassed but that the artist is underestimating dot gain.

Other telltale areas: purplish skies, lack of shadow detail, and a general muddy appearance. Skies have more cyan in them than magenta; as the color gets deeper, the magenta component deepens faster. And the muddy look is usually caused by a relatively heavy black plate, coupled with misguessing black dot gain.

If you're inclined to try your hand at this, several of the CMYK images that printed in Chapters 2 and 3 are included on our CD. Can you alter your own Custom CMYK to make your screen match the book?

Of Numbers and Blunders

At least three different mathematical models of dot gain exist, the details of which would put a volcano to sleep. The most widely accepted one, the Murray-Davies equation, sensibly requires measurements not just of the blank paper, one perfectly imaged and one real-life pattern of 50% dots, but a swatch of 100% as well. In this version, the dot gain number derives not just from the difference between theoretical and actual 50%, but between actual 50% and actual 100%.

This discussion is getting messy, so let's get to the bottom line. You will recall that the introduction of Photoshop 5 created considerable trouble by, without warning, changing the meaning of the dot gain numbers. The new model, which Photoshop 6 also employs, doesn't use this 100% measurement. Its numbers therefore need to be set lower than industry standards. Photoshop 4 and earlier versions needed to be set *higher* than industry standards.

For a North American magazine printed on a web press using coated publication stock, dot gain ought to be about 22%. Such, at any rate, is the view of two standards groups, SWOP and GRACOL. This number, however, converts to about 17% in Photoshop.

Even that's an oversimplification. SWOP and GRACOL actually say that dot gain is 22% only in magenta and cyan. In yellow they suggest 20%, and in the critical black plate, 26%. And, horrors, they say we should expect differences of plus or minus five points, depending on the printer, the stock, the phase of the moon, and other factors.

The way they get these numbers is itself highly suspect. Color-measurement instruments are fairly good at evaluating solid patches, but notoriously inaccurate at reading printed dots, especially in poor print conditions. Plus, there are several complicating factors, such as ink purity and transparency, that can cause the illusion of a different dot gain than even a precise measurement would predict. And even if you could miraculously generate an accurate number, it would likely be valid only for the particular imagesetter that handled your sample. Different brands make different dot shapes, and different dot shapes make for different dot gain.

Of Ghoulies and Ghosties

All this should indicate that the theory of dot gain is tenebrous at best and that the settings themselves are guesses, about as reliable as Tarot card readings. This leads to the question of whether it makes any sense to pay attention to them at all.

If you work only in RGB, you needn't. But if you are converting RGB to CMYK, it affects the separation process. Once a file is in CMYK, changing the setting no longer changes the file, but it will affect the monitor preview. Once you have converted a file, you can no longer blame the service bureau or printer: the onus is on you.

Yes, the concept is difficult. Yes, plenty of people create good color without understanding it. Yes, the methods of Chapters 2–9 will make your images look better whether you have a correct dot gain setting or not.

But, once you get it, changing the settings is so easy! What on earth is the point of having every picture print darker than the monitor shows? Why lose detail in the darker areas of every image because the original separation stank? Why have every face print too red? Why, when you can make the adjustment in seconds?

I suggest that allowing these things to happen is stupid, and offer the following recommendations.

In Custom CMYK, start the guesswork by entering the dot gain value suggested by the box on Page 244—14% for this direct-to-plate book.

That box says nothing about color copiers and other non-impact printers. Such devices usually have more dot gain than a press—but vendors often hide this by an internal routine that lightens all incoming files, in an attempt to emulate the look of commercial printing. Since there's no way of predicting whether this may be happening, we're better off assuming that it is a press, until proven otherwise.

Next, you need some printed samples. If you really are trying to profile a press, you need a *lot* of printed samples, because just two or three may not be typical. If you're trying to outguess a large-format printer or digital proofer, you don't need quite so many, as most of these devices are more stable than any press.

Try to use humdrum stuff for the samples, not spectacular "calibration" images like Photoshop's "Olé No Moiré." or Figure 11.3. Remember, brilliant colors are immune to dot gain's caress.

Assuming that you have a monitor that otherwise is in reasonable shape, with the sample CMYK images open on your system, compare them to the printed results. If the screen image always looks lighter, you need to increase the dot gain setting. If the screen looks too dark, you need to lighten it. Again: fooling around with the dot gain setting on a document that's already in CMYK doesn't change the file, only the way it looks on screen.

Why, you may ask, doesn't the printer, or somebody else, just tell me what the dot gain setting should be?

Well, do you suppose that if you plug somebody else's dot gain into your monitor, however great the care you have may taken in calibrating it, that it will look the same as his? On a Macintosh, there are at least six different hardware and software controls that may impact monitor appearance. Under Wintel, there aren't quite as many, but still more than enough to derail any great precision in the monitor tweaking department.

Some will tell you that all you need is to drop a few thousand dollars on calibration equipment and a consultant to run it, and your monitor's very mother wouldn't be able to tell it from another similarly ravished screen. This is, not to use a stronger term, rot. It's quite OK for the same files to look more accurate at 18% dot gain on one calibrated monitor and 20% on another.

In fairness, it's possible to so mess up a monitor that it will seem that 3%, or 40%, is the right dot gain for sheetfed printing. If so, you need more help than this book can give.

And Four-Channeled Beasties

Having established an overall dot gain number, we need to turn attention to the individual inks—especially black.

In all CMYK work, black gain is higher than the others. On digital devices this may only be 3 or 4 points, but on presses it can be more.

It's also important to get a handle on what's happening with magenta. For things other than presses, it's fairly safe to assume it behaves like cyan. But on press, its dot gain is often higher, and as the paper gets worse, the effect gets more pronounced.

In principle, magenta shouldn't be as vital as black, but there's a catch. Dot gain is

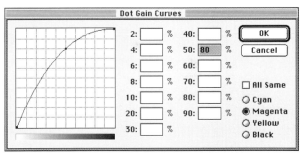

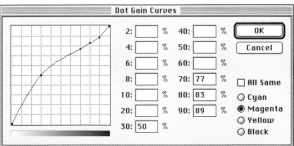

Figure 12.5 *When dot gain is extreme, as in newspaper printing, the normal curve (top) is somewhat inadequate. The custom curve at bottom is usually more accurate—but remember, it's all basically guesswork.*

greatest in the middle ranges. If a certain object is between 35^K and 55^K, it will be a fairly subdued color, unlikely to be the most important thing in the picture. But objects having between 35^M and 55^M are likely to be skin, and skin often *is* the most important thing in the picture.

Purists should assume yellow has a couple of points less dot gain than the other three. Don't hold your breath waiting to see a practical impact of this; yellow is a weak ink. We have a lot of leeway to get it wrong. Black and magenta, that's another story.

In Custom CMYK, change dot gain from "Standard" to "Curves." Up will pop the curve for cyan, and another testimonial to how difficult the whole concept is.

The MYK curves raise 50% by the dot gain amount in Custom CMYK. In Figure 12.5, where that value is 30%, the magenta curve moves 50% to 80%. The cyan curve, however, will be four points higher—in this case, 84%.

In other words, the presets assume that cyan has more dot gain than do the other three inks. As far as I know, there are no printing conditions on this planet of which this is true.

Nobody at Adobe knows how this howler got perpetrated, as it dates from many versions ago. Having analyzed how Photoshop's separation algorithm works, I think I know: it was a counterkludge for a self-inflicted problem with gray generation. But that's irrelevant; what counts is that it's wrong. As a start, reduce cyan to be equal to the magenta, set the midpoint of the yellow 2 points lower than either, and black 4 points higher.

Beyond this, it's a matter of twiddling. Frequently the magenta should go a little higher. Also, in many cases the results will be slightly better if the curve has a control point at 40% rather than 50%, steepening its light half and having a smoother slope in its darker half as in Figure 12.5.

Of these moves, by far the most important is the increase in black. In offset printing, black density is inconsistent, and sometimes is much heavier than expected. Two default CMYK settings should be changed, to cater to this unhappy fact.

The traditional high-end black plate is a "skeleton" with little weight in colored areas. Either UCR or Light GCR will get this. The default, Medium GCR, makes more sense on something like an Iris printer, where ink density is more consistent. On a press, however, it's a chancier proposition.

Press or printer, however, you should change the default of 100% black ink limit to 75% to 85%, to avoid having shadow detail close up.

If most of your work goes to a single printer, you may find that certain tweaks are helpful. For example, magenta dot gain often seems higher in the quartertone than in the midtone. If you see this occurring, you can compensate by putting an additional point in the magenta dot gain curve. Assuming again 16% overall dot gain, this second point might raise 20 to 34, leaving the 50 to 66 point alone.

If you are dead set and determined to make use of these curves, and if your work prints in a newspaper or other high dot gain environment, here's a tip. Use the curve shape shown in the bottom half of Figure 12.5. When dot gain is high, the effect is more noticeable in the quarter- to midtone range and less in the shadows. With the default curve shown at top, too much detail will be lost in the mid- to three-quartertone in the conversion.

DOT GAIN AND CUSTOM CMYK

✓ The key issue in calibration of CMYK files is understanding the difficult phenomenon of dot gain. Dot gain can roughly be described as a darkening effect that varies in intensity from device to device. However, it's more complex than that, and often affects colors as well.

✓ Changing the dot gain setting in Custom CMYK does not affect the integrity of files that are already in CMYK. It does, however, make them appear darker on screen. Files that never enter CMYK are unaffected by changes in the setting.

✓ At the moment of separation, the dot gain setting is critical. The higher the setting, the lighter the separation will be. This is deceptive, because it won't *seem* to be darker on screen: the same setting that lightens the separation also darkens the monitor display.

✓ Presses are so variable that many samples are needed before coming to any firm conclusions about dot gain behavior. More stable devices such as digital proofers don't have this problem.

✓ Nevertheless, one is often called on to estimate dot gain based on woefully incomplete information. Therefore, developing guesstimating skill is important.

✓ Starting with Photoshop 5, the meanings of the dot gain numbers were changed. If you are upgrading from Photoshop 4 or previous versions, you need to review information on the enclosed CD. Neither set of dot gain numbers agrees with the methodology used by leading industry sources such as SWOP.

✓ Measurements of dot gain with artificial instruments are inherently unreliable, particularly as printing conditions deteriorate. Using the eyeball method—if the printed results consistently look too dark, raise the dot gain setting, and vice versa—is not just simpler, but more accurate.

✓ As with all calibration issues, don't act until you see a consistent pattern. If some of your images print too dark and others too light, this is a problem of process control, not your dot gain setting.

✓ Files already in CMYK can be repurposed for different CMYK conditions—such as a desktop proofer—by using Photoshop 6's Convert to Profile command, specifying a new Custom CMYK with different dot gain settings as the destination.

The Key to Calibration

Accurate dot gain adjustment opens many doors. Appropriate settings are the only way to get a monitor to give a believable preview of what a job will look like in print, and are far more important in calibration than is accuracy in rendering color. Besides being the simplest way to calibrate a desktop printer, this is also the most effective: your eyes will do a better job of gauging dot gain than any artificial instrument. No need to hire someone to make a custom profile!

Unlike past versions, which required frequent changes in CMYK Setup with the attendant possibility of working a file with the wrong settings, Photoshop 6's Color Settings needn't be tinkered with once we have them where we want them. Instead, when we need something unusual, we go to the Convert to Profile command.

If, for example, you're trying to make your desktop inkjet behave like a contract proofer, it's easily done—provided you can come up with valid Custom CMYKs for both your device and for the job's eventual printer. And that, of course, depends almost entirely on whether you understand this dot gain business.

Once you have these Custom CMYKs, you can save them into System Folder/ColorSync Profiles (Macs) or [Windows or Win NT]/[System or System 32]/Color Folder. They will now appear regularly in the Convert to Profile dialog, just like any other Photoshop-supplied profile.

When the time comes to proof your files, copy them into a folder, and use Convert to Profile to get them into the shape your desktop device wants. This can even be automated further with Photoshop's powerful File: Batch command.

An Act of Imagination

A facility which prided itself on how well its monitors matched the print once invited me for a visit. When I got there I had to reach for my sunglasses. Every screen was wildly yellow.

Once they scraped me off the ceiling, I had to concede that perhaps they had a point. Pretending that a monitor matches a piece of paper is at best an act of imagination. Training the eye to ignore a yellow cast seems to me as easy as ignoring the huge difference in contrast.

Not, however, if the dot gain setting is wrong. These people had it right.

So ends our three-chapter discussion of the puzzling phenomena of calibration, calibrationism, separation settings and color management, of which compensating for dot gain is the most important part.

If sufficiently anal, one can go crazy with all these controls, measuring and tweaking each curve ad infinitum. I have nothing against this, but there are better ways to expend energy.

On the other hand, being able to guess at dot gain—perhaps on the basis of only one or two samples—is a skill that is going to become more important. Noncontact printing is growing fast, but it isn't a mature technology. Every new machine has its own characteristics. If you think each vendor is qualified to write a profile that will compensate for them, may I suggest you are living in a fool's paradise.

The crapshoot nature of the printing game dictates that we will be disappointed some of the time. But if you are getting disappointed all of the time, there's something wrong. Look to dot gain, and take your best guess.

13

Friend and Foe in Black and White

Before taking a color picture into black and white, be Orwellian. Realize that all channels are equal, but some are more equal than others. But be Machiavellian, too: find out which one is your enemy—and proceed to eliminate it.

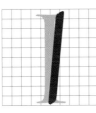

n the good old days, color photos implied color printing. Jobs that were to appear in black and white—which were the majority, given the high cost of color—were generally shot in black and white as well.

Nowadays, however, nearly every picture is shot in color—but quite a lot of them still need to print in black and white. The good news is that Photoshop provides a number of ways to make a really sparkling conversion.

The bad news is, in the old days the client could only compare the printed result to a black and white original. Today, there's a *color* original floating around, ready to thumb us in the eye, laughing at how futile our conversion technique is.

This is a considerably deeper topic than many people think. But I would like to suggest a method that will greatly improve the process. It's based on understanding what gets lost during the conversion—and then putting some of it back again.

To start with, a small quiz. Think back to the brilliantly colored parrot we've seen earlier. Figure 13.1 offers two different B/W renditions, each done quickly. Which do you think is better? When you've made up

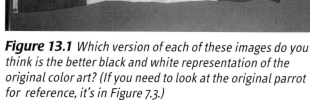

Figure 13.1 *Which version of each of these images do you think is the better black and white representation of the original color art? (If you need to look at the original parrot for reference, it's in Figure 7.3.)*

your mind, consider the two B/W versions of the Canadian flag, and answer the same question.

I've presented this choice to several large audiences. The vote isn't quite unanimous, but upwards of 95% agree. Given the brilliant reds, blues, and yellows of the parrot the top B/W version is fairly bogus. The bottom version is more faithful to the original. Similarly, the top flag clearly stands out better against the sky than does the bottom one.

I intentionally didn't print the color original of the flag, to avoid calling attention to what it has in common with the parrot. We'll get back to that original later; meanwhile, let's talk about contrast, and the lack thereof in black and white.

The Fatal Flatness in B/W

Color pictures almost invariably appear flat when they go to B/W. A lot of the contrast we saw in the color original is gone, and we can no longer distinguish some of the subtler details. It's our job to get them back.

Eventually, we have to make a mode change into grayscale. In doing so, Photoshop uses a weighted-average method based on RGB values, even if the image we are converting is in CMYK. Each new B/W pixel gets about 60 percent of the value of the green component of the RGB, 30 percent of the red, and 10 percent of the blue. As usual, some calibrationists, seduced by anything that seems to have a mathematical formula in it, claim that this will always give the most "accurate," and hence best, rendition of a color photograph.

Figure 13.2 is a little test of this assertion. Let's see what happens when we convert this "picture" to B/W using this infallible formula.

In a proper conversion, the B/W image should be crisp and legible. The viewer should be able to form a mental picture of what the color image looks like. If these are our objectives, we have obviously failed miserably. What went wrong?

Poor understanding of color management and color theory, that's what. Figure 13.2 is basically an illustration of the HSB colorspace discussed in Chapter 8. In the left third of the image, there is a big contrast in hue between the red and the blue square. Unfortunately, hue contrast is worth deedledy-bop in B/W, so the conversion doesn't work too well.

In the center third, there is a big contrast in saturation between the two greens. As saturation is a meaningless concept in B/W, this conversion is lamentable as well.

In the right-hand third, the contrast is neither hue nor saturation, but luminosity. Bingo! Luminosity not only counts in B/W, it's the *only* thing that counts. So this conversion is quite acceptable.

If the color image is full of luminosity contrast, we're in good shape. If not, we have to take action. We have to find the contrast that will vanish, and convert it into the kind of contrast that won't.

It's useful to think of B/W in terms of HSB—we just have to remember that H and S are now worthless.

If we start with the bottom version and try to correct it, we will get nowhere fast. We have to do something, but whatever it

Figure 13.2 Certain types of contrast convert well to black and white, but other varieties completely dry up.

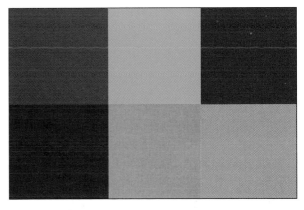

Figure 13.3 *Images have three kinds of contrast: hue, or basic color; saturation, or purity; and luminosity, or brightness. The first two kinds vanish in B/W. Photoshop layers can be set up in Hue or Saturation mode (below). If any objects are clearly defined—as the parrot and its wings are—that's contrast that will be lost during conversion. You should be thinking of how to get it back.*

is, it has to be done to the color version, before we make the switch to black and white. This is a most important concept. A good 4/c image can produce an unacceptable B/W one. Sometimes it takes an unacceptable 4/c image to produce a good B/W one.

Foreseeing What Gets Lost

Success in this endeavor depends on three things: identifying what will be lost when hue and saturation vanish; deciding approximately what the final result *should* look like; and figuring out how to get there.

In B/W, there is contrast between the white and dark parts of the flags, and between both and the sky, which is somewhere in the middle.

But there isn't *enough* contrast, because some got left by the wayside during the conversion. In the color original, we would perceive that the flag was dark and the sky light, but we would also perceive

that the flag is red and the sky blue. That hue variation makes the flag stand out against the background much more sharply.

And so, the bottom version comes up a bit short. Not that there's no contrast between flag and sky—the flag is definitely darker—but there isn't as much as we're looking for.

We therefore must add contrast. As luminosity, or darkness contrast is the only kind that counts in B/W, that's the kind we have to add. In the top version, the flag gets darker, the sky gets lighter, and it looks more natural. A suggestion of the hue variation has been retained.

In the flag image, the contrast between red and blue is obvious, and it's also obvious that the red is currently the darker of the two. So, we know which to lighten and which to darken.

The parrot also has a red vs. blue issue, but the solution isn't so simple. If the picture were any more complicated, it might be really tough to figure out what needs to be done.

If you haven't done a lot of this before, a good way to begin is with a Photoshop layers trick. Set the image up as two identical layers, but replace the bottom one with bright green—if you're in RGB, $0^R255^G0^B$. The overall image won't look any different, because the top layer takes precedence.

Now, however, we can commence our investigation, by

changing the layer method from Normal to something else. Figure 13.3 illustrates what happens when we select Hue, Saturation, and Luminosity. The first two, though blurry, show the contrast that will be lost in black and white.

A certain amount of thinking is necessary here. Hue can show worthless variation, such as the blue blotch in the upper left corner of the image. You have to examine this and decide to ignore it. On the other hand, when objects are well defined—as the shape of the parrot is in both Hue and Saturation modes—some compensation is going to be necessary.

Two other contrast problems suggest themselves. The blue feathers are well defined in Hue mode, and the parrot's claw is visible in Saturation.

At this point, we move to a picture that's black and white and green all over, by switching the layering method to Luminosity—which is another way of saying, black and white. This helps in two ways. First, we can decide that there is already so much contrast in certain areas—such as the parrot's claw against its body—that we don't have to worry about it. Second, it can guide us to the best way of augmenting contrast.

Our two images both present the problem of differentiating something blue from something red. The red flag is plainly darker than the blue sky. In the parrot, however, it's *not* obvious whether the red chest is darker than the blue wings. That's why we often need to look at the Luminosity layer (or the Info palette, set to read LAB values).

That tells us that the wings are very slightly darker than the chest. As in the flag image, we need to enhance the difference between the two. And, since we have no hue or saturation to play with, we'll have to suggest contrast by varying darkness. We'll have to lighten the reds and darken the blues—the opposite of the move required in the flag image.

This is, incidentally, why I didn't want to show a color original. The red of a Canadian flag isn't precisely the same as the red of the parrot's chest, but it's very similar. And, in the default B/W versions of each in Figure 13.1, the two reds are indeed close, which is what one might expect.

But they shouldn't be! What those reds *used to be* is history. Maybe they were identical once, in a colorspace far, far away. There is no earthly reason for them to be identical now.

Putting a Hand on the Scale

For black and whites, we need a file with only one channel. Unfortunately, files that are in color start it with at least three. To

B/W and Duotones

Photoshop provides an excellent selection of prepackaged duotone and multitone curves, located in the application's Presets folder. The key to any good multitone image, however, is a good black and white. Accordingly, if you are taking color images and making duotones of them, you urgently need to study this chapter.

In past editions, we've had a full chapter on the problems of multitones, which are defined as any image in which each channel is based on a common ancestor, and on treatment of fifth and subsequent spot colors generally. These are topics of limited interest, and there weren't significant changes between Photoshop 5 and 6.

We've therefore, to conserve space, moved that chapter into PDF on the enclosed CD. If you need twenty pages on duotones in depth, you'll find that PDF in the Chapter 13 folder.

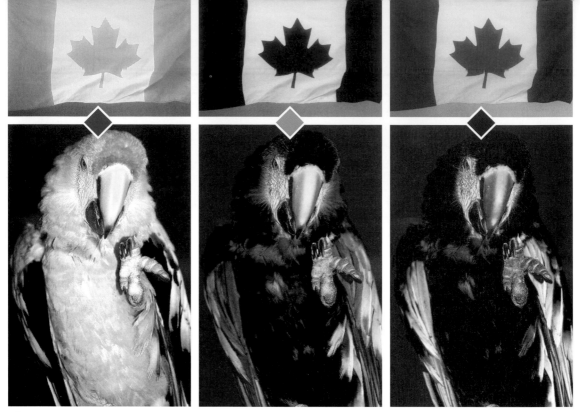

Figure 13.4 The conversion to black and white averages the red, green, and blue channels, but they aren't given equal value. The green is twice as important as the red, and six times as important as the blue.

make the switchover, we could use one of the color channels and throw away the others, or take some kind of average of all the color channels.

The channel blending I'm about to describe is the most important part of the conversion. Curves, sharpening, and CMYK trickery also come into play, but I didn't use any of them to correct either the parrot or the flag.

The single-channel approach is usually advanced by aging scanner operators, who use the green channel of RGB, throwing away the red and the blue. (Some people suggest converting the file to LAB and trashing the A and B channels, but this is essentially the same as converting to gray-scale directly.)

For several reasons, using the green is more likely to be correct than anything else.

Many times, however, this isn't true. Two of these times appear in Figure 13.4.

Suppose that we have to choose the best black and white in each case. In the flag, the green isn't bad, but the blue is better. In the parrot, all three channels are terrible, but if someone points a gun at us and tells us to choose the best one, it's the red for sure.

In short, choosing a single channel to work with is occasionally worthwhile. Taking the blue channel only of the flag might work, but taking the red of the parrot would not. An averaging method makes more sense.

That doesn't mean the averaging should always be by the Photoshop formula, in which the green channel is worth around twice as much as the red and six times as much as the blue. Instead, we should feel free to stick a heavy hand on the scale.

Who's Not with the Program?

Machiavelli wrote: "A prince ought either to be a true friend or a true enemy. He should stand wholeheartedly behind his friends, and just as wholeheartedly against his enemies. This is always smarter than remaining neutral."

Although he was not a Photoshop user, Machiavelli would have done just fine with his B/W conversions. Success often depends on finding out who your enemies are, and arranging to have them liquidated, or at least eviscerated.

In short, we need to ask: friend or foe?

In the flag image, we've concluded that we need to darken the flag and lighten the sky. Unfortunately, the red channel has a different agenda. It is the foe. The green is somewhat lacking in detail, but it's our friend. The blue is our *good* friend.

In the parrot, the wings must be darker than the chest. The green and blue channels are on a different wavelength. They are the foe. They need to find out who's boss. Our only friend, the red, will teach them.

There are many different ways to get this lesson across. Mostly, it's just a matter of remembering the recipe: six parts green, three parts red, one part blue.

One of the simplest solutions, albeit not the most intuitive, is to switch channels. Red is three times as important as blue, so switching the good blue with the bad red in the flag will improve matters. Green is twice as important as red, so switching the good red with the bad green in the parrot will give the contrast between wings and chest that we're looking for.

This can be done easily with Image: Adjust>Channel Mixer. As shown in Figure 13.5, just define the green as being based 100% on the red, and vice versa.

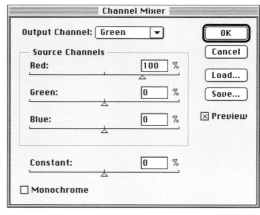

Figure 13.5 *The Channel Mixer can add contrast before the B/W conversion. Here, the green channel is replaced altogether by the red.*

This method can yield funky-looking results, such as the green parrot of Figure 13.6. Plus, my Canadian friends are still sore over an incident in a recent World Series where representatives of the U.S. armed forces undertook to display the flag of Canada upside down. What will they think when they see Figure 13.7 and find out I've made it blue?

To pacify them, the original is alongside it. Even if you don't follow the averaging process, do you see what will happen when these two go to B/W? The blue flag seems to us darker than the red one; the blue sky darker than the orange one.

The Channel Mixer isn't the only way to get this result. One could also, for example, save a copy of the RGB original, convert the copy to B/W, and then blend the best original channel into it. For that, one can't use the Channel Mixer, which only works within a single document. Instead, one could (1) paste one channel on top of the other and change the opacity in the Layers palette; (2) use the Image: Calculations command; (3) use Image: Apply Image (my favorite, because it's simpler).

There is no colorspace limitation on Apply Image blends; we can combine an RGB with a CMYK channel. This capability becomes important as the images get more complex. The flag and the parrot are fairly straightforward and there are lots of ways to attack them. Both parrots of Figure 13.6 will produce about the same B/W. The pinkish one on the right was produced by a single Apply Image, 60% of the red into the green.

Complications can arise when a channel we wish to weaken also has critical detail, where the overall range of the image is incorrect, or where there is a sharpening issue. Then, we may need to cross colorspaces. Let's go on to something tougher.

The Lion and the Fox

It goes without saying that both example images could have been made a whole lot better by the use of all the techniques of Chapters 2–4. We haven't even set a highlight or shadow. For most B/W conditions, good target points would be 3^K and 90^K.

Similarly, targeted curves and creative sharpening are concepts that work as well in black and white as in color.

In the corrected flag image, we could go further by using a curve that was steep in highlights and shadows, flatter in the midrange. This would add contrast to both the light and dark areas of the flags, while flattening out the sky, over which loss we will presumably lose no sleep. Also, sharpening would be in order, but we'd probably have to use the complex darken-more-than-lighten strategy shown back in Figure 4.13.

This is stuff you can work out for yourself. Without the preliminary blends, though, you're unlikely to get satisfactory results. Let's end with a no-holds-barred exercise.

There is plenty of color in Figure 13.8, but it is all relatively light, and full of the kind of contrast that is great in 4/c and terrible in B/W. The dark windows will certainly convert well, and the bricks will be moderately successful, though some of the color-related contrast in the bricks will vanish.

In order of importance, the major problems are:

- The sign hanging over the

Figure 13.6 *Two ways of accentuating contrast between the blue wings and the red chest. Left, swapping the red and green channels. Right, replacing the green channel with a new one that is a 60–40 blend of the old red and the old green. This can be done with the Channel Mixer, Calculations, or Apply Image commands.*

Figure 13.7 *The red channel is three times as important as the blue in the conversion to B/W. One solution to the flag problem, therefore, is to swap them. The bottom version is strangely colored, since it uses the blue channel in the red position and vice versa, but it will also convert to B/W better than the one at top.*

to exaggerate this difference before it vanishes in the conversion to B/W.

Inspection of the individual plates (Figure 13.9) shows bricks in all plates, but the sign is heaviest by far in the yellow, and the shutters are concentrated in the cyan.

In image enhancement, there is a time for delicate instruments and a time for sledgehammers and crowbars. This is one of those latter instances.

The fastest way by far to make an object darker is to get some black ink into it. Therefore, my first step was to blend 20% of the yellow into the black. The black was now much darker overall, but more importantly, it had a pronounced sign. Since this move also put some unwelcome black in the image highlight, I wrote the curve shown in Figure 13.9. This blew out the black where it wasn't wanted, but steepened the area in which the bricks and the sign fell.

This left less black than before in the bricks, so to compensate, I increased magenta above the midtone, but I killed the magenta highlight. This made the light areas even whiter and thus gave more contrast to the bricks.

Next, I went to the magenta and increased contrast by lightening the highlight and darkening the bricks. In the magenta, the shutters were already much lighter than the bricks, and this move exaggerated the difference, just as planned.

But not enough. The idea being to get

door is likely to disappear into the background bricks.

• In the color image there is great contrast between the light blue shutters and the red bricks, but this will go away in B/W.
• Maintaining some semblance of life in the doors.
• Helping out the bricks.

The shutters vs. bricks problem raises the interesting issue of which should wind up darker. If we want differentiation in B/W, we will have to make a choice.

In such cases, set up the Info palette (using its eyedropper tools) so that it reads LAB as well as Actual Color, currently CMYK. We find typical values of 73^L in the blue shutters and 71^L in the bricks. The readings in the A and B channels, being color-related only, are irrelevant. Since, in the L, a lower number is a darker one, we start off with the bricks being very slightly darker than the shutters. We need

Figure 13.8 *This image is full of the kinds of contrast that cause headaches when converted to B/W.*

shutters much lighter than the windows, I blended 50% of this magenta into the cyan, where the shutters were strongest. This left the cyan plate with shutters and bricks roughly equal. Since in the other three plates the bricks were much darker than the shutters, I called it quits there and converted to grayscale.

To Those Who Understand

Looking at the final results in Figure 13.10, you must agree that there would be no hope of ever correcting the top image to equal the one at the bottom.

If you want your B/Ws to look their best, you must logically also agree that initial corrections must be done in color. Taking it further still, you must also agree that the quality of Photoshop's CMYK-to-grayscale conversion is really a secondary issue.

Recall that all we are doing when we go into grayscale is forcing our image into a smaller colorspace of drastically different shape. It is precisely analogous to an RGB- (or LAB)-to-CMYK conversion.

If you concur that the corrected B/Ws in this chapter are overwhelmingly superior to the default conversions, you have become an anti-calibrationist. In Chapter 11, we discussed how there can't be a perfect separation algorithm, largely because CMYK doesn't have a blue and RGB and LAB do.

Black and white is simply an expanded version of this problem. In addition to not having a blue, it doesn't have a green, red, or turquoise either, among other inconveniences. But the idea is exactly the same. We're trying to stay as faithful as possible, given the limitations of the process. This is every bit as much a color management

issue as is the conversion of a color image into CMYK.

The demonstration is somewhat more dramatic—the greater the difference between the original and the colorspace we have to convert it to, the more intervention will be necessary—but the point is the same. The 6–3–1 formula is probably the best for a generalized RGB to B/W conversion. But if you rely on that exclusively, you'll get fifth-rate results.

This jigsaw puzzle has many solutions. You may not agree with the blending percentages I used, or you may use other methods that accomplish the suppression of the poor channels in favor of the contrasty ones.

If you don't do *something* along these lines, however, you are fated to have dull B/Ws. If that isn't in your travel plans, you need to keep a few things in mind:

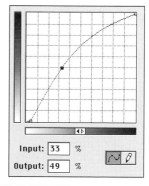

Figure 13.9 *Left, top to bottom: the original cyan, magenta, yellow and black plates of Figure 13.8. Bottom right: the black after 20% of the yellow was blended into it, followed by an application of the curve at right.*

Input: 33 %
Output: 49 %

Figure 13.10 A default conversion of Figure 13.8, top, and one using the methods advocated in this chapter.

FRIEND AND FOE IN BLACK AND WHITE

✓Any time an image goes from color to B/W viewers complain that it loses contrast. This is inaccurate. The image loses those types of contrast that are associated with color, but it fully retains light/dark distinctions.

✓Photoshop's default conversion to B/W takes no account of the individuality of the image. If we were not allowed to color-correct before conversion, it would probably be the best formula. As matters stand, however, practically every image can be improved by moves in color before going to B/W.

✓Conversion candidates should be examined carefully for the kinds of contrast that *don't* convert well. Different colors that are of roughly the same lightness (e.g., the reds and blues in the flags of various nations) will reproduce as nearly the same shade in B/W. Similarly, different saturation values of the same color are readily distinguishable in CMYK, but not B/W.

✓Having identified the areas of a color image that will not convert well to B/W, decide on a strategy for introducing luminosity contrast in them. Usually, this will call for certain major objects to get lighter and others darker.

✓Once your strategy is finalized, examine the individual channels to see which ones seem to be in compliance with it, and which ones take an opposite tack.

✓Having identified your friends and foes among the color channel, the next step is to blend channels to weaken the foes. This can be done with the Channel Mixer, Calculations, or Apply Image commands.

✓The actual conversion to B/W gives the green twice the weight of the red and six times that of the blue. Therefore, although the blue is a good source for blends, there's little point in blending into it. Concentrate on the green, and to a lesser extent, the red.

✓If the color image is in CMYK, the black plate tends to have more shape than the other three and is a good candidate for blends. For this reason, many RGB images should go to CMYK first before conversion to B/W.

✓Don't worry about strict adherence to highlight/shadow settings in making the first correction. These can easily be fixed once we get to B/W, but whatever contrast we lose on the way will be gone forever.

- Know what you're losing in the conversion. Examine the original for places where the contrast you perceive is one of color and not of brightness.

- Get away from thinking that this is some kind of literal, formulaic conversion. It's perfectly all right for the same red to be of different darknesses in different B/Ws, It's perfectly all right for your idea of how dark each red should be to vary from mine.

- Similarly, forget a one-size-fits-all averaging method. In the flag image the red was bad; in the parrot image the green was. The popular misconception that the green channel is the best one to use probably came about from images involving flesh-tones, where the green is indeed usually the best of the three.

- "But my intention being to provide something of use to those of understanding," Machiavelli wrote, "it appears to me better to head for the truth of the matter than to something intangible. Many have imagined republics and principalities the like of which have never been seen or known to exist in reality; for how we live is so far removed from how we ought to live, that he who abandons what has to be done for what ought to be done, will rather learn to bring about his own ruin than his preservation. One who wishes to make a profession of goodness in everything must surely come to grief among so many who are not good. Therefore a prince must, in self-defense, learn how not to be good, and to use or refrain from using this knowledge, according to the necessity of the case."

As in the management of graphic arts firms, you sometimes need to be ruthless. When you encounter an individual—or a channel—with an attitude problem, if persuasion doesn't work, elimination is the next step. Your employees, and your B/Ws, will thank you for it.

14

Resolving the Resolution Issue

Many very different types of resolution are expressed by the same ambiguous acronym. At times, a high resolution is necessary. At others it's a waste of disk space and computing power, if not an outright quality-killer.

Graphic arts is notorious for its ambiguous terminology. *Trap* can mean a prepress technique or a pressroom anomaly. *PMT* describes a variety of scanner or a type of positive proof. *Shadow* means one thing to a photographer and another to a retoucher. A typeface called *Gothic* is a bold sans-serif—unless it is a medieval blackletter, such as Old English. *Web,* to a printer, is quite a different animal from the worldwide variety. Even *red* means something different to a pressman than it does to the rest of the world.

But of all the semantic snares we set for the unwary, the most insidious has to be the innocent-sounding *dpi,* which plagues us throughout our process and sometimes is used as a synonym for a second bugaboo, resolution.

Consider all the different things that DPI connotes, and understand why novices—and some experts—get confused. 300 DPI may be a type of scan or a laser printer. 2,400 DPI may denote a different type of scan or an imagesetter. 72 DPI may measure the number of phosphors in a monitor, or a newspaper's screen ruling.

In choosing the various flavors of resolution for a certain job, it's silly to assume that bigger is better. Unnecessarily high resolutions, at best,

eat storage space and bog down networks. If we are not so lucky, they may bring a RIP to its knees, or worse, produce poorer quality than if we had used the proper resolutions to begin with.

And what are these correct resolutions? They depend on the job, but they also depend upon each other.

First of all, even defining *resolution* is not that easy. It means, more or less, how far apart the smallest distinct parts of the subject of discussion are. Frequently, these small parts are all of the same size, as in the individual pixels of a Photoshop file. But in nondigital parts of the process, they aren't, as in the case of film grain, which is, one might say, the resolution of film, or the halftone dot, which might be termed the resolution of a printing press.

Figure 14.1 suggests what happens when we print without enough press "resolution," in other words, with a halftone screen that is too coarse. The grainy-looking center image is more appropriate for newspapers than for a book. The smaller the dots, the less obtrusive they are, and the more the final product looks like the original photograph it is supposed to recall.

Anyone who thinks that if a fine screen is good then a finer one must be better, is a moron. The finer the screen ruling, the smaller the dots, but the smaller the dots, the harder they are to print properly. If they are on the cusp of what the press can tolerate, the following irritating things happen:

• Darker areas start to plug up, resulting in a perceived lower maximum shadow.

• The minimum acceptable highlight dot goes up; at some point, a dot simply gets

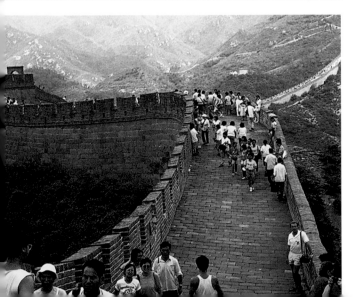

Figure 14.1 *Top, an image printed at press resolution (oops, screen ruling) of 133 dots per inch; center, at 65 DPI; and bottom, at 300 DPI.*

too tiny for the plate and the blanket to hold. Overall, detail in the highlight will become inconsistent.

• The image will begin to appear soft as transition areas become less distinct.

• Dot gain will appear to increase.

Now, at what point does all this unpleasantness start to kick in? In newspaper printing, as a rule it happens at about 100, so most newspapers print with an 85-line screen, and 65-line is not uncommon. Some, however, do use a 100-line screen, and I know of at least one that has successfully used 120 lines.

As paper starts to get a little better and as we migrate to commercial presses, the tolerance goes up. Reasonable uncoated papers can easily hold a 120-line screen, and there can be some success with 133. Magazines that use coated paper generally use 133, and some try 150.

High-quality commercial printing, such as annual reports, uses more expensive coated papers and usually is done at 175, sometimes even 200. And waterless offset, a relatively new approach, appears to make it much easier to hold small dots. There have been reports, which I can't vouch for, of success with screens of over 1,000 lines.

The sad truth is that many printers overstate their own capabilities. A large part of my career has involved preparing color ads for reproduction in national magazines. Most magazines will accept either 133 or 150. My observation is that overall the ads printed at the coarser screen have had a quality edge.

Many people get fooled by their contract proofs, which are far easier to control than a press. The bottom version of Figure 14.1 looks just fine on mine. On press, assuming I can slip it by the printer's preflight department, I predict it will look like a cartoon: all brilliant colors. Where an ink is heavy, it will in fact print as solid, since the press won't be able to maintain dot integrity. The weakest colors, which would temper the brightness of these colors, will be missing altogether, as the tiny dots that theoretically compose them blow away.

This will be the first of several examples of how too much resolution can be harmful. Most people assume that the reason an excessive resolution would be counterproductive pertains exclusively to the press.

It doesn't. All resolutions depend upon one another. Too fine a screen may cause more quality problems with the imagesetter than the press.

Out of Spots, Dots

The term DPI stands for dots per inch. In printing, that's just what we are describing, dots. Infuriatingly, this is the one instance where the term DPI is *not* frequently used; most reserve it to describe situations in which it would be just as accurate to say bananas per inch as dots. But in talking about presswork, people don't say 65 DPI, but a 65-line screen, and they abbreviate it as 65 LPI. Yet we have dots, not lines.

To find out how those dots get there, we need to discuss another kind of resolution.

Whether from a $500,000 platesetter or a $300 inkjet printer, the halftone dots we've been talking about are made up of tinier dots. How tiny those tiny dots are governs how effectively the bigger dots can be drawn. The size of those tiny dots, which I will henceforth refer to as *spots,* represents the resolution of the device.

We've barely begun, and already the terminology is tripping us up. This will never do. In the first edition of this book, after griping about it over several paragraphs, I caved in to the conventional and used DPI indiscriminately. No more. I am older and more set in my ways now. This time, as in the last edition, I'm taking a hard line. Where appropriate acronyms don't exist, I've invented them. And, as you can see, I'm using SPECIAL TYPE to set the various acronyms off.

I shall therefore, use DPI to describe a dots-per-inch screen ruling, but never to describe measurements that don't involve dots. The rest of the world can use sloppy terminology and be damned, for all I care. You don't like it, buy a different book.

End of rant. Imagesetters made in the United States usually have a resolution of at least 2,400 DPI—oops, 2,400 *spots* per inch. If made elsewhere, the usual resolution is at least 2,540, which happens to be 100 spots per millimeter. Note that spots, unlike dots, never vary in size. They are either off or on; they're either there or they're not.

The spots are too small for most of us to see, which may make them just about the right size to construct halftone dots with, as Figure 14.2 shows. But it may not: the size relationship between spot and dot is critical, and if it's out of whack, quality will suffer. To know what "out of whack" means, we have to consider yet another species of resolution, the ability of the human eye to resolve differences in color and tonality.

Nobody really knows how great that ability is. Some reputable sources have suggested that typical humans can only perceive around 2,500 different shades of color. On the opposite extreme are folks like myself who say that some individuals are capable of differentiating a million or more.

For realism, whatever printing method we choose should be able to portray at least as many colors as typical

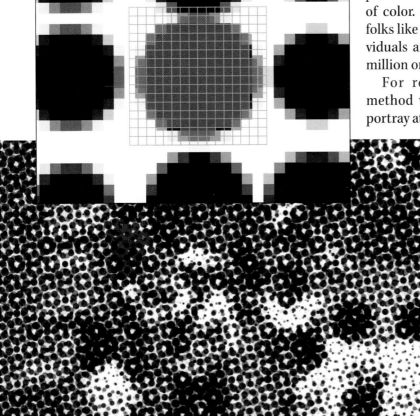

Figure 14.2 *Dots and spots: Below, a blowup of Figure 14.1 shows its dot structure clearly. The imagesetter constructs each dot, inset, by turning spots off and on in a grid. Here, the grid has 256 such spots available for each dot, which is just right—in theory.*

humans can perceive, and preferably quite a few more, in case we start moving things around with curves. We need to be able to make very fine adjustments, therefore, in the size of the halftone dot. The smaller the imagesetter spot is, the more flexibility we'll have. On the other hand, constructing dots out of spots is not a trivial calculation. Having spots that are too small will snarl the most powerful RIP.

It certainly makes sense to have at least 200 different sizes of dot available, probably more. If the halftone dots are at 150 DPI and the imagesetter resolution is 2,400 SPI, this will be possible.

150 is $1/16$ of 2,400. The spots that the imagesetter can potentially paint will be rectangles where each side is $1/2400$ of an inch, or .00042". Those rectangles will be exactly $1/16$ of the maximum width of the halftone dot. There will be 16 rows of rectangles across and 16 columns down, for a total of 256 rectangles. Depending upon how many of these actually get painted, there are 256 possible darknesses of the halftone dot, or 257, if you count zero.

256, is, coincidentally, a key number in yet another kind of resolution.

The Blind Man's Eyeglasses

Tonal information also has a resolution, in a manner of speaking. An original photograph is said, rather inaccurately, to be *continuous-tone.* Digital files aren't. They only can portray a certain number of varieties of tone, frequently 256. Printable Photoshop files have 256 VOT *per channel,* which is why so many different colors are possible. A standard RGB file can accommodate 16,777,216 different colors, this being 256 to the third power.

To add to the exponential chaos, a second term, *bit depth,* is often used in preference to VOT, with different numbers that mean the same thing. A 256 VOT file is also known as an 8-bit file. In keeping with the spirit of the rest of this chapter, it gets a more precise name, 8 BPC, for bits per channel. This refers to the computer storage space required per pixel, in this case eight binary bits: eight zeros or ones. With eight zeros or ones the total number of possible variations is two to the eighth power, which is, conveniently, 256.

Most scanners and some other devices can operate at higher bit depths. A 12 BPC

Dots & Spots: a Glossary

Much confusion is caused by the use of a single term, *dpi,* to refer to wildly different genera of resolution. In an act of rebellion against this practice, different abbreviations will be used in this chapter. Unfortunately, in some cases, I have had to invent them. Here is an alphabetical list of the acronyms you'll find here. These don't agree with industry practice, and there is no suggestion that you should use them. But at least they are more accurate than calling everything dpi.

BPC Bits per channel, in a digital image file.

BPI Black or white bits per inch, in a bitmapped graphic file.

DPI Dots per inch, in a halftone screen.

PLD Total pixels in the long direction of a digital file.

PPI Pixels per inch, in a digital file.

SPI Spots per inch, the smallest area that can be marked by an output device such as an imagesetter or film recorder.

SSPI Scanning samples per inch.

TPC Total pixel count of a digital file.

VOT Varieties of tone, sometimes called levels of gray, the maximum number of shades of gray in a single channel of a digital file.

scan has 4,096 VOT. Some manufacturers would have us believe that a greater bit depth implies better scan quality. Don't believe it. If a scanner can't see detail in shadow areas, a 12 BPC scan won't help. We may have 4,096 VOT, but in this case, VOT stands for varieties of trash. To see why, let's compare the work of three very expensive pieces of hardware.

For the past quarter century, drum scanners have been the standard for those desiring the highest quality. They continue to be the best today, but not by much. Their photomultiplier tubes have certain advantages over the charge-coupled device technology used in flatbed scanners and professional digital cameras. CCD devices are particularly vulnerable to a loss of detail in the darkest areas.

They've been getting better, though. Seven years ago, no scanner costing less than $10,000 was even remotely in the same quality league as a drum scanner. Today, $2,000 buys a very strong desktop unit that, if not capable of the same enlargement, is almost as good otherwise.

To assess the state of the technology, in 1996 I arranged a shootout between a drum scanner from the early 1980s and two professional-level (i.e., they cost about $50,000 apiece) CCD units. I refrain from naming the products, because all three vendors make better scanners today.

Anyway, the idea was to have expert operators of each scanner try to milk the most from a dozen moderate-to-difficult chromes. They were given identical printing and sizing specifications. If they did not like the scans for any reason they could do them over. When they were satisfied, all 36 versions would be assigned random letters and proofed next to one another. The proofs would go to a panel of ten experts who, working in separate light booths, would evaluate which of the three versions of each original was the best, without knowing which ones came from where.

I expected this exercise to prove that the CCD scanners had basically caught up. It didn't. Of 120 first-place votes, Brand X (you and I know it's the drum scanner, but the jurors didn't) got 98, Brand Y 12, and Brand Z 10. In 7 of the 12 contests, Brand X swept all ten votes.

Figure 14.3 is one of those in which the vote was unanimous. I'm showing a piece of it, then enlarging it, and then applying a drastic contrast-enhancing curve to it, so that we can evaluate just how well these three beasts are holding the shadows.

Figure 14.3 *The ability to retain shadow detail is a major test of a scanner. Opposite, normal-size repro-ductions of scans of the same original by, left to right, Brands X, Y, and Z. Above, the shadow areas magnified (left) and with contrast in the shadows greatly enhanced (right). Top to bottom, the Brand X, Y, and Z scans.*

This is easiest to judge in the three right-hand versions. The problems are the center of the tree and the car beneath it.

Brand X is the only one that is having any luck with the car. If you look hard, you can even see that the taillights are red. In the tree, which is darker still, it's a lot more of a struggle. Brand X is obviously at its wit's end, but it is still a drum scanner, and a cut above the other two in such shadow areas. Brand Y posterizes the inside of the tree, whereas Brand Z freaks out. The whole center of its tree is featureless.

The final output of these scanners is an 8 BPC file, but all three interpolate that down from an original with more data. Brands Y and Z are 12 BPC scanners. Brand X is analog; its original scan is a series of voltage readings that in principle carry an infinite variety of tonality. More modern versions of this scanner are fully digital, and also give 12 BPC files.

So, Brand Z can portray 4,096 levels of tonality in each channel. A fat lot of good it did. In this image, endowing the scanner with extra bits is like handing a blind man a pair of eyeglasses. If Brand X were an 8-bit scanner, yea, verily, if it were a *six*-bit scanner capable of only 64 VOT, it would still have the best version here. If you're buying a scanner or a digital camera, forget this bit depth balderdash, and look at a few tough samples.

Comes the Quintillion

The above discussion is no endorsement of drum scanners. Experts looking at these images closely found enough difference to say that Brand X was better. I concur, and so do you, presumably. The question is, though, how *much* better? Going back to the real originals, the smaller versions in Figure 14.3, I'd have to say, a little better, but very little.

So, while the drum scanners have a theoretical advantage, in real life it doesn't amount to much, at least not in comparison to a mid-five-figure CCD scanner. In a race like this, the difference is going to be the jockey, not the horse.

Of even less practical significance is the use of the extra bits in Photoshop. If we

Figure 14.4 *Theoretically, working with 16 BPC should give smoother transitions, even though the file must be reduced to 8 BPC for printing. In practice, it doesn't work that way. At left, a file from a high-end CCD scanner, originally at 16 BPC. Opposite page, RGB curves are applied that are many times more violent than the norm. Top left: the curve applied to the 16 BPC file, which is then converted to 8 BPC; top right, the original converted to 8 BPC first before the application of the same curve. Bottom: the blue channels of the two files, which should show the greatest advantage for 16 BPC. A histogram would show the difference, and if the image is blown up to three or four times its size, the 16 BPC image looks better—but can you see the difference here?*

have a scanner that can save files with more than 8 BPC, Photoshop 6 can work with them to a limited extent. We can apply curves, but only a few filters and no retouching tools except the rubber stamp, before converting them to the 8 BPC that all output devices require.

Theoretically, this is tempting. When we apply a curve to an image, we reduce its VOT, for the following reason. Suppose we have a B/W file with 256 VOT. It happens to be a picture of a white cat, so we jack up the center point by, say, 10%. Originally, 128 of our tones fell below the midpoint, and 128 above it. But now, we have stretched the light tones, and compressed the dark ones. Only about 115 real tones now fill the first 128 available spaces. On the other hand, there will be 141 real tones competing to fill the second 128 spaces. The surplus has to be discarded. Hence, only 243 real tonal values remain of the original 256.

If we work, instead, with the extra bits, this criticism will not apply. Photoshop's two options (under Image: Mode) are 8 or 16 BPC. While no scanner extant gives 16 meaningful bits, if we start to fool around in LAB or do various other things, it's possible that we may fill those extra bits up with something other than garbage.

This makes our file size twice as large. It also gives us, er, a bit more information. To be precise, each channel now has a resolution of 65,536 VOT. How many discrete CMYK possibilities can this produce? The answer is so impressive that I can't bear to use numerals, I have to just say it. Eighteen quintillion, 446 quadrillion, 744 trillion, 73 billion, 709 million, 600 thousand, that's how many.

If we apply a curve to such data, we still throw away a few of these possibilities. We will miss this about as much as Bill Gates misses the quarter he spends on his morning newspaper.

For those calibrationists to whom a good-looking histogram is more important than a good-looking image, this cinches it. We must work in 16 BPC whenever possible, to avoid that fearful bogeyman, data loss.

To be honest, I used to think that there was merit in this belief. I thought, if the curves we apply are extreme enough, that extra information could help.

The more I've played with extra-bit files, unfortunately, the less I've been able to justify the extra processing time and disk space. In fact, I've been unable to see any practical difference at all, even under extreme testing conditions.

The left half of Figure 14.4 is an 8 BPC file; it has to be or I wouldn't be able to print it. But it was originally a 12 BPC file produced on a high-end CCD scanner.

In the right half, the image goes through a torture test. This is not a color correction, but a drastic curve applied to open everything up much as was done in Figure 14.3. I did this with two copies of the 12 BPC RGB file, which became a 16 BPC file in Photoshop. In the left-hand sample, I applied (and saved) the curve to the 16 BPC file, and then converted it to 8-bit CMYK for printing here. In the right-hand version, I first went to 8 BPC, then applied the curve, then converted to CMYK.

Theoretically, the version on the left should be superior. But as a practical matter, is it? The detail-filled blue channel should show the difference more than the composite original.

The calibrationist response to this is that the difference can clearly be seen in the image's histogram, and it can. That of the left-hand image is smooth and beautiful. The one for the right-hand image looks like a comb. (As a matter of policy, I refuse to include histograms and similar irrelevancies in a serious book, so you'll just have to take my word for it.)

When we start printing histograms alongside our final work, then the eventual viewers will know for sure how bad our work actually is. Until then, they will have to rely on how the images *look*. To me, they look the same.

Incidentally, not all channels are created equal: we can get away with murder sometimes. The JPEG format saves so much file size with so little loss in quality essentially by bulldozing the B channel of LAB into around 6 BPC. That sounds pretty draconian, but it works.

Quality, Not Quantity

In the 21st century, we are all photographers, we are all scanner operators, we are all retouchers.

If you're buying a digital camera, you should consider the same points that you would if you were buying a desktop scanner. They use, after all, the same CCD technology. The digital camera is little more than a portable scanner with a variable focal length and a flash mechanism.

I tortured the $800 digital camera I purchased in early 2000 (I won't name it, as again the manufacturer now makes even better models) with the image of Figure 14.5. This is from Capitol Reef National Park. It is a gypsum sinkhole some 200 feet deep. I know this, because I almost fell in, which would have saved you the trouble of reading the rest of this book.

Figure 14.5 *The quality of the data is much more important than the number of bits per channel. This image contains only 20 to 25 values per channel (called VOT in text) but, with the exception of the blown-out foreground areas, it's acceptable for printing.*

Well, actually, what it looked like originally was Figure 14.6—utterly black. That's what the camera saw. Figure 14.5 is what happens when the image is opened up as much as possible with curves.

When I first saw this result, I flipped. I could not believe that the camera was getting data this good. The image looks natural—yet there are only around 20 VOT in the red and green channels and 25 in the blue. This file, then, only needs *five* BPC, let alone eight. It's the quality of the capture that matters, not the number of bits. If you don't believe this, flip ahead to Figure 17.3, which is a digital capture of about the same darkness but is catastrophically noisy when the range is opened.

The obsession that some have with the extra bits matches their paranoia about switching from one colorspace to another. Both are cases of Bill Gates worrying about losing quarters. 256 VOT is more than enough for practical color work. 100, or even 80, is quite sufficient, although one would like more in black and white. Remember, in an RGB file, even 100 VOT produces a million different colors. That may not be 18 quintillion, but let's not be piggy.

By all means, if you are planning to apply 20 different curves consecutively to a certain image, do it with an extra-bit file. And if you sometimes take images out of CMYK so as to work on them in other colorspaces, try to limit yourself to no more than ten or twenty conversions per correction.

In real life, you are not going to do either of these things. Don't worry about histograms. Worry about making the image look good. 256 VOT is far more than enough—for photographic images, that is. But if you are making gradations, you have to look at resolution in yet another way.

And the Band Played On

Banding in gradients has been a headache since the first days of PostScript. In the middle of what seems to be a smooth gradation, there is a systemic burp, a sudden, annoying jump from one tonality to another, ruining a job.

"How can this possibly have happened?" shrieks the hysterical artist, "when I specified 256 steps for the blend?"

Two ways. The likeliest is that the blend was originally made in RGB and involved colors close to the edge or outside of the CMYK gamut. The other is, of course, a resolution problem.

If a blend goes from say, 10% to 20% in a certain channel, the output device will only have about 25 VOT available. It won't matter whether the input has 256 or 256 million VOT. Furthermore, some of the 25 are probably not available, due to rounding error, so banding is likely to show up, especially if the blend covers a wide area on the page.

In principle, an output device that can create 256 VOT itself has exactly enough resolution. In practice, that isn't quite true. The dots are angled, which can reduce the number of spots available. More important, although both file and imagesetter are at 256 VOT, the two 256s won't line up exactly. Certain values that are different in the original file will result in identical dots, and certain dots that are theoretically possible will actually be inaccessible.

So, how many VOT are actually available at 150 DPI on a 2,400 SPI imagesetter? Chances are, 220 or so. If photographs are the only thing we print, neither we nor anybody else will be able to tell the difference between 220 and 256 VOT. If, however, we start introducing fine gradations, it may make quite a difference indeed.

Banding can be defeated by adding a small amount of randomization (noise) to the digital file. This is why photos don't band: there is always enough natural noise to obliterate the problem.

Photoshop 6 introduces an anti-banding method into its separation algorithm—a dither, a very fine amount of noise applied in areas banding is likely to occur. It's on by default, and should be left that way if you have banding problems. If you don't, but you do blend channels from time to time, I would turn it off.

With dithering off the seps will match those generated by Photoshop 5 almost exactly. I think it's very unlikely to make a difference either way, but if it ain't broke, why fix it? (To turn the dither option off, the Advanced Mode box in Edit: Color Settings has to be checked.)

Other methods of overcoming banding are to use a higher-resolution imagesetter or to reduce the screen ruling. 150 DPI blends on a 2,400 SPI imagesetter tempt fate. 133 DPI blends are more reliable.

Figure 14.7 shows how many VOT are actually available at normal DPIs for some common SPIs of laser printers and imagesetters. I'd avoid any number under 150.

This is why photographic reproduction on laser printers is so lousy, even on today's better 600 SPI units. And yet there's a resolution paradox. This book is imaged on a 2,400 SPI platesetter. If we were to substitute output from a 600 SPI laser printer, the images would be a joke—but few people would notice that anything was wrong with the *type*. How can the same resolution be so terrible in one case and so nearly undetectable in the other?

Figure 14.6 *This is the raw capture that was modified to produce Figure 14.5. It comes from an $800 digital camera purchased in early 2000. Although the depths of this sinkhole are almost completely black, the camera was able to see an impressive amount of detail.*

Spots, Dots, & Tonality:
DPI vs. SPI vs. VOT

IMAGESETTER RESOLUTION (spots per inch)

	300	600	1200	2400	3600	
65	21	85	256	256	256	
85	12	50	199	256	256	
100	9	36	144	256	256	SCREEN (dots per inch)
120	6	25	100	256	256	
133	5	20	81	256	256	
150	4	16	64	256	256	
175	3	12	47	188	256	
200	2	9	36	144	256	

Figure 14.7 Realistic photographic images are impossible if the output device can't generate enough varieties of tone. For professional work, one needs at least 100 vot, and many would say at least 200. Here's how many levels of tone imagesetters of various resolutions can theoretically produce at some common screen rulings.

The Resolution That Isn't There

Unlike the images we've been considering so far, type contains no grays, only black letters on white paper. The type still has to be painted using the same imagesetter spots, but now it's much easier. The glory of PostScript is that it allows certain kinds of graphics to have an entirely different variety of resolution, to wit, none at all.

Objects that can be described in terms of curves or other mathematical shapes (and typefaces can be so described) eventually need a resolution. An imagesetter doesn't print mathematical concepts, only spots. But a RIP's whole function is to map out those spots. When a file comes in saying, "I am a bunch of curves, map me however you think best for your imaging engine," not only can the RIP do this, it can do so much more smoothly than if the file already carried its own bitmap.

Since type and similar line graphics contain no grays, only blacks and whites, Figure 14.7 is not relevant. The only question is, how many spots per inch does the printer need to construct the curves and fine lines of text type accurately?

Older laser printers generally have a resolution of 300 SPI and produce type that's obviously inferior to what you're reading here. At 600 SPI, the type is pretty good—one has to look closely to see the difference between it and type output from a 1,200 SPI imagesetter, which, in turn, is indistinguishable from 2,400 SPI without a loupe.

When it's necessary to scan type or other graphics because digital versions don't exist, yet another kind of resolution comes into play. We now have a file that can be expressed in bits per inch, each bit being either white or black. If a 600 BPI file is sent to a 600 SPI printer, the printer's RIP has to remap it. The results will not be quite as good as if a resolution-independent file were sent to the same printer.

So, at what resolution should one scan type and other line graphics? Half again the resolution of the output device is my rule, to a maximum of 1,800 SSPI—scanning samples per inch.

If you've ever wondered why type always looks fuzzy in a photograph, it's that old devil resolution again. In Figure 14.8, you will observe that 300 BPI is inadequate for type—and most color images are scanned at less than 300 SSPI. The type in such images isn't quite as jagged as the example, because screening tends to soften images, but it still will be pretty bad.

One way to make it better, naturally, is to scan at a higher resolution. The higher the scanning resolution, the softer and smoother the curves will be. The problem with that is, so will everything else.

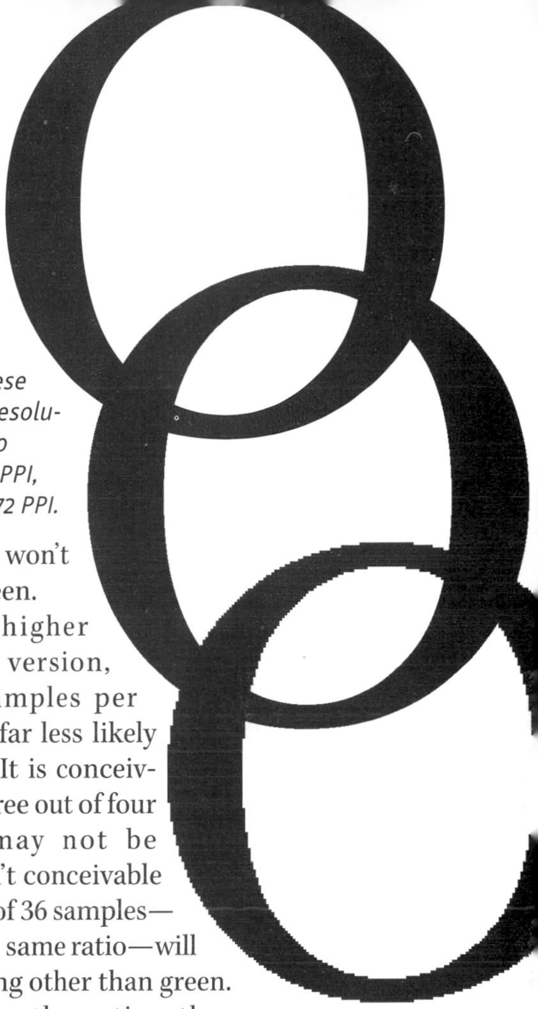

When scanning type only, excessive resolution eats up disk space, overburdens the imagesetter, clogs up communication, and is generally a complete waste of time. Other than that, it doesn't hurt. But with a photograph, too much resolution, in addition to the shortcomings enumerated above, actually *does* hurt. Which of the two images of grass in Figure 14.9 do you like best?

If we want something that looks like blades of grass and not AstroTurf, the bottom version seems clearly better. But it's the lower-resolution scan! Doesn't high resolution equate to more detail?

Of course it does. But here, we don't want detail, we want the *illusion* of detail. That's what the bottom one provides. Let me try to explain how and why.

The bottom image's resolution is approximately four scanning samples per halftone dot. That's in line with the conventional wisdom, which is that it should be between 1.5 and 2 times the screen ruling. The dots are roughly $\frac{1}{133}$" apart, the scanning samples roughly $\frac{1}{266}$". That squares up to four samples per dot: two across, two down.

The top image has three times this resolution. The samples are roughly $\frac{1}{700}$" apart. The file is nine times as large. There are now 36 scanning samples per halftone dot, rather than four.

The grass, obviously, is predominantly green. Parts of it are gray, black, yellow, or brown. But at either of these scan resolutions, probably three out of four samples will find green.

In the lower resolution image, therefore, which has four samples per halftone dot, the chances are that three of them will be green, but sometimes all four will be, and sometimes zero or one. In such cases the re-

Figure 14.8
How much resolution is needed for smooth-looking type and similar graphics? These letters have resolutions of, top to bottom, 1800 PPI, 300 PPI, and 72 PPI.

sulting dots won't produce green.

In the higher resolution version, with 36 samples per dot, this is far less likely to happen. It is conceivable that three out of four samples may not be green. It isn't conceivable that 27 out of 36 samples— which is the same ratio—will be something other than green. A rule of mathematics: the more samples, the less variance from what the law of averages predicts. If we flip a coin four times, it may well come up heads three out of the four, although two heads is more likely. If we flip four *hundred* times, 300 heads couldn't possibly happen.

The higher the resolution, the more uniform the color will be: the closer it will approach whatever the average color of the grass is. There is a lot more variation in the lower resolution version. That variation, or action, suggests the blades of grass that our imagination is telling us are actually there.

In scanning, moving to a lower resolution is a move toward action and variability. This is a fine concept, but if the resolution

Figure 14.9 *Does resolution equal detail? The top version seems soft, even though it was scanned at three times the resolution of the bottom version, and takes up nine times as much disk space. In areas of one color, like the grass, the higher the resolution, the more even the color will become.*

gets too low, the image will become harsh and jagged.

A higher resolution is a move toward smoothness and consistency. This is also a laudable goal, but if it gets too high, the image will look soft and defocused.

It follows that there is no one "correct" scanning resolution. A woman's face generally should be scanned at a higher resolution than a man's, because we accept more roughness in a man's face. An image of furniture requires more resolution than

does grass, because furniture has diagonal lines that shouldn't look too harsh. A damaged, noisy, or prescreened original also is helped by higher resolution. And, certainly, if you think there is a good chance you'll be upsizing the image, give yourself some extra resolution in the original scan.

Many people, refusing to believe that too much resolution can hurt, obdurately scan everything at 300 SSPI. This explains why so many newspaper photographs look so soft. It also makes the vendors of disk drives very happy. File size increases with the square of the resolution. If, for magazine work, you go with 250 SSPI rather than 300, your files will only be $^2/_3$ as large—and quality will probably be *better.*

Resampling and the Rogue Pixel

The foregoing discussion concerns scanning resolution, which is expressed in SSPI. The resolution of the Photoshop file is not necessarily the same kind of resolution. We express this in PPI—pixels per inch. A pixel is the smallest building block of a file. You can see them clearly in Figure 14.10.

When a raw scan is opened directly in Photoshop, at that moment the SSPI equals the PPI. That equality does not necessarily continue, because at some point the scan may get *resampled.* Plus, with many desktop scanners, what seems to be the raw scan isn't any such thing: it may already have been interpolated.

Photoshop itself allows us to change the number of pixels in a file, using the dialog box shown in Figure 14.12, accessed by Image: Image Size.

When the Resample Image box is unchecked, changing the numbers changes only the nominal size of the image, not any data. A 4"×6" file at 150 PPI is exactly the same as a 2"×3" file at 300 PPI. One changes size without resampling for the sake of convenience. For example, images in Photo CD format start at a nominal resolution of 72 PPI. They have more than enough pixels to use for this book, provided I place them in the page layout file at a quarter of their nominal size, which would make their effective resolution 288 PPI. To avoid this hassle, I change resolution to 250 PPI, without resampling. That, I know, will make the image close to the size I need.

Resampling *down*—that is, throwing some of the data away—is appropriate when there's more than enough for whatever use you intend. It's ridiculous to post a 5-megabyte image file for Web viewing, just as it's ridiculous to use a 15-megabyte file for the top half of Figure 14.9.

To resample down, check the resample box, and enter a lower size, resolution, or both. But keep two things in mind. First of all, unless you're positive you'll never need to print the image at a larger size, save a copy of the original. Downsampling is a one-way street.

Second, realize that a downsampled image isn't equivalent to an original scan of the same PPI. The downsampled version will be softer, like the bottom third of Figure 14.10.

The lower the resolution, the more chance that a rogue pixel will appear, an area where the scanner picked up really

Figure 14.10 *What passes for detail is often nothing more than variation. Pixels in the top two images (blowups of the two images of Figure 14.9) seem to have the same amount of variation, but this is an illusion. If the high-resolution version, top, is downsampled to match the resolution of the middle version, the result is the image at bottom, which is much softer.*

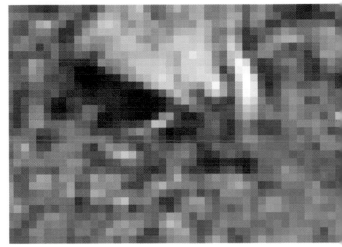

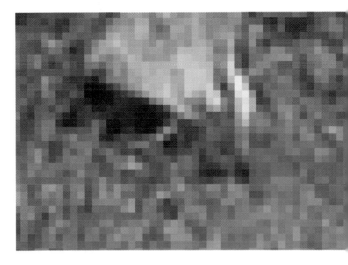

SOME RESOLUTIONS ABOUT RESOLUTION

✓Many different kinds of resolution are often described by one ambiguous term, *dpi.* Photoshop users have to know what each kind of dpi means.

✓Excessive resolution is often as harmful as not having enough. This is true in the screen ruling of a printed image, and in scanning, where too much resolution yields an overly soft result.

✓Graphics and type prepared in vector programs such as Adobe Illustrator, Macromedia FreeHand, and CorelDraw, are resolution-independent: the output device will draw the graphics in the optimal fashion. Once imported into Photoshop, though, the graphics are turned into pixels and lose this attribute.

✓The choice of screen ruling shouldn't outstrip the capabilities of either the press or the imagesetter. If the imagesetter isn't capable of at least 150 varieties of tone at a given screen, go to a coarser screen.

✓The industry consensus is that scan resolution for an image that is to be printed at same size should be 1.5 to 2 times screen ruling. As the screen ruling goes up, the effect of inadequate resolution goes down.

✓Scanning at a relatively high resolution guarantees smoothness and consistency. If overdone, however, images become soft. Lower resolution is a move toward action and variability. If overdone, however, images become harsh and jagged.

✓Type and other line graphics should generally be scanned at 1.5 times the printer or imagesetter resolution, or greater.

✓Many manufacturers of scanners and digital cameras trumpet how many bits per channel they capture. This is very interesting but has little bearing on the critical question, which is how accurately the device sees into shadow areas.

✓Photoshop allows several operations on files that contain 16 bits of information per channel. Although many scanners can provide such files, it is questionable whether there is any advantage to working on them in this mode.

✓Inkjet printers, which tend to give softer-looking reproductions than presses do, don't need as much resolution in the input file.

atypical information. Such a thing usually translates into a halftone dot that looks out of place, almost like a speck of dust. The greater the density of scanning samples—resampled or not—the less likely this is to occur. And the higher the screen ruling, the less noticeable the effect of such a rogue pixel will be.

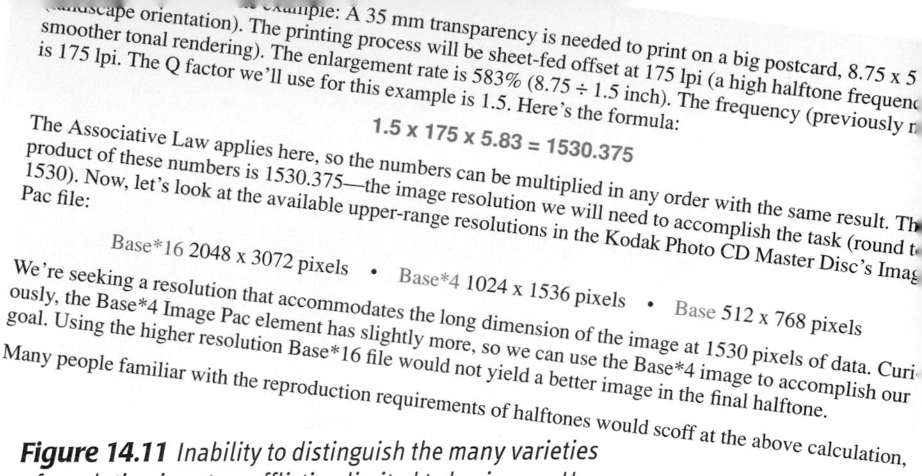

The conventional wisdom is that resolution should be 1.5 to 2 times screen ruling times magnification. If your images have been downsampled you really don't need that much (1.3 to 1.7 ought to do it). Also, with screens of 175 DPI and up, or stochastic screening, you can get by with less.

Inkjet printers as a class don't require as much resolution. Images from such printers look a bit soft anyway, and aren't as likely to show the harshness of low resolution as a press would be.

You can also get by with less on certain types of image. In this early part of the Web age, when we still have to worry about holding image size down, this can be a big factor. This is one reason for the ability to cut images into slices with the knife tool: if you can isolate areas of nearly flat color, you can cut their resolution drastically.

And one can cut corners on certain kinds of image. Figure 14.9 is a very soft subject. I've printed it successfully with the scanning resolution as low as .8 of the screen ruling. For a picture as busy and full of fine detail as Figure 14.1, that would be disastrously low.

example: A 35 mm transparency is needed to print on a big postcard, 8.75 x 5 (landscape orientation). The printing process will be sheet-fed offset at 175 lpi (a high halftone frequency smoother tonal rendering). The enlargement rate is 583% (8.75 ÷ 1.5 inch). The frequency (previously n is 175 lpi. The Q factor we'll use for this example is 1.5. Here's the formula:

$$1.5 \times 175 \times 5.83 = 1530.375$$

The Associative Law applies here, so the numbers can be multiplied in any order with the same result. Th product of these numbers is 1530.375—the image resolution we will need to accomplish the task (round t 1530). Now, let's look at the available upper-range resolutions in the Kodak Photo CD Master Disc's Imag Pac file:

Base*16 2048 x 3072 pixels • Base*4 1024 x 1536 pixels • Base 512 x 768 pixels

We're seeking a resolution that accommodates the long dimension of the image at 1530 pixels of data. Curi ously, the Base*4 Image Pac element has slightly more, so we can use the Base*4 image to accomplish our goal. Using the higher resolution Base*16 file would not yield a better image in the final halftone.

Many people familiar with the reproduction requirements of halftones would scoff at the above calculation,

Figure 14.11 *Inability to distinguish the many varieties of resolution is not an affliction limited to beginners. Here, Kodak gives users some incorrect, and quality-damaging, advice on how to use Photo CD, based on a misunderstanding of two types of resolution.*

Millions and Millions of Pixels

The concept of PPI is closely related to another species of resolution: total pixel count. Film recorders, digital cameras, and certain types of scans express their resolution in terms the total number of pixels per image, not per unit of measurement, probably because their vendors like to impress people with a lot of zeroes. A high-end digital camera may have a resolution of 20,000,000 TPC, but it is less bulky to quote it as 5,000 PLD by 4,000 PSD—pixels in the long (short) direction.

Figure 14.12 *The Photoshop resampling dialog box, accessed under Image: Image Size.*

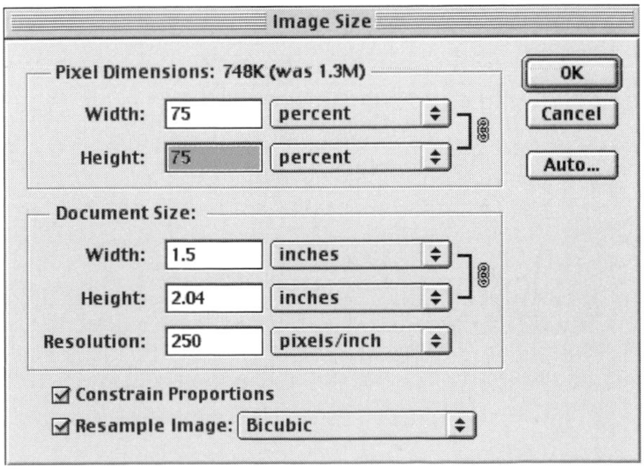

Throwing around all these types of resolution can be confusing even for experts. If your head is swimming, take heart: even Kodak sometimes doesn't fathom these distinctions, as Figure 14.11 shows.

This gaffe, excerpted from a Kodak document on how to prepare Photo CD images for press, offers the following example: given a 35 mm original ($1\frac{1}{2}$" wide), which of several Photo CD resolutions should we choose, if we intend to print the image $8\frac{3}{4}$" wide at a 175 DPI screen?

The author of this document observes that "Many people familiar with the production requirements of halftones would scoff" at his answer. That is definitely correct, but not for the reason he thinks. We scoff, instead, at those who are so busy with Q factors and associative laws that they miss the basic concepts. Here, Kodak has mixed up two kinds of resolution. Let's try to help the Great Yellow Father out.

Kodak suggests 1.5 here for the ratio of resolution to screen ruling. This is certainly reasonable. The magnification factor is 583%; the screen factor is 175. Multiply the three together, and the answer is 1,530.

Since one of the possible Photo CD resolutions has a width of 1,536, Kodak concludes that it is nearly a perfect fit, and that this is the resolution of choice.

But no, as the doctor said to Hercule Poirot. No, no, and again no! That is an explanation that will not hold water!

The desired resolution of 1,530 is in pixels *per inch*. The Photo CD alternative of 1,536 is in pixels *in the long direction*. The original being $1\frac{1}{2}$" wide, we need to multiply that 1,530 by 1.5 to get an appropriate PLD. Since Kodak's choice of 1,536 is too low, we need to go to the next higher alternative, which is 3,072 PLD.

That 3,072 figure gives us the happy ratio of 2.0 times the screen ruling. 1,536 would yield a 1.0 ratio, and print quality would go down the tubes, Kodak's feelings to the contrary notwithstanding.

Some Final Resolutions

The genesis of this chapter was a magazine column I reluctantly wrote in response to the requests of novices who didn't understand the difference between the "DPI" of scans and laser printers. I began with the idea that it was a throwaway, for beginners only. Once I read the first draft, however, it struck me that this is the most baffling and confusing topic I've ever written about—even though it doesn't even touch monitor resolution, the resolution of Web images, or of film recorders. That was when I decided to highlight each occurrence of phrases like yet another species of resolution.

Like many professionals, I had made the mistake of assuming that this was all intuitive. After observing just how many highlighted phrases there were (and after reading an extraordinary volume of correspondence after the column appeared), I had a much better understanding of why some artists find themselves buried under a blizzard of soft images, jagged edges, strangled networks, and unhappy RIPs.

The way to resolve one's resolution difficulties can be simply stated: don't ask for too much, don't provide too little.

You may find it easier to do that if you refrain from using that deceptive DPI term.

Declaring that we will never let those three deadly letters pass our lips is probably impractical. I don't really advocate that. But even if you *say* DPI, don't *think* DPI. Keeping the true meaning in mind is one of the best resolutions you can make.

Math, Moiré, and the Artist: A New Angle on Descreening

Whenever two patterns overlap in print, a weird-looking interference is possible. Mostly this happens with prescreened originals, occasionally with patterned objects. Usually, moiré can be avoided by keeping two words in mind: thirty degrees.

Faced with a messy moiré like the one on the right side of Figure 15.1, the temptation is to look for a magic bullet. This atrocity represents a problem we all face from time to time, although we would rather not: reproduction of a prescreened original. People recommend all sorts of magic bullets for dealing with it. Frequently the bullets wind up in their feet.

Can you guess what I did to correct the file to produce the resounding improvement shown at the left?

Nothing. I did nothing at all.

The two versions are exactly the same. They access the same file, are cropped identically.

For identical pictures, that is rather a dramatic difference in print quality. It indicates that prescreened originals present some unique problems, many of which can be solved by keeping two words in mind: thirty degrees. That's the real magic bullet.

Before getting into descreening technique, we'd better have a quick review of what this screening stuff is all about.

Limiting ourselves for the moment to black and white, successful reproduction depends on achieving a full range of tone: whites, blacks, dark grays, light grays, medium grays. Unfortunately, we have no gray ink to work with on press, merely black ink and white paper.

A little legerdemain is therefore in order. By subtly laying down smallish quantities of black ink in conjunction with showing smallish amounts of white paper, we can fool viewers into thinking they are perceiving gray.

There are several ways of doing this. Randomly placed dots will work. If such dots are intended to be readily visible, we call the result a *mezzotint*. If they are too small to be seen easily, we call it a *stochastic screen*.

Overwhelmingly, though, the printing industry uses some kind of regular pattern of ink coverage that gets darker or lighter to portray different shades of gray. Nowadays that pattern is almost invariably one of dots that vary in size but not in distance from one another. The pattern is called a *screen;* the number of dots per linear inch is the *screen frequency* or *ruling*. A higher ruling implies better print quality: the pictures of Madeleine Albright are screened at 65 dots per inch, which is more appropriate for newspapers than a book. (In this book, the normal screen is 133 DPI.)

The dot pattern is modestly more pronounced if the rows of dots are exactly horizontal and vertical with respect to the

Figure 15.1 *The moiré in the image opposite is absent in the version to the left. What's the secret that makes this corrected version so much better?*

page. Therefore, it is customary to angle them. The exact angle makes not a whit of difference, unless the picture is being printed with more than one ink—or unless we are trying to reproduce a prescreened image.

The Thirty Degree Solution

Most of us have some kind of vague comprehension that cyan, magenta, yellow, and black are customarily printed at four different screen angles. It is normally completely irrelevant whether we know what those angles are or why. If, however, we have to work with prescreened originals, understanding the theory of angling is critical.

Whenever two regular patterns are superimposed on one another, there will be some kind of interference, or moiré. The moiré can range from spectacular, as in the right half of Figure 15.1, to almost unnoticeable. Obviously, we prefer the latter. However, if we print all the CMYK inks at the same screen angle, we are guaranteed to get one of the former variety.

Color printing has been around long enough for a lot of experimentation. In that time printers have learned that, while a lot of angle combinations work, the most reliable is one where they are 30° apart.

The Photoshop convention in referring to angles is that a vertical line would be at 0°, a horizontal one at 90°. If you think about it, you will realize that only three

inks can be 30° apart from one another. If an ink were angled at 90° (i.e., a row of dots is perfectly horizontal) it also would be 0°, since a row of dots would also be perfectly vertical. We could have a second ink at 30° and a third at 60°, but we'd have to scramble for a fourth angle.

Fortunately, yellow is so much lighter than the other three colors that it really doesn't matter what its screen angle is. (For want of anything better, it's usually set at 0°, the same orientation as the page.) As long as the cyan, magenta, and black are 30° apart from one another, we're home. Conventionally, the magenta is at 75°, the black at 45°, and the cyan at 15°, but it's the 30° relationship of the three that's important, not these particular numbers.

Now, back to Secretary Albright. The original appeared in a newspaper that uses the above angles. Its black is therefore at 45°. My scan captured its dot pattern, and although I may not have had the original exactly straight when I scanned it, the pattern probably is somewhere between 43° and 47°.

On top of that, we impose this book's black screen, which is also angled at 45°. This is why the right image resides in Moirésville. The left version is vastly better, because instead of two screens at around 45°, there is one at 45° and another 30° away at 15°. The book's angle didn't change. The image's did.

This demonstration should convince you that if you are dealing with prescreened B/W originals, you will improve quality decisively by rotating them all 30° on the printed page. Regrettably, that is a somewhat unrealistic method.

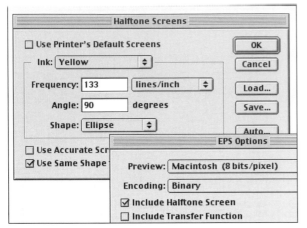

Figure 15.2 *The two steps in embedding a screen angle in a Photoshop file: background, the Screens submenu of Edit: Page Setup; foreground, saving an EPS file.*

Confronted with a moth that persisted in trying to throw itself into a lighted candle, archy the cockroach remarked, "why do you fellows pull this stunt/because it is the conventional thing for moths or why/...have you no sense [?]"

Take it to heart. The 45° black angle is, indeed, the conventional thing. But the mountain need not come to Mohammed. If the original art and the new screen both have the same angle, and you can't rotate the original art, rotate the screen.

If we save the image in EPS format rather than the more customary TIFF, we are allowed to choose a screen angle and/or frequency that will override the image-setter's default. If we want our Albright image to be oriented vertically but not have that revolting moiré, all we have to do is set the black screen angle to 15° or 75°, either of which is that magic 30° away from the original screen.

The method of embedding angles is shown in Figure 15.2. The first step is File: Page Setup>Screens, to enter the frequency and angle of the screen we've decided to use. Then, when saving, choose Photoshop EPS as a format, and the second dialog box shown will pop up automatically.

Changing screen frequencies and angles can be devastatingly effective. It can have devastating effects of an entirely different nature if you or somebody else later picks up the image and uses it for something else. Photoshop issues no warning that an EPS file has embedded screens.

Therefore, you should issue your own. Name the file *albright.screens.in* or something else that unambiguously indicates what is going on. This practice is likely to save your local police department a lot of money, because they will not have to figure out which of the frustrated subsequent users was the one who murdered you.

PageMaker 6.5's Print>Color Options, and InDesign 1.5's Print>Color allows us to change the angle and frequency in the same way, without the dangerous practice of embedding them in the image file. The print menu of QuarkXPress 4 has similar features. Earlier versions of the program do not.

Embedding a Screen

With black and white images, we should feel free to embed screen rulings that minimize moiré. With color images, there is considerably more risk, and this should be an experts-only tactic. But in B/W, nothing much can go wrong if we change the angle to 15° or 75°, which are optimal if the pre-screened original was at 45°, as it almost always is.

But while doing this, we ought to think about screen *frequency* as well, because this is another case where prescreened originals should be treated in a way completely foreign to what we are used to.

The image of President Clinton in Figure 15.3A illustrates why we should not be overly intent on destroying every dot. Although it's an uncorrected scan of a pre-screened image, and I haven't fiddled with the angles, the moiré is scarcely noticeable. It is in fact scanned from the same newspaper as the Albright image.

The only variable is that Albright is re-screened at 65 DPI, whereas Clinton is at the standard 133. The coarser the patterns, the worse the moiré. The finer the output screen pattern, the better off we'll be.

The flip side is, the smaller the dots, the less controllable they are on press. If the printer can't hold dot integrity, the picture will start to go blurry. Ordinarily, that is a terrible thing, but in the case of a pre-screened original, it's a good thing. Ordinarily, we trust what the printer says about maximum screen ruling—but not when we're trying to fight a moiré.

Magazines, for example, recommend a 133-line screen. If you are submitting a pre-screened B/W piece, however, I recommend that you embed a 150-line screen—and with a black angle of 15°, not 45°.

There is an interesting test of this in Figure 15.3B. That particular image sports a 200 DPI screen, which the printer of this book would likely have a heart attack over if he knew in advance it were there. Web presses like the one that is slated to print this book are not meant for such abuse; even the finest sheetfed presses using the best stock have difficulty with 200-line screens, as do imagesetters.

There's a similar example in Chapter 14, but that one (Figure 14.1) uses a finer rul-ing, an unscreened original, and a color image. Here, there's a lot more of a case for it. This set of images has already printed in four different magazines, moiré avoidance being a major concern worldwide. In the original article that accompanied them, I predicted that Figure 15.3B had a good chance to look acceptable when ink actu-ally hit paper.

In three out of four magazines, it did. And in every printing of *Professional Photo-shop 5*, it also was reasonable. Then again, this book goes direct-to-plate, which gives sharper dots that are easier to hold.

Thirty Degrees Again

In addition to the angle of the original and that of the imagesetter, there is a third angle that must be taken into account: the angle of the scan.

Scanners take their samples in a per-fectly horizontal pattern, or, to make it consistent with previous terminology, at an angle of 90°. They are not exempt from the 30-degree rule. Just throwing pre-screened art into the scanner, as I did with the Albright image, is highly inferior. For best reproduction, the scan must be angled as well. If the original is mounted straight up and down, there will be an unacceptable 45° between its screen pattern and the angle of scan. We therefore rotate the orig-inal by 15°. Whether the rotation is clock-wise or counterclockwise is irrelevant in a B/W image; either way, the scan angle will be off by 30°, which is just what we want.

Angling the scan is one of the more com-mon magic bullets being offered for your delectation by various authorities, most of whom recommend trial and error. If the original is as bad as it can possibly be, angling it can't make it worse, I'd have to agree. But why guess? Why choose a random angle, when the 30-degree rule suggests one that is better than all others?

Instead of popping the original into the scanner at an angle chosen by Providence because you are desperate, pop it in at 15° because you are confident.

All this horsing around with angles and frequencies will solve most of your B/W de-screening problems. These easy steps may give you all the quality you require out of a prescreened original. If so, there is no need for you to read further. The rest of this chapter is for the folks who have time to spare and need to make rescreened images look not just OK, but as good as possible.

Figure 15.3 *Different approaches to a prescreened original. A: an uncorrected scan. B: the same file with a 200-line screen embedded. C: the same image scanned and corrected with the methods recommended in this chapter. D: the same file with 150-line screen at a 15° black screen angle. E: version A treated with an automated range correction and descreening routine.*

Those Dots: Rules and Exceptions

Any attempt at further improvement starts with the realization that the embedded dot pattern is a two-edged sword. On the one hand, it deters us from trying to add contrast to the image by threatening us with a ruinous moiré if we try. On the other, it holds all the detail. We don't need to eliminate it, just subdue it somewhat as we add range overall.

Exactly how much to play down the dot pattern is an image-by-image decision. I'll give you a recipe that usually works, but you may have to modify it in certain cases. Before I give you that recipe, here are some general concepts:

• Always scan prescreened art at the highest possible resolution, then resample it down. Very high scan resolutions are usually bad because they make images overly soft, but if the original has a pattern, softness is just fine, thank you.

• Learn to read the angles of the original. This takes practice, especially when dealing with color. Examine the original under a loupe, and imagine a box, or an L-shape, as shown in Figure 15.5. Rotate it until straight rows of dots match its sides, and you'll know the angle. With few exceptions, you'll find that black is at 45° and that cyan and magenta are at approximately 15° and 75°, respectively. But it isn't always so, particularly in older publications or those printed in Europe. Once you have verified the angle, use the 30-degree rule in both scanning and imaging.

• Build yourself a scanner template, with a line showing you where 15° is. Admittedly, you will never set the angle perfectly in a scanner, but why be off by five degrees?

• Don't use unsharp masking. The whole problem with prescreened originals is they are *too* sharp. Generally we want to blur them to some extent, and it is possible, nay likely, that we may want to go into local areas with the sharpening tool thereafter. For example, a person's eyes or jewelry will lose sparkle during the blurring. This should be attacked with the tool, not an overall filter. If you blur so much that you have to sharpen globally, the sharpening is a bandage to put over the magic-bullet wound in your foot.

• Don't use automated descreening software. Some, like the routine illustrated in Figure 15.3E, are pretty good, but none will give the same quality as careful human intervention. There are some successful descreening algorithms for film, but once

ink hits paper, there are enough variables to make the results of automated descreening mediocre at best.

And now, the recipe. First, go back to the Albright moiré, and convince yourself that it isn't as bad as you first thought. Her jewelry is fine as is. Her dark dress and the background are also more or less acceptable. The really disgusting moiré happens only in the face. That is very typical. It's the middle range of the picture we need to worry about, not the two ends.

Second, break the image into two parts in your mind. On the one hand, the dots, which have detail, on the other, the white space between them, which does not. We definitely have to reduce the difference between the two, but doesn't it make sense to handle these two hugely different phenom-

Figure 15.4 *Deemphasizing the dots is best done in separate lightening and darkening steps. A: a blowup of part of Figure 15.3.A, with contrast increased. B: a Gaussian Blur on a copy of version A. C: the blurred version B applied, Darken mode, to version A. D: the Dust & Scratches filter run on a second, darkened copy of version A. E: version D applied, Lighten mode, to version C.*

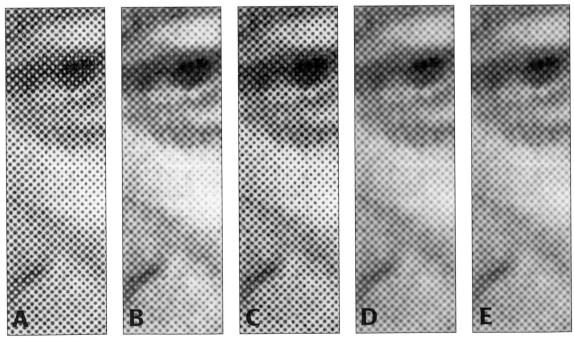

ena in two different ways, rather than with a single cataclysm?

With these thoughts in mind, you may follow what happens in Figure 15.4.

• Take your properly sized and rotated grayscale scan and increase its contrast to your taste, ignoring the fact that this makes the dot pattern worse.

• Make two duplicates of the resulting image. To avoid confusion with the lettered versions of Figure 15.4, I will refer to these as Copy X and Copy Y.

• Going to Copy X, apply a Gaussian blur filter at Radius 1.0. This will fill up the white space, which we want. It will also badly damage the dots, which we don't. Not to worry. This is Figure 15.4B.

• Back to the original. With Image: Apply Image, apply Copy X in Darken mode. This will not affect the dots, which will necessarily be lighter in Copy X than the original. We are now at Figure 15.4C.

• Trash Copy X, and turn to Copy Y. Apply a curve to bring up the highlight to a minimum of a 20^K dot.

• With the newly darkened Copy Y, apply Photoshop's Dust & Scratches filter, Radius 1. This will diminish the dots but hold their shape more or less, except for the lightest dots, which will be history. The result is Figure 15.4D.

• Back to the original. Apply Copy Y, this time in Lighten mode. The point of the earlier darkening of Copy Y now becomes clear. The lightest fifth of the original will be unaffected by this move—Copy Y is guaranteed darker. The big action is in the midtone. Copy X brought up the background, and Copy Y subdues but does not kill the dot pattern, yielding Figure 15.4E.

• If it seems appropriate, increase contrast again.

Figure 15.5 *Finding the screen angles can be tough, especially in a color image. Below, an enlarged scan of a printed image. Above, the original digital image with a perfect screen imposed. To find the cyan angle, for example, imagine an L-shape, and angle it until the lines of cyan dots follow it both up and down. Insets: the two cyan plates, showing how much detail is lost because of printing and rescanning.*

If you can proof the image before actually going to press with it, be conservative with the above recipe. It's a lot easier to reduce moiré on the second pass than to restore detail.

Figure 15.6 *Striped shirts are notorious for being subject to moiré, as in the original above. This is commonly—and wrongly—blamed on screening. As the enlarged sections of the cyan plate below show, moiré was already present, thanks to the scanner.*

The Good Old Days

If the 200-line screen, which we know to be ridiculous, is even close to being acceptable, that's a strong vote in favor of using 150 or even 175. This is a fairly risk-free technique with B/W originals, less so with color. Prescreened color originals are easier, in the sense that the dot pattern is not as pronounced, but they are also harder, in that we have to spend a lot of time worrying about the possibility of goofy colors creeping in.

The age of Photoshop has given us so many advantages over traditional methods that it is somewhat sobering to hear that the old way was better. Our forefathers would merely stick the prescreened original into a process camera and "fineline" it. The result would then be merged by hand into the final film for the job. In other words, they would let the original screen also be the final screen. We, having no choice in a PostScript world but to screen the original

again when we place it in our pages, are not so lucky.

That camera method doesn't work if the original screen is drastically different from the final desired one, as in the Clinton image, which was originally 65 DPI yet had to be repurposed to match the 133 found in the rest of the book. In such a case, the traditional high-end method is to scan at an extremely high resolution, which we can do to some extent with our desktop scanners, and to scan just slightly out of focus, which we can't. We can never equal the quality of starting with a continuous-tone original, true. But *acceptable* quality? I think so. The Clinton series, remember, is done at same size from an original printed in a 65 DPI newspaper. That's about as bad as it gets. How unreasonable is the corrected version?

It would be nice never to have to work with prescreened art, but it sometimes can't be avoided. Original photographs get lost or damaged; historical photos are only available in printed form, and so forth. It would also be nice to have some of the high-end tools of yesteryear to deal with them. But we can make do.

A Pattern of Deception

Moiré isn't limited to cases where an original is already screened—the image's subject can be the culprit. Whenever two or more patterns overlap, unusual things can but do not always occur, as in Figure 15.7. These subpatterns are interesting, but they aren't exactly what we want to see on the printed page.

We who work with print are particularly vulnerable to variations on this disagreeable interference theme, because in reproducing artwork, we generally impose a pattern ourselves, in the form of rows of tiny, evenly spaced dots, otherwise known as a screen ruling. If some kind of pattern also exists in the original art, as it does in the striped shirt of Figure 15.6, ugly things can begin to happen.

There is, however, a third potential contributor. As the enlarged sections of the cyan plate demonstrate, the moiré is already an integral part of the image, courtesy of the *scanner*. Even a stochastic screen, which has no pattern, would not help at this point.

The mathematics of moiré are moderately complex. But for our

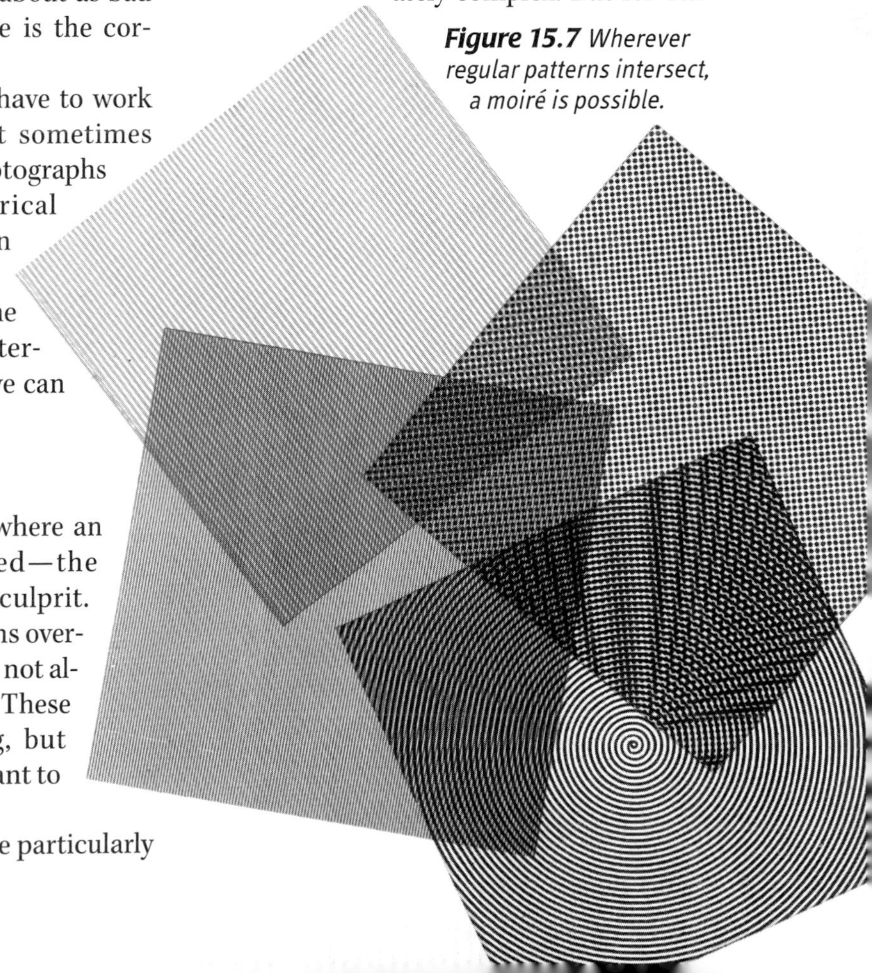

Figure 15.7 *Wherever regular patterns intersect, a moiré is possible.*

purposes, one grand oversimplification will do. Remember the lesson of the black and whites we just did. Assuming two straight-line patterns, having them 30° or 60° apart from one another is best; the same angle, or 90° apart, is worst.

The vertical stripes of the shirt have an angle of 0°, disastrous because the scanner does its thing at an angle of 90°, leaving the deadly 90° difference.

If you don't believe that this is the cause of the problem, have a look at the sleeve. I measure it at 126°, a very happy 36° away from the scanning angle, and, by gosh, there isn't a moiré!

The moral is that striped shirts only produce moirés when the scanner operator falls asleep. Here, all that had to be done to avoid moiré was to rotate the original by 30° prior to scanning it, intending to reverse the rotation in Photoshop later. By using that angle, the stripes would have been at −60° with respect to the scan and the sleeve at 66°, both of which are nearly optimal.

Color images are a little easier to de-screen than black and whites, and also a little harder. Easier, because moirés will ordinarily not be in

Figure 15.8 *Top left, an original digital file as printed in a magazine. Bottom left, a scan of the actual printed result done as though it were an ordinary piece of reflective art. Bottom right, a different scan of the printed piece using an automated descreening package. Top right, a reproduction of the printed piece using the methods advocated in this chapter.*

all plates. Harder, because if one or more plates has a serious moiré, image quality will suffer even if we can't easily see the moiré in the image as a whole.

And the same, because they are still subject to the 30-degrees-is-best rule; because the idea is to subdue the dots without wiping them out entirely; and because with reasonable care one can get much better results than by using some sort of automated descreening program.

To illustrate, in Figure 15.8 I'll work with an image I used in a magazine article. Naturally, I have the original file, which is shown for reference. Every version with a B in the upper right is actually a scan from the printed magazine.

The image of the shirt had a subject moiré—there was a pattern in the shirt proper, having nothing to do with the printing process. In principle, there is no such pattern in the woman's face, but the fact that it has been previously screened introduces not one, but four patterns, one for each CMYK ink. We need to compensate for that during reprinting, but especially during scanning.

The Unimportance of Yellow

Figure 15.9 has a moiré, but it isn't a prescreened original: it's the same file as the original in Figure 15.8, but with something strange going on with the screens. I have swapped the magenta and yellow angles. The purpose of this is not to prove that random screen angles don't work as much as that we shouldn't get terribly agitated over the fate of the yellow plate.

A reminder: only three inks can have angles 30° apart. Naturally, we let those three be our darkest inks, cyan, magenta, and black. The yellow is a singleton; conventionally its angle is pure horizontal. This sandwiches it between the magenta and the cyan, 15° away from either and 45° away from the black, but in reality the yellow angle is irrelevant.

If you don't believe this, have a closer look at the misangled version. Can you explain why there is moiré in the background and the hair, but not so much in the face?

This magenta plate isn't 30° away from anything. But the angle is only relevant if there's something to conflict with it. Cyan and black are doing a good job of that in the background. But the face is almost entirely magenta *and yellow,* and yellow isn't strong enough to create a moiré.

Given the normal angles of 15° for the cyan plate, 45° for the black, 75° for the magenta, and 0° for the yellow, if we mount a prescreened original in a scanner at the usual angle, 90°, *none* of the screens will be 30 degrees away from it. We therefore should mount at an angle, but what that angle should be is open for discussion. For the same reason that only three printing inks can be 30° apart from one another,

Figure 15.9
The original file printed with magenta and yellow screen angles reversed. Note the color variation from the original, although the files are identical!

only two can be 30° away from the scanning angle. Which leaves us with some choices to make.

The best scanning angle for prescreened color is usually 45°, which is 30° away from both magenta and cyan. Black and yellow will unfortunately thus be at relatively bad scanning angles.

The importance of these choices is demonstrated starkly in Figure 15.10. This scan was made at a 45° angle and then rotated back to vertical in Photoshop. Shown, greatly enlarged, are the resulting RGB channels.

The red and green channels are shaped by the cyan and magenta components, respectively, of the original. Do you see the characteristic 15° angle of the dots in the red, and the 75° angle in the green?

The dot structure, however, is crisp and well defined. Compare that to the blue channel, which is based on the yellow component of the original. Moiré has struck! As, indeed, mathematics suggests. The yellow screen angle is zero; rotating the scan as I did places it at 45° relative to the scanner, which is not good.

This plate will hurt quality, but we'd much rather have a good cyan and magenta than a good yellow. We can recover from a bad yellow, as I'm about to demonstrate. If we don't take care in choosing the scan angle, though, we'll have *every* channel looking like the blue one does in Figure 15.10, and that will be a mess.

Resolution, and Other Resolutions

With that mathematical introduction out of the way, let's first resolve not to accept the atrocities shown in Figure 15.8 of either a normal scan or an automated descreen. Both have too many problems to repair. The

first has an incipient moiré nearly everywhere; the sledgehammer applied to the second has blown away detail.

Let us further resolve that this is not to be an all-day affair. With unlimited time, one can reconstruct almost anything.

Finally, let us remember that the dots that make up this image may not be much, but they're all we have in the way of detail, and we can't afford to damage them. That means, no festivals of resampling, blurring, despeckling, and resharpening, no added noise, and no other sledgehammers. Instead, let's:

• **Scan at maximum resolution, and at the proper angle**. The high resolution softens the image. Of course, you should also downsample it to the desired resolution before printing; see Chapter 14 for guidelines. The proper angle keeps the moiré manageable. For monochrome images, the proper scan angle is 15° or –15°; for color, 45° is usually best, sacrificing a little in the black channel in the interest of better cyan and magenta. In certain darker images, –15°, which sacrifices magenta, or 15°, which sacrifices cyan, may work better. Figure 15.11 puts the choices in graphic form.

• **Convert the image to LAB, and blur the A and B channels**. This is a critical step. LAB separates color from contrast, and the A and B define color only. Blurring the A and B eliminates the big color transitions that dots of colored ink cause, without damaging detail in the image. Note how much better the blue channel above is once this blurring is done and the image is reconverted to RGB.

Choose a Gaussian blur value that will eliminate the dot pattern in the channel, which you should be able to see easily. The amount of blur will usually be more in the B channel than the A. Here, I used a Radius of 1.4 in the A and 2.0 in the B. Because of the need to use two different Radii, doing this in RGB or CMYK and fading back to Color mode isn't an adequate substitute.

• **Create a black plate immediately**. Make a copy of the LAB document as is, and convert it to CMYK. You may discard the CMY channels if you like; this version of the document is useful only for its black. The idea is to preserve all the detail possible in the black—the next step will suppress some of the dot pattern in the other plates, but the black is the backbone of the printed image, and we want it to be as close to the original in detail as possible.

• **Reduce the dot pattern in the L channel**. Returning to the original LAB document, open the L channel and descreen it as though it were a black and white image, using the same recipe

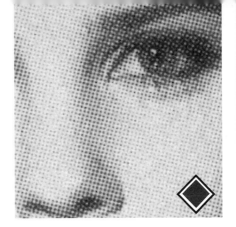
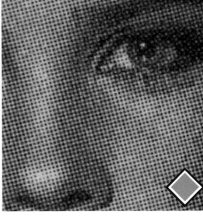

Figure 15.10 *The angle of scanning is critical in dealing with prescreened color originals. A 45° angle is optimal in most cases, and will yield the best capture of the cyan and magenta dots. Above, greatly enlarged, are the red and green of a 45° scan. Note the excellent dot structure in the red, which is based on cyan, and in the green, which is based on magenta. Below left, however, the blue channel has a bad moiré. This happened because the blue is based on yellow, and 45° is a poor angle for yellow. Had this image not been scanned at an angle, in all probability the red and green channels would look like this as well. Below right, the same blue channel after the document had been temporarily converted into LAB and the A and B channels blurred.*

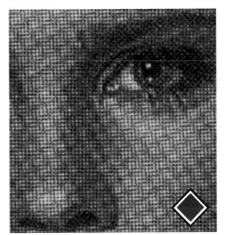
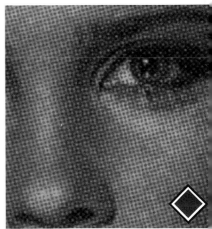

described in our discussion of the Clinton image of Figure 15.3.

• **Correct color and convert**. How you go about this is up to you, but if you are able to set range using the L channel of LAB, that's the best way for a prescreened original. All the rescreened versions in Figure 15.8 suffer to some extent from color hot spots, which an L correction wouldn't exaggerate.

• **Replace the black plate**. Since some degradation will have taken place in the last two steps, replace the new black plate with the black plate generated earlier.

• **Ask yourself, where is detail unnecessary**? In more places than you might think. In the current picture, we'd like to hold detail in the hair, the eyes, the eyebrows and eyelids, the lips, the earrings, and the garment. But that only amounts to a small

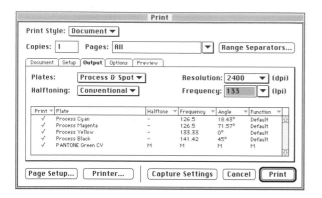

Figure 15.11 *The graphic below shows the conventional 4/c screen angles, and offers some suggested scanning angles. Not every image-setter, however, uses precisely these angles. In any application that is capable of loading PostScript Printer Descriptions (PPDs), we can read what a specific imagesetter will do. Above, a menu from QuarkXPress 4, which, unlike past versions, allows screens to be overridden.*

fraction of the image's geography. If the skin and background, which cover a much larger area, somehow got smoother, that would be just fine.

Accordingly, if you are comfortable with the use of masks, make a copy of the picture and blur it. Then, merge the two versions together, masking out the portions of the original that have critical detail. If you are uncomfortable with this method, an alternative is to use the blur tool to soften up the face.

A better technique, in my opinion, is to place the original as a layer on top of a blurred version. Then, by Layer: Add Layer Mask>Reveal All, establish a mask on which you can, in effect, airbrush in detail from the bottom version.

In the corrected version in Figure 15.8, you can, if you look carefully, detect graininess in the hair, which needs detail. The woman's face, which does not, is smooth.

- **Consider manipulating the screen angles.** In a black and white image, as we've seen, the original screen is almost sure to be 45°. It's virtually automatic, therefore, to change the output screen to 15° or 75°, assuring there will be the magic 30° difference.

  The argument also applies (albeit less strongly) to color work. In finely detailed or color-neutral images, it pays to make, for example, the cyan output angle something other than the angle of the cyan in the original. In a case like the image of the woman, which is not very subject to moiré in the first place, I wouldn't recommend it.

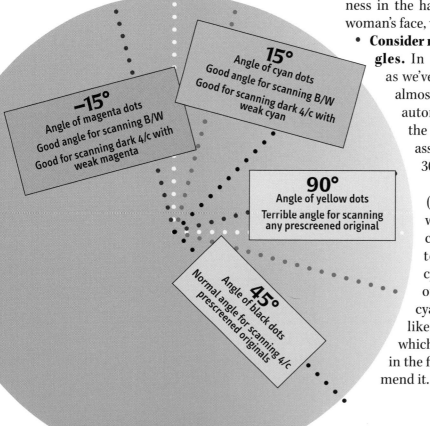

Quick & Dirty

MATHEMATICS, MOIRE, AND THE ARTIST

✓ Whenever two regular grids are imposed on one another, some type of interference pattern will result. This interference is somewhat unpredictable. It may be unnoticeable, or it may cause an obvious moiré.

✓ When we print anything that contains tone, we impose a pattern, or screen. If we scan a printed piece and try to reprint it, we impose a second pattern on top of the one that is already in the image, and moiré is the likely result.

✓ Patterns are much less noticeable when offset from one another by 30°. This rule applies just as much to the pattern of a striped shirt as it does to a row of dots.

✓ Reprinting a prescreened black and white, without intervening, will cause moiré, because there will be two sets of screens, each with an angle of 45°, which is the conventional black angle.

✓ Photoshop, QuarkXPress 4 and up, PageMaker, and InDesign allow us to override normal screen angles. In the case of a prescreened black and white, we would substitute a new output screen angle of 15° (or 75°), to stay 30° away from the screen that is part of the original art.

✓ The cyan, magenta, and black inks are customarily printed with screen angles 30° apart from one another. There is no room for a fourth such offset, but this doesn't matter, as the yellow is too light to create any moiré.

✓ The 30-degree rule also applies to scanning. The original should be mounted 30° away from the screen angle of the most prominent ink(s). A prescreened or patterned original should never be mounted perpendicular to the scanner, as other art would be. After the scan, rotate the file back to vertical in Photoshop.

✓ In correcting a prescreened file, the goal is to tone down the dot pattern, not eliminate it. The dots are what define all detail. If you can no longer see the dots, the image is too soft. For best results, consider the file as two separate images: one containing the dots and one the white spaces between them.

✓ Don't apply overall unsharp masking to a prescreened file. If the file needs it, you have probably blurred the image too much in a needless effort to kill the dots. Use the sharpening tool if needed on critical areas such as eyes.

A Self-Fulfilling Prophecy

My statement that the correct angles are 15°, 30°, 75°, and 90° isn't quite accurate nowadays. Each imagesetter has different characteristics, and manufacturers recommend slight differences not just in angle, but in screen frequency as well.

The imagesetter that set the original of Figure 15.8, for example, runs its cyan at an angle of 18.43°, not 15°, and at a frequency of 126.5 lines per inch, not the 133 the magazine advertises. The black is at the normal 45°, but at a frequency of 141.42 DPI. If you feel the need to swap angles, I suggest you just swap the magenta and cyan, which will be simple and effective. If you are ambitious, there will be cases where a more aggressive approach will work.

In a perfect world, we would never have to work with a prescreened original, any more than we would have to repurpose an indexed-color image from the Web for press, any more than we'd have to restore a 19th-century photograph, or take a 2-megabyte file up to poster size. But today we get asked to do this kind of thing more than ever before.

A number of practitioners assure us that it is impossible to get adequate results from such originals. They they proceed to make this a self-fulfilling prophecy by first scanning at the wrong angle, followed by an obliteration of the dots, possibly with some unsharp masking thrown in, and finally outputting the whole mess at the wrong screen angle.

Those dots are your friend. They become your enemy only if you allow them to moiré. Remember the magic words—thirty degrees—and they won't.

Every File Has Ten Channels

Introducing a powerful new technique! Think about each color image as though you were going to convert it to black and white. Look for areas where you'd like to adjust the relationships between the darknesses of objects. You can do this with a method that works as well with excellent originals as with poor ones: a blend before the application of any curves, followed by a reversion to the color of the original.

olor correction is like chess.

There are certain basics that almost always work. The hotshot chessplayer shoots for an early development, safety for the King, control of the center, and open diagonals for his bishops. The successful retoucher is after good light and dark points, long ranges for the objects of interest, control of neutrality, and a powerful dose of sharpening. If these are the only things you know you will be both a very good chessplayer and a very good retoucher.

Both disciplines, however, can be much deeper. A good grasp of normal tactics is fairly easy. The hard part is developing strategies for individual situations and against individual opponents. So many weapons, so little time to figure out which to use!

As one gets more experienced one tends to see a bigger picture in which everything is interrelated. That's when you see the scintillating sacrifices and mating combinations, or the brilliant resurrections of seemingly hopeless images.

The irritating thing is, if you don't know someone capable of executing them, you never know that such things can be done. And, in that case, you can think you are milking the most out of your position

already, because this, being so dark, is a tough customer.

By now, you should be accustomed in situations like this to think of color and contrast separately. The color of the original is somewhat too yellow, but the real problem is one of darkness and flatness. That suggests an initial correction in LAB, not CMYK. The form of the curve in the L is a straightforward drop in the quartertone. The A and B are straight lines, slightly steepened in the manner shown in Chapter 8, and both moved a bit to the left to compensate for a small yellowish-green cast. By now we should consider that the whitest clouds are more reliably neutral than the shirts, due to the harsh sunlight. So we should zero the A and B channels there.

or your picture, when in reality a much stronger game is available.

Let's play a game of speed chess—er, color. The rules say, no use of tools, no selections or masks. The opponent is the top version of Figure 16.1. It starts in LAB and we are required to make a CMYK version.

It's a good thing that we're in Chapter 16

If you are familiar with the strengths and weaknesses of LAB, it should only take you a few seconds to analyze the image in this way. If not, don't feel embarrassed if you have to take a few minutes just staring at the original. Either way, the big clue is: the lightest point of the image is obviously the white clothing. But what's the *second* lightest point? Whether it's a point in the clouds or the shirt of the guy in the foreground, it's way darker than the light shirts. Our task will naturally be to reduce the wasted space between the two, by sharply lightening the clouds or whatever.

Speaking of sharpening, you should also realize that this should probably be sharpened in the L, rather than in selected CMYK channels. There is no dominating color, no facial detail. If you're a real sharpening whiz, you should note that many of the transition areas feature relatively dark colors butting one another, which suggests the trick of emphasizing dark sharpening shown in Figure 4.13.

But, as an expert, you have to be ready to turn on a dime. Originals this dark often become quite noisy when lightened. Sharpening the L looks like the right thing to do, but it doesn't happen to work with this shot. So, you go to Plan B, which is to sharpen the black plate after the conversion to CMYK.

While we're thinking about the separation, now's the time to figure out whether we need one that's out of the ordinary. You ask whether it would be very bad if bright colors appeared in the final

picture. You look for critically important detail in the blacks. You look for an object that absolutely has to be kept as neutral as possible. And, finding none of these things, you decide on a normal, skeleton black.

Your CMYK curves, in addition to setting proper endpoints (did you remember to have an extra-dark shadow, considering that the darkest area, the ranger's pants, doesn't have important detail?), should try to steepen the range of the detail in the canyon. And, as planned, you sharpened the black.

If you have made all these careful moves, you are an expert. If you took this original image to a prepress house, 99 percent would not be able to get a result as good as the bottom half of Figure 16.1.

In chess, they also have an official ranking of "expert." An expert can whip about 99 percent of normal chess players. Unfortunately, then there are masters, and even

Figure 16.2 *This version is created in the same manner as the bottom of Figure 16.1, but with the addition of a step before the LAB curves. Can you guess the step that brought out the extra punch?*

Figure 16.3 *If the assignment is to convert this RGB image to B/W, the issue will be that the sky will wind up being approximately the same darkness as the stadium.*

grandmasters, who simply eat experts for lunch when they face them.

And so it is here. The bottom half of Figure 16.1, good as it is, doesn't compare to Figure 16.2. I'll explain what the key move was, but first let's change the subject entirely, reverting to the theme of Chapter 13.

The Grayscale Gambit

Figure 16.3 is an excellent professional shot with a fine tonal range. Unhappily, our assignment is to convert it to black and white. The original is in RGB.

We've learned previously what to do. We have to analyze the image to see if any high-contrast areas are really due to contrast in hue and/or saturation, these things being worthless in black and white. Then, if we find them, we create a plan to change that contrast into a variation in luminosity.

The problem here is obvious. The build-

ings, especially the stadium, are about the same darkness as the sky. Convert this to B/W, and we'll get mud.

If the background buildings didn't exist, we'd scratch our heads over whether to make the sky darker and the stadium lighter or vice versa. But since the buildings are there and they are already darker than the sky, our plan has to be to lighten the sky and darken everything else.

Given that agenda, we now analyze the RGB channels to find out whether they are friend or foe. Since we need the sky lighter than the stadium, the red is the foe. The green is a neutral party, and the blue is clearly an ally.

The exact blending method would be up for debate. Mine started with minor curve moves in the light part of both the red and the green to accentuate the clouds. I was afraid of losing these during the blends.

Figure 16.4 *Top, a default conversion of Figure 16.3 into B/W. Bottom, a version prepared by blending to minimize the impact of the red channel, in the manner suggested in Chapter 13.*

Figure 16.5 *This is the blended file that was converted into B/W to create the bottom half of Figure 16.4.*

I then blended 75% of the green into the red. After doing so, I blended 40% of the blue into the green, knowing that the green carries inordinate weight in the conversion to grayscale. But I used Lighten mode, because I wanted to retain contrast in the background buildings.

I then converted. The result is in Figure 16.4 below a default conversion. Normally I would have looked for a sharpening opportunity before going into B/W, but I had a particular reason not to do so here.

That reason is, I am conscious that you are wondering what the point of this exercise is. We've already covered this elsewhere; perhaps you never even have to convert color into black and white.

Well, when I said the idea was to convert this image into B/W, that was a lie. The truth is, I wanted to do a *color* correction.

Gaining a Tempo

Let's back up one step, to the moment before the conversion into B/W. At this point, we have Figure 16.5. The desired lightening

of the sky is there, but so is some pretty wretched color.

That, however, isn't relevant. The color of the original was good. There is no need to trouble ourselves with it further. All we have to do is something similar to the move we saw much earlier in the raspberries image of Figure 9.3. We paste Figure 16.5 as a layer on top of the original, and change the layering mode from Normal to Luminosity.

Increasing the contrast between sky and structure is something the photographer is likely to want to do. But without the initial blend, there's no way to get to the bottom half of Figure 16.6. No curve or Hue/Saturation adjustment would so transform the top version. The only other option would be a selection, which takes far longer and is hard to keep looking natural.

Now do you get what went on with that ranger image? The bottom of Figure 16.1 is good, but the ranger's face isn't nearly as well defined as in Figure 16.2.

In Figure 16.7, have a look at the three RGB channels. Think of how we would convert this image to B/W. The red channel is clearly a friend. The blue is the foe. The green is somewhere in the middle.

Therefore, the first step in RGB is to set up a duplicate layer and start blending away. The layer mode is set to Luminosity, meaning that the bottom image, the original, will be used for color and the top one for contrast. When satisfied, Layer: Flatten Image, convert to LAB and *then* do all of the expert stuff you used to produce the bottom half of Figure 16.1. That first move, gaining depth in the face, is the key to the whole combination.

This preliminary luminosity blend isn't right for all images, but when it is right it's just as right for an excellent original like

Figure 16.6 *Top, the original image; bottom, when Figure 16.5 is placed on a layer on top of it and layering mode is set to Luminosity.*

Figure 16.7 The red, green, and blue channels of Figure 16.1.

this one as it is for that ugly ranger shot. You should therefore start off by examining the individual RGB channels, even if you normally do your work in another colorspace. That goes double for one very common, very important class of image: faces.

The Flatness Counter-Gambit

Flat-looking faces are one of the banes of our existence, the source of many client complaints. We've already discussed, in Chapter 5, various kinds of CMYK blending to beef up the contrast in the weaker channels. We can get even more with a preliminary RGB/luminosity move that's a lot easier than the ones so far.

We've been looking for channels that are outright foes, such as the blue in the ranger image or the red in the picture of the stadium. Sometimes we've found that the remaining two channels, as in the stadium, have different strengths and weaknesses. Sometimes, as in red of the ranger, both channels are friends, but one is clearly better.

That's what usually happens with faces. The channels always go, from lightest to darkest, red, green, blue. If we consider each channel as a separate black and white, none is exactly the foe; however, the green is always better-looking than the red, and most of the time than the blue as well.

So, try this recipe with your next skintone problem:

- Starting in RGB, make a duplicate layer.
- With Image: Apply Image, apply the green channel to the RGB composite. Did you know you could do that? It results in a black and white image. In true gambit fashion, the red and blue channels have been sacrificed. The green is now the only piece on the board.
- In the Layers palette, change the mode from Normal to Luminosity. This restores the color of the original, while retaining the contrast of the green. If you think the effect is too harsh change opacity to something lower than 100%.

I saw no need to do that in the two faces of Figure 16.8. Both bottom versions faithfully follow the above recipe, at 100% opacity.

Mind you, these versions are not final corrections. None of the by-the-numbers and sharpening stuff we've learned has happened yet. It still needs to. But whatever further corrections you have in mind are going to get considerably

Figure 16.8 *The green channel is almost always the best in a face shot. Therefore, to add snap, one can, on a layer, replace the entire file with the green only, mode Luminosity.*

better results if you start the process with the bottom versions instead of the top.

Checkmating the Defect

Now that we have this weapon in our arsenal, it's more important than ever to think about overall strategy before starting work on the image. This kind of wholesale replacement by a single channel has its dangers. The woman in Figure 16.8 looks better in every way, in my opinion, after the correction, because the original green channel was clearly better than the others. The man looks better also, but his shirt is actually a little worse. That's a fair price to pay here, but often the defect in the blending channel is serious enough to keep us in check.

Let's plan strategy for Figure 16.9. At first glance, it looks a lot like the canyon shot in Figure 8.10, which responded nicely to LAB curves. But there's one little complication that wasn't present in the earlier image: this one has a sky. That means the lightest point of the image isn't the lightest point of the canyon.

Figure 16.9 *The idea here is to bring out detail in the rocks without obliterating the sky. Right, the original RGB channels.*

The eventual idea will be to extend range in the canyon by lightening its lightest point, thus making the whole thing fall in a steeper area of the curve. That will be too bad for what feeble detail we have in the sky, which, being lighter than the canyon, will fall in a flatter area.

If we're going to apply that curve we have to figure out a way to beef up the sky. Adding cyan and magenta to all blues in Adjust: Selective Color might work in certain images, but not this one, because parts of the canyon are also blue.

So, a luminosity blend suggests itself. We make the sky stronger, knowing it will probably lose a little when we apply LAB curves later.

The analysis of the skies in the RGB channels unmasks one friend and two foes. If we apply the friendly red to the duplicate layer in Luminosity mode as we did with the faces, that will produce a much better sky. Lamentably, it'll also eviscerate the reddish peninsula of rock on the left of the image. In that peninsula, the red is considerably worse than the other two channels.

That's not a fair exchange. I'd settle for a bad sky before I did that. But there's a way to queen one's pawn and have it, too.

The way we did the faces was, Duplicate Layer, then Apply Image, Normal mode. This time, we'll apply the red to the entire image, not in Normal, but Darken mode. This replaces areas of the image where the red channel is darker. But it doesn't do it based on a weighted average of

Figure 16.10 *The version below will be much easier to correct. It uses the color of Figure 16.9 but the luminosity of the version at right, which was produced by blending the red channel into the whole file in Darken mode. The background is monochrome because the red was the darkest of any channel there. After reverting to the original color, the sky was blue again, but with much stronger detail.*

the other two channels: it can replace both of the others, one, or neither.

The top of Figure 16.10 is the result. The sky, and the darkest areas of the background canyon, are now monochrome, because the red is darker than both the green and the blue there. Certain areas of the background canyon are now magenta, because the red is darker than the blue but not the green. And the foreground formations don't change color at all because the red is lighter than both the others.

At this point, we change the layering mode to Luminosity, getting the bottom version of Figure 16.10 with its rich sky, awaiting our pleasure in LAB.

Figure 16.11 *The desired result here is to increase contrast in the canyon walls, but also to make the tree stand out more.*

Controlling the Open Diagonal

That canyon picture would look OK if we just converted it to B/W. The image of Figure 16.11 is a different canyon, and the same can't be said of it. If we converted it directly to B/W the tree at bottom right would vanish into the canyon, for want of a difference in lightness.

Looking at the RGB channels, if the idea is to break the tree away from the canyon walls the blue is the only friend we've got.

If we use it, we'll get better canyon walls and a better tree. Unfortunately, though, it has no sky at all. Also, it seems like a bad idea to wipe out the hiker. This can all be avoided with another Darken blend, with a slight variation.

In the canyon walls the blue channel is so much darker than the other two that the blend may make the walls look unnatural. Therefore, after making the duplicate layer, I applied a curve to the blue channel, dropping its midpoint. This lightened the channel, but it also added contrast to the walls and the tree, which fall in the dark half of the curve. It hurt contrast in the hiker, which matters not a fig, as she will be unaffected by the final blend.

After the curve, I applied this new blue to the entire duplicate layer. That produced the top of Figure 16.12. The hiker and the sky are unaffected. The tree is monochrome because the blue channel is much heavier than the other two. Parts of the canyon walls are also monochrome; there are also patches of color where the blue, lightened by my curve, is no longer darker than one or both of the other two.

Figure 16.12
Right, a version prepared by blending a modified blue channel of Figure 16.11 into the entire document, Darken mode. The version below uses 75% of its luminosity coupled with the color of Figure 16.11.

The bottom half of Figure 16.12 is, of course, with the top layer switched to Luminosity mode, restoring the original color while keeping the new contrast. This time, however, I couldn't use 100% opacity for the top layer. The tree would have been nearly black otherwise. So I used 75%. You might have picked some other number. It depends on how strongly you feel about the role of that tree.

The CMYK Endgame

About 300 pages ago, I remarked that most Photoshop users make selections far too often. This chapter offers a more sophisticated—and more effective—alternative.

Selections and masks are surely necessary from time to time. If we're merging images or making truly major artistic changes, there's no getting around them. In color correction, though, there's always a slight aura of artificiality when one section of the image is treated differently from the rest. This is why, when using a selection, we have to try to make any curve move as subtle as possible.

In the last canyon example, in effect we were selecting the tree and changing its color, but there's none of the usual telltale evidence, because there never was any time that the tree was isolated, except by the natural, unexaggerated "mask" found in each channel, which is undetectable.

Let's finish with another tree, in a situation that most retouchers would handle with a selection.

If you've never seen the Utah state capitol, you might think Figure 16.13A has a slight green cast. It doesn't; that's the natural color of the building. The colors of the original are by and large good, with the screaming exception of the tree at right,

which is for some reason having to do with sunlight an eerie yellow.

Trying to make that tree more green with curves is hopeless. Depending on your choice of colorspace, you'd be darkening the midrange of the cyan, darkening the upper range of the red, or moving the neutral point of the A toward green. All three of these moves fail because the tree has too much in common with the front of the building, which will become too cyan in RGB or CMYK or too green in LAB.

Making the change with Hue/Saturation or Selective Color wouldn't work either. You'd have to target Yellows—remember, the tree is yellow now, not green; the values in the second version are around $40^C46^M95^Y5^K$. But if you ask Photoshop to move yellows toward green, that will hammer the steps and parts of the dome, which are both yellow.

So, we're stalemated: stuck with a selection of the tree—unless we know our colorspaces and our blends. We start with an RGB original; the objective is a CMYK file. First question: which of the images we've worked on in this chapter does this one remind you of?

For me, this is the same problem we encountered with the first canyon of Figure 16.9. We want to open the foreground object in LAB. This will regrettably kill the sky, which is lighter.

Figure 16.13 (opposite) Version B is a luminosity blend of A, using the red channel, Darken mode. After conversion into CMYK, replacing the cyan channel with the yellow produces C, which then goes on a layer over B, Darken mode, opacity 40%. This changes the color of the tree, but little else, as the pink sky and the gray building are both lighter in C than in B. D is the final result.

The solution is the same: a luminosity blend using the red channel, Darken mode. This darkens the building slightly, does nothing to the trees, and adds much depth to the sky and clouds.

Now, onto LAB for the contrast-building curve, and also sharpening. This picture doesn't have the dominant color that would argue in favor of doing that in CMYK.

Before converting, I observe that the most important object in this image is light and rather neutral. This suggests using more GCR than usual, and I chose Medium. After conversion the highlights and shad-

ows were correct as is, so I had arrived at Figure 16.13B.

I now created a duplicate layer, and replaced the cyan channel with a copy of the yellow. The result is Figure 16.13C. The sky is now magenta because it no longer has any cyan. The tree is a funky bluish color because in nature the yellow is supposed to be significantly higher than the cyan and here it is of course equal.

The final step was to set the layer mode to Darken. Very little is affected now but the tree. I chose 40% opacity to create what I thought was an appropriate green.

Compression Artifacts: Beware the Blue Blend!

If your files are in JPEG format or have been compressed in some other way, be careful with luminosity blends using the blue channel. Most digital camera captures and most Web graphics have gone through some kind of "lossy" compression process. *Lossy* means that some data gets thrown away. The idea is to throw away things the viewer won't notice when the image is restored.

If you think about it, the least evil place to lose data is the blue (RGB), the B (LAB), or the yellow (CMYK). These channels are so weak that we'll forgive quite a bit of harshness. Accordingly, many algorithms will smash these channels into smithereens if you demand a file small enough.

To see a primitive compression at work, take an LAB image and save its three channels as individual grayscale documents. Leave the L alone, but cut the resolution of the A in half and the B by two-thirds. The size of the three together is now 45% of what it used to be, but if you res the AB back up to original size and recombine the image, it'll probably be just as usable as the original.

Once you convert to RGB, however, you'll probably notice artifacts in the blue—maybe enough to bite you in the behind if you use it in a luminosity blend. Here's an image that's been JPEGged

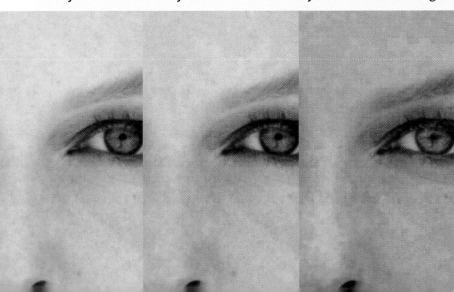

down to an eighth of its original size in Photoshop. The original, left, isn't all that choppy. You can even luminosity-blend it with the green, center. But try it with the blue, right, and be prepared for an evening of retouching out the damage.

EVERY FILE HAS TEN CHANNELS

✓ The techniques used to convert a color image into black and white are often also useful in correcting color. Even if an original has good tonal range there may be an advantage in changing the darkness relation between certain objects.

✓ When wishing to reallocate contrast, it can make sense to do the blending in advance, before applying any curves. This is done by creating a duplicate layer, executing the blend(s) there, and changing layering mode to Luminosity.

✓ Luminosity blends usually work better in RGB than in CMYK, because the CMY channels lack shadow detail and because CMY's compensation for the poor cyan ink restricts blending opportunities.

✓ It's perfectly possible to blend one channel into the composite color image. This will make the image momentarily black and white, but putting it on a luminosity layer will restore the original color.

✓ The downside of luminosity blending is that one channel is often better than the others in most, but not all respects. This calls for careful evaluation before pulling the trigger. Look to the possibility of blending in Darken or Lighten mode to exclude the poorer parts of the source channel.

✓ One can't generalize about which channel will be the best one for blending. Critical detail may be found anywhere.

✓ Nevertheless, in faces the green channel is almost always better than the other two, especially the red, in images of faces. Therefore, it usually makes sense to apply the green to the entire image on a luminosity layer.

✓ Be cautious about blending from the blue or yellow channels. These often have more noise than the others. Also, if an image has gone through JPEG compression, its blue or yellow often has ugly, blockish artifacts.

✓ Occasionally preblends are also useful to change the color of certain objects, or to strengthen detail that is expected to be harmed later by curves.

✓ A luminosity blend isn't just for poor originals. A photographer doesn't always have control of luminosity relationships in the original composition. Therefore, this technique can assist even images that are technically excellent.

Every Square on the Board

Knowing that the RGB channels are very similar to their CMY cousins, you might ask why I didn't just correct the tree in RGB, by darken-blending the blue into the red, as I later did with the yellow into the cyan in CMY. The answer is, interestingly, for the same reason that all the other blends were done in RGB.

Not that they couldn't have been done, or at least attempted, in CMYK afterwards, rather than RGB beforehand. Some of them would work, but there would be a problem in the darkest areas.

As we saw in Chapter 6, the ink limits in CMYK make the CMY channels, especially the magenta and yellow, have lousy shadows, with detail suppressed. This is not an advantage in blending. Furthermore, in RGB neutral colors imply channels of equal strength, but in CMY they imply a heavier cyan. So, for example, the initial move in this image, darken-blending the red into the image to get a better sky, wouldn't work as well in CMY. Darken-blending with the cyan channel, the red's relative, would make the building too dark. Remember, in a roughly gray object, the red matches the green and blue, but the cyan is higher than the magenta and yellow.

The CMY problems turn out to be advantages for the blend that made the tree green. The shadow weakness isn't a factor. And the CMY imbalance works in our favor here. In RGB, the dome is darker in blue than in red. In CMY, the yellow and cyan are about the same. That excludes the dome from the blend, just what we want.

If you think all the way back to Figure 1.4, you might have wondered what the point was of asking you to distinguish the red from the cyan from the L. The point was, you can do good color correction if you stick primarily to either RGB or CMYK. You can do *very* good color correction if you add a knowledge of LAB. But if you really want to reach the pinnacle, you have to lose all pretense of colorspace-centricity, and achieve a Zen-like mental state where all files appear to have ten channels. Only then can you develop the proper strategy for each opponent.

It might be expected that the ten-channel approach would be effective in dealing with poor originals, such as the grossly dark ranger image, Surprisingly, it's also a powerful way of improving very good originals, such as those taken by professional photographers. Take a look again at the original Utah capitol of Figure 16.13A. What is the criticism? It's not like one of the horrors we started with in Chapters 2 and 3. The highlight and shadow values are perfect; the color balance is reasonable; there's no suppression of any detail that a client might be object to. There is nothing professionally wrong with the image.

It just isn't all it could be.

A chessplayer who decided only to use 61 of the board's squares would never become a master. Similarly, if you won't go to RGB when you encounter a picture like the ranger; if you won't go to CMYK when you work with an image with critical shadow detail like in Figure 6.11; if you decline to use LAB for things like the canyon of Figure 8.10, well...

While that sentence hangs unfinished, let's end our color correction adventures with some unusually poor originals.

There Are No Bad Originals

Food for thought in a final chapter: how we are too soon old, too late smart; how to create a silk purse from a sow's ear; and a libation to remember. Plus, a two-page guide to how to approach an image: the strategy of the thinking retoucher.

Prerelease software often contains what programmers consider to be humor: hidden messages, insider jokes, Easter Eggs, swipes at competitors. If you know how to make the Big Electric Cat burp, for example, you are an aficionado.

To avoid confusion with the shipping product, Photoshop betas always have a different startup screen. Past versions have been named *Tiger Mountain* and *Strange Cargo,* in addition to the aforementioned BEC. I have no clue as to what any of these refer to, but I have one about the name of the Photoshop 6 beta, which was *Venus in Furs.* This was the title of the principal literary work of one L. von Sacher-Masoch, unlikely to be found on the bookshelves of your public library.

It is unclear who the allusion was intended to apply to. Perhaps the programmers feel that they themselves must be masochistic, or perhaps they are referring to those who attempted to make the color management settings of Photoshop 5 work. Or it may be a comment on the general state of the graphic arts: as time goes on, the quality of the digital original seems to get worse and worse, to the point that only a masochist would attempt to correct it.

If so, the programmers have cited the wrong perversion. Those supposedly poor originals can only inflict pain if we allow them to do so. The successful retoucher is a disciplinarian, not a slave. But without the knowledge of Photoshop's intricacies, it's no more than a fantasy. How many times have we looked at some bloodcurdling original, known perfectly well what it *should* look like, and been forced to say something like the following, as did a certain marquis some time ago:

> Is it *possible* to commit crimes such as those our minds yearn after, crimes like those you mention? For my part, I must confess that my imagination has always outstripped my capabilities; I lack the methods to carry out what I would like to...I despise Nature who, while giving me the desire to outrage her, has always deprived me of the means.

*   *   *

This final chapter will discuss some of these means. In *Professional Photoshop 5,* I used older, damaged originals. Nowadays, there's no need to search archives; we have more than enough bad scans and digital captures to work with. Let me start with a bit of self-flagellation.

For Better or for Worse

The word *impossible* is not to be confused with the phrase *too difficult for me.* Unfortunately, many experienced Photoshop users can't keep the two straight. If you don't know how to execute a certain correction, it's only natural to suppose that nobody else knows either.

The idea of professional quality from substandard originals is one that I have long been associated with, and criticized for. The first edition of this book appeared in 1994, and caused howls of protest from professional prepress operations over my statement that many scans from inexpensive desktop units could be brought to the point where they rivaled drum scans. Especially, I was castigated for being so upbeat about the Kodak Photo CD process, although to be fair to the skeptics I had included an impossible scan where there was nothing that could be done to bring the Photo CD version to the standard of a drum scan that I also showed.

I was also called to task for being so silly as to suggest that the typical originals we work with would get worse. But scanners are getting *better,* I was assured. And people are getting more knowledgeable about Photoshop.

True enough—but six years later, we're working with worse originals nonetheless. Color has become so cheap that many projects are initiated on a shoestring budget. Professional photographers still exist, but a smaller percentage of the images we work with are shot by professionals. Cheap stock photography is a wonderful innovation, but its technical quality is, shall we say, variable. Consumer digital cameras are now of high quality, but are often operated by people who just point in the general direction of the subject and click the shutter. And then there are prescreened originals, the images without enough resolution, and the digital restorations.

The problem I and everyone else had in 1994 was that we had limited experience with really poor originals. If somebody had asked a prepress house to take a video capture and make a presentable picture out of it, that would have been considered far more humorous than Jerry Seinfeld.

Within two years, however, it had become clear that clients were from time to time going to provide garbage and insist that it be drastically improved. And the more we worked on them, the more we realized the limitations of a traditional correction method that was never designed to deal with such ghastly input.

Now, don't get me wrong. By-the-numbers works. Setting proper highlights, shadows, neutrals, and fleshtones is an absolute prerequisite to quality results. Precision curves using CMYK are also the best way to bring out detail in an important object.

Where CMYK falls short is in making monstrous changes to monstrous originals. I was beginning to realize this in 1994, and suggested in a couple of cases a move in the L channel of LAB. In 1996 I published a reasonably complete philosophy of working in LAB in a series of magazine articles. By 1998, for the second edition of this book, it was much refined.

In preparing that edition, I noted a couple of instances where I had learned better ways of doing things. Notably, I brought back the Photo CD original that I had declared in 1994 was impossible, corrected it, and showed it next to the drum scan.

The point was proven. The impossible original was competitive with the drum scan. Yet, it fell short of my fantasies. My imagination had outstripped my capabilities. I still thought the drum scan a bit preferable. So, I've tried again. It may have required a new millennium, but I think the original is now *better* than the drum scan. All four versions are in Figure 17.1. Let's discuss the strategies that produced them.

Too Soon Old, Too Late Smart

Although this is a professional photograph, it has a very limited tonal range, as do most pictures of cloudy mountainsides. Such images are not the best advertisements for

Photo CD, which makes no adjustment whatever for the character of the image. This is as opposed to drum scanning, where the operator would automatically have applied curves to open the image up.

So, how to compensate in Photoshop? We have to assume that any use of selections or tools would constitute unsportsmanlike conduct. Drum scanners can't do that. This is why my versions are so full of dust and hairs. Things like Adjust Hue/Saturation, however, are analogous to drum capabilities, and are perfectly kosher.

As a further handicap, we have to start with a CMYK original, the Photo CD itself having evidently grown legs with the passage of time and walked out of my office.

Here's the progression of my thinking over the years:

- **1994**. What are you, a comedian? Get a grip. It can't be done.
- **1998**. It *can* be done. The major problems suggest an LAB correction. The extreme lack of detail can be fixed up with a steep L curve. The lack of color suggests the sort of steep AB curves shown several times earlier, notably in Figure 8.7. I kept both as straight lines, but I made the B cross the center line toward the blue side, because the clouds originally had a reading of 8^B or so, quite yellow.

This done, I made a copy of the image and converted the original to CMYK and the copy to RGB. I did not apply unsharp masking in LAB, as I would have done ordinarily, because there wasn't yet enough contrast in the trees to make it worthwhile.

Instead, I strengthened the magenta channel by blending in 75% of the green channel from the RGB copy, and the cyan by blending in 50% of the red.

As for the yellow, I blended 75% of the

Figure 17.1 *The original art was a professionally shot chrome of this challenging subject. Above left, a professional drum scan. Below left, a Kodak Photo CD capture of the same film, which a book about color correction said was hopeless and could not be made to compete with the drum scan. The images on this page (above, 1998; below, 2000) attempt to prove that book wrong. Which is the best version?*

blue, not to add contrast (because yellow is such a weak ink, it doesn't contribute much detail) but because I felt that the greenery was unnaturally blue. Natural greens have more yellow than cyan. In both the original Photo CD scan and the drum version, the inks are about equal: I downgrade the drum scan for that reason.

Next, I applied curves to the CMYK file to set highlight and shadow. The only thing out of the ordinary I did was to lower the midpoint of the magenta curve to allow the greenery to become more saturated, without affecting the bridge, which is lighter in the magenta plate.

Finally, I sharpened the cyan, magenta, and black individually. The latter two got much more than the cyan, for the reasons stated in Chapter 4. As cyan is a dominant color in this image, it is home to more noise than the weaker magenta and black.

The final result of this is Figure 17.1C.

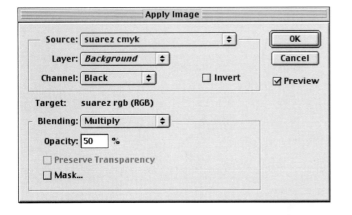

• **2000**. Taking a fresh look two years later, I felt that neither the drum scan nor my 1998 version did justice to the lush greens of Puerto Rico. The drum has the poorer overall color of the two, but it did better at differentiating the relatively red foliage from the background greenery. The sharpening is better too, and there is more of a sensation of three-dimensionality: the foreground trees are more pronounced.

Although the 1998 version is a huge improvement over the original, and it has better color than the drum scan, there's still a cast. In retrospect, going into LAB first was the right thing to do—whenever we see this much greenery in an image we should be thinking LAB—but trying to compensate for a color cast was not.

Most casts pervade the entire image, appearing in all ranges. Now and then, an exception like this shows up. The clouds indeed start out yellow—but the deepest shadows measure $(5)^B$, which is blue. I thought I could get away with an even bluer shadow, so, in 1998 I hamhandedly tried to knock out the cast in LAB. This would have been right had the shadow been yellow as well. But here, it made the darkest parts of the image too blue and deadened the redder foliage.

In 2000, I again converted to LAB and did about the same thing to the L channel.

Figure 17.2 *The black channel of Figure 17.1B looks hopeless, but can be used for a most unusual channel blend (above).*

I again steepened the A and B to get more variation in the colored areas, but avoided any attempt to kill the cast. For that, I changed gears and switched to RGB.

The point was to try to force more detail into the image by using the luminosity-blend technique of Chapter 16. And indeed, I found that the red channel was slightly better than either of the other two. So, Duplicate Layer, followed by an application of the red channel to the entire top layer, changing the layering mode to Luminosity, and flattening the image.

That helped a bit, but the key move involved an unexpected interloper. My very first move last time was to move the image into LAB. This time, I took a *copy* into LAB, because I realized there was a good use for the seemingly hopeless CMYK original.

That original is so light and so flat that its black channel is nearly nonexistent, as you can see in Figure 17.2. But the foreground trees are there, and darker than the background. This suggests a trick that appears nowhere else in the book. I now blended that black channel into the RGB file, mode Multiply, opacity 50%.

Multiply mode, which forces the resulting image to be darker than either parent, isn't normally too useful in color correction. Every now and then it helps in retouching areas with critical highlight detail. In those cases, we can create a copy of the document and apply it to itself in Multiply mode. That will enhance the highlights (and massacre everything else). Those highlights can then be insinuated into the original by a variety of methods, such as through a layer mask.

If the black channel is light enough one can occasionally consider this kind of maneuver as well, usually at a very low opacity.

The depth of the 2000 version is better than it was in 1998 in consequence.

Next, the color correction. Since the idea was not to add contrast so much as normalize colors, there wasn't a reason to avoid doing it in RGB. My curves neutralized the shadow and seriously lightened the green channel. Not only did this lighten the image overall—it was at this point too heavy because of all the blending—but it made the green purer. Also, I went a bit overboard in the highlight, forcing the darker parts of the clouds to become blue. This was no mistake; I had a CMYK plan in mind.

That plan continued with a three-pronged application of Adjust: Hue/Saturation. First, I made those blues darker. Second, I saturated the greens even more. And last, I selected yellows, and moved them toward red. The point was to isolate the reddish greenery—the only thing in the image that really qualifies as yellow.

Sharpening was also a bit more accurate than last time. Still in RGB, I observed that the green channel showed much more detail in the foliage than either of the others. Therefore, I decided to sharpen only it. I created a duplicate layer, hit the green with USM settings of 500,1.5,15, and changed the layering mode to Luminosity.

But before doing so, I made a copy of the unsharpened RGB image. I then converted both to CMYK. I replaced the black in the sharp version with the unsharpened one, trashing the unsharpened CMY channels.

Of course, this was a prelude to a heavy sharpen of the new black. Resharpening something is a good way to produce ugly artifacts. By starting with a relatively soft black, I was able to use settings of 500,1.3,8.

In CMYK now, highlight and shadow values were close enough that no further curve

Figure 17.3 *The advent of cheap digital cameras (and people who don't know how to use them) means that today's artist has to be prepared, from time to time, to correct an original that looks like this.*

to be able to assail the sun, snatch it out of the universe, create a general darkness, or use that star to scorch the world! Now, that would be a *crime,* I tell you, and no petty misdemeanor..."

Now that we've corrected the petty misdemeanor, let's take a whip to the crime.

The Dangerous Phrase

The most dangerous phrase in our frustrating, unreasonable, and mistake-prone industry is, "I don't see how it could get much worse than this."

Over the years, artists, photographers, printers, supervisors, Web designers, and clients who have uttered these fatal words have usually found out that God is not merely a great educator, but also a creative and witty one. Doubt that things can get much worse, and He is always pleased to demonstrate how it is possible.

was necessary. I did, however, use Adjust: Selective Color. There, I made greens more intense by adding yellow and subtracting magenta from greens. I further isolated the off-color foliage by subtracting cyan from yellow. And, having previously set up the clouds for this correction, I added black to and subtracted cyan from cyans.

Granted, this multistep process took 15 minutes or so. That, however, isn't any slower than what drum scanning used to be: it was fairly typical for the operator to analyze the original for ten minutes or so before spinning the drum.

A reasonable shot, to be sure, but hardly the stuff of which fantasies are made.

"There are," said Curval, "but two or three crimes to perform in this world, and they, once done, make further discussion unnecessary; everything else is inferior. Ah, how many times, by God, have I not longed

Right up there as an invitation to catastrophe is "After all, how bad can it be?" This one usually emerges from the lips of a salesperson or other desperado who has just accepted, sight unseen, a job from an unknown or unreliable client who has alluded to the fact that a problem exists.

I recently got such a call, asking if I might try to correct a digital image that was purportedly not very good. Nonchalantly, I said to send it over and I'd take care of it, saying to myself, "After all, how bad can it be?"

My reward was Figure 17.3. Being experienced in these matters, I did not compound things by saying, as I examined it,

"I don't see how it could get much worse than this." Otherwise, it would have had to go up to poster size as well.

For those who think that the best strategy might be to throw this original back in the face of whoever provided it, I'm sympathetic, but in this case it really wasn't possible. The image is from the Spring 1999 Seybold conference. On the right is Craig Kevghas, president of CPR Marketing, a public relations firm. He is presenting an award to the graphic arts editor of the year, Tom McMillan, of *Electronic Publishing* magazine. His wife, Nancy, is seated at left.

Figure 17.4 *A corrected version of Figure 17.3. For details of this complicated procedure, read on.*

Let's get the sad part out of the way. Tom was dying when he received this award, and everybody in the room knew it. I owe Tom a lot, and so do you, if you've been getting anything out of this book. He was the one who, in 1992, envisioned the series of columns that were the seeds of every edition of *Professional Photoshop.*

Figure 17.3 was, believe it or not, the best available image of this heartrending ceremony. One can't exactly say no to an assignment like this.

The Importance of Planning

Along with the blazingly yellow woman of Figure 9.17, this is the most difficult correction in the book. A number of tools and colorspaces are required to get to something like Figure 17.4, at least in my experience. I've had around 50 students attack this in classes and nobody else has gotten a decent result yet.

The problem with images like this is that there are so many things wrong that it is tempting to wade in and start correcting willy-nilly. This can quickly degenerate into a document with so many extra channels and layers that one runs out of disk space in the process of producing a horrible mess. The sensible approach is the conservative one. Selections imply artificiality. They need to be kept to a minimum—and you should know in advance what areas are going to be selected, not make it up as you go along.

If only we'd had a drum scanner here! They see miraculously well into deep shadows. If somebody had given us a piece of, er, film that looked like Figure 17.3, a good drum scanner operator would have been able to save it without undue difficulty.

But this is a twenty-first century problem. There's no film, because it's a capture from a consumer-level digital camera.

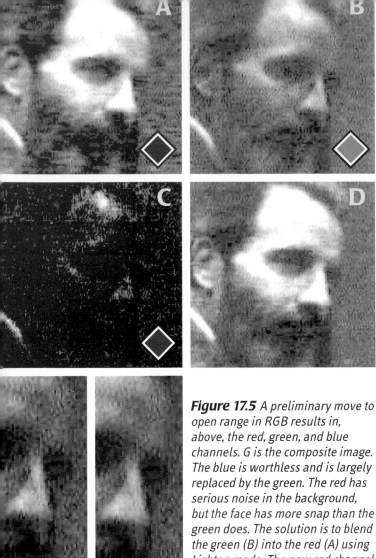

Presumably, it was operated in this case by a consumer, as a professional photographer might have been expected to know the purpose of the device's flash mechanism.

Is trying to correct this a form of masochism? Sure, but get used to it. Digital cameras are the wave of the future. Most images won't be as bad as this, but some will.

Successful image strategists hate selections, but they look at Figure 17.3 and see one staring them in the face. They know instinctively that the box containing the prize must be handled separately. In the original, it's much lighter than anything else. That can't be. Everything else needs to be lightened so drastically that the box will be blown away. We have to assume that the box will be pasted in later, and go for a white point in Craig's collar.

We start with an RGB file of unknown origin. Opening the overall range of the image seems obvious enough, but unless you have a grasp of Photoshop's color management, the best way of doing it may elude you.

From time to time, I've jeered at the calibrationist contention that applying curves somehow damages the picture by throwing away critical data. It takes a ridiculously extreme case for that to be true.

This is a ridiculously extreme case.

Not wishing to squander so much as a pixel of real information, I indulged in a little color management, although perhaps not what the advocates of that tenebrous concept usually think of.

I thought back to the four pictures

Figure 17.5 *A preliminary move to open range in RGB results in, above, the red, green, and blue channels. G is the composite image. The blue is worthless and is largely replaced by the green. The red has serious noise in the background, but the face has more snap than the green does. The solution is to blend the green (B) into the red (A) using Lighten mode. The new red channel is D. The new composite color file is H. Center left, greatly enlarged: there's still colored noise in the background of E, but it's missing from Version F because of a blur of the A and B channels in LAB.*

of the pool in Figure 11.6. Remember how lying to Photoshop by saying that a file was in Adobe RGB, or sRGB, when it actually was in Apple RGB, caused Photoshop to think the file was too dark? This was because Apple RGB has a lower gamma, 1.8, than the 2.2 used in the other two.

What we need here, plainly, is a lie that makes it not darker but lighter. In Edit: Color Settings>Working Spaces>RGB, I chose Custom RGB. (To do so, the Advanced Mode box in Color Settings needs to be checked.) I then changed the gamma setting from 1.8 to 1.0. Then I converted the file from RGB to LAB, having first, for technical reasons, applied a very small curve to lighten the highlight.

Figure 17.6 *After LAB curves aimed at increasing contrast in the faces and jackets and reducing the yellow cast, the image stands as above. The white splotches represent areas where the original was absolutely black, no detail at all in any channel.*

I then restored the original RGB settings and reconverted the file to RGB. Wanting now to establish the white point in Craig's collar, to save time, I clicked on the white eyedropper tool in the Curves dialog box and then clicked into the collar, establishing a zero point there.

That put me at Figure 17.5G, a yellowish entity considerably better than Figure 17.3, yet considerably short of acceptability. Its component channels are nauseating. The red has adequate contrast, but a revolting pattern of noise in the background and hair. The green has no specific defect, other than being flatter than a pancake that has been run over by a steamroller. And the blue is like a John Grisham novel: it has its amusement value, but otherwise is without redeeming social importance.

The blue should be largely replaced by another channel. I've chosen here to blend in 75% of the green. As will be the case throughout this correction, you might choose a different percentage yourself.

This move can't be bad, because it helps color as well as detail. Figure 17.5G is so yellow because the blue is so dark.

As for the red channel, the difficulty is killing the noise without damaging the faces, which have more snap than in the green. The solution is to blend the green, which has a darker face but little noise, into the red in Lighten mode. The improved red channel is Figure 17.5D.

In Figure 17.5G, Tom's green beard is not just color imbalance, but a revolting patterning of red and green that pervades the entire picture.

Fortunately, there's a way to get rid of it.

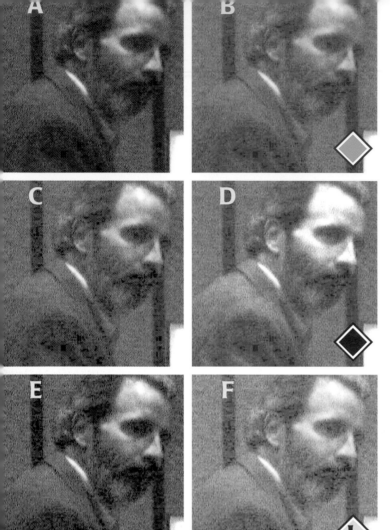

Figure 17.7 *The idea of this luminosity blend is to get more differentiation between the jacket and the background, and to gain contrast in the face. In the green channel there isn't much of either, so it's blended with the red and the L of LAB. This changes the existing image from A to C, but the luminosity blend yields E.*

needed. One hates to do this. It should probably be limited to the background, which we can afford to defocus, and the faces.

Both men, especially Craig, practically vanish into the background. We have to do something to combat this, perhaps with a channel blend, perhaps by finding a way to make the background less colorful.

Above all, we need to gain contrast. The normal way of doing this is by engineering an ultra-peppy black plate. This is usually a routine matter but in a nearly hopeless case like this special handling is in order.

A setting of UCR in Custom CMYK, with a maximum black of 100% and a dot gain set to 0%, is a very nonstandard way of doing things. It is, however, the way to get the highest-contrast black possible. One can't just make an entire separation this way; it would be far too dark. Instead, we need two copies of the RGB (or LAB) file, one taken into CMYK normally, the other with these weird settings. We use the CMY from the normal separation and the black from the other, trashing the remainder.

One of the things that this demonstrated

I converted the file to LAB and applied a Gaussian blur of 2.0 to the A channel and 2.8 to the B. That's the difference between Figures 17.5.E and 17.5F.

All these moves together have brought us to Figure 17.5H, a substantial improvement over 17.5G, let alone the original.

Pushing the Background Away

This concludes the easy part. Now, given Figure 17.6, it's time to do some serious planning. Despite the AB blur, the image remains so grainy that further blurs seem was the obvious, that the image is full of garbage. In Figure 17.6, I've whited out the parts of the original that were absolutely black, zero in all three RGB channels. These areas are as free of detail as the Gulf of Mexico is of icebergs. You can bet that in such circumstances there will be many more places that are saved from total blackness only by a point or two in a single channel and realistically have no detail either. Such an image, when opened up, will be granular beyond all names of granularity.

By using a 100% black ink limit, a lot of that noise finds its way into the black channel, where it can be targeted fairly easily. There are several methods of doing so. Mine was to make a rough selection of the men and invert it so that only the background was selected. I then blended the yellow into the

Figure 17.8 *Another luminosity blend, this one aimed at the magenta. Top row: the color is approximately correct, but the face is still too flat. Middle row: the L of LAB has been blended into the magenta, gaining contrast but making the overall image too gray. Bottom row: reverting to luminosity restores the original color and retains some of the extra pop in magenta.*

black, Lighten mode. As the only parts of the background where the black was darker than the yellow would represent noise, this worked well. Then, the snappy black was further corrected with curves.

A Pair of Luminosity Blends

Pictures as poor as this one cry out for treating contrast and color separately. The color of Figure 17.6 is close to acceptable. The detailing is obviously not, and the drastic moves required to fix it may knock the color for a loop.

The solution is that of Chapter 16: establish a duplicate layer, work the contrast-enhancing curves or channel blending on

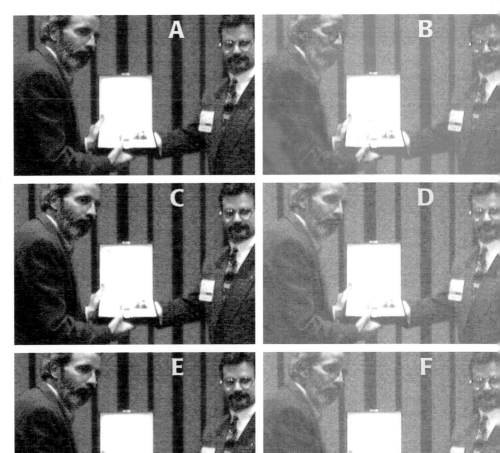

it, and then change the layering mode from Normal to Luminosity. Often the best approach is to make a copy of the image, convert it to LAB, and use the L channel as a source for certain blends, trashing the copy when finished.

This has happened twice here. In Figure

Figure 17.9 *Retouching is most effective when it adds the suggestion of contrast either in color or in darkness. In an enlarged comparison of sections of Figures 17.3 and 17.5, do you see where hand work has been done?*

17.7, still in RGB, the idea is to break Tom's jacket away from the background. The green channel doesn't help with this. The L does. I made an LAB copy of the image and blended 50% of the resulting L into the green. As you can see in Figure 17.7C, this creates rancid color. But changing the layer mode to Luminosity in Figure 17.7E created the desired result.

Later on, I tried the same thing in CMYK. Figure 17.8A's faces look flat. I made another LAB copy (this one was better than the one shown as Figure 17.7F, due to all the intervening horsing around). I set up a duplicate layer in the CMYK document and blended the L channel 50% into both the magenta and yellow, and 35% into the cyan, which was more reasonable to begin with. Then, I again reverted to Luminosity, yielding Figure 17.8E. We're starting to get close.

Where to Commit the Crime

Criminals know enough to try to restrict their activities to places where no one is looking. The same goes for retouching, which is always detectable if somebody looks hard enough. The trick usually is to do it where they won't be looking too hard.

Accordingly, we should try to avoid fooling with the important parts of the image. One can often accomplish the same things by working the background.

Similarly, although making selections is inevitable in an image like this, one tries to make small moves. When necessary, it looks more natural to change color in the selected area than to change detail. This is why the earlier channel blends were so important, to avoid having it look as though the two men were cut out and pasted in.

I've indeed made a selection of the background here, and lightened it a bit. It's also moved toward blue, to differentiate it more from the men, and blurred slightly.

To my mind the bigger background move is to add apparent snap. A lot of times, what the viewer thinks is contrast depends not on the whole picture but on certain small areas such as those shown in Figure 17.9. No matter that there weren't any bright colors in the original; the viewer will still think the result looks monochromatic. So one creates bright colors somewhere, anywhere. I gave Nancy a blue blouse, and Craig a more colorful tie. Also, I built up his nametag. The viewer isn't likely to be concentrating on any of these three, so the scam is less likely to be detected.

The tool of choice here is the paintbrush, set to Color mode, meaning it can't alter detail. Also, the paintbrush, unlike the airbrush, doesn't increase its effect the more one applies it. Noticing that Tom's jacket had lost its reddish hue everywhere except in the shoulders, I picked up that color and painted it into the rest of the jacket. Because this doesn't affect the darkening of the fabric, it looks natural.

Likewise, the apparent detail in Tom's hair is a trick. I lightened the natural areas of gray with the dodge tool set to highlights, forcing in more contrast.

Only a couple of steps remained, for which three supplemental versions had to be made. The award box itself had to be pasted in, using Figure 17.10A, which had to be produced from a copy of the original image, as all corrected versions had blown the box away. As the faces were a bit too pink, the darker, yellower Figure 17.10B came into play. Merged through a layer mask, it gave a healthier glow to the flesh.

I still felt the image was muddy, and blamed the contrasty, black channel that I

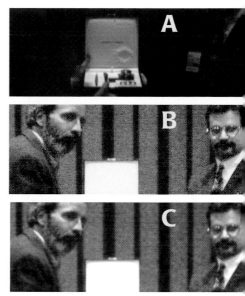

Figure 17.10 In an image this complex, several alternate versions are often used for specific purposes. Top to bottom: a much darker version for the box; a darker, yellower version for the faces; and a blurred, desaturated version for the background.

was at such pains to create earlier. I resolved to fix it, but first I decided to show how important the black is. So I made Figure 17.11 by deleting black ink completely.

I'd intended to correct the black with curves, but the colorful blackless version gave me an idea. I put it on a separate layer, and blended it into the existing document using Soft Light mode.

This lightens the gradation, and brightens the color, in the lighter half of the image. It also gave a better-looking result than I could get with a curve to the black only. Whaddaya know! A new technique!

There has been so much new material in this book that I felt it only right that this chapter be done from scratch. And I proposed to end it by reminding you of how far we have come from the monkey work of Chapter 2, and also of the words of a possibly recognizable song:

All the monkeys aren't in the zoo;
Every day you meet quite a few,
So you see, it's all up to you:
You can be better than you are...

THE STRATEGIES FOR APPROACHING AN IMAGE

THE EVERY-IMAGE TOOLS

If you haven't done these things every time, you won't have first-quality images.

Full Range
No Impossible Colors
Proper Shaping of Curves
Good Black Plate
Good Unwanted Color (channel blend if necessary)
Good Sharpening

THE OPTIONS

Here are some of the unusual techniques that show up from time to time.
This is your arsenal of weapons. They aren't appropriate for every image.
Look for the right opportunity to bring them into play.

GCR maneuvering, including reseparating a CMYK image.
Channel blending to change color
Steepening or flattening the AB curves
Altering the picture to put in a cast and then putting in a false highlight
Selecting the background and desaturating it
Sharpening in some unorthodox way, such as emphasizing the darkening
False reseparation
Putting in a false highlight or other detail via a layer mask
Using an unusual black plate to emphasize shadow detail
Saturating and desaturating for a sense of depth
Selecting an area and correcting it locally
Correcting once for color and once for contrast
Plate blending in luminosity mode

THE CHECKLIST

Ask yourself these questions before you do ANYTHING.

• **What is the object of the correction?** This is such an obvious question most of the time that when the exceptional case comes up there's often a problem. So, before starting, try to look at the image from a different perspective. What, from the client's point of view, is likely to be the objective? What parts of the image need to be spruced up, and which can be sacrificed?

• **Are there obvious problems that need to be fixed?** This will govern your overall strategy. If there's one crying problem with the image, go with the method that fixes it even if other strategies might otherwise be appropriate.

• **Is there any critical highlight detail that an aggressive correction may damage?** If there is, be careful about correcting outside of CMYK.

- **Are the shadows in this picture important?** Look also at the three-quartertones. Is there any delicate gradation to black there that you'd be afraid of losing? If not, jack up the shadow value by adding more black.

- **Does the image have problems with color, contrast, neither, or both?** If only color or only contrast is a problem, think about a correction in LAB. If both color and contrast are wrong, ordinarily think RGB or CMYK. Before using LAB to correct color make sure that the cast you are correcting is uniform, that is, that it affects highlight and shadow in the same way.

- **Are bright colors bad?** If so, think about heavier GCR. Most pictures look better with bright colors; if you have the exceptional one that won't, compensate with a heavier black plate.

- **Is the most important object at least a midtone in darkness?** If so, normal sharpening may not work well. Consider a multistep sharpening process that emphasizes dark haloing.

- **Is the most important object light and neutral?** If it is, think heavier GCR, to prevent any color cast from developing and to make bringing out the detail with curves a bit easier.

- **Are you reasonably certain you know what the colors should be?** If you aren't, this suggests the use of LAB (and perhaps the Hue/Saturation command), both of which are easy to experiment with.

- **Is some type of local correction going to be necessary?** If you discover halfway through the correction that you need a selection, you didn't plan well. If a selection will eventually be necessary this will make life much easier: you can in effect work on two separate images.

- **Is one color by far the most important in the image?** If so, this suggests avoiding sharpening the darkest channels. Think about sharpening black plus the weak color. When colors are of more equal importance an overall sharpening reverted to luminosity mode, or in the L channel of LAB, is usually better.

- **Is the original halfway decent, or are major moves going to be needed?** The worse the original, the more you should avoid starting in CMYK. Try to bring the image closer in LAB or RGB before converting it.

- **Is there an atrocious color cast?** If so, it suggests LAB, but before doing so, see if you can minimize the cast with an RGB channel blend. For example, if the image has a gross yellow cast, it can often be softened by blending some red into the blue.

- **Is there critical detail in the darkest shadows?** This suggests special handling of the black plate. Remember that detail in the CMY channels will be suppressed because of the total ink limit. Consider starting with a weak black plate and then applying a drastic curve. Also consider, at the end, using Image: Adjust>Selective Color to reduce the CMY component of blacks. Even though this will lighten the shadow, it will probably add detail.

- **Is there a lot of greenery?** Think steepening the A, and possibly the B, channels of LAB.

- **Are there important fleshtones?** This is the only major class of image where bringing out detail is usually undesirable. Never sharpen the blue, green, magenta, or yellow channels. Expect to have to do a channel blend into the cyan. Think about a preliminary luminosity blend of the green into the entire image. Avoid taking fleshtone readings in any area where makeup may be present. Be prepared at the end to minimize hot spots that the camera may have picked up in the face.

Figure 17.11 *The final correction, with the black plate removed.*

creates art where others see mere numbers.

If you have traveled with me so far, you are surely included. And with that, I return you to the better ending of *Professional Photoshop 5.*

Getting the Fizz Back

This book has emphasized the use of traditional methods, updated for the needs of today's images. Having come to the end, I suggest that we honor another long-standing graphic arts tradition by celebrating with a cold beer.

Unfortunately, the beverage of Figure 17.12 resembles apple juice more than it does the kind of thing I'd like to down after a long day of Photoshop work. The color is approximately correct, but what happened to the fizz?

Is it a bad original? It can't be, if it can be brought to the state of the pint on the right. Particularly, if it can be brought there in a minute or less, scarcely enough time for the head to settle.

The image starts in LAB. Recalling a similar experience with a yellow pepper in Figure 9.6, we save a copy, and convert the original to RGB. An examination of the channels (Figure 17.13) indicates that the bubbles in this beer exist only in the green. The head in the green is adequate but not as good as in the blue. The red channel, like certain of my relatives, occupies space without serving any useful purpose.

We now know that we will be working this image at least partially in RGB, because two problems are conveniently isolated.

Indeed, with these methods, you can be swingin' on a star, color-wise. This result is not as good as a drum scan—yet. In the next edition, I think it may be. Three weeks before the book went to press, way too late to change anything, I realized I had missed an opportunity way back on page 331. Next time, I'll tell you what it was.

Learning this deepest of all graphic subjects is an endless cycle of considering new options, adopting some, rejecting others, saving still others for a better day. There is no shame in admitting that, having considered this new ending, I think the one from the last edition is better.

I therefore bid farewell with a tip of my hat to da Vinci, to Ogden Rood, to Chevreul, Darwin, Newton and to all others who struggle to grasp what color means and how best to use it—and to everyone who, by thinking hard about the science of what we see and about the emotion it makes us feel,

The red channel needs to be liquidated before it contaminates every channel in CMYK, and the green must get special sharpening attention because in it, we have isolated the bubbles we are so interested in improving.

First, we need to make the two useful channels even better. The steeper the curve, the more the contrast, so we apply the curves of Figure 17.13, steepening the green where the body of the beer falls and the blue where the head is. As for curving the red, forget that. That channel is history.

The blue and the green are two separate sharpening problems. In the green, we are trying for the bubbles in the beer. They aren't subtle, so we need a wide Radius of 3.5, with a 400% Amount, Threshold of 5. The foam that is the blue's strength, on the other hand, has fine gradations that a wide threshold would kill. So, we lower the Radius to 1.5.

Now it's just a question of getting the blends right. I chose to replace the red with a 65–35 blend of green and blue, feeling that the beer was more important than the

Figure 17.12 *The original beer at left looks flat in more ways than one. The correction, right, adds fizz.*

head. For the same reason, I then blended 25% of the green into the blue.

The situation at this point is Figure 17.14. Happy St. Patrick's Day! But we are long since past the point where such trivialities as green beer cause us grief. We simply convert to LAB, where a copy of the original awaits us. The old and the new L channel are compared in Figure 17.15. Replace one with the other, convert to CMYK, and we're done.

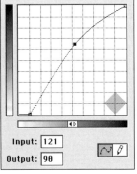

Input: 121
Output: 90

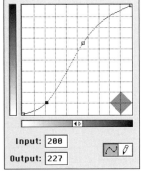

Input: 200
Output: 227

Figure 17.13 *Below, the red, green, and blue channels of Figure 17.12. Above, the curves applied to the green and blue channels (the red having been discarded).*

A Toast to Professional Color

And with that, we come to the end of a long journey. This image is an appropriate one to finish with, not so much because it is an effective correction but because it is an easy one—for those in the know.

Although our field is in many ways a highly technical one, it's very different from most technical fields. It takes someone with a background in numbers to know whether a mathematician's work is credible. It takes a background in music to understand why Vladimir Horowitz played piano better than Liberace. But with us, it isn't that way. What expertise does it take to tell that the right side of Figure 17.12 looks a lot better than the left side?

Not too much—that's why we call it a *correction.* You know it's better, I know it's better, even if we can't put our finger on why. And, as we are talking *professional* Photoshop, this presupposes that we have clients. They will think the corrected beer is better, too; how could they not?

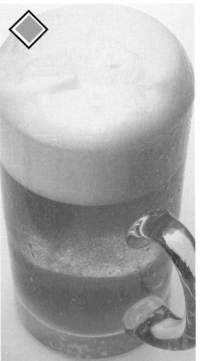

This image had no highlight, no shadow, no neutrals, no fleshtone, and no unwanted color. It's therefore a most atypical problem, and this may account for why professionals do so badly with it.

Throughout this book, I've tried to suggest a general way of approaching correction by the numbers. That is indeed the best way, the timeless and time-proven way, to give your images the snap they deserve. Special treatment is sometimes required, in

Figure 17.14 *After the curves and channel blending, the beer is appropriate to serve on St. Patrick's Day. But the skilled Photoshop user has no problem restoring the original color.*

which case experience with this kind of image helps. If we've worked recently on the seltzer image of Figure 8.2, for example, we're a long way toward understanding the problems of bubble-bearing beverages.

But there's so much to keep in one's head! So many tools, so many tricks, and so little time to decide on the right one to use!

On Pages 336 and 337, I've attempted to summarize the thought process one goes through *before* picking up the mouse. Much of it seems automatic. When in doubt, however, it may be useful to just go, er, by the numbers down that list.

For example, here we should ask ourselves:

• What is the object of the correction? (To make the beer look appetizing.)

• Are there obvious problems that need to be fixed? (You can't see the bubbles.)

• Is there any critical detail that an aggressive correction may damage? (The lightest area of the foam.)

• Are there problems with color, contrast, neither, or both? (Just contrast; the original color is acceptable.)

• Is some type of local correction going to be necessary? (Not here.)

• Is the original halfway decent, or are major moves going to be needed? (The original is terrible.)

All these answers suggest both an LAB correction and that sharpening will be a critical issue.

Figure 17.15 *The L channels of the files that became Figure 17.12.*

But no matter what strategy you use, no matter what colorspace you work in, no matter what your workflow, no matter what version of Photoshop you use, certain goals are constant. Ignore them, and you condemn yourself to mediocrity. Achieve them, and you'll have professional color. They are:

• A full tonal range.

• Interest areas falling in steep parts of the correction curves, where possible.

• Strong detail in the unwanted color, if there is one.

• Accurate unsharp masking.

• The right kind of black plate.

Do these things, and you will be able to shrug off changes in Photoshop and laugh at what some call bad originals.

If you don't foresee spending a career working on images, may those that you do correct be vivid, lifelike, full of detail. And if this is going to be your lifetime interest area, may it always fall in the steepest portion of fortune's curve. Let's raise our glasses to that.

Notes & Credits

Most images in this book come from what used to be called the Corel Professional Photos collection of stock photography. Originally, these were chosen because they are variable in quality and represent many of the problems one faces in real life, and because they were easily accessible at very reasonable prices through Corel as well as many mail-order and on-line sources.

Shortly before this book was released, however, Corel sold the rights to the library to Hemera Technologies. As yet, Hemera has not announced its plans for them. But as the Corel CDs are still often available through Web auction sites, I'm continuing to list the disk title for each image. Monitor www.hemcra.com for updates.

From past editions, we've retained images from five other vendors, two of whom are, as best I can determine, now out of business. The others: Photodisc, Inc., 800-528-3472 or www.photodisc.com, and competitor Digital Stock Corp., 800-545-4514 or www.digitalstock.com, have extensive libraries of disks on a variety of subjects. The Photodisc images shown here are from their very earliest releases and do not reflect the high quality of their current offerings. Artbeats, 800-444-9392, 541-863-4429, or www.artbeats.com, specializes in backgrounds, e.g., textured images, such as marbled paper, wood, and stone.

Where a disk title appears without further identification, it means the image came from the aforementioned Corel/Hemera series. "Unavailable" means it came from a vendor we believe is defunct.

CHAPTER 1

The opening shot of Grand Canyon National Park is from *Grand Canyon*. Hawaii's Kilauea volcano is from *World Landmarks,* and the rhododendron shot is mine.

The baby picture of my niece Rebecca is one I've used for many years. Rebecca is nine now, and is even prettier, if possible.

CHAPTER 2

The shot of the lobsters with the wine bottle in the background is from *Grapes and Wine*. The Montréal street scene is from *Construction*. The shot with the pronounced blue cast is from *Women in Vogue*. The statue known as Christ of the Andes comes from *South America*. The statue used to test neutrality is from *Garden Ornaments*. And the statue that symbolizes the United States is found in New York Harbor and in *World Landmarks*.

The horses come from PhotoDisc 5, *World Commerce and Travel*. The torero plies his art in *People II*.

CHAPTER 3

The various house cats are from *Cats and Kittens*. Their larger cousin is from *Tigers;* the people standing in the snow from *O Canada;* the bobcat from *Wildcats;* the darkened room from *Office Interiors;* and the photo of the pool area at the Bellagio Las Vegas is mine.

The quotation alleging that bad originals cannot be compensated for is from Bridgewater and Woods, *Halftone Effects*, (Chronicle Books, 1993).

CHAPTER 4

The car is from *Museum Children's Toys.* The Sphinx appears in *World Landmarks.* The bottle of red wine is from *Grapes & Wine* and the empty green bottles from *Still Life.* The oversharpened woman appears in *Women by Jack Cutler,* and the soldier in *Army.* The shot of the Mormon temple in Salt Lake City is mine.

El Greco's *Christ with the Cross* hangs in the Museo del Prado in Madrid.

CHAPTER 5

Complete Poems of Emily Dickinson (Johnson, editor; Little Brown & Co., 1951) is the source of the poetry. In order of appearance, the assertion about trying to be a rose and failing is in Poem #442; about nature's use of yellow #1045; about our adjustment to lighting contitions #419; and about how to gain the good will of a flower #845.

The rose is from *Beautiful Roses;* the woman's face from *Hairstyles II;* the lime from *Food Objects;* and the woman standing in front of the door from *Women in Vogue.* I shot the lush greenery in a Costa Rican rainforest.

The marbled paper pattern is from Artbeats' "Marbled Paper Textures" CD. The artist is Phil Bates. The Aruban dancer with the red feathers is unavailable.

The closing quotation is from Yule, *Principles of Color Reproduction* (John Wiley & Sons, 1967).

CHAPTER 6

The background of Figure 6.1 is from Artbeats' "Marble and Granite" CD set.

The images of the Erechtheion and the Chinese tapestry are found on PhotoDisc 5, "World Commerce and Travel."

The shishkebab image appears in *Cui-sine;* the bride in *Weddings;* the apple in *Food Objects,* and the old printed cover in *Sheet Music Cover Girls.* The black cat testing shadow detail is found in *Cats and Kittens.* The woman wearing the dark clothing is from *Hairstyles.*

CHAPTER 7

The beach scene is from *Jamaica;* the parrot is from *Island Vacation;* the channels of the children come from the image shown in its entirety at the top of Figure 10.3.

The MiG-31 fighter is from *Aviation II.* The giant leaves are mine, again from the Costa Rican rainforest. The two final diving images are found in *Under the Red Sea.*

CHAPTER 8

Strephon and Phyllis's love duet is from the first act of *Iolanthe.*

The sparkling water comes from *Beverages;* the canyon scene from *Images of the Grand Canyon;* and the graffiti from *Graffiti.* The cowboy is mine, as is the picture of the distant New York City skyline, taken from a park near my house.

The shot of the bighorn sheep, along with the car window, is the responsibility of my father. He may also have photographed the peacock, a print of which I found buried in a box in his house.

CHAPTER 9

The image of chocolates is from *Food Textures.* Both the raspberries and the yellow pepper come from *Food Objects.* The model with the ghastly yellow cast is from *Women by Jack Cutler.*

The picture of the three musicians, perhaps the most reproduced image in the world, is included in the "Kodak Color Reproduction Guides," otherwise known as the Q-60 set, available from Eastman Kodak Corp.

The mundane image of the green tile, and the spectacular one of the statue with the starry backdrop, are both mine.

CHAPTER 10

The simultaneous-contrast graphic first appeared in Adams and Weisberg, *The GATF Practical Guide to Color Management* (GATFPress, 1998).

The squire attempted to pull the wool over Moses' eyes in Goldsmith's *The Vicar of Wakefield.*

The review that rated the calamitous Illustrator 9 "freakin' awesome" appeared in *MacAddict,* September 2000. The five-star review of Photoshop 5 appeared in *Publish,* September 1998.

My review of Photoshop 5, skewering its color handling (though very positive about all other features of the program), appeared in *Electronic Publishing,* July 1998.

The comment saying that I would be sunk like the typesetters was posted to the newsgroup comp.apps.graphics.photoshop in July 1999, by Adobe's Chris Cox, who states that his views do not necessarily represent those of his company.

The statement that service bureaus were starting to adopt color management in 1996 appeared in "Pushbutton Color Still in the Shadows," by Bruce Fraser, *MacUser* magazine, June 1996.

The six-month prediction for universal adoption of an RGB workflow was made by Brian Lawler at the VuePoint conference, April 1997.

The children in the GCR demonstration are from *Jamaica.*

Santayana issued his famous epigram in his *Life of Reason.*

Da Vinci's cryptic remarks on shadow neutrality, inviting the reader to verify them by looking at the darkest parts of strongly-colored paintings inside a dimly lit church, came in random writings which have since been published as his *Notebooks.*

Newton's *Opticks* (1704) is the most influential text in the history of color, but Chevreul's *De la Loi du Contraste Simultané des Couleurs* (1839) is deeper, and Rood's *Modern Chromatics* (1878) is, in my view, the best color book ever written.

Darwin's tribute to the human visual system is found in *Origin of Species.*

CHAPTER 11

The gamut drawing of Figure 11.1 was supplied by Pantone, Inc. The complicated Figure 11.3 is from a set of images used to calibrate Scitex scanners.

The blue and yellow forest scene is from Digital Stock's *Nature & Landscapes* set of CDs.

The fruit basket is from *Food.* The pepper is the same one that appeared in Figure 9.6, with the cyan and yellow plates having been transposed.

The images of Costa Rica's Poas volcano, the Bellagio pool, and the mule deer are all mine.

CHAPTER 12

Copies of the full Specifications for Web Offset Publications are available from SWOP, Inc., 60 E. 42nd St. Suite 721, New York, NY 10165; 212-983-6042.

The General Requirements for Applications in Commercial Offset Lithography may be ordered through www.gracol.org.

The magazine page is from *Electronic Publishing,* October 1998. The harbor image is from *Cornish Riviera.*

CHAPTER 13

The parrot is the same one seen in Chapter 7. The Canadian flag is from *Flags of the World,* and the Chart House is unavailable.

Machiavelli's, er, principe-al work, *Il Principe,* is the source of all the quotes.

CHAPTER 14

The image of the Great Wall of China is un-available. The horse was photographed by Franklyn Higgs. The sinkhole is mine.

The Kodak document referred to is enti-tled "Optimizing Photo CD Scans for Pre-press and Publishing," accessible as a PDF file from various Web locations.

Dr. Constantine's comment to Poirot came after the great detective, in *Murder on the Orient Express,* had deliberately offered an incorrect solution to the crime.

CHAPTER 15

The image of the bareshouldered model was scanned from *Electronic Publishing* magazine, January 1996.

archy's plaintive question, "have you no sense" appears in Don Marquis' *archy and mehitabel.* The moth replies,

> plenty of it
> but at times we get tired of using it
> we get bored with the routine
> and crave beauty
> and excitement
> fire is beautiful
> and we know that if we get
> too close it will kill us
> but what does that matter
> it is better to be happy
> for a moment
> and be burned up with beauty

> than to live a long time
> and be bored all the while

This is, of course, an excellent philosophy for color correction.

CHAPTER 16

The ranger's lecture is on *Grand Canyon.* The woman's face used to illustrate the green>RGB luminosity blend is in *Lovely Ladies.* The man's is in *Fashion.*

The photograph of the Cleveland Browns' stadium under construction is by Stan Kohn. The two canyon shots and that of the Utah state capitol are mine.

CHAPTER 17

The cloud-shrouded bridge in Puerto Rico was photographed by René Suárez. I don't know who took the heartrending shot of Tom McMillan; doubtless that person would not want credit for it anyway. The closing image of beer is from *Beverages.*

The dialogue between Durcet and Curval is from Sade's *Les 120 Journées de Sodome.*

The oft-parodied *Swinging on a Star,* by Johnny Burke and Jimmy Van Heusen, was wildly popular during World War II.

> *When first you're starting it may take*
>   *some nerve,*
> *To trust your fortune to a single curve,*
> *But if you think that it's not too much*
>   *to ask,*
> *You'll never need to make a mask.*

Reaching the Author

Readers are invited to send text messages—no images or other attachments, please—to 76270.1033@compuserve.com; also DMargulis@aol.com.

Index

A Note on the Type

The face in use in this book is a variant of Kepler, a 1996 design release of Robert Slimbach of Adobe Systems. Kepler is extraordinary in a number of respects. Generically, based on its slight diagonal slant and its relatively strong contrast between thick and thin strokes, it would be classified as a transitional type, the same general grouping as, say, Baskerville or Caledonia. But transitional types are not noted for their legibility, and Kepler, as you can see, is very easy on the eyes.

The face also incorporates detailing very atypical of such faces, such as an open *P* that is more typical of sculpted-look Venetian oldstyles such as Palatino. Kepler uses Adobe's Multiple Master technology, allowing an infinite number of variants along three axes: width, boldness, and optical weight. For this edition, I chose a slightly emboldened and condensed version.

In an end-of-millennium column in December 1999, I named Palatino the typeface of the century—and Kepler the typeface of the decade.

A Legal Note on the CD

CUSTOMER NOTE: IF THIS BOOK IS ACCOMPANIED BY SOFTWARE, PLEASE READ THE FOLLOWING BEFORE OPENING THE PACKAGE.

This software on the attached CD contains files to help you utilize the models described in the accompanying book. By opening the package, you are agreeing to be bound by the following agreement:

This software product is protected by copyright and all rights are reserved by the author, John Wiley & Sons, Inc., or their licensors. You are licensed to use this software as described in the software and the accompanying book. Copying the software for any other purpose may be a violation of the U.S. Copyright Law.

This software product is sold as is without warranty of any kind, either express or implied, including but not limited to the implied warranty of merchantability and fitness for a particular purpose. Neither Wiley nor its dealers or distributors assumes any liability for any alleged or actual damages arising from the use of or the inability to use this software. (Some states do not allow the exclusion of implied warranties, so the exclusion may not apply to you.)